SAMS
Teach
Yourself

CSS

in 24 Hours

Kynn Bartlett

SAMS *800 East 96th Street, Indianapolis, Indiana, 46240 USA*

Sams Teach Yourself CSS in 24 Hours

International Standard Book Number: 0-672-32906-9

Library of Congress Catalog Card Number: 2006920653

Printed in the United States of America

First Printing: May 2006

09   08   07   06   4   3   2   1

Trademarks

Warning and Disclaimer

Bulk Sales

Sams Publishing offers excellent discounts on this book when ordered in quantity for bulk purchases or special sales. For more information, please contact

U.S. Corporate and Government Sales

1-800-382-3419

corpsales@pearsontechgroup.com

For sales outside of the U.S., please contact

International Sales

international@pearsoned.com

Acquisitions Editor
Linda Bump Harrison

Development Editors
Jon Steever
Songlin Qiu

Managing Editor
Patrick Kanouse

Project Editor
Mandie Frank

Copy Editor
Margo Catts

Indexer
Heather McNeill

Proofreader
Elizabeth Scott

Technical Editor
Michelle Jones

Publishing Coordinator
Vanessa Evans

Multimedia Developer
Dan Scherf

Book Designer
Gary Adair

Page Layout
Juli Cook

Contents at a Glance

Part V: Mastering CSS

Part VI: Appendixes

Part VII: Bonus Content

Table of Contents

Part III: Styling Text with CSS

About the Author

Kynn Bartlett has been using the Internet since 1986, and has been a web developer since 1994. Self-taught in HTML, CSS, XML, and many other web technologies, he passes this knowledge along to others through authoring books, teaching online classes, and giving seminars and presentations. His specialty is web accessibility: making websites that can be used easily by people with disabilities.

Kynn was a key board member in building the HTML Writers Guild, a non-profit educational association of web developers from around the world, and helped create the Guild's online education program. He also served as the Guild's representative on several World Wide Web Consortium working groups.

From 1995 to 2005, Kynn was the co-owner and Chief Technologist of Idyll Mountain Internet, in Fullerton, California. Currently, he lives with his wife Liz and cat Eowyn in Tucson, Arizona, where he writes books and does digital photography in addition to web consulting.

Kynn's personal website is http://kynn.com/, and you can write to him about this book at kynn@css24.com.

Dedication

For my mother, Vicky Bartlett.

Acknowledgments

A book isn't really created by the person whose name is on the cover. It's actually the result of a lot of help, encouragement, and support from a sizeable group, and I'm going to take this space to thank them.

First, of course, is my wife and partner Liz, without whose assistance you wouldn't be reading this. The rest of the family—my mom, Vicky; my dad, Bud; my grandmother, Dot; my mother-in-law, PK; my sister, Denise; my "sister," Eve Shaffer—were very supportive, even if many of them didn't quite understand what I was writing about. Eowyn, our cat, provided constant encouragement along with demands for food.

As for people who worked on this book, I want to thank the whole Sams team including Michelle Jones, Linda Bump Harrison, Jon Steever, Mandie Frank, Margo Catts, Songlin Qiu, and Mark Taber. Special thanks to Lynn Haller, Korynn Bohn, and everyone at Studio B agency.

The support of my friends has meant much to me. Thanks to Nick Mamatas, R. Francis Smith, James Kiley, Matthew Rhoten, Noel Gorelick, and the rest of the Surly Dinos. Thanks to Dawud Zafir and Gwen Low for putting up with dropped social gatherings due to book deadlines.

Also, in no particular order, thank you to Joe Crawford, Matt Brown, Michael Dayah and Halle Berry, Dwayne McDuffie, Lea Hernandez, Amber Greenlee, and everyone on my LiveJournal friends list.

This book was written in Tucson, Arizona. Thank you to everyone at Applebees, Ironwood Terraces, Rainbow Planet, Bentley's, and Something Sweet who provided me with working space, power outlets, wi-fi connections, and cherry cola. Thank you to the Arizona-Sonora Desert Museum and the Dunbar Project.

Thank you to everyone who fights for peace, equality, and justice in an unfair world.

We Want to Hear from You!

As the reader of this book, *you* are our most important critic and commentator. We value your opinion and want to know what we're doing right, what we could do better, what areas you'd like to see us publish in, and any other words of wisdom you're willing to pass our way.

You can email or write me directly to let me know what you did or didn't like about this book—as well as what we can do to make our books stronger.

Please note that I cannot help you with technical problems related to the topic of this book, and that due to the high volume of mail I receive, I might not be able to reply to every message.

When you write, please be sure to include this book's title and author as well as your name and phone or email address. I will carefully review your comments and share them with the author and editors who worked on the book.

Email: webdev@samspublishing.com

Mail: Mark Taber
            Associate Publisher
            Sams Publishing
            800 East 96th Street
            Indianapolis, IN 46240 USA

Reader Services

Visit our website and register this book at www.samspublishing.com/register for convenient access to any updates, downloads, or errata that might be available for this book.

Introduction

We've come a long way in the CSS world.

Way back in 1998, I was all set to teach an online course on Cascading Style Sheets—but there weren't textbooks available. In that dark, prehistoric time, all we had to work with were the arcane and confusing CSS specifications from the W3C. And almost nobody was using CSS; HTML attributes and tables for layout and single-pixel spacer images dominated what passed for advanced web design.

I asked around to various publishers and authors about the situation, and I was told quite plainly, "CSS just isn't ready yet." Publishing companies hadn't heard of it, browsers didn't support it, and web developers didn't want to learn about it.

Jump ahead to 2002, and the first edition of this book. CSS was no longer a great mystery, known unto a few; it was starting to pick up steam and become popular for styling websites—but always with an important caveat. You couldn't do much of anything really cool with it, because the older browsers were just so bad at CSS that it was like playing craps with your design. Would it work? Would it degrade nicely? Or would it just produce a multi-colored mess, like that time your dog ate your crayons?

Now, as this book is written, we're in a new age of CSS. The browser companies are almost finished cleaning up their acts. The cool kids of web design have abandoned the tables-for-layout, the single-pixel hacks, and the proprietary browser code, to utilize the awesome power of a fully operational standards-based design approach. (What took you guys so long?) The accessibility benefits of CSS are touted not only by advocates for people with disabilities but by top web developers.

The environment in which we write CSS has also changed. It's been over ten years since Netscape 4 was introduced, and the browser statistics make it clear that the Web has moved on from that buggy model. No longer will pages and pages of this book be devoted to a decade-old program. (We are stuck with older versions of Internet Explorer, however!) New browsers are available that didn't exist a few years ago—Mozilla's browser has evolved into the popular Firefox, and Apple has introduced the Safari web browser for Mac OS X computers.

The CSS language has evolved as well—CSS 2.1, although not yet a formal recommendation, provides a solid, reliable update to the CSS Level 2 recommendation. And top CSS designers have spent years developing standards-based techniques for styles that were once thought impossible under CSS.

It was time for a new version of *Sams Teach Yourself CSS in 24 Hours*, as well.

The goal of this book is to give you a solid, practical foundation in Cascading Style Sheets. You'll not only learn what the CSS specifications tell you, but you'll also learn how those specs have been implemented in the browsers. In each hour, your knowledge of CSS will increase, and by the time you're finished with the book, you'll be quite proud of how much you've learned. More than just a reference book, this is a tutorial that will guide you to an understanding of what CSS can do for your web designs.

How to Read This Book

The title of this book, *Sams Teach Yourself CSS in 24 Hours*, comes with a promise to you, the reader. The promise is that in 24 hours—or less—I'll have you up and running with CSS, producing your own style sheets that rival those of web grandmasters. To do this, I've broken down that 24-hour period into 24 lessons of one hour or less.

Now, let's be honest—you really should not try to do everything in the book in 24 hours straight. I suppose if you have the stamina, and your loved ones don't mind too much, you *could* try, but really I suggest learning at a pace that's healthy for you and appropriate for your life's schedule.

This book is divided into five parts. In Part I, "Introduction to CSS," you'll learn the basic knowledge you need to understand what CSS is and how to use it. Part II, "Core Principles of CSS," explains the theory behind CSS, which will help you understand the rest of the book. In Part III, "Styling Text with CSS," you'll learn the types of style rules that can change font properties and color. Part IV, "Layout with CSS," teaches you how to use CSS properties to lay out a page on the screen, without using HTML `<table>` tags. And Part V, "Mastering CSS," covers advanced uses of CSS, including accessibility and browser hacks.

Other Ways to Use This Book

You don't necessarily have to read through this book in sequential order. Each lesson is designed to stand alone, and you can skip over entire hours, jump ahead to things that interest you, or go back to pick up something that catches your interest. Naturally, you'll get the most out of the book if you eventually read the whole thing, but often you only have time for the answers, so I've written this book with your needs in mind.

Here are some different ways to use this book:

▶ To get started quickly, read all of Part I and begin adding styles to your web pages. There are basic styles in Hour 2, "Getting Started with CSS," to let you hit the ground running. Total time commitment: 4 hours.

▶ If you've worked with CSS informally before and want to sharpen your skills, jump directly to Part II and Part III. Total time commitment: 10 hours.

▶ To learn about CSS-based layout and replace your <table> tags with positioning properties, read Part IV. You'll also want to read Part II to brush up on advanced selectors, and then see Hour 24, "Troubleshooting and Browser Hacks," for useful filters around broken browsers. Total time commitment: 11 hours.

▶ If you're primarily learning CSS to increase your site's accessibility for people with disabilities—perhaps because of the U.S. government's Section 508 regulations or similar policies—start with Part I and Part II then skip ahead to Hour 22, "Accessibility and Print Media." Finish up with Appendix A, "Replacing Presentational HTML with CSS." Total time commitment: 10 hours.

▶ To become a true expert on CSS, read the whole book! It's not that difficult, and you'll soon be the envy of your fellow web designers who are not as well read. Total time commitment: 24 hours.

What's in Each Hour

To make it easy for you to learn exactly what you need to learn, each hour is structured along the same basic outline.

At the start of each hour, I'll tell you exactly what you'll learn in the next 60 minutes. Then we launch into the body of the lesson with plenty of examples and illustrative screenshots. At the end, I'll summarize the material to help put everything in perspective.

Most chapters will have one or more Try it Yourself sections. These are step-by-step tutorials to take you through a simple project to illustrate a CSS concept or technique that you've just learned.

The Workshop is designed to be completed within the hour of time you've set aside for each lesson and is a way to test and apply the knowledge you've gained. The Q&A section at the end of each hour is a mini-FAQ, answering Frequently Asked Questions you may have. The Exercises section suggests step-by-step activities to help you learn more about the topic, and Quizzes enable you to self-test your mastery of the subject.

Who Should Read This Book

I'm going to assume that you know the basics of HTML and have created web pages before; that you know how to run a text editor, save files and publish them on the Web, and do all the normal tasks related to making a website. If the concept of web design is completely new to you, Sams publishes some excellent introductory books, including *Sams Teach Yourself HTML and CSS in 24 Hours*.

As you go through the 24 lessons of this book, you'll learn practical CSS that you can put into practice immediately. By the time you finish the whole book, you'll know everything you need to know about Cascading Style Sheets, from browser support to the most effective ways to integrate CSS into your web development process. We'll make an expert out of you, in 24 hours or less!

What You Need

To display your CSS-based web designs, you need a web browser that has a reasonably good implementation of the Cascading Style Sheets specifications. The following browsers are recommended; you should have at least one of the following browsers installed on your system:

▶ Internet Explorer 6.0 or 7.0 (or higher) for Windows (http://www.microsoft.com/windows/ie/)

▶ Safari 1.3 or 2.0 (or higher) for Mac OS X (http://www.apple.com/safari/)

▶ Firefox 1.5 (or higher) for Windows, Linux, or Mac OS X (http://www.mozilla.com/firefox/)

▶ Camino 1.0 (or higher) for Mac OS X (http://www.caminobrowser.org/

▶ Opera 8.5 (or higher) for Windows, Linux, or Mac OS X (http://www.opera.com/)

These are most recent versions of each browser at the time this book is being written, and offer the highest level of support for CSS to date. Check the appropriate websites for newer updates of these browsers.

You will probably want to maintain a suite of additional browsers for testing purposes; older browsers have varying degrees of support for CSS. You'll learn more about browsers and their CSS implementations in Hour 3, "Browser Support for CSS."

In addition, you need some kind of editing software that allows you to create text files. This could be something as simple as TextEdit or Notepad, or as complex as an integrated web development suite. Any HTML editor that enables you to edit the source code works as a CSS editor; as I'm assuming you can create HTML files, anyone reading this book should have access to a text editor. In Hour 2, I list some CSS editing programs you can use.

The Book's Website

This book has a companion site hosted at Sams Publishing. At this site, you'll find:

▶ Two bonus chapters: Bonus Hour 1, "CSS and JavaScript," and Bonus Hour 2, "CSS and XML."

▶ Downloadable copies of code samples in the book

▶ Style sheets you can download and use

▶ Updates and additions to book material

To get to this content, all you need to do is go to www.samspublishing.com/register and register this book (enter this book's ISBN without the hyphens, 0672329069).

In addition to the official site, the author (that's me, Kynn) maintains an unofficial website for the book at www.css24.com.

Conventions Used in This Book

To make this book easier to understand, different typefaces are used in each hour to identify specific types of information.

New terms are set off in *italics* when they're first defined.

Screen captures for this book were created almost entirely with Firefox used on a Mac OS X computer. This isn't to suggest that such a setup is the only one worth using; rather, Firefox provides the most reliable CSS support and is readily available on Windows, Mac OS X, and Linux platforms.

CSS rules, properties, and values; HTML elements, attributes, and values; and other snippets of code are presented in a monospace font, `like this`. Placeholder values are shown in `italic monospace`. Longer code appears in a formal listing, which is also available on the website. For example:

LISTING 0.1   Code Listing Example

```
body
{
    color: white;
    background-color: maroon;
  }
```

In addition, several boxed elements appear throughout the book: By The Way, Did You Know? and Watch Out!

By the Way

By The Way is a short side comment from me that provides additional information or calls attention to something important. I'm usually chattier in a note than I am in the body of each hour.

Did you Know?

A Did You Know? is a useful bit of advice that may not be immediately obvious. These expand on the knowledge of the hour's text and give you new uses for what you've just learned.

Watch Out!

Watch Out! is exactly what it sounds like—it's a classic "Danger, Will Robinson!" warning alarm. If there's a possibility of you turning down the wrong path, I'll be there to steer you clear of it. If there's a bug in a browser's version of CSS support, I'll warn you with Watch Out!

Ready, Set, Go!

Are you eager to start? Ready your browser, sit yourself in front of your computer in a comfortable position, and go on to the first hour!

Let me know how well you've done at teaching yourself Cascading Style Sheets; drop me an email at kynn@css24.com. I'll try to respond to each letter, although I can't guarantee I'll be able to give personal web design advice to everyone. Just remember—by the time you finish this book, you'll know about as much about CSS as I do!

Good luck, and have fun styling!

—*Kynn Bartlett*

PART I

Introduction to CSS

HOUR 1

Understanding CSS

What You'll Learn in This Hour:

▶ What style sheets are and what the term "cascading" refers to

▶ How the Cascading Style Sheets standard was written and what the two levels of CSS refer to

▶ How CSS is used with HTML and XML and when to use it

▶ The types of style effects you can produce with CSS and what you can't do

▶ How browser support for CSS affects what you can do with style sheets

Cascading Style Sheets (CSS) can open up a whole new dimension to your web designs, delivering power and flexibility beyond what's available in plain HTML.

What Are Cascading Style Sheets?

Cascading Style Sheets is the name of a simple language that enables you to declare how documents are displayed by web browsers. This language is used extensively on the Web and can be applied to HTML as well as to newer XML-based languages.

Through the application of CSS, you're able to change many aspects of how a web page is displayed—the fonts, the colors, the layout, the graphics, the links, and more. Cascading Style Sheets enable content—your HTML markup, text, graphics, and multimedia—to be separated from presentation.

Defining Style Sheets

The concept of style sheets did not originate on the Web; it has been used extensively in computing for years now. The most familiar application of style sheets off the Web is the formatting styles used in word processors, such as Microsoft Word.

Microsoft Word allows you to assign parts of your file to specific styles, such as "Heading" or "Note," and then decide what sort of formatting should be applied to each style. For example, a Heading style should be larger and bold, with extra line spacing after the heading and in a specific heading font. This book, in fact, was composed in exactly that way; each part of the book, from headings to text paragraphs to tips and notes, has a specific style that I set as I composed the manuscript, and those styles eventually determined how you see the printed page today.

In the same way, Cascading Style Sheets let you, the web designer, assign specific styles to different types of HTML elements. You might want to make all your text one color, to make all your headings a specific font, and to specify that all notes should be centered in a box with a thin outline. You can do some of this in HTML by using <font> tags and various attributes, but that can get cumbersome and difficult to maintain. When you define your presentation styles in CSS, it becomes quick and easy to apply new styles that can affect all styles on a page or even the whole site—without editing the source HTML at all!

Defining Cascading

The term *cascading* in Cascading Style Sheets refers to a specific way in which browsers determine which styles to apply to a specific part of the page. This method is called "the cascade," and it's from the cascade that CSS takes its name.

When I'm designing something that I know is going to be used in a fixed medium, such as the printed page or this book, I can be pretty confident that the styles that I choose will show up exactly like I expect them to. All copies of this book will look exactly the same; the page layout won't vary from reader to reader, and the same fonts will appear in each copy. Page 57 of your copy of this book is identical to every other page 57 in existence.

When you're designing for a variable medium such as the Web, however, you don't have that certainty. The appearance of a web page (designed with CSS or not) depends on a number of factors, including the characteristics of the user's display device, his computer's color resolution, the version of the browser he's using, and even his preferred font size.

Did you Know?

Some users might not even be using monitors at all! People with visual disabilities routinely use the Web as a primary source of information, relying on software known as screen readers, which vocalize the content of a page. You'll learn more about how CSS benefits users with disabilities in Hour 22, "Accessibility and Print Media"; you can also read more at the International Center for Disability Resources on the Internet website at http://www.icdri.org/.

This lack of absolute control over the final presentation can be somewhat disconcerting for designers who are used to fixed mediums; how can you fine-tune your design if you don't know how it will eventually look? It's important to keep in mind that this isn't a design flaw in CSS—it's a deliberate feature. Creating designs that adapt to the user's environment and preferences widens your audience and enables more people to access your content.

The *cascade* is the set of principles that tells browsers how to merge together a number of presentation choices: the web developer's designs for the site, the web browser's capabilities and default settings, and the web user's preferences or requirements for display. In the cascade, items that are higher up in priority affect other properties with lower priorities, with the values "cascading" down like a waterfall. You'll learn more about this in Hour 7, "Cascading and Inheritance," but for now it's enough to understand that in CSS, the final presentation is an active collaboration between designer, browser, and user.

The Origin of Cascading Style Sheets

The Cascading Style Sheets language was created through a collaborative effort between web developers and browser programmers under the auspices of the World Wide Web Consortium (W3C for short).

The W3C is an international industry group, comprising hundreds of companies, research institutions, and web development organizations, that issues technical specifications for web languages and protocols.

W3C specifications are called *recommendations* because the W3C is technically not a standards-issuing organization, but in practice this is usually an issue of semantics. W3C recommendations are taken as defining a standard form of a web language, and they are used by web developers, software tool creators, browser programmers, and others as a blueprint for computer communication over the Web. Examples of W3C recommendations include Hypertext Markup Language (HTML), Extensible Markup Language (XML), Extensible Stylesheet Language (XSL), and Scalable Vector Graphics (SVG).

The CSS Specifications

The W3C recommendations issued by the Cascading Style Sheet working group are collectively the official specification for the CSS language. The CSS working group consists of a number of experts in web development, graphic design, and software programming, representing a number of companies, who all work together to establish a common styling language for the Web.

Two full recommendations have been issued for Cascading Style Sheets so far; these are called Cascading Style Sheets Level 1 (CSS1) and Cascading Style Sheets Level 2 (CSS2). An update to CSS2, CSS 2.1, has been drafted and is gaining acceptance. Work is under way currently on Cascading Style Sheets Level 3, but these are only draft proposals at the time of writing.

CSS Level 1

The Cascading Style Sheets Level 1 (sometimes called CSS1 for short) specification was officially issued as a W3C recommendation in December 1996. The URL for this specification is http://www.w3.org/TR/REC-CSS1.

If you try to read the W3C recommendation for CSS1, you may end up confused. That's because W3C documents aren't written as a general introduction to a subject but rather as precise language definitions for software developers. Most W3C recommendations are quite opaque to most normal people, although the CSS1 specification isn't too bad compared with some. Later in this hour I'll give some tips on how to read a W3C recommendation if you need to dive into it.

CSS Level 1 defines a number of simple text formatting properties, along with properties for colors, fonts and boxes, principles of the cascade, and the linking mechanism between CSS and HTML. CSS1 may be used to create some impressive results, but it doesn't deliver the full range of function found in CSS Level 2.

CSS Level 2

CSS Level 2 was published in May 1998 (at http://www.w3.org/TR/REC-CSS2) and extends the power of CSS considerably. CSS Level 2 enables the web developer to use CSS to lay out a page, replacing HTML tables; to create style sheets for specific output devices, such as printers or even Braille devices; to have fine control over which parts of the page receive styling; and to designate a wider range of effects, such as text shadows or downloadable fonts. CSS Level 2 includes and extends all properties and values defined in CSS Level 1.

CSS Level 2.1

The W3C published a working draft in June 2005 called Cascading Style Sheets, Level 2 Revision 1 (http://www.w3.org/TR/CSS21), more commonly known as CSS 2.1 This update to the CSS2 specification is not yet a formal W3C recommendation, but was written to reflect a snapshot of the current state of CSS implementation in browsers. CSS properties and values that were not widely supported by the browsers were cut from the specification, a few widely supported values were added, and various problems in the definition of the CSS language were fixed.

CSS 2.1 has been adopted as a de facto standard, if only because it gives a good approximation of the most workable features in CSS2. Generally speaking, nearly all CSS 2.1 style sheets should work properly in the newest versions of the major browsers, and most web developers are writing in CSS 2.1 (even if they haven't read the official specification). For those reasons, this book focuses on CSS 2.1 when there is a conflict between the CSS2 and CSS 2.1 languages; CSS 2.1 is the safer, saner version.

Other Style Languages

CSS isn't the only style language, but it's the primary one used on the Web. Some other style languages include Document Style Semantics and Specification Language (DSSSL) and Extensible Stylesheet Language (XSL).

DSSSL is an older and more complex styling language developed for Standard Generalized Markup Language (SGML), an ancestor of XML and the basis for HTML syntax. DSSSL is rarely used on the Web, just as other SGML technologies (besides HTML) are extremely uncommon.

XSL is a group of related languages intended for styling XML documents. *XSL Transformations (XSLT)* is a method to describe a transformation from one XML-based language to another. XSL Formatting Objects (XSL-FO) is one such language; an XML document can be converted to XSL-FO with XSLT. XSL-FO files contain XML formatting objects, which can be used by browsers or printing software to lay out the appearance of a document precisely, most commonly for print media.

CSS in Web Design

Because the Cascading Style Sheets language was designed to be used primarily with HTML, CSS is ideally suited for use in web design. The language is simple and flexible enough to encompass all common web presentation effects, and the concepts should be familiar to anyone who has used HTML before. To use the CSS language effectively, it's important to understand how it's used, what it can do, and what it can't do.

How CSS Is Used

In CSS, the term *style sheet* refers to a file consisting of a number of CSS rules. A *rule* is the smallest unit of CSS, defining one or more style effects. Each rule identifies which parts of the web page it selects and what properties it applies to that section of the page. The web document then links to that style sheet, which means the browser downloads the style sheet and applies the rules when it displays the web page. A single CSS file can be linked to by any number of documents, so one style sheet can control the look of the entire site or a portion thereof.

CSS can be used with several different markup languages, including HTML and XML-based languages.

CSS and HTML

The *Hypertext Markup Language* (*HTML*) consists of a series of tags that mark up specific elements within a document. Each of those elements has a default presentation style, which is provided by the browser, based on the formal specification for HTML. You can apply a style sheet to an HTML page by linking to it or even by including the style sheet within the HTML file, and the presentation style for each element can be redefined.

A hypothetical style sheet can be created that states that all <h1> tags should be presented on a green background with white text, and all <p> tags should be indented 25 pixels and the text justified. This would change the appearance of any web page that links to that style sheet.

HTML pages can contain attributes and tags that set presentational styles, but their versatility and utility are limited compared with CSS. Style sheets can be used either in conjunction with HTML presentational markup, such as <font> or color="red" attributes, or can replace presentational tags and attributes entirely.

For example, CSS is used extensively to define the colors, look, and layout of this book's author's personal site (http://kynn.com/). In Figure 1.1, no style sheet has been applied to the site, and so the appearance is quite plain. No HTML attributes have been used for formatting because the site relies on Cascading Style Sheets for presentation effects. The fonts are all browser defaults and the colors are very basic. Despite the somewhat boring appearance, all information is clearly visible and the page can be used easily. All that it needs is a style sheet to make it look better.

Figure 1.2 is the author's site as it appears in a browser that understands Cascading Style Sheets. The style sheet not only specifies more attractive fonts for the page, but it also reformats the navigation bar, lays out the page in columns, and aligns the content attractively. The overall effect of the style sheet is to enhance the appearance considerably, making the site appear more friendly, identifiable, and usable.

What does CSS look like? In Figure 1.3 you can see an example of the CSS "source code" used to style the web page in Figure 1.2. As you can see, the CSS language is very different in form and syntax from HTML.

FIGURE 1.1
The author's website without CSS.

FIGURE 1.2
The author's website with style sheet applied.

CSS and XML

Cascading Style Sheets are also designed to work with *Extensible Markup Language* (*XML*). XML languages often don't have an inherent presentation defined, and CSS files can be applied directly to XML files to add presentational styling.

FIGURE 1.3
Viewing a style sheet's CSS codes.

```
body { background-color: white;
       color: #333333;
       font-family: Verdana, sans-serif;
       margin: 0;
       padding: 0;
       }

a:link { color: #DD8800; text-decoration: none; }
a:visited { color: #CC8866; text-decoration: none; }
a:hover { color: lime; }

#layout { padding: 1em; }

#nav { position: fixed;
       top: 0px;
       left: 0px;
       padding-top: 3px; padding-bottom: 3px;
       background-color: #333333;
       color: white; width: 100%; text-align: center;
       text-transform: lowercase; }

#nav .section, #nav .shead, #nav .sitem, #nav h1 { display: inline; }

#nav .section { font-size: 90%; }

#nav .shead, #nav .sitem { padding-left: 1em; padding-right: 1em; }

#nav h1 { font-size: 1em; background-color: #333333; color: white; }

#nav a:link, #nav a:visited, #footer a:link, #footer a:visited {
   text-decoration: none; color: #CCCCCC; }

#nav a:hover, #footer a:hover { color: lime; }
```

By the Way

> For most of this book, I'm going to assume you're using CSS with HTML. The techniques for using CSS with XML are pretty much the same as using CSS with HTML. Specific issues related to XML are covered in Bonus Web Hour 2, "CSS and XML," available on this book's website (described in the Introduction).

What CSS Can Do

As you see on the author's site, the application of a style sheet can drastically change the appearance of an HTML page. CSS can be used to change anything from text styling to page layout, and can be combined with JavaScript to produce dynamic presentation effects.

Text Formatting and Colors

CSS can be used to produce a number of text effects, such as

- ▶ Choosing specific fonts and font sizes

- ▶ Setting bold, italics, underlines, and text shadows

- ▶ Changing text color and background color

- ▶ Changing the colors of links or removing underlining

- ▶ Indenting or centering text

- ▶ Stretching and adjusting text size and line spacing

▶ Transforming sections of text to upper-, lower-, or mixed case

▶ Adding drop-capitals and other special effects

These are all accomplished by creating CSS rules to set properties on text.

Graphical Appearance and Layout

CSS can also be used to change the look of the entire page. CSS properties for positioning—sometimes called CSS-P—were introduced in CSS Level 2 and enable you to format a web page without using tables. Some of the things you can do with CSS to affect the graphical layout of the page include

▶ Setting a background graphic, controlling its location, tiling, and scrolling

▶ Drawing borders and outlines around sections of a page

▶ Setting vertical and horizontal margins on all elements, as well as vertical and horizontal padding

▶ Flowing text around images, or even around other text

▶ Positioning sections of the page in precise locations on the virtual canvas

▶ Redefining how HTML tables, forms, and lists are presented

▶ Layering page elements atop each other in a specified order

Dynamic Actions

Dynamic effects in web design are those that are interactive, changing in response to being used. CSS lets you create interactive designs that respond to the user, such as

▶ Mouseover effects on links

▶ Dynamically inserted content before or after HTML tags

▶ Automatic numbering of page elements

▶ Fully interactive designs in Dynamic HTML (DHTML) and Asynchronous JavaScript and XML (AJAX)

What CSS Can't Do

Although CSS is powerful, it does have certain limitations. The primary limitation of CSS is that it is restricted to working mainly with only what is present in the markup file. The display order can be somewhat altered, and a small amount of text content can be inserted, but to produce major changes in the source HTML (or XML), you need to use another method—such as XSL Transformations (XSLT).

Also, CSS is a younger language than HTML by about five years; this means that some of the oldest browsers don't understand styles written in CSS, or might not load a style sheet at all. CSS is also of limited use on simple text browsers, such as those written for cell phones or mobile devices.

The Cascading Style Sheets language was designed to be backwards compatible, which means older browsers don't refuse to show your web page if they aren't able to display your styles. Instead, the default HTML presentation is used, and if you've designed your CSS and HTML properly, the page content is usable even if your CSS styles aren't shown. This allows older browsers to access even advanced CSS pages.

When to Use CSS

After you start learning to create Cascading Style Sheets, you probably will never want to stop using them! You can start using CSS today, as a supplement to your presentational markup, and then gradually move toward purer CSS presentations as you learn more.

Reading W3C Specifications

You may find yourself referring to the CSS recommendations from time to time—as well as the HTML and XHTML specifications as well. As they define the language, a specification is considered the definitive source for that language. After you get the hang of reading the CSS 2.1 specification, it makes a useful reference—but there's a learning curve.

A W3C recommendation is different from most other types of technical writing. Most technical works you're familiar with, from user manuals to books like this one, are written as documentation. Documentation is a user resource, something that helps you understand how to use a program or language. Tutorials, reference works, and textbooks are all written with that goal.

Standards, including the de facto standards of W3C recommendations, are written differently. The purpose of a standards document is to be definitive. A specification explicitly defines what is contained within a given set of technology. The key to comprehending a spec is not only understanding how it is organized but also understanding the intended audience and use of the specification.

In nearly all cases, the intended audience of a W3C specification is not you. It's not web developers, even though the languages defined by these specs are written for use by web developers. As a web developer, you'll definitely be able to gain useful knowledge from the W3C's recommendations, but that's just an ancillary effect.

Figure 1.4 is an example—this is part of the CSS 2.1 specification; specifically, the part that defines a property called `clip`. Does this make sense to you? Probably not, because it's full of technical jargon, links to other parts of the specification, and advice on whether or not any "user agents" (browsers) must support a given feature.

11.1.2 Clipping: the 'clip' property

A *clipping region* defines what portion of an element's border box is visible. By default, the element is not clipped. However, the clipping region may be explicitly set with the 'clip' property.

'clip'
Value:	<shape> I auto I inherit
Initial:	auto
Applies to:	absolutely positioned elements
Inherited:	no
Percentages:	N/A
Media:	visual
Computed value:	For rectangle values, a rectangle consisting of four computed lengths; otherwise, as specified

The 'clip' property applies only to absolutely positioned elements. Values have the following meanings:

auto
The element does not clip.
<shape>
In CSS 2.1, the only valid <shape> value is: rect(<top>, <right>, <bottom>, <left>) where <top> and <bottom> specify offsets from the top border edge of the box, and <right>, and <left> specify offsets from the left border edge of the box in left-to-right text and from the right border edge of the box in right-to-left text. Authors should separate offset values with commas. User agents must support separation with commas, but may also support separation without commas, because a previous version of this specification was ambiguous in this respect.

<top>, <right>, <bottom>, and <left> may either have a <length> value or 'auto'. Negative lengths are permitted. The value 'auto' means that a given edge of the clipping region will be the same as the edge of the element's generated border box (i.e., 'auto' means the same as '0' for <top> and <left> (in left-to-right text, <right> in right-to-left text), the same as the computed value of the height plus the sum of vertical padding and border widths for <bottom>, and the same as the computed value of the width plus the sum of the horizontal padding and border widths for <right> (in left-to-right text, <left> in right-to-left text), such that four 'auto' values result in the clipping region being the same as the element's border box).

FIGURE 1.4
Why you don't want to just start reading the specifications.

The real audience for W3C recommendations is the software developers who create programs that use the protocols and languages in the specs. The CSS 2.1 specification, for example, was written primarily for implementers at Microsoft, Opera, Mozilla, Apple, and other software companies producing web-related software. In other words, people who already have a basic understanding of what the language does, and how other languages work with it.

One consequence of being written for those already in the know is that the W3C specifications aren't written linearly but circularly. To make sense of what's written in section two, you need to have read not only section one, but also sections three, four, and five, plus the appendix and about a half dozen related specifications. For a definitive work, that's actually quite appropriate; you can't read a dictionary straight through, either, and all terms in a dictionary are defined with other dictionary terms. W3C recommendations are written in the same manner, so you'll probably have to read through several times—following hyperlinks instead of just proceeding linearly—to fully grasp everything.

To approach a W3C recommendation, first understand the structure of the document. Nearly all are written with the same general outline. The first part of the structure looks like a bit of legalistic fluff, but is actually quite important; it identifies when the document was written and what status it holds in the W3C's hierarchy of technical recommendations. The W3C Process is a procedure for moving a working group's documents from draft to officially approved recommendation, and there are a number of steps along the way. The status of the document is stated at the very beginning.

A short introduction usually follows, which states the purpose of the recommendation. A glossary of terms might be provided at the front, but most commonly it is at the end; read it before the main content so you'll recognize the terms, even if they don't make sense until you've read more. Also at the end you'll find a list of references; W3C documents don't usually link directly to other sources but instead link to their reference lists. These references include the links out to other materials you can find on the Web, many of which are essential to making sense of what you're reading.

The main content is in the middle, of course, and is usually divided into sensible categories, although if you start following links within a recommendation, you'll find yourself skipping randomly through the text, which can be disorienting. The best W3C recommendations have small menu bars at the top that allow you to page between sections or, more usefully, to jump directly to an alphabetized table listing all elements, attributes, or properties. The index at the back of a long recommendation also proves invaluable when navigating the structure of the W3C specification.

Browser Support

Unfortunately for those of us who want to reap the full benefits of using CSS, the browser manufacturers were slow in providing support for CSS in their software. This meant that people who programmed authoring software didn't bother to produce CSS (after all, which browsers could display it?) and web developers didn't bother to learn CSS because it was a pointless exercise.

Early browsers that understood Cascading Style Sheets, such as Internet Explorer 3 and Netscape 4, had only incomplete implementations, meaning that even simple style sheets using rules defined in CSS1 might not have displayed consistently. This meant that CSS was considered unreliable for several years after the recommendations were issued.

Thankfully, the Dark Age of CSS didn't last forever, and current browsers have decent support for the CSS standards. Recent versions of Firefox, Internet Explorer, Opera, and Safari all have good implementations of the Cascading Style Sheet specifications. We're entering a new age of CSS, one where you can design safely and confidently, knowing that your style sheet won't confuse some old browser with buggy CSS implementations.

Workarounds for Browser Limitations

However, some older browsers still exist and are used by a number of web surfers, despite the poor and quirky support for CSS—most notably Internet Explorer versions 5, 5.5, and 6. Furthermore, not even the newest browsers adhere 100% to the specifications, although they come very close. In Hour 3, "Browser Support for CSS," you'll learn more about what some of those limitations may be.

For these reasons, it may be necessary to employ workarounds or browser hacks in your CSS or HTML to ensure that your style effects come through as intended. These are described in Hour 24, "Troubleshooting and Browser Hacks," and specific implementation problems are mentioned throughout the book when you need to know about them.

Summary

Cascading Style Sheets are files that describe how to present specific effects when displaying a web page. They're so named because they follow a specific pattern, called the cascade, which determines the order in which style effects are applied. The CSS language is a web standard, defined by the World Wide Web Consortium; the current version is CSS Level 2, updated by CSS 2.1.

A style sheet consists of CSS rules that define styles to apply to specific parts of the page. Style rules can change the color, font, and other qualities of the text of a page; they can define the layout and graphical appearance; and they can add interactivity to a site.

Although Cascading Style Sheets are quite powerful and useful, care needs to be taken to apply them in ways consistent with current browser implementations. Not all browsers have good CSS support, and using CSS without understanding the support issues can lead to problems if you're not careful.

Workshop

This workshop contains a Q&A section and quiz questions to help reinforce what you've learned in this hour. If you get stuck, the answers to the quiz can be found after the questions.

Q&A

Q. *Which version of CSS should I use?*

A. Cascading Style Sheets Level 2 is the most current W3C recommendation; it contains all the CSS1 properties and gives more complete definitions for them, in addition to defining new properties that weren't included in CSS1. Very few browsers (if any) supported only CSS1; most of them supported either a subset of CSS1 or a set chosen from CSS1 and CSS2 properties, so the division between the two is not really meaningful when you look at browser support. Because CSS 2.1 updates CSS2 to fix some problematic definitions and remove unimplemented property values, CSS 2.1 is your best bet for current and future compatibility. However, there are still implementation problems even with CSS 2.1, and so you have to test all your style sheets on a wide variety browsers.

Q. *So what's so cool about CSS anyway?*

A. Because Cascading Style Sheets let you encode your style effects separately from your HTML, this promotes separation of presentation and content. That means that the look of the page is independent from the information on the page, and that's cool for a number of reasons. You can create a single style sheet that styles the entire site at once. You can develop alternate style sheets for specific output devices, such as printers. You can ensure greater accessibility for people with disabilities. In addition, Cascading Style Sheets also afford a measure of control over the presentation, which simply is not available in traditional HTML web design.

Q. *What's the most important thing to know about Cascading Style Sheets?*

A. Browser support is the critical issue in CSS design. You will see this theme repeated throughout the book. Lack of browser support has seriously hindered the use of CSS, and many of the really great things you can do with style sheets continue to be limited in many browsers. Fortunately, the browser companies are working hard to improve their programs, and are getting ever closer to full, correct implementation of the CSS specifications.

Quiz

1. What is the cascade in CSS?

2. Which markup languages can be used with CSS?

3. What's the current version of Cascading Style Sheets?

Answers

1. The cascade is the set of rules that order how style preferences are combined together. The effects of higher-priority rules cascade down like a waterfall.

2. CSS was designed to work with HTML as well as with any XML-based markup language.

3. The current version of Cascading Style Sheets is CSS Level 2, updated by the CSS 2.1 draft.

HOUR 2

Getting Started with CSS

What You'll Learn in This Hour:

- ▶ What kinds of tools, from text editors to CSS software, you can use to write your style sheets
- ▶ How to create, name, and save a style sheet
- ▶ What the different parts of a CSS rule are and the function of each
- ▶ How and when to add comments to a style sheet
- ▶ Which simple rules you can use to create a basic style sheet
- ▶ How to apply your style sheet to a simple HTML file
- ▶ Which browsers to use to test your style sheet

Creating a Style Sheet

A Cascading Style Sheet, as you learned in Hour 1, "Understanding CSS," is simply a file made up of style rules. CSS files are ordinary text files, just as HTML files are ordinary text files. This means that you can use a wide variety of programs to create a style sheet, from simple text editors to specialized software written just for creating and maintaining style sheets. Anything that can be used to create a text file can create a style sheet.

Because Cascading Style Sheets are pretty simple to write, you don't need to use complex tools to create a basic style sheet. Many web developers will write CSS by hand, meaning that they type out the text of each rule; however, authoring tools exist that can make this task easier.

Software Tools for CSS

Your editing environment is the program or set of programs that you use to create your style sheet. You'll want to choose the editing environment that works best for you, be that a text editor, a style sheet editor, or a web development tool. I use a text editor myself, and I recommend starting simple, at least until you've learned enough about the basics of CSS to understand how editing tools can help you.

Text Editors

Every operating system comes with a basic text editor, and because CSS is just basic text, it's a good match for one of these programs. A text editor is a simple program that just produces plain text files, which means it can also be used to create HTML or CSS files. Unlike word processing software, text editors don't save formatting with the text; that's why they are said to produce plain text. Text editors are ubiquitous and don't get in the way of your learning about CSS, so this is probably where you want to start. You probably already know how to use one of the text editors on your computer. Some basic text editors include

▶ Notepad or WordPad on Microsoft Windows

▶ TextEdit on Macintosh

▶ vi, vim, or emacs on Linux or Unix

Figure 2.1 shows a style sheet being edited in Notepad on Windows; this is the style sheet from the author's personal website, which was shown in Hour 1. Don't worry too much about reading and understanding the properties; the style sheet is rather complex and has a lot of properties from the middle or end of this book.

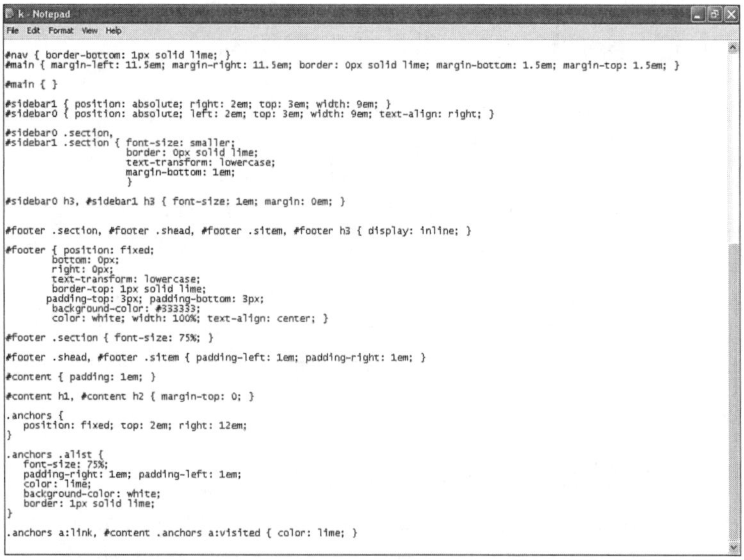

FIGURE 2.1
Editing a style sheet in Notepad.

```
#nav { border-bottom: 1px solid lime; }
#main { margin-left: 11.5em; margin-right: 11.5em; border: 0px solid lime; margin-bottom: 1.5em; margin-top: 1.5em; }

#main { }

#sidebar1 { position: absolute; right: 2em; top: 3em; width: 9em; }
#sidebar0 { position: absolute; left: 2em; top: 3em; width: 9em; text-align: right; }

#sidebar0 .section,
#sidebar1 .section { font-size: smaller;
                     border: 0px solid lime;
                     text-transform: lowercase;
                     margin-bottom: 1em;
                     }

#sidebar0 h3, #sidebar1 h3 { font-size: 1em; margin: 0em; }

#footer .section, #footer .shead, #footer .sitem, #footer h3 { display: inline; }

#footer { position: fixed;
          bottom: 0px;
          right: 0px;
          text-transform: lowercase;
          border-top: 1px solid lime;
          padding-top: 3px; padding-bottom: 3px;
          background-color: #333333;
          color: white; width: 100%; text-align: center; }

#footer .section { font-size: 75%; }

#footer .shead, #footer .sitem { padding-left: 1em; padding-right: 1em; }

#content { padding: 1em; }

#content h1, #content h2 { margin-top: 0; }

.anchors {
          position: fixed; top: 2em; right: 12em;
}

.anchors .alist {
          font-size: 75%;
          padding-right: 1em; padding-left: 1em;
          color: lime;
          background-color: white;
          border: 1px solid lime;
}

.anchors a:link, #content .anchors a:visited { color: lime; }
```

You can use a word processing program, such as Microsoft Word, to create text files, but you need to remember to save your files as plain text without any special formatting. It's probably easier to just use a text editor, although most of them lack the advanced features found in word processors, such as advanced find-and-replace and word counting. Fortunately, you'll rarely need those features when editing CSS.

Style Sheet Editors

Some software has been written specifically to create CSS style sheets; these have advanced features such as color-coding of rules and properties, syntax checking, and more. These are great tools, and I highly recommend them when you're doing serious CSS development; if you're just beginning, though, they may be more than you need right now and could overwhelm you with options. After you understand the principles and language of CSS, however, a style sheet editor is invaluable. Some of the CSS editors available include

▶ TopStyle, for Windows; http://www.bradsoft.com/topstyle/

▶ Style Master, for Windows and Mac OS X; http://www.westciv.com/style_master/

▶ CSSEdit, for Mac OS X; http://www.macrabbit.com/cssedit/

▶ JustStyle CSS Editor, for all Java-enabled computers; http://www.ucware.com/juststyle/

The screenshot in Figure 2.2 shows the author's style sheet being edited in Style Master, one of the CSS editors listed here. As you can see, a style sheet editor offers a lot more in the way of development features compared to a simple text editor, but it's also more complex to use.

HTML Editors and Web Development Software

Because CSS is an integral part of web design, web design packages that let you create HTML often support CSS editing. Visual editors let you set styles and create the style sheet behind the scenes, whereas those with source editing modes enable you to edit the style sheet directly. As with CSS editors, I recommend using these after you've become familiar with the basics of CSS syntax. Your favorite web editing environment may already include CSS support; some that do include

▶ Microsoft FrontPage, for Windows; http://www.microsoft.com/frontpage/

▶ Macromedia Dreamweaver, for Windows and Mac OS X; http://www.macromedia.com/software/dreamweaver/

FIGURE 2.2
Editing a style
sheet in Style
Master.

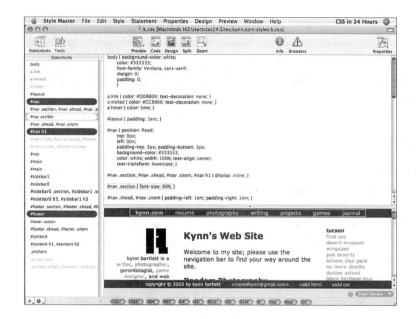

FIGURE 2.2
Editing a style
sheet in Style
Master.

▶ Adobe GoLive, for Windows and Macintosh; http://www.adobe.com/products/golive/

▶ CoffeeCup HTML Editor, for Windows; http://www.coffeecup.com/editor/

▶ BBEdit, for Mac OS X; http://www.barebones.com/products/bbedit/

Naming and Saving a Style Sheet

However you edit your style sheet, the basic principle will be the same: You create a text file that contains the CSS rules, and you save that as a CSS file. Your style sheet's filename shouldn't contain spaces, so that it will be easier to use on the Web.

The extension you should use is .css, so your files should be named something like test.css or sitedesign.css. While you're learning and practicing, you'll probably want to keep the .css file in the same directory as your HTML pages. After you've got the hang of CSS, you'll probably want to store your style sheets in a designated directory on your website; I usually create a /styles/ directory for mine.

Writing CSS Rules

The building blocks of any style sheet are the CSS rules that compose it. Each rule is a single statement that identifies what should be styled and how those styles should be applied. Style sheets are then composed of lists of rules, which the browser uses to determine what a page should look like (or even sound like).

The Basic Structure of a CSS Rule

A *CSS rule* consists of two sections: the selector(s) and the declaration(s). A declaration is made up of a property and a value for that property. A simple CSS rule would therefore look something like this:

```
selector { property: value; }
```

One important thing to note is that CSS ignores extra whitespace, just as HTML usually does. This means that as far as CSS-enabled browsers are concerned, one space is equal to twenty spaces or even five spaces, four blank lines, and four more spaces. So the rule could be written like this and still mean the same thing:

```
selector
  {
    property:
      value;
  }
```

You should feel free to use whatever spaces and lines you need within your CSS to make it easy to read and maintain. For example, I usually indent the property and value pairs quite a bit by inserting spaces; this makes it easier for me to see at a glance where one rule ends and the next begins. By being consistent in how you use blank spaces in your style sheets, you can keep them easy to read and maintain. There is no one best way to write a style rule, and you may end up using different spacing in different situations. As long as it works for you, that's what matters.

The Selector

The *selector* part of the rule tells which section of the document the rule covers. The simplest type of selector is a type selector that indicates a specific markup element, such as the <p> tag in HTML. You write a type selector by just giving the name of the element without the <> brackets, as in the following:

```
p { property: value; }
```

Such a rule would select the styling of all <p> tags.

The Declaration

The next part of the rule is the *declaration*. Declarations are enclosed in {} braces. Within the braces, the property name is given first, followed by a colon, and then a property value. An ending semicolon is optional but recommended for reasons that will become apparent later this hour. The entire rule is concluded by the ending brace.

Properties

Properties are defined by the official CSS specifications; these are the specific style effects you can define and expect to be supported by CSS-compliant browsers. Most browsers are likely to ignore properties that aren't part of the CSS specification, although some browsers recognize nonstandard properties that are not part of the formal language specification. It's best to not rely on these proprietary extensions, but browsers that don't recognize them simply overlook them. In Hour 3, "Browser Support for CSS," you'll learn more about how browsers handle or don't handle CSS.

Values

The *value* of the declaration follows the property name, after the colon, and defines exactly how that property should be set. The range of values for each property is also defined in the CSS specifications. For example, the property named `color` can take values that consist of color names or codes, as in the following:

```
p { color: blue; }
```

This rule declares that the content of all paragraph tags should have their `color` properties set to the value `blue`. So all <p> text would turn blue.

> What happens if you don't set the `color`? Well, you can probably guess from your work with HTML that a default will be chosen—one set by the browser or the user's preferences. The color might also be set by the text attribute on the <body> tag, or on a <font> tag. CSS adds additional ways to determine the color, including writing a rule with the <body> tag as the selector, which would then apply to all <p> tags within the <body>—that is to say, it would apply to all paragraphs on the page.
>
> The specific process CSS uses to determine the color of the text or of any other property settings is called the *cascade*. You'll learn more about how the cascade works in Hour 7, "Cascading and Inheritance."

Combining CSS Rules

You can combine two CSS rules that share the same selector by listing their declarations within the curly braces. The ending semicolon is no longer optional between two rules combined this way; it's a necessary separator between the two declarations. For ease of editing and combining, I suggest always including the semicolon even if your braces contain only one declaration.

Here's an example of two CSS rules with the same selector:

```
p { color: blue; }
p { font-size: large; }
```

These rules can be combined into one rule like the following:

```
p { color: blue; font-size: large; }
```

I could have also written the rule like this:

```
p
  {
    color:          blue;
    font-size:      large;
  }
```

That particular style of spacing makes it a little easier to cut and paste entire lines while writing or testing the CSS. The browsers don't care about the whitespace—it's there to help you organize your style sheet in whatever manner works best for you.

You can also combine rules if they have the same declarations and different selectors. You combine selectors by putting them in a list, separated by commas. For example, the following rules have the same declarations:

```
p { color: blue; }
address { color: blue; }
```

You can write them as one rule, as follows:

```
p, address { color: blue; }
```

This rule says, "The content of <p> tags and of <address> tags should be colored as blue text."

You can use multiple selectors together with multiple declarations; that is perfectly legal and very common. You can also write additional rules to further style those selectors together or separately. Here's what that might look like:

```
p, address
  {
    color:          blue;
    font-size:      large;
  }
p
  {
    font-family:    Arial;
  }
```

CSS Comments

Like many other languages, including HTML, CSS allows you to embed *comments* in the source code. A comment is a special bit of code that you embed in your CSS that is completely ignored by the browser. Comments serve as a way of adding to the source notes that are meant for the author of the style sheet or someone maintaining it. The user doesn't ever see comments, and they won't affect the style of the page; they are significant only when reading or editing the style sheet itself.

Comments can be used to describe what your style sheet is doing at a particular point, or perhaps why it's doing it, so that when you come back to the style sheet later, you can recall why you wrote it that particular way. Comments are also useful for hiding sections of code that you feel you don't need any more or that you want browsers to ignore; this is known as *commenting out* your code. Comments can also be used to identify the author and the creation date of the style sheet and to provide a copyright notice.

Comments in CSS begin with the characters /* and end with the characters */. Anything between the start of the comment and the end is ignored. Here's an example of a comment:

```
/* Let's turn all the paragraph text blue */
p { color: blue; }
```

Your comments can appear anywhere you like, even inside a rule:

```
p
  {
    color: /* make it less blue */ purple;
    font-size:  large;
  }
```

You can comment out parts of a declaration if you decide you don't want that particular part of the style rule to be applied, but you don't want to delete it. This is useful for testing various options when developing your style sheet. For example, this comments out the font-size declaration:

```
p
  {
    color: /* make it less blue */ purple;
    /*   font-size:    large;     */
  }
```

However, you can't *nest* comments, meaning that if you try to enclose one comment within another, both comments end at the first */. For example, imagine that you want to comment out the color purple instead; if the comment markers are in the wrong place, as in the following, it doesn't work:

```
p
  {
    /* color: /* make it less blue */ purple; */
    font-size:     large;
  }
```

In this case, the comment ends after `blue`, not at the end of the declaration. This leaves the word `purple` floating there outside the comment. CSS browsers will probably ignore it because a `purple` by itself doesn't have any particular meaning in CSS, but that's just lucky this time. You need to be careful when placing your comments so that you don't accidentally try to nest them.

Simple CSS Properties for Text Formatting

As you've probably surmised from the previous examples, there are CSS properties that can be used to set the text color, the size of the font, and the family of the font—`color`, `font-size`, and `font-family`, respectively. These are some of the simplest and yet most useful CSS properties; collectively, they perform the same function as the HTML `<font>` tag. Another very useful property is `background-color`, which sets the color of the background.

The `color` Property

The `color` property is used to set the foreground color of the element, which is the property controlling the color of the text. For example,

```
h1 { color: lime; }
h2 { color: red; }
```

This makes all `<h1>` elements a bright, lime-green color and makes all `<h1>` elements red. As with HTML, you can use one of 17 standard color names, or you can give an RGB value, such as #FF0000. The color names and their corresponding RGB values are shown in Table 2.1.

TABLE 2.1   Color Names in CSS

Color Name	RGB Value	Color Name	RGB Value
aqua	#00FFFF	olive	#808000
black	#000000	orange	#ffA500
blue	#0000FF	purple	#800080
fuchsia	#FF00FF	red	#FF0000
gray	#808080	silver	#C0C0C0
green	#008000	teal	#008080
lime	#00FF00	white	#FFFFFF
maroon	#800000	yellow	#FFFF00
navy	#000080		

The background-color **Property**

You can use the background-color property to set the background color. The values are the same as for the color property—color names or RGB values. To set the background color for the whole page, use the <body> tag in your selector; you can set backgrounds on any other elements as well. For example,

```
body { background: silver; }
h1 { background: #FFFF00; }
```

> When you set the background color, make sure you've also set a foreground color that is visible against it! Otherwise your text may be very hard to read.

The font-size **Property**

The font-size property enables you to specify the size of the text that's displayed to the user. One of the easier ways to specify font sizes is to give a value relative to the user's default text size; this respects the user's preferences as set in the browser.

The default text size has a value of normal; larger sizes go up in increments of about 20% to values of large, x-large, and xx-large. Smaller sizes decrease by 20% to small, x-small, and xx-small. You can also use the relative values larger and smaller to indicate one step up or down the scale from the current size. Here are some examples:

```
dl { font-size: large; }
caption { font-size: small; }
em { font-size: larger; }
```

The font-family **Property**

You can use the font-family property to set the font face of the text. So why is it called font-family and not font-face? When you designate a font, you're really designating a whole family of related variants within the same font family. So when choosing Arial font, you're actually choosing the Arial family of fonts, each one slightly different in size.

CSS also uses *generic font families*. The generic font families are sans-serif, serif, monospace, cursive, and fantasy. These aren't names of specific fonts, but rather a broad class that can be used as defaults if the browser doesn't know what a font name represents. If you choose a font that isn't installed on the user's machine, the browser uses just the normal font, so make sure you designate a generic font family as well as a specific one. You indicate the generic font by listing it after the specific font, separated by a comma.

Common web fonts and their generic families are shown on Table 2.2.

TABLE 2.2 Common Font Families

Font	Generic Font Family
Arial	sans-serif
Times New Roman	serif
Courier New	monospace
Verdana	sans-serif

If the name of the font family has more than one word, enclose it in quotes. Here are some examples of CSS rules that use font-family:

```
body { font-family: Arial, sans-serif; }
h1 { font-family: "Courier New", monospace; }
h2 { font-family: "Times New Roman", serif; }
```

You'll learn more about font families and font sizes in Hour 9, "Fonts and Font Families."

A Simple Style Sheet

Using just the simple properties and values you've learned so far this hour, you already can create a basic style sheet; an example of a complete style sheet is shown in Listing 2.1.

LISTING 2.1 A Basic Style Sheet with Color, Size, and Font Declarations

```
/* basic-2.1.css */
body     { font-family: Arial;
           color: black;
           background-color: white; }

/* I think Verdana looks nice for headlines */
h1, h2, h3, h4, h5, h6
         { font-family: Verdana, sans-serif; }

/* This makes the largest heading have a background */
h1       { background-color: silver; }

/* This puts the even numbered headings in gray */
h2, h4, h6
         { color: gray; }

table    { background-color: white; }
th       { background-color: black;
           color: white;
           font-size: smaller; }
td       { background-color: gray;
```

LISTING 2.1 Continued

```
        font-size: smaller; }

address  { font-family: "Courier New", monospace;
           font-size: larger; }
```

You can find a copy of this style sheet on the book's website.

Linking a Style Sheet to an HTML Page

A style sheet by itself doesn't really do anything except sit there on your hard drive or web server. If you try to load it in your browser, it displays as just plain text. To actually use the CSS rules, you need to have a file with markup, such as an HTML page, and you need to add an HTML tag to link the CSS file to the web page.

A Simple HTML Page for Styling

Listing 2.2 shows the structure of a basic HTML page like one you might find on the Web; it has headlines, paragraphs, horizontal rules, and even a table on the side. You can download a copy of this file from the book's website—because that's easier than typing in the whole thing.

LISTING 2.2 A Simple HTML File that Needs Styling

```html
<!-- authorbio-2.2.html -->
<html>
  <head>
    <title>Kynn.com</title>
  </head>
  <body>
    <h1>Kynn.com</h1>
    <table align="right" width="25%">
      <tr><th><h3>New Stuff</h3></th></tr>
      <tr><td>
        <ul>
          <li>Pictures of <a href="http://www.desertmuseum.org/">
              The Arizona-Sonora Desert Museum</a> from
              <a href="/gallery/2006/02/desertmuseum/">February
              2006</a></li>
          <li>The <a href="/projects/heritage-tour/">Black
              Heritage Tour of Tucson, Arizona</a></li>
        </ul>
      </td></tr>
    </table>
    <h2>Kynn Bartlett's Web Site</h2>
    <p>Welcome to my site!</p>
    <h3>Biography</h3>
    <p>Kynn Bartlett has been using the Internet since
       1986, and has been a Web developer since 1994.
```

LISTING 2.2   Continued

```
      Self-taught in HTML, CSS, XML, and many other Web
      technologies, he passes this knowledge along to others
      through authoring books, teaching online classes, and
      giving seminars and presentations.  His specialty is
      Web accessibility:  Making Web sites that can be used
      by people with disabilities.</p>
    <p>Kynn was a key board member in building the HTML Writers
      Guild, a non-profit educational association of Web
      developers from around the world, and helped create the
      Guild's online education program.  He also served as the
      Guild's representative on several World Wide Web
      Consortium working groups.</p>
    <p>From 1995 to 2005, Kynn was the co-owner and Chief
      Technologist of Idyll Mountain Internet, in Fullerton,
      California. Currently, he lives in Tucson, Arizona, where
      he writes books and does digital photography in addition
      to Web consulting.</p>
    <hr>
    <address>
      <a href="mailto:kynn@css24.com">kynn@css24.com</a>
    </address>
  </body>
</html>
```

As shown in the screenshot in Figure 2.3, web browsers display this simply, without any CSS styles. It's not ugly, but it's not very interesting to look at, either.

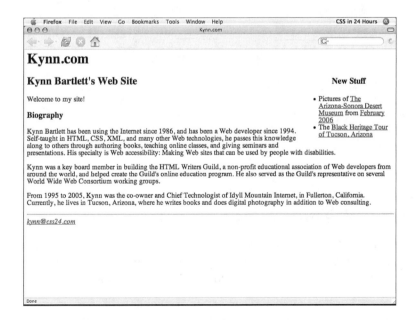

FIGURE 2.3
Firefox's default rendering of authorbio-2.2.html.

Linked Style Sheets in HTML

To apply the style sheet to the HTML page, you need to tell the browser which style sheet to use. You do this by using the `<link>` element of HTML, and in this case the `basic-2.1.css` file from Listing 2.1.

The `<link>` tag can appear only within the `<head>` section of the HTML page. To link the style sheet, I open the HTML file and add the following line (shown in bold):

```
<head>
  <title>Kynn.com</title>
  <link type="text/css" rel="stylesheet" href="basic-2.1.css">
</head>
```

You can see the effect of applying the style sheet in Figure 2.4; compare this with Figure 2.3 to see the difference CSS can make in the appearance of the page.

FIGURE 2.4
Styles change the appearance of the plain HTML page.

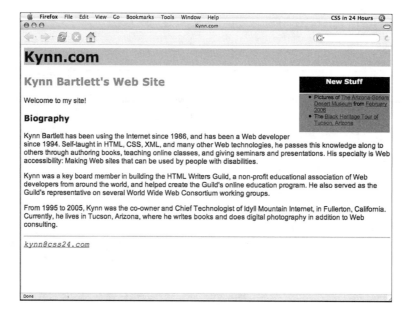

Viewing Your Style Sheet

After you've created a style sheet, you'll want to take a look at it to ensure that it works. Uneven browser support for CSS means that it's important to check how it appears in various browsers, as well as to make sure you got the syntax correct.

To view the style sheet, simply view the HTML file that links to your CSS file. Don't try viewing the CSS file directly; it just looks like source code in many browsers. The way to know whether it worked is to look at the HTML page that's being styled.

Recommended Browsers

You'll want to verify your style sheet in at least the major browsers because they represent the greatest number of users who may access your page. You'll also want to test in browsers that have good support for the CSS standard. Browsers can vary between operating systems; Internet Explorer on Microsoft Windows handles CSS quite differently from Internet Explorer on a Macintosh.

Naturally, it's difficult for one person to have access to every different browser combination available, but the more you're able to use, the better your results will be. I recommend a standard testing suite consisting of three or four of the following browsers:

▶ Internet Explorer (6.0 or higher for Windows)

▶ Safari (1.3 or higher for Mac OS X)

▶ Firefox (1.5 or higher for Windows, Mac OS X, or Linux)

▶ Opera (8.5 or higher for Windows, Mac OS X, or Linux)

▶ Lynx (2.8 or higher; Windows, Macintosh, or Linux)

These browsers represent a good cross-section for testing, and are generally widely available on most popular operating systems. In Hour 3 you'll learn more about these browsers and how to install them on your computer.

Try it Yourself ▼

Creating Your First Style Sheet

Learning by doing is the key to understanding Cascading Style Sheets, and building your own style sheet is the first step in the process. Follow these instructions to create and test your own CSS:

1. Select an HTML page to style. This could be one you've created before, a brand new one, or perhaps the `authorbio-2.2.html` file used earlier this hour.

2. Create a new CSS file, using the text editor of your choice. Using the style properties you learned this hour, add style rules to apply to your HTML page. Change the color of the text, the background color, the font sizes, and the text font. Save this file with a `.css` extension.

3. Use the `<link>` tag in your HTML to associate the style sheet with the HTML page. Be sure the HTML and CSS files are in the same directory, or else the browser might not be able to find the CSS file. (You can use full URL paths if you want, but for now, it's easiest to have HTML and CSS in the same location.) ▼

▼

4. Open your page in your primary web browser and view the results of your work. You may want to go back and tweak the CSS to see what effect additional styles have; go right ahead, and then reload the page!

5. If you have any of the other recommended browsers, try the page with those. You probably won't see much difference because the CSS properties introduced in this hour are relatively safe and reasonably well supported.

▲

Summary

In this hour, you learned about using text editors and specialized software to create and edit style sheets, which are just ordinary text files of CSS rules. You learned the general structure of a CSS rule and its component parts, including the selector, the declaration, the property name, and the property value. You learned how and why to include comments in your CSS files. You got to see a few simple styles change an HTML page, setting the text color, size, and font, and you learned how the HTML <link> tag associates a style sheet with a web page. Finally, you learned how to display your page in your browser and see your CSS in action.

Workshop

The workshop contains a Q&A section, quiz questions, and activities to help reinforce what you've learned in this hour. If you get stuck, the answers to the quiz can be found after the questions.

Q&A

Q. *I'm not sure what the "RGB" values used for colors are. Can you explain?*

A. Sure! RGB triples are one of the most common ways to specify color on the Web, in both HTML and CSS. RGB stands for Red-Green-Blue and is a standard way to specify a color as a composite of three values: the amount of red, the amount of green, and the amount of blue. In HTML and CSS these are written in hexadecimal numbers (base 16), which start with 0, go up to 9, and then continue on to A, B, C, D, E, and F. If you don't know how to use RGB hexadecimal values, you can use the rgb() function to specify colors, like this:

```
h1 { color: rgb(100%, 50%, 25%); }
```

Q. *Can I set the* `font-size` *to a specific value, such as 12 point?*

A. Yes, you can; 12 point is written as 12pt (no space). This is what's known as an absolute font size, though, and it can cause problems for users who need to adjust their preferences to account for visual impairments. For now I recommend sticking with the relative values given earlier in this hour, like `larger` and `x-small`, but if you want you can read ahead to Hour 9 for more about font size units.

Quiz

1. What kind of software is needed to create a CSS file?

2. What is the name of the part of a CSS rule that goes within the curly braces?

    a. The selector

    b. The declaration

    c. The property name

    d. The property value

3. You want to make all your HTML headings (<h1>, and so on) blue and in Arial font. What CSS rule(s) do you write?

Answers

1. Because CSS files are just ordinary text files, anything that can create or edit text files can make a style sheet. This includes text editors, style sheet editors, web development tools, and word processors. The important thing is to save the files as plain text, usually with a `.css` file extension suffix.

2. The declaration, which consists of the one or more pairs of property names and values, is the part of the CSS rule between curly braces.

3. Here's the easiest way to make headings blue and Arial:

```
h1, h2, h3, h4, h5, h6
  {
    color:        blue;
    font-family:  Arial;
  }
```

You could also write this as several rules—as many as 12—but this combined form is the easiest way to do it.

Exercise

You now know how to make the easiest types of style sheets—those that can be applied to HTML pages to change the colors, background colors, and fonts of HTML tags on the page. Test your new skills by creating several web pages that use the same style sheet. You will soon notice you're running into some limitations—you have to style all elements the same way. In Hour 4, "Using CSS with HTML," you'll learn how to expand your repertoire of selectors.

HOUR 3

Browser Support for CSS

What You'll Learn in This Hour:

▶ How web browsers fail to support CSS correctly

▶ The consequences of browser failure

▶ What the Acid2 test is and what it measures

▶ What a layout engine is and how it affects your web page

▶ How current browsers implement Cascading Style Sheets

▶ How screen readers work with browsers to speak web pages to blind users

CSS rules are always interpreted by web browsers, just as the HTML pages those rules style are interpreted. The HTML and CSS standards give specifics on how browsers should display those rules—but they're not always followed. To design pages with CSS, you not only need to know the standards, as presented in the CSS specification, but also understand how browsers' quirks and flaws will affect your web design results.

The Browser Problem

A web browser is the essential Internet access tool of the early twenty-first century. Browsers are now indispensable to business, education, and personal communication. They create a common platform upon which web-based applications can be built, with an HTML framework driving e-commerce, business-to-business transactions, web-based learning, and online communities. Hundreds of thousands of pages of new information are added to the Web each day. Cascading Style Sheets play a crucial role in this communications medium by not only providing a pleasant visual layer on the surface of these web applications, but also by potentially reshaping the entire user experience.

So what's the problem? In short: web browsers have been inconsistent in their support for CSS.

There are many reasons for this. Some early browsers, such as Netscape 3, were created before the CSS specification was published. Some browsers jumped the gun. Microsoft is notorious for rushing ahead and using draft specifications of standards in their browsers, and then the specifications get changed. And sadly, some browsers are just plain bad. They may seem to function normally, but when it comes to consistent and standardized support for CSS, they fall very short.

The good news is that the problem is being solved. Slowly but surely, each new major browser release is better than the last, and you can get pretty decent CSS implementations from Firefox, Opera, Safari, and other browsers.

How Browsers Deal with CSS

When a browser encounters anything—from CSS rules to HTML, JavaScript to Flash multimedia—it has several choices as to what it can do. If the browser has been programmed to understand the thing it has encountered, it attempts to display it according to the specification. If it has no idea what it has come across, it can ignore it. Both these options can be considered "doing the right thing." Or the browser can do the wrong thing. It can get confused; it can display in some nonstandard way; it can even crash, although that's rare. Doing any of these wrong things, of course, is the least desirable and is at the root of our problem.

Cascading Style Sheets were designed from the start to degrade gracefully. This means that if your CSS rules aren't recognized for some reason, your page is still usable and the content accessible. Because presentation is separated from content, the content should be able to stand on its own, albeit not as beautifully, after the presentation is removed. At least, that's the theory.

In practice it's not nearly as easy as that. To be an effective CSS author, you need to know not only what works in any given browser—or in most or all of them—but also what happens when it doesn't work. Is it as simple as your style not being applied correctly and a bit of decoration being lost, or is it as serious as your entire layout being disrupted and content being lost?

Compliance and Lack Thereof

You need to understand what happens in each case of browser failure to know how to approach each browser. When a browser fails to correctly understand and apply a CSS rule, the browser may just ignore the rule and your design will be fine. Or, because of a browser quirk or bug, it may ignore the rule and your page could become unreadable. As a designer, you need to weigh each style rule carefully and know what effects will result if browsers don't understand and apply it.

In some cases, you may want to use CSS properties that aren't well supported; you may figure that you don't mind some users missing out on a special styling if it improves the site for those users with more advanced browsers. In other cases, you may decide you can't take that chance, and you'll have to make a choice whether to support the broken browsers with workarounds or ignore that audience.

For example, consider a CSS rule that makes the first letter of each section stand out large in a stylized font. This may just be simple decoration, and if the font is normal sized in some browsers, so be it; it may not affect at all the way your page functions.

In other situations, you may be forced to either abandon certain types of style rules that are perfectly valid and useful simply because some major browsers don't support them. An alternative to this approach is to make special modifications, called browser hacks, which allow your style sheets to work despite browser problems. The most common of these is called a filter; a filter prevents certain browsers from reading specific CSS rules that might cause them problems. You'll learn more about browser hacks and filters in Hour 24, "Troubleshooting and Browser Hacks."

To understand how browsers deal with CSS, I've divided them into four categories: ancient browsers, which pre-date the CSS specification and thus ignore it completely; broken browsers, which try to provide CSS functionality but fail horribly in some manner; quirky browsers, which have generally decent CSS support but a number of "gotchas" where they don't quite measure up; and compliant browsers, which do a good job of presenting CSS as it's meant to be. Each category of browsers treats style sheets differently, and it's important to understand what those differences are and how you can design for those browsers.

Ancient Browsers

Ancient browsers are those that existed before Cascading Style Sheets were even a glimmer in the W3C's collective eye. Netscape 3 is the classic example of an older browser, and it does exactly what it's supposed to do: It ignores CSS entirely. If you use Netscape 3 to visit a web page styled with CSS, the browser doesn't notice a single rule. The style sheet doesn't even load.

This is actually ideal behavior for older browsers; with CSS designed for backwards compatibility, most CSS-based websites should still work, although they may be somewhat boring in appearance. Because Netscape 3 is ignoring all Cascading Style Sheets rules, you know exactly what it will do with them; there's no guesswork necessary on the part of the author. You don't have to do anything special to support these types of browsers, except for testing your designs to see whether they still function without CSS.

Some ancient browsers are:

- ▶ Lynx

- ▶ Mosaic (no longer in widespread use)

- ▶ Netscape 3 (no longer in widespread use)

Broken Browsers

The worst kind of browser is one that is simply broken when it comes to CSS, despite whatever claims the provider makes to standards compliance. A broken browser is one that, when given perfectly legitimate Cascading Style Sheets rules, doesn't present a web surfer with anything useful, but instead displays a mishmash of styles where information gets lost. The difference between an older browser and a broken browser is that older browsers don't try to display CSS, and broken browsers try and fail horribly.

Internet Explorer 3 was the first browser to implement any CSS, but it did an overall bad job at it, based in part on the fact that they coded to a specification that was still being written at the time. When the final version of CSS Level One came out, it was quite different from Internet Explorer 3's attempt to implement CSS support.

Fortunately, Internet Explorer 3 has almost passed into memory, replaced by newer versions of Internet Explorer that are closer to the CSS specification, meaning that the buggy CSS implementation in Internet Explorer 3 really isn't a factor in current CSS usage.

To account for the broken browsers out there, it's necessary to understand how they're broken and what happens when you give each browser some CSS rules that it doesn't understand. In some cases, the broken browser just ignores your CSS, as is the case with a limited or older browser; in others, it may do something horribly wrong.

There are two approaches to dealing with broken browsers. First, you can code around the problems by using a filter or other browser hack to prevent the browser from mangling your page. And second, for some browsers that are just so old that few people use them any more, you could just no longer support those browsers on your website.

The list of broken browsers includes:

- ▶ Internet Explorer 3 (no longer in widespread use)

- ▶ Netscape 4 (no longer in widespread use)

▶ Various minor releases of browsers that had serious bugs, and thus are no longer available

Quirky Browsers

Between the downright broken browsers and the compliant ones is a category of web browsers that have the best intentions, but just don't get it quite right. These browsers are generally compliant but have serious problems that come out when you start doing complex styles—for example, when using CSS to lay out a web page. We'll call these quirky browsers.

Unlike broken browsers, these are still in use, especially Internet Explorer versions 5 through 6. This means that as a web designer you can't just ignore them, nor can you simply lay the blame on the programmers who created the browser. It's your website (or your employer's, or your client's), and you need to take responsibility for how it appears in common browsers.

The way to deal with these browsers is to understand their quirks and bugs and work around them. One strategy is to use only "safe" CSS code in your designs, even if that limits the effects you can produce in more fully compliant browsers. Another method for dealing with a quirky browser is to use filters and other browser hacks to tailor the style rules given to that browser; techniques of this sort are described in Hour 24.

Some browsers with quirks include:

▶ Internet Explorer 6, 5.5, and 5

▶ Internet Explorer for Mac (no longer in widespread use)

▶ Opera 5 and 6 (no longer in widespread use)

▶ Netscape 6 (no longer in widespread use)

Compliant Browsers

A compliant browser is one that follows the CSS and HTML specifications to the letter. Well, that's not really true—as of early 2006, no browser can legitimately claim 100% standards compliance. However, there are browsers that get very close, to the extent that they can be treated as basically compliant. This is the category we'll call compliant browsers, although if you want to be pedantic, you can think of this as the "almost compliant" group instead.

When designing for compliant browsers, you don't have to do anything particularly special other than follow the CSS 2.1 specification. The selectors and properties you'll learn in later chapters of this book will work as described; text styling and even complex layouts don't present any major obstacles. You won't need to use filters or other browser hacks to deal with compliant browsers.

However, you need to keep in mind that not all browsers out there are compliant. The quirky browsers, in particular, are still around and may require special attention, even if the compliant browsers are going to be well behaved.

The following are generally compliant browsers:

▶ Firefox 1.5

▶ iCab

▶ Konqueror

▶ Mozilla 1.7

▶ Opera 8.5

▶ Safari 1.3 and 2

Web Standards and the Acid2 Test

As you learned in Hour 1, "Understanding CSS," the CSS language is defined by the Cascading Style Sheets Level 1 and Level 2 recommendations from the World Wide Web Consortium, and updated by CSS 2.1. These recommendations function as standards for the CSS language.

Standards are a good thing for developers; the more the browsers support the standards, the easier it is for us to create expressive and attractive designs in CSS and know they'll work reliably. Increased support from standards, the browser makers, the web developer community, and the web software manufacturers will only make our jobs easier.

One group of web designers decided to take their support for standards public and founded the Web Standards Project to encourage browser makers to adhere closely to the CSS recommendations and other web standards. In addition to their advocacy work, the Web Standards Project site contains useful FAQs and links on standards support. Their URL is http://www.webstandards.org/.

In 2005, the Web Standards Project developed the Acid2 test. Acid2 is a web page created with some rather complex CSS rules that hit key parts of the CSS and HTML specifications. If a browser successfully interprets and displays the CSS rules according to the standards, a happy face is displayed. Figure 3.1 is the reference picture showing how a compliant browser should display Acid2.

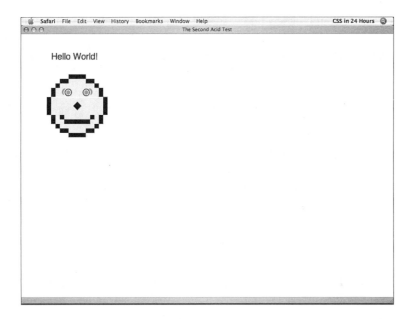

FIGURE 3.1
How the Acid2 test is supposed to look; shown in Safari 2.

Figure 3.2, on the other hand, is an example of a failed test. Internet Explorer 6 doesn't display the happy face according to the specifications.

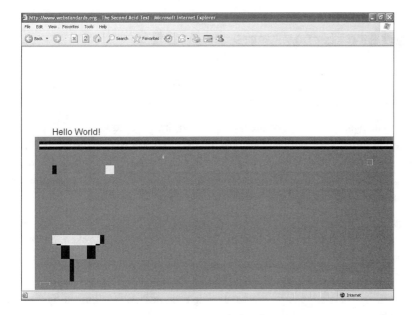

FIGURE 3.2
Internet Explorer 6 quite clearly fails the Acid2 test.

As of early 2006, four browsers had passed the Acid2 test; in order: Safari, iCab, Konqueror, and Opera. Acid2 isn't the ultimate test of CSS support—it's possible to pass Acid2 and still have serious CSS bugs or quirks—but it is an important benchmark for measuring progress toward standards compliance.

Browser Compatibility Charts

A *browser compatibility chart* is an invaluable resource for anyone doing serious CSS work. What is it? A compatibility chart lists every CSS property in a matrix, cross-referenced with a number of different browsers (including various version numbers and platforms). For example, if you want to know whether version 5.5 of the Internet Explorer browser supports the text-transform property, you can consult a compatibility chart. For each property you look up, you'll see whether or not it's supported by the browser, and if there are any special notes or known bugs in the implementation.

There are several sources of CSS browser compatibility charts; one that's particularly nice to use is David Hammond's chart at http://www.webdevout.net/. Bookmark that site and refer to it when testing your CSS-based designs. Brian Wilson's Index DOT css site at http://www.blooberry.com/indexdot/css/ hasn't been updated for several years, but it's still useful if you need to dig back through history for information on older browsers.

Modern Browsers and CSS

From the perspective of a CSS designer, the most important part of the web browser is not the menu bar, the tabbed window interface, or even the security and privacy features. The true heart of a web browser is its layout engine.

The *layout engine* is the part of the browser program that reads an HTML page and applies the browser's default style rules, the user's personal style sheet (if any), and the style sheets associated with the page being displayed. The colors, fonts, page layout, and other properties controlled by HTML and CSS are all applied by the layout engine, which presents the page content to the user.

This is also where you find browser bugs and quirks that affect CSS usage. The layout engine is the primary determinant of whether a browser is broken, quirky, or compliant.

In modern web browsers, the layout engine is modular and can be used by other applications. For example, the layout engine used in Firefox is known by the code-name Gecko. (All layout engines have code-names which are, essentially, arbitrarily chosen and don't really mean anything in particular.) Gecko is an open-source layout engine—meaning that the code used to create the program is available on the Web for anyone to read—and it has been used in other programs, such as the browsers Camino, K-Meleon, and Epiphany, as well as the email program Thunderbird. From a CSS designer's perspective, these browsers are all effectively the same as Firefox; they display CSS in the same way, and share any quirks and bugs found in Gecko.

The rest of this hour is a snapshot of the major browsers in the first part of 2006 (and some minor browsers), grouped by layout engine. Older versions of these browsers are listed as well, with advice on how these browsers will affect your web design practices.

Internet Explorer

Microsoft's Internet Explorer 6 is currently the most popular web browser; recent browser statistics show that more people use IE than all other browsers combined.

On the other hand, Internet Explorer is probably the least favorite current browser among designers who use CSS extensively. There are a number of bugs and other problems in Internet Explorer, which force it into the category of "quirky browsers." You're going to need to make special provisions for Internet Explorer if you use more complex CSS, such as advanced selectors or CSS for layout.

You can download Internet Explorer 6 from http://www.microsoft.com/ windows/ie/. It's available on the Windows platform only; see later this hour for details on the now-defunct Internet Explorer for Mac.

Did you Know?

The layout engine used in Internet Explorer is code-named Trident. As the part of the web browser responsible for the display of web content, including HTML tags and CSS rules, Trident is also the source of the bugs and quirks in IE. These include problems calculating the dimensions of sized content (the "box model bug"), lack of support for advanced CSS selectors, and a number of display quirks ranging in importance from trivial to serious. You can get a list of CSS bugs from the website Position Is Everything (http://www.positioniseverything.net/).

At the time of this book's writing, a preview version of Internet Explorer 7 is available for testing. Some, but not all, known CSS bugs in Internet Explorer 6 are being fixed in the new version. Because of the unstable nature of pre-release software, this book doesn't cover any Internet Explorer 7 CSS quirks or bugs.

By the Way

Internet Explorer Shells

An Internet Explorer shell is a browser which uses the Trident layout engine from Internet Explorer but provides its own user interface framework—the buttons, bars and menus that drive the program. This means that the look of the browser may not resemble Internet Explorer at all, but under the hood, it displays websites just as Internet Explorer would. Early IE shells were created for corporate branding purposes, but recent browsers based on Trident have focused on providing a better browsing experience for the user.

Maxthon from MySoft (http://www.maxthon.com/) is an example of such a shell. It adds features from other browsers such as tabbed browsing and ad blocking, while using the Trident layout engine for HTML and CSS display. This means that Maxthon inherits all of Internet Explorer 6's CSS quirks and bugs.

Fortunately, you don't need to do anything else to support users of Internet Explorer shells than you're already doing for IE 6 itself. Maxthon users don't need special attention beyond any browser hacks you might put in place anyway.

Other examples of Internet Explorer shells include America Online's AOL Explorer (http://downloads.channel.aol.com/browser) and Avant Browser (http://www.avantbrowser.com/).

Older Versions of Internet Explorer

Internet Explorer 3 was the first major browser to implement cascading style sheets—or rather, it was the first to attempt to do so. By all measures it failed horribly in the attempt, producing nightmares for many early adopter web designers who tried to use CSS. Internet Explorer 4 was almost as bad, but things started slowly getting better in IE 5 and 5.5.

The early, buggy versions of Internet Explorer are all but gone from the Web, but you may still have to deal with Internet Explorer 5 and 5.5. These versions had decent CSS support but a number of serious problems related to page layout. In Hour 24, you'll learn several ways to selectively hide or target CSS rules for those versions of Internet Explorer.

Firefox

One of the earliest graphical browsers was called Netscape. Netscape was the top dog of browsers until Microsoft threw its market dominance around and knocked Netscape out of the competition. The Netscape browser eventually became part of the open source movement, in a project code-named Mozilla.

Mozilla Firefox is an open-source browser developed by the Mozilla Foundation and is available on a wide variety of platforms, including Microsoft Windows, Mac OS X, and Linux and other Unix-like operating systems. The most recent version, as this book is being written, is Firefox 1.5. Firefox provides standard features found on most browsers such as tabbed browsing, pop-up blocking, and good support for user style sheets.

You can download Firefox for a wide variety of platforms from http://www.mozilla. com/firefox/.

Did you Know?

Firefox has very good overall CSS 2.1 support, which is one reason why it's used for the screenshots in this book. (The other reason is that it's one of the few current browsers available on all major operating systems, meaning it's very likely that anyone who picks up this book will be able to run Firefox.) There are a few quirks and bugs in Firefox, but in general you won't make big changes to your CSS or HTML to support Firefox users.

At the time of this book's writing, a preview version of Firefox 2 is available for testing. Because of the unstable nature of pre-release software, this book doesn't cover any Firefox 2 CSS quirks or bugs.

By the Way

Other Gecko-Based Browsers

The layout engine used in Firefox is called Gecko, and it has been incorporated into a number of other browsers, some of them open source, and others that are closed but use the layout engine. Because Gecko provides a solid base for CSS implementation, you don't have any extra worries from Gecko-based browsers—no more than those you have for Firefox bugs.

Netscape Browser version 8.1 (http://browser.netscape.com/ns8/, Windows only) is an example of a browser that is Gecko-based—it is proprietary software developed by Netscape Communications (part of America Online), the current owners of the "Netscape" trade name. The user interface shell is closed source, but it uses the Gecko engine. Interestingly, it also can use Internet Explorer's Trident layout engine as well on certain pages.

Making the Gecko family tree even more complicated is the Mozilla browser (http://www.mozilla.org/products/mozilla1.x/), part of the Mozilla Application Suite, which is different from Mozilla Firefox and is currently at version 1.7. Mozilla-the-browser is now giving way to the open-source project codenamed SeaMonkey, which released version 1.0 (http://www.mozilla.org/projects/seamonkey/) in January 2006.

The Gecko layout engine is also used on several projects that give a "native" user interface environment, rather than Firefox's more generic, cross-platform user interface. Camino (http://www.caminobrowser.org/) is an open-source browser for Mac OS X that feels more like a native Macintosh application, with the Gecko engine doing the HTML and CSS display. K-Meleon (http://kmeleon.sourceforge.net/) does the same for the Microsoft Windows operating system, and Epiphany (http://www.gnome.org/projects/epiphany/) is the native Linux and Unix-like browser with a Gecko layout engine foundation.

Other examples of Gecko-based browsers include Flock (http://flock.com/) and Galeon (http://galeon.sourceforge.net/).

Older Versions of Netscape

Ancient versions of Netscape—sometimes also called Netscape Navigator and Netscape Communicator, depending on the corporate policy of any given time—had no CSS support; Netscape 3 wouldn't recognize CSS rules or related attributes and elements. This actually made it a good test case for web developers who wanted to see how their sites would work without style sheets. These days, however, nobody uses Netscape 3 or earlier versions.

Netscape 4 was released in June 1997 and had notoriously bad CSS support. Version 4.02 contained a bug that would cause the entire browser to crash upon reading certain perfectly valid CSS rules. Later versions of Netscape in the 4.x series gradually improved their support for CSS, but even by the release of Netscape 4.8, it was still a very buggy browser that required major work-arounds to do complex CSS layouts.

Fortunately for web developers, Netscape 4 is all but dead. These days it is used by so few people that there's really little point in using the classic work-arounds and browser hacks for Netscape 4. Unless you are very conscientious, or somehow dealing with a group of primitive users who run Netscape 4 on stone computers, you won't have to make changes to your CSS or HTML to deal with Netscape 4.

Netscape 5 actually wasn't released; the browser developers skipped the numbering to "catch up" to Internet Explorer 6. Netscape 6 was the first Mozilla release, using the new Gecko engine developed by open source developers. The Gecko support for CSS started out strong and has gotten stronger since. In general, there are very few times in which you'll need to use browser hacks to deal with bugs in Netscape 6.2 or later.

The Netscape website has an incomplete archive of old versions of Netscape for testing. As of early 2006, this appears to be unavailable, but you can find archived versions of Netscape browsers at http://browsers.evolt.org/.

Opera

The Opera browser was developed by Opera Software of Oslo, Norway, and runs on Microsoft Windows, Mac OS X, and Linux and Unix-like operating systems. The current version is Opera 8.5, and it uses a layout engine named Presto. Presto has good support for CSS, which isn't that surprising considering that Håkon Wium Lie, one of the creators of the CSS specification, is a long-time Opera employee. Opera is also very customizable, and has good support for user-defined style sheets and user configuration options.

You can download Opera for a wide variety of platforms from http://www.opera.com/.

In general, there are very few situations in which you will need to provide special code for Opera only. Opera's CSS 2.1 support is generally quite solid and it does CSS-based layout without major problems.

At the time of this book's writing, a preview version of Opera 9 is available for testing. The new version of Opera promises even better support for CSS; in late March, 2006, the Web Standards Project announced that Opera 9 passed the Acid2 test. Because of the unstable nature of pre-release software, this book doesn't cover any Opera 9 CSS quirks or bugs.

Early versions of Opera quickly gained a reputation for excellent CSS support—relative to the existing browsers in the market. The 5.0 and 6.0 versions have seen Opera drop back into the middle of the pack for CSS support; there are some serious CSS limitations and bugs in Opera versions before Opera 7.

Fortunately, Opera users tend to be well informed about new browser releases and transition relatively quickly to newer, less buggy versions. For this reason, the older versions of Opera are not a serious problem at this time and rarely need any special attention.

Safari

Safari is Apple Computer's web browser for the Mac OS X operating system. The layout engine in Safari is called WebCore and is based on the KHTML layout engine from Konqueror (which you'll learn about in just a moment). There are two current versions of Safari—Safari 2 runs on Mac OS X version 10.4, and Safari 1.3 is for Mac OS X version 10.3. The layout engine is almost the same between the two versions, so for CSS purposes they're effectively the same browser.

Safari supports nearly all of CSS 2.1, including advanced selectors and CSS-based layout. You won't have many problems from Safari when you write standard CSS. In April 2005, it was reported that Safari 2 had successfully passed the Acid2 test.

Older versions of Safari had numerous CSS bugs, but Apple's software developers have been diligently rooting them out. The Safari browser is included with the Mac OS X operating system, and is automatically updated by Apple's software update program. This means very few users will have-out-of date versions of Safari; you won't have to worry about older, buggy versions.

Apple's website for Safari is http://www.apple.com/safari/, and you can also install the most recent version through Software Update.

Konqueror

Konqueror is an open-source browser developed as part of the K Desktop Environment (KDE) by volunteers for Linux, BSD, and other Unix-like operating systems. In addition to being a web browser, it also functions as a file manager and file viewer.

Konqueror uses a layout engine called KHTML, which was incorporated into Apple's WebCore layout engine. Konqueror also can operate in a mode where it uses Mozilla's Gecko layout engine.

In general, Konqueror's support for CSS is good, thanks in part to the contributions of Apple's WebCore developers back into the KHTML project, and in part because of the efforts of KDE's volunteers. In June 2005, Konqueror passed the Acid2 test from the Web Standards Project. Because of this high level of CSS support and Konqueror's small user base, you likely will never have to pay any special attention to Konqueror.

You can download Konqueror from the KDE website at http://konqueror.kde.org/.

WebCore

WebCore is the name of Apple's KHTML-derived layout engine for Mac OS X, which has been incorporated into other applications that need HTML rendering functions. Such applications have no more and no fewer problems than does Safari when it comes to CSS display; whatever you do for Safari will benefit these browsers as well.

The OmniWeb browser is one of the older small browsers still around, originally written in 1995 for the NeXTSTEP platform. Created by the Omni Group, OmniWeb first used its own proprietary layout engine, but in 2003 switched to using Apple's WebCore.

OmniWeb is available for Mac OS X from http://www.omnigroup.com/applications/ omniweb/.

Did you Know?

Other Browsers

In addition to the major browsers listed here, there are a number of smaller, less frequently used browsers you should be aware of. A huge list of many browsers can be found at the Evolt browser archive, http://browsers.evolt.org/. It's also important for you to understand screen readers, a type of assistive technology employed by users who are blind.

Lynx

Lynx is an old classic browser, which is most commonly used at a shell window or command prompt. Versions of Lynx can run on any system, although it is most commonly used on Unix-like operating systems, such as Linux or Mac OS X.

Lynx doesn't display images. It doesn't display colors. It doesn't do tables. It's the prototypical text-only browser—and it definitely doesn't do CSS. This actually makes it ideal for testing your CSS-based designs to ensure that the underlying page can be used even if the style sheets are not understood.

Figure 3.3 is an example of how Lynx displays the author's website—by ignoring the style sheet. You can compare this with Figure 1.2 in Hour 1, which shows the same site in Firefox.

The download site for Lynx is http://lynx.isc.org/, and the browser runs on many operating systems.

Did you Know?

Many people use Lynx because it provides a faster and simpler interface to the Web, without the extra download time of a graphical browser. Other examples of similar text-based browsers include Links (http://links.sourceforge.net/) and w3m (http://w3m.sourceforge.net/).

FIGURE 3.3
Lynx displays the author's personal website.

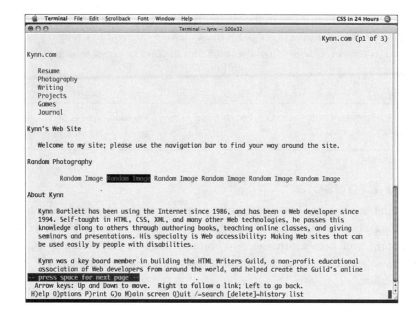

iCab

iCab is a web browser created by Alexander Clauss of Germany, and is available for both Mac OS X and for earlier versions of Mac OS, making it the primary browser for Macintosh users who have not upgraded beyond Mac OS 9. The CSS support in iCab is good, and in June 2005 it was reported that iCab was the second browser to pass the Acid2 test. This high level of CSS support plus the small user base of iCab mean that you are not likely to need to make special considerations for iCab.

You can download iCab for Mac OS X (or earlier versions of Mac OS) from http://www.icab.de/.

Internet Explorer for Macintosh

Even though they both originated at Microsoft around the same time, Internet Explorer for Windows and Internet Explorer for Macintosh are literally different pieces of software that confusingly share the same name. Internet Explorer for Mac was bundled with new Apple computers for years, and for a while was the best browser for Macs. In fact, it was probably the best browser for any operating system in 2000.

Internet Explorer for Mac was developed separately from the Windows version, and had a number of features that its Windows counterpart didn't have. From a CSS perspective, the most important of these was the layout engine, code-named Tasman, which provided superior (but quirky) CSS support, especially when compared with Trident, the equivalent in Internet Explorer on Windows.

You'd have to worry about providing support for Internet Explorer for Mac, except for one thing: It's officially dead. The last version for Mac OS X was 5.2.3, and 5.1.7 for Mac OS 8 and 9—both released in June 2003. Microsoft no longer has programmers working on it, Apple no longer bundles it with new computers, and as of January 2006 you can't even download it from Microsoft's site. They tell you to use Safari instead.

That's kind of a shame, really, but it makes your job easier as a web developer—very few people are using Internet Explorer for Mac, and so you probably won't need to use the Mac IE workarounds from Hour 24.

Screen Readers

A screen reader is a specialized piece of software that works between the operating system and applications to read out a program's output to a user who is blind or visually impaired. This allows someone to access and use your website even if she is unable to see it.

The term "screen reader" is descriptive; most screen readers literally read only whatever they see on the screen. A screen reader needs to work with a browser to access the Web. The most common screen readers, such as JAWS or WindowEyes, are available only for Microsoft Windows, and work primarily with Internet Explorer.

This means that someone using a screen reader not only has to deal with the quirks of the screen reader and possible inaccessible web design techniques in the HTML, but also the CSS quirks of the browser. Hour 24 has advice on how to make specific sections of your site available only to users with screen readers.

You'll learn more about access by people with disabilities in Hour 22, "Accessibility and Print Media."

Try it Yourself

Test Drive a New Browser

The more browsers you use for testing, the better you'll be able to understand how your CSS works with those browsers. To get some hands-on experience with new browsers, follow these directions:

1. Choose one or more browsers from earlier in this hour that will work on your operating system. If you've already used them all, download an older version or an alternate browser from the Evolt browser archive.

2. Install the browser and fire it up for surfing the Web.

3. Visit several websites that use CSS, including the site for this book, and the Web Standards Project, home of the Acid 2 test (http://www.webstandards.org/action/acid2).

4. How does your experience using these browsers differ from your experience using your normal browser-of-choice? Note whether the CSS support is better or worse, and rank the browser you're using as "ancient," "broken," "quirky," or "compliant."

Summary

Browser support is the key issue to understanding how to use Cascading Style Sheets effectively. Older browsers ignore CSS, compliant browsers support CSS, and other browsers provide either broken or quirky support for the standards. Knowing how to deal with the different types of browsers makes your style sheets more effective across a variety of platforms and browser versions.

The layout engine is the most important part of the browser, from a CSS perspective, as it determines how a web page is displayed—and thus how web designers deal with that browser. The Acid2 test was developed as one benchmark to measure a browser's conformance with CSS.

Internet Explorer (for Windows) is an example of a quirky browser—one that requires special attention from the web designer. Firefox, Opera, Safari, and related browsers are generally compliant with the web standards. Web designers need to be aware of these browsers and others when using CSS.

Workshop

The workshop contains a Q&A section, quiz questions, and an exercise to help reinforce what you've learned in this hour. If you get stuck, the answers to the quiz can be found after the questions.

Q&A

Q. *Which browsers should I use?*

A. For your own personal use, you're free to use any you prefer! I like Safari and Firefox, myself. For testing purposes, as described in Hour 2, "Getting Started with CSS," a good minimal set of browsers consists of Internet Explorer, Lynx, Firefox, Opera, and/or Safari. If you have access to additional platforms, you'll want to get appropriate browsers for those. In short, testing on as many browsers and platforms as possible will always be to your advantage.

Q. *Are there more browsers out there than just those you've listed? What about older versions?*

A. It turns out there are dozens and dozens of browsers that run on a wide variety of operating systems and configurations. You can find these alternate browsers, as well as older versions of more popular browsers, at the Evolt browser archive at http://browsers.evolt.org/.

Q. *What do I look for when testing a web page with a browser?*

A. Well, the most obvious thing to check for is simple access to information. Are you able to read what's on the screen and get at the content of the HTML? Next, check for functionality. You may find that some browsers make it impossible to follow links or submit forms if your style sheet is not understood. Finally, check for aesthetics: Does the page look as you want it to look, or a reasonable approximation? If so, you're in luck; if not, you may want to change your style sheet by adding or removing properties. The workarounds in subsequent hours of this book can help you figure out how to make effects work in specific browsers.

Q. *I don't have access to every browser ever created, and I certainly don't have multiple computers with a variety of operating systems. What can I do, short of spending a fortune on new hardware?*

A. For starters, you can join any number of web forums or mailing lists that support web developers. Experienced designers are usually more than happy to help out new folks learning CSS. Another resource is BrowserCam (http://www.browsercam.com/) which, for a fee, offers screenshots and even remote access on a wide variety of computer and browser combinations.

Quiz

1. What will an older browser do if it encounters Cascading Style Sheets? Is this a good thing or a bad thing?

2. Which browsers are the closest to being fully compliant with the CSS specifications?

3. Why is it important to test in Internet Explorer 6?

Answers

1. An older browser—one written before the CSS recommendation was issued—won't understand anything about Cascading Style Sheets. This is not great, but it's not bad either because CSS is designed so that if you design your style sheets correctly, your web pages will still function even with CSS unavailable. The presentation may look dull or even awful, but your message will still shine through.

2. The best browsers for CSS support currently are Firefox 1.5 (and derivatives), Opera 8.5, and Safari. Internet Explorer 7 and Opera 9 are very promising, but were not yet officially released as of the time this book was written.

3. It's important to test your designs in Internet Explorer 6 because it's still used by a sizable number of web surfers, and because it contains serious problems that can render your designs unusable because of quirks and bugs.

Exercise

This would be an excellent time to assemble your test suite of browsers. Using the information provided in this chapter, assemble your own set of programs that you'll use to check your designs. A variety of browsers—ancient, broken, quirky, and compliant—is a good approach. Will you include minor browsers in your test suite? How will you deal with programs that don't run on your primary computer? If you use Microsoft Windows, you can't easily test on Safari. Write down your testing decisions and procedures.

HOUR 4

Using CSS with HTML

What You'll Learn in This Hour:

▶ What the different types of HTML are and how to use them with Cascading Style Sheets

▶ The three ways to link CSS to styles and when to use each

▶ How to create an external style sheet for your entire website

▶ How to embed style sheets directly in your HTML

▶ How to create CSS rules based on the HTML attributes of `class` and `id`

In previous hours, you've used Cascading Style Sheets to style your HTML pages by linking in an external CSS file. The true power of CSS and HTML really shines through only when you understand both of these complementary languages, how they relate to each other, and how they can be used effectively.

HTML and CSS blend together well not by coincidence but by design; they literally were made for each other. Using that designed synergy is the key to creating effective presentations on your websites.

Types of HTML

To fully understand how HTML and CSS work together, it's important to know what we're talking about when we talk about HTML. Hypertext Markup Language is defined by formal recommendations issued by the World Wide Web Consortium (W3C), just as the Cascading Style Sheets language is.

HTML 4.01

The most recent version of HTML is HTML 4.01. HTML 4.01 is an updated version of HTML 4.0, which itself was an improvement over HTML 3.2 and 2.0. (There was no official version numbered 1.0; the first version of HTML was a quickly changing ad-hoc language put together primarily by World Wide Web creator Tim Berners-Lee. When efforts began to standardize HTML, numbering started with 2.0.)

HTML 4.01 comes in three "flavors"—Strict, Transitional, and Frameset. The type of HTML used on your page is indicated by the DOCTYPE statement you place as the first line of the page. Each flavor has a set of tags and attributes that are allowed and disallowed; they're like a variant of spoken human languages, in a way.

What's the difference between the three? HTML Strict relies entirely on CSS for presentational styling; HTML Transitional includes some HTML attributes and elements for presentation effects; and HTML Frameset is used to create frames.

Strict

HTML 4.01 Strict is a version of HTML that removes nearly all the presentational markup—the <font> tags, the color and link attributes on <body>, the border attribute, and other old standbys that have been used for years to make pages more visually appealing. So what's a web developer to do if she doesn't want boring pages?

The answer should be clear to anyone reading this book: Use Cascading Style Sheets! The Strict variety relies heavily on CSS for presentation; that's why it's considered strict.

To declare your page as using HTML Strict, put the following at the very top of your HTML file as the first line:

```
<!DOCTYPE HTML PUBLIC "-//W3C//DTD HTML 4.01//EN"
        "http://www.w3.org/TR/html4/strict.dtd">
```

You'll want to use HTML Strict if you're designing primarily for newer browsers or if you don't mind giving unstyled pages to older browsers that ignore CSS.

Several recent browsers have a special compatibility mode for HTML and CSS where they adhere more closely to the published standards. Firefox and Internet Explorer turn on this mode when they encounter a valid DOCTYPE for HTML Strict and for a few other DOCTYPE declarations; other pages are shown in a "quirky" mode for backward compatibility with older browsers. For more information, see the following URLs:

> ▶ http://www.mozilla.org/docs/web-developer/quirks/
>
> ▶ http://msdn.microsoft.com/library/default.asp?url=/library/en-us/dnie60/
> html/cssenhancements.asp

Transitional

HTML 4.01 Transitional adds back in those presentation markup tags and attributes, although some, such as the `<font>` tag, are considered deprecated. What's deprecated mean? That's W3C-talk that means "This is still within the formal specification, but you really should not use it, and it won't be in future versions of this language." Not all presentation markup in HTML 4.01 is deprecated, and you can freely use those nondeprecated elements and attributes as part of HTML 4.01 Transitional.

Transitional HTML is so named because at the time the HTML 4.0 specification was released, few browsers had particularly good CSS support, which meant Strict wasn't really usable on most websites, unless you wanted plain gray or white backgrounds, black text, and default fonts.

Transitional is intended as a temporary measure until browsers catch up. So far, the browsers have been slow in catching up; Transitional HTML is therefore what I suggest for most web development. If you are concerned about delivering your design to the majority of browsers out there, you should use HTML Transitional.

> You can use CSS and Transitional HTML together, and in fact that's highly recommended; CSS rules are followed if the browser understands CSS, and if not, it looks at the HTML attributes or elements instead. This enables you to have "fallback" presentations in the HTML markup for older or limited browsers that don't support CSS.

By the Way

This is the `DOCTYPE` statement for HTML 4.01 Transitional; it should be the very first line of your document:

```
<!DOCTYPE HTML PUBLIC "-//W3C//DTD HTML 4.01 Transitional//EN"
        "http://www.w3.org/TR/html4/loose.dtd">
```

Frameset

The Frameset variety of HTML 4.01 is intended for use only in creating frameset pages—those that use the `<frameset>` element, along with `<frame>` and `<noframes>`, to lay out different windows within the page. It's otherwise identical to Transitional HTML; you need to use this only on the page that establishes the

frames, not on the frames contained within that set (unless they define other
<frameset> elements, of course).

You'll want to use HTML Frameset whenever you're creating a frame presentation
and at no other time otherwise.

The DOCTYPE for HTML 4.01 Frameset is

```
<!DOCTYPE HTML PUBLIC "-//W3C//DTD HTML 4.01 Frameset//EN"
        "http://www.w3.org/TR/html4/frameset.dtd">
```

XHTML

XHTML 1.0 is a version of HTML 4.01 written as XML, which means it follows the
very specific rules and structure imposed on XML documents. The tags are all the
same as in HTML, but how you write them may be different. For example, all
XHTML tags are lowercase, and all attribute values have to be quoted. XHTML 1.0
comes in the same three varieties: Strict, Transitional, and Frameset. The next version, XHTML 1.1, is available only in a Strict flavor and thus relies entirely on CSS
for presentation.

Using CSS with XHTML is pretty much the same as using CSS with HTML. Because
XHTML represents a move forward to an XML-based web, you may end up migrat-
ing from HTML to XHTML sometime in the future. For this reason, I recommend
writing all your CSS rules so that element names are written in lowercase letters. It
doesn't matter in HTML, but it will in XHTML, and making this a habit will save
you time now if you choose to use XHTML in the future: You won't need to rewrite
all your style sheets.

Validating HTML

Validating your HTML means that you run your page through an HTML validator,
which is a program to analyze HTML code and ensure that the code you write is in
compliance with the HTML specification. In this way, an HTML validator is like a
spellchecker or grammar checker for HTML.

By validating your HTML, you can catch errors in your code, such as misspelled
attributes (like aling or scr) or closing tags you've accidentally left out. Validation
also improves your compatibility with browsers: Valid HTML code is closer to what
browsers—especially newer ones—are expecting. You can validate against your chosen variety of HTML (Strict, Transitional, or Frameset) to ensure that you're using
only tags and attributes that are within that subset of the language.

From the standpoint of troubleshooting your style sheet, it's much easier to catch
CSS errors if you know you don't have many HTML errors. I've spent many hours

chasing down what I thought were mistakes in my CSS when really I'd just written an HTML attribute or element incorrectly.

I recommend always making sure your HTML is valid. Valid code conforms to the appropriate HTML Document Type Definition, which is a formal specification of HTML syntax. You use the DOCTYPE statement as the first line of your HTML file to indicate the correct version of HTML.

To check your HTML, you can use one of the validation services listed here:

▶ W3C's HTML Validator (http://validator.w3.org)

▶ Web Design Group's HTML Validator (http://www.htmlhelp.com/tools/validator)

If a validator locates a problem with your HTML files, you can correct them by hand, in an HTML editor, or by using the HTML Tidy program created by Dave Raggett of the W3C. You can download HTML Tidy for free for various operating systems from http://www.w3.org/People/Raggett/tidy/. It's well worth the time.

Try it Yourself

Validate a Web Page

The process of checking your HTML is so important to creating good CSS that you should take the time out now to get familiar with it:

1. Choose a validator from the list just given and go to that site.

2. Enter the URL of a web page you've worked on, or upload the file directly from your computer.

3. Make sure your web page contains a DOCTYPE statement as the first line, preferably Transitional (if you use HTML attributes for appearance) or Strict (if you use pure CSS).

4. Check the validation results. You may have tags that aren't closed, obsolete elements or attributes, or plain, ordinary typos. What would it take to fix your page?

5. Make those changes and revalidate until your page passes. Congrats—you're writing valid HTML.

6. For fun, validate other websites, including major destinations on the Internet such as search engines or news portals. How serious are they about valid HTML?

The code examples given in this book don't include the DOCTYPE statement, so technically they aren't valid. This was done deliberately to conserve space as well as attention; a complex DOCTYPE at the beginning of an HTML example can distract from whatever point I'm trying to make by providing the HTML code. However, I do ensure the code is otherwise valid, and I ask for your forgiveness for lack of DOCTYPE. Do as I say, not as I do, in this specific case.

Style Sheets in HTML

The Cascading Style Sheets language was specifically designed to work with HTML to build web pages. CSS rules can appear within linked style sheets, embedded style sheets, or inline style attributes.

The CSS rules that you will write for each method are generally the same, but the way your HTML and your CSS work together depends on the method you used. So far, you've worked with linked external style sheets, as that's the most useful way of dealing with Cascading Style Sheets and offers the most flexibility.

Examples in this book, unless stated otherwise, generally assume you're using a linked style sheet, and complete listings are shown as external CSS files. CSS rules (and declarations, for inline styles) are written the same regardless of how they're applied to HTML, so you'll get the same styling effects if you use linked, embedded, or inline style rules.

Linked Style Sheets

In Hour 2, "Getting Started with CSS," you learned about how to create external style sheets and link them with the <link> element in HTML. Linking style sheets in this manner gives you the greatest portability and ease of maintenance when designing your styles for your website.

Many sites use one or more global style sheets that are linked from every page on the site. Using a global style sheet lets you make changes to one file that will affect the appearance of every page on your site. With a simple change, you can switch the colors, fonts, sizes, and more across your whole website.

External style sheets let you separate your content fully from your styles, which means it's easy to replace those styles with something else. For example, you could easily change the appearance of a site by replacing the old style sheet with a new set of rules under the same name.

You can also link in specific style sheets for specific uses, such as one style sheet per company division, as well as a global style sheet for the whole company, on a corporate website. You can link style sheets for specific types of output devices as well, using styles written just for those types of devices. For example, you could create a style sheet specifically for handheld wireless devices, screen readers, or printers. In Hour 22, "Accessibility and Print Media," you'll learn more about designing for alternate output devices.

As seen in Hour 2, you can create linked style sheets by using the HTML <link> element in the <head> section of the page. A number of attributes can be used with the <link> element, but for our purposes only the following options are important:

```
<link rel="relationship" href="URL"
     type="content-type" media="media-type">
```

The <link> tag is actually an all-purpose linking element; it doesn't just define style sheets but also can be used to create any link between the entire document and some other URL location. To use it to identify a linked document as a style sheet, you need to specify what the relationship is. Other types of relationships include contents (specifying the location of a table of contents), alternate (an alternate version of the page for specific types of output devices or languages), and glossary (for a glossary of terms). To indicate a style sheet, however, you need only rel="stylesheet".

The href attribute indicates the location of the style sheet and is a normal web URL. The location can be relative or absolute; without a directory path, it's assumed to be within the same directory, but you can use any URL path (and machine name), as with any other link in HTML.

Your style sheet even can reside on a different web server than your HTML file; in fact, this is a good way to quickly and easily add style to a web page. However, this isn't a license to merely steal someone else's work, any more than viewing the HTML source is an invitation to swipe source code. Use an offsite style sheet only if the site operator has explicitly given permission for it to be used in such a manner. Keep in mind that many web hosting services charge for bandwidth usage, so you may be costing someone money each time you use that style sheet without permission. Also remember that because you don't control the style sheet, it could affect the look of your web page if it's changed or removed.

The World Wide Web Consortium offers a number of style sheets for public use at http://www.w3.org/StyleSheets/Core/. You can use these to test styles on your pages by applying them as linked style sheets.

Did you Know?

The content-type attribute of the <link> tag indicates the styling language of the linked style sheet. For Cascading Style Sheets—Levels 1, 2, and 2.1—this should be text/css. This is also the MIME type that your server should return when serving up CSS files. All modern web servers recognize the file extension .css as being a CSS file and send an appropriate MIME type. If you name your file something ending in .css, the server sends it as text/css. If you think your server doesn't do this properly for some reason, you should consult your web server administrator or the documentation for your server software. Also, if you write a server-side script to create a CSS document in, for example, Perl, ASP, or PHP, you should make sure you set the content-type HTTP header line to text/css.

The media attribute tells the browser with which types of media or output device categories the style sheet should be used. A browser applies different style sheets depending on the media—for example, one style sheet for printing and another for onscreen display. Style sheets for other media are ignored, and those rules aren't applied.

For the most part, we are concerned with the media-type screen, which means visual, onscreen display. Because screen is assumed to be the default, you don't need to specify this unless you're linking a style sheet for another type of output device. Other media types include printer (for printed documents), braille (for tactile Braille devices), aural (for speech synthesizers), and all, which covers all media types. You can list more than one media type by separating them with commas, such as screen, printer.

By the Way

> You'll learn more about the media types printer, braille, and aural in Hour 22.

Embedded Style Sheets

Another way to apply CSS to HTML is by embedding the CSS directly within the HTML file with the <style> tag. Your CSS rules are then part of the same file as the HTML, which makes editing easier, at least at first. An embedded style sheet also is useful for rules that apply only to a specific page and don't need to be used by other parts of the site, which helps keep the size of your global style sheet relatively small. For example, if you have a rule that applies only to the front page of the site, you don't need that in a site-wide style sheet that is accessed by every page, even those that don't use the rule.

On the other hand, it's also harder to maintain and update a site only with embedded style sheets; you have to edit every single page when you want to make a change in the appearance of the site.

For this reason, I prefer linking instead of embedding CSS, but in many situations it's easier or more appropriate to use an embedded style sheet. For example, when testing CSS rules or developing a style sheet, it may be easiest to use an embedded style sheet and then convert it to an external style sheet for production use.

> How do you convert an embedded style sheet to an external one? Simple: You just cut the content of the <style> tag and paste it into a new file with a name ending in .css. Here's the tricky part: If there are any URL references (such as background images) in your CSS, you need to make sure that they apply relative to the new style sheet and not the original document. To convert an external style sheet to an embedded one, just paste it into a <style> element and check the URLs again.

Did you Know?

To embed a style sheet, use the <style> tag, which can be used only within the <head> of a web page:

```
<style type="text/css" media="media-type">
  ... CSS rules go here ...
</style>
```

The type attribute is required. Theoretically, this is because a different style language could be used with HTML, although in practice only CSS is ever used. The media attribute is optional; the default is screen. As with the <link> element, you can set multiple media types by listing them with comma separators.

You can have more than one <style> element within the <head> section of the page if you like; for example, you could have one for screen and one for printer. (You could have two for printer, if you want, but it usually makes more sense to combine them together in a single <style> tag.)

Hiding CSS Code from Older Browsers

Browsers shouldn't ever reveal the contents of a <style> tag. Even if a browser doesn't support CSS, it shouldn't display the rules to the user. However, some very ancient browsers were written before CSS was created, and because these browsers don't know what the <style> tag is, they just display it as HTML text, which is just a mess. The best way to avoid this is by wrapping your CSS rules within HTML comments:

```
<style type="text/css" media="screen">
  <!--
  ... CSS rules go here ...
  -->
</style>
```

The older browsers interpret this as just a normal comment, whereas the modern browsers understand the CSS. As nearly every browser used these days understands the `<style>` tag, it's not particularly necessary, but it doesn't hurt anything to do it, either. The examples in this book don't include comments.

Inline Style Attributes

You set inline styles on HTML tags by using the `style` attribute. Such a style applies to that particular element, or possibly to that element's children, if the rule's properties can be inherited.

> In Hour 7, "Cascading and Inheritance," you'll learn more about how HTML tags inherit CSS properties from other tags.

The `style` attribute can be set on nearly any HTML tag that is displayed by a browser. The attribute contains the declaration of a CSS rule but not a selector; the tag itself (and its content) serves as the selector.

Here's an example of using inline styles to set some CSS properties:

```
<table style="font-family: Arial; font-size: large">
  <tr>
    <th style="color: blue">
      Writer's Name
    </th>
    <th style="color: green">
      Primary Genre
    </th>
  </tr>
  <tr><td>Kynn</td><td>Technical (Web Design)</td></tr>
  <tr><td>Nick</td><td>Fiction (Horror)</td></tr>
  <tr style="color: red">
    <td>R. Francis</td>
    <td>Non-Fiction (Podcasting)</td>
  </tr>
</table>
```

As you can see, the selector is unnecessary; the style is applied to the tag on which the `style` attribute is set. Also, there are no ending semicolons on the rules. Within `style` attributes, the ending semicolon is optional. I usually write it myself because it makes it easier to add additional rules if I need them.

Style attributes are most useful for single-point changes, such as changing the color of an announcement to make it stand out, like this:

```
<h1 style="color: red;">
  Just Added: New book signing at City Lights on Feb. 5.
</h1>
```

As you're building a web page, it may seem easier to use inline styles rather than to create a separate style sheet; you won't have to go back to the <style> section or an external style sheet, but can just type the declaration directly into an attribute. However, in the long run it's harder to maintain inline styles because they'll be scattered throughout your HTML source.

Ultimately, the use of inline styles reduces the separation of content from presentation because it mixes the two together within the same markup. It makes more sense to use HTML for structure and content and CSS for presentation; in this regard, inline CSS is just a single step up from HTML presentation attributes.

In general, you should avoid using inline styles unless you have a very specific use in mind. If you have to style more than one part of your page the same way, it's better to use an embedded or external style sheet and define a class instead.

It's perfectly valid to use all three methods for using CSS rules within one document—for example, an external style sheet for the entire site applied with a <link> tag; an embedded style sheet inside a <style> tag for rules specific to that web page; and inline styles set on individual elements with the style attribute.

Classes and IDs

In addition to setting styles based on HTML elements, CSS allows for rules based on two optional attributes in HTML: class and id. Each of these can serve as the selector part of a CSS rule and can be set on any visible HTML tag.

For even more selectors you can use with HTML and CSS, see Hour 5, "Selectors," and Hour 8, "Advanced Selectors."

The <div> and <span> elements really come into their own with the class and id selectors. Through the use of class and id attributes, <div> or <span> tags can be made to have nearly any effect and presentation, which is often good but sometimes bad. When using class and id markers, you shouldn't neglect other markup tags that might be better suited for the task at hand. For example, you might decide to create an emphatic class for emphasizing portions of your text, and then use a CSS rule to make it bold. It's better to instead just use the <strong> tag in HTML and apply CSS to style it as you want—<strong> already has a meaning in HTML (which is "emphasized text"). Use <div> or <span> only if there are no appropriate HTML tags you can style or restyle.

The `class` **Attribute in HTML**

The `class` attribute is used to define a related group of HTML elements on a page. They might have the same function or role, but in a CSS context, it means they have the same style rules applied to them. (The `class` attribute could be used for more than just styling, but in practice it's rarely used for any other purpose.)

The elements within a class can be of any type; one might be a <p>, another a <span>, and a third an <img>. That's perfectly fine; they will have the same style rules applied to them, but the fact that each one has a default presentation (defined by the browser or the HTML specifications) means those styles will be applied relative to the way they're normally rendered.

To create a class, you simply have to give it a name. A class name may be nearly anything, but has to be one word; in practice, it's best to stick to letters and numbers. Avoid using underlines, periods, and other non-alphanumeric characters when naming your classes.

You can name a class anything you like; it's basically just an arbitrary word used to group these items together. A descriptive name is good, especially one that describes function instead of presentation. For example, `class="detail"` makes more sense than `class="bluetext"`; if I can't come up with a good descriptive name, I'll use something arbitrary instead, such as the names of planets or the seven dwarves. Class names are not inherently case sensitive, but you should try to use the same case of characters when writing your HTML and your CSS rules.

After you've chosen a name for your class, you just have to assign HTML elements to that class by setting the class attribute on each. A given HTML element can be part of one or more classes if they are separated with spaces. Here are some examples:

```
<div class="p1">
  <h2 class="q2">Meeting Times</h2>
  <p class="r3">
    We will be meeting every other Wednesday, at
    <span class="q2 j4">7:30 p.m.</span>
  </p>
</div>
```

In this example, the <div> is part of the p1 class. The <h2> and the <span> are both part of the q2 class. The <p> is part of the "r3" class, and the <span> is also part of the j4 class.

Class Selectors in CSS

After you've defined a class in your HTML, you can use it as a class selector in CSS. Class selectors are indicated by a period (.) before the name of the class, like this:

```
.q2 { color: blue; }
.r3 { font-family: Arial; }
```

You can combine an element selector with a class selector; the result selects only those members of the class that are of that particular element. (Or, it selects only those elements that are members of that particular class—same thing.) Just put the name of the element directly in front of the period and then the class name. For example:

```
span.q2 { font-size: large; }
p.r3 { color: green; }
```

The first refers to all <span> elements with class="q2"; the latter to all <p> elements in the r3 class. You can combine together several classes within a rule to select only elements that have those classes listed (separated by spaces, as described before) by separating them with periods, as shown here:

```
.q2.j4 { font-family: Arial; }
```

This rule would select the <span>, which is part of both class q2 and class j4.

A complete example of using class selectors is shown in Listings 4.1 and 4.2, and the result of displaying in a browser is presented in Figure 4.1.

LISTING 4.1   HTML Code Illustrating Class Selectors

```
<html>
  <!-- This is class-4.1.html -->
  <head>
    <title>
      Class Selectors in Action
    </title>
    <link type="text/css" rel="stylesheet" href="5-3.css">
  </head>
  <body>
    <h1 class="mercury">
      Welcome!
    </h1>
    <div class="mars">
      <p class="saturn">
        This is a short page to tell you about our writers
        group. We meet in the bookstore every other Wednesday;
        our meetings are at <span class="mercury">7:30 p.m.
        sharp.</span>
      </p>
    </div>
  </body>
</html>
```

LISTING 4.2   CSS Code Illustrating Class Selectors

```
/* This is class-4.2.css */
.mercury     { color: white; background-color: black; }
.mars        { font-family: Arial; }
.saturn      { color: black; }
h1.mercury   { font-family: Verdana; color: silver; }
```

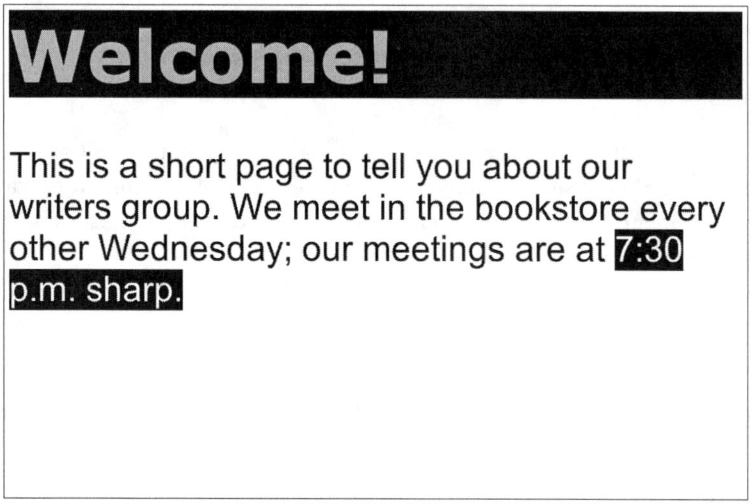

FIGURE 4.1
Firefox displays
the style rules
defined with
class selectors.

The id **Attribute in HTML**

The HTML attribute id is similar to the class attribute—it can be set on nearly any tag and can be used as a CSS selector—but is much more restricted. Only one tag on a page can have a given id; it must be unique within the page and is used to identify just that element. An id attribute's value has to begin with a letter and can be followed by letters, numbers, periods (.), underlines (_), hyphens (-) or colons (:); however, if you're using it as a selector in CSS, it's safest to stick to just letters and numbers. Case matters, so be consistent in the case of your id attributes. Here's an example:

```
<a href="next.html" id="next">The next page</a>
```

id **Selectors in CSS**

An id selector is indicated by a # (the hash, also called the pound sign) before the value of the id. For example:

```
#next { font-size: large; }
```

Why would you want to use id selectors and not class selectors? Good question. A class selector is more flexible; it can do anything an id selector can do and more. If you want to reuse the style, you can do it with a class selector by adding new elements to the class, but you can't do that with id selectors because an id value must be unique in a document, and only one element on the page can have that value.

An id selector is useful if you know that you have to identify one unique item within a page—for example, the Next link, or maybe a common navigation or layout element that appears on each page. In general, id selectors are less useful than class selectors when you use CSS with HTML. When using CSS with XML, however, id attributes play a larger role because XML uses id attributes more than HTML does.

Try it Yourself   ▼
Using CSS with HTML

To apply what you've learned this hour, why not create an HTML page, create an external CSS file and link it to the HTML file, and add embedded and inline styles? This will make you familiar with the ways HTML and CSS are used together in web design.

1. Create a basic HTML document with headers, paragraphs, `<div>` and `<span>` tags, and other markup. Be sure to set some `class` and `id` attributes on your tags. Save this HTML file.

2. Create a CSS file with rules based on element selectors, `class` selectors, and `id` selectors. Save this CSS file.

3. Use `<link>` to apply the CSS style sheet to the HTML file. View the results in an HTML browser that supports CSS.

4. Add more styles directly into the HTML file by creating a `<style>` element in the `<head>`; view the results.

5. Create some inline styles using the `style` attribute, and check your creation in a browser.

You'll have successfully completed the activity if you're able to use CSS with your HTML in each of the ways discussed this hour—with external style sheets, embedded style sheets, and inline `style` attributes—and if you can utilize `class` and `id` attributes as selectors in your CSS rules.   ▲

Summary

In this hour, you learned about the three flavors of HTML 4.01 and how CSS is used in each, and you learned about the benefits of validating your HTML code. You learned about three tools for applying Cascading Style Sheets to HTML pages: external style sheets that use the `<link>` tag, embedded style sheets defined inside a `<style>` tag, or specific styles set with the `style` attribute. You learned how to set `class` and `id` attributes in HTML and how to create rules using `class` and `id` attributes as selectors.

Workshop

The workshop contains a Q&A section, quiz questions, and activities to help reinforce what you've learned in this hour. If you get stuck, the answers to the quiz can be found after the questions.

Q&A

Q. *Will there be such a thing as HTML 5?*

A. No, and yes, and kind of. The W3C has stopped work on developing HTML and is concentrating on XHTML instead. The next version of HTML will be XHTML 2.0, and in addition to being composed of distinct modules, it will have new elements and attributes that don't currently exist in HTML. You can track the progress of XHTML 2's development at http://www.w3.org/Markup/.

In addition, a group called the Web Hypertext Application Technology Working Group (WhatWG), a group of browser developers and other interested parties, is working on what they call Web Applications 1.0—an extension to XHTML 1.0, which is informally referred to as "HTML 5." Whether these efforts will bear fruit as a replacement for HTML 4.01 is unclear; you can follow the WhatWG's progress at http://www.whatwg.org.

Q. *Can you use selectors with inline styles? For example,* `<div style=".dot { color: black; }">`?

A. No; a style attribute contains only the declaration part of a CSS rule, not the selector portion. The selector is the content of the element itself.

Q. *You said I could use style attributes, embedded style sheets, and linked style sheets on the same HTML page. What happens if they have different values for the same property?*

A. When two or more rules conflict, the method of resolving the conflict is known as the cascade. You'll learn more about this in Hour 7, but the general principle is that the more specific rule usually wins.

Quiz

1. What HTML tag is used to insert an embedded style sheet? What are the primary attributes of that tag?

2. What HTML tag is used to associate an external style sheet with an HTML tag? What are the primary attributes of that tag?

3. What is the default value for the media attribute?

4. What is the difference between a class selector and an id selector? When would you use each?

5. What are the three "flavors" of HTML, and which one relies on CSS for nearly all presentation styling?

6. What does HTML validation check for?

Answers

1. The `<style>` tag is used to embed a style sheet in an HTML file. The main attributes are type, which should be text/css, and an optional media attribute.

2. The `<link>` tag can be set in the `<head>` of an HTML file to link to an external style sheet. The primary attributes used with CSS are type, media, rel="stylesheet", and href.

3. The default value of the media attribute is screen.

4. An id selector applies to only one element within each document, whereas a class selector can be used to select any element within that class. You'd use class when you needed to select multiple elements, and id if you wanted to select only a single, unique element.

5. The three types of HTML 4.01 are Strict, Transitional, and Frameset. HTML Strict has almost no presentational markup and depends on CSS to provide styling instructions.

6. HTML validation checks your HTML code against the formal specification and DTD for the HTML language.

Exercise

Create your own web page and use what you've learned so far to style your page. Choose your type of HTML, set a DOCTYPE, and validate the page. Use <link> and <style> tags to set up your style sheet, and add inline rules with the style attribute.

You'll have successfully completed the activity if you're able to use CSS with your HTML in each of the ways discussed this hour—external style sheets, embedded style sheets, and inline style attributes—and if you can utilize class and id attributes as selectors in your CSS rules.

PART II

Core Principles of CSS

HOUR 5

Selectors

What You'll Learn in This Hour:

▶ More about simple selectors you've already been using

▶ How to use `class` and `id` selectors

▶ What the universal selector is and when to use it

▶ What pseudo-classes and pseudo-elements are and how they can be used

▶ How to specify styles that affect hypertext links

As you learned in Hour 2, "Getting Started with CSS," selectors are the part of the CSS rule that identifies the target of the styling. Putting the power of selectors to use is vital for getting the most out of CSS.

Simple Selectors

You've seen the simplest type of selectors already: type selectors, `class` selectors, and `id` selectors. In this hour, you'll look at how you can use them more effectively.

So far you have learned how to create CSS rules using simple selectors: type selectors based on the HTML tag, and `class` or `id` selectors based on attributes in the HTML.

A type selector is simply the name of an HTML tag minus the <> angle brackets. For example:

```
h1 { color: blue; }
```

This selects all <h1> tags and specifies that they're the color blue. Type selectors are the easiest to use because they're so straightforward, but they're also very limited. What if you want only some of the <h1> tags to be blue and others to be green? That's when you'd use `class` and `id` selectors.

Although I said type selectors had to be HTML tags, I must admit that's only half true. They actually have to be any sort of legitimate element for the language you're styling; this is how you can use CSS with XML, for example. And in fact, you don't have to have the actual tag present! HTML (but not XML or XHTML) lets you leave out certain tag declarations entirely, such as the <body> element. These are *implied* tags. The opening and closing tags are implied. If you have a rule based on body, such as 'body { font-family: Arial; }', a CSS-compliant browser will still apply your font to the implied <body> even though no tags are present.

In Hour 4, "Using CSS with HTML," you learned how you can set class and id selectors in your rules based on HTML attributes of class and id, such as

```
#here      { font-size: large;      }
.there     { color: green;          }
```

An id selector uniquely identifies part of a page, whereas a class selector allows you to identify specific tags as being part of a certain set you've defined.

Using class and id Selectors

You can combine class selectors or id selectors with <div> tags to designate specific sections of a page that should receive special styling. For example, consider the HTML page shown in Listing 5.1, which has a class or id attribute set on each <div> tag.

LISTING 5.1   HTML Sections Set via <div> and class

```
<!-- imgtip-5.1.html -->
<html>
  <head>
    <title>Image Accessibility</title>
    <link type="text/css" rel="stylesheet"
        href="tips-5.2.css">
  </head>
  <body>
    <div id="breadcrumb">
      <a href="http://kynn.com">Kynn.com</a> &middot;
      <a href="http://kynn.com/writing/">Writing</a> &middot;
      <a href="http://kynn.com/writing/tips">Tips</a> &middot;
      Images
    </div>
    <div id="header">
      <h1>Image Accessibility</h1>
      <h2>Making your graphics accessible</h2>
    </div>
    <div class="tips">
      <p> Here are some helpful tips on making your graphical
          content accessible to users who can't see images: </p>
      <ul>
```

LISTING 5.1   Continued

```
            <li>Always include an <tt>alt</tt> attribute on your
               <tt>&lt;img&gt;</tt> tag.</li>
            <li>The <tt>alt</tt> attribute should contain a short
               replacement for the graphic, in text. If the image
               itself has text, list that in <tt>alt</tt>.</li>
            <li>If the image is purely decorative and doesn't convey
               any additional information, use <tt>alt=""</tt>.</li>
            <li>If there is more information in the graphic than you
               can convey in a short <tt>alt</tt> attribute, such
               as the information in a graph or chart, then use
               the <tt>longdesc</tt> attribute to give the URL of
               a page that describes the graphic in text.</li>
         </ul>
      </div>
      <div id="footer">
        <address> Copyright &copy; 2006 by Kynn Bartlett </address>
      </div>
   </body>
</html>
```

As you can see, I linked in an external style sheet, `tips-5.2.css`, using a `<link>` tag. That style sheet defines a style for each section of the page; the sections are `breadcrumb`, `header`, `tips`, and `footer`. The style sheet is shown in Listing 5.2.

LISTING 5.2   Sectional Styles Using Classes and IDs

```
/* tips-5.2.css                    */
      body
        { color: black;
          background-color: white; }

      #breadcrumb
        { font-family: Verdana, sans-serif;
          color: black;
          background-color: silver; }

      #header
        { color: white;
          background-color: maroon;
          font-family: "Courier New", monospace; }

      .tips
        { color: white;
          background-color: gray;
          font-family: Arial, sans-serif; }

      #footer
        { color: silver;
          background-color: black;
          font-family: "Times New Roman", serif; }
```

The effect of applying these styles is shown in Figure 5.1. You'll notice that I've used background colors to make some of the <div> sections visible; in practice, this can be a somewhat unattractive effect; some of my examples are written simply to illustrate a principle rather than to be aesthetically appealing, especially in the limited black, white, and gray shades available in this book. Each section gets its own font, background color, and foreground color.

FIGURE 5.1
Firefox displays sectional styles set by <div>, class and id.

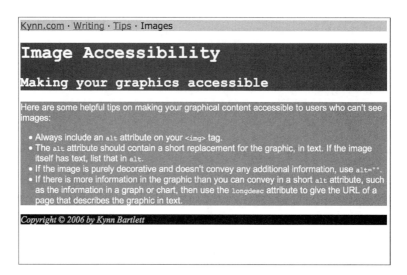

In this example, id selectors were used for the breadcrumb trail, the header, and the footer, and a class selector for the tips. Why?

Simple: You can (and probably should) use id whenever you can be sure that the id will be unique on a page. A page may contain multiple tips, but just one breadcrumb trail, one header, and one footer. The style sheet could still be written with class; it doesn't really hurt anything to use class instead of id, but style sheets are simpler and more specific if they use id.

The Universal Selector

In addition to type, class, and id selectors, CSS also defines a *universal selector*. The universal selector applies to all tags and content within a page and is represented by an asterisk (*). Here's an example of a universal selector rule:

```
* { color: blue; }
```

If you're writing a rule that uses the universal selector and there's something else to that rule, such as a `class` or `id` selector, you can leave out the asterisk. In fact, the general way of writing class selectors is just a special case of the universal selector with the asterisk omitted. The following two declarations are identical:

```
*.there    { color: green;          }
.there     { color: green;          }
```

You may wonder why there's a need for a universal selector; as you've seen before, you can affect the style of an entire page by using a selector of the <body> tag. It's important to understand that the universal selector sets the style on all elements and doesn't just set an inherited default. What do I mean? Consider the following style sheet:

```
* { color: green; }
h1 { color: blue; }
```

Let's assume you'll link that to an HTML file that includes this:

```
<h1>This is <em>very</em> important</h1>
```

What color will the word "very" be? It will be green and in the middle of a blue headline because the universal rule says everything has the color green explicitly set, just as if there were a rule for every possible element, reading

```
element { color: green; }
```

In practice, you'd probably want the color of the <em> to inherit from the <h1>'s style, so you need to be very careful about when and where you use a universal selector. You would have gotten a very different result if you did the following:

```
body { color: green; }
h1 { color: blue; }
```

This would also make the default text green and the <h1> heading blue, but the embedded <em> would inherit the color from the <h1>. You'll learn more about inheritance in Hour 7, "Cascading and Inheritance."

Combining Simple Selectors

To get the most utility out of your CSS rules, you'll want to write combined rules. You've already learned a little about grouping selectors together; now you'll see how you can use descendant selectors as well.

Grouping Selectors

As you learned in Hour 2, you can combine rules by listing the selectors together, separating them by commas. You can combine any sort of selectors in this way, such as in the following rule:

```
/* Anything that is sorta heading-like is in Arial;
   only even headings are maroon and the rest are green */
h1, h2, h3, h4, h5, h6, dt, .heading, .standout, #headline
  { font-family: Arial; }
h1, h3, h5, dt, .heading, .standout, #headline
  { font-color: maroon; }
h2, h4, h6
  { font-color: green; }
```

Alternately, you could have written the same set of rules in another way by grouping them differently:

```
/* Anything that is sorta heading-like is in Arial;
   only even headings are maroon, and the rest are green */
h1, h3, h5, dt, .heading, .standout, #headline
  { font-family: Arial;
    font-color: maroon; }
h2, h4, h6
  { font-family: Arial;
    font-color: green; }
```

Writing it the first way makes it easier to change the font family if you need to; the declaration font-family: Arial; appears in only one place in your document. The way you group your rules can improve the ease with which you can modify them. Note, though, that there's a drawback to this approach, as well; to change how one type of selector is rendered (say, anything in the standout class), you need to edit several rules. There are no hard-and-fast guidelines, therefore, about how you can group your rules in modules; as you gain experience with CSS, you'll form your own methods for style rules grouping.

Descendant Selectors

One of the most useful ways to group selectors together is to use a *descendant selector*. A *descendant*, in HTML and XML, is an element that's completely contained within another element's content. As an example, the <h2> is a descendant of the <div>, and the <cite> of the <h1>, in Listing 5.3. The <cite> is also a descendant of the <div>, as it's contained by both the <div> and the <h1>, and they are all descendants of the <body> element.

LISTING 5.3   Descendants in HTML

```
<!-- babe-5.3.html                      -->
<html>
  <head>
    <title>Babe: Best Movie EVER</title>
    <style type="text/css">
      /* add style rules here */
    </style>
  </head>
  <body>
    <div class="header">
      <h1>Movie Review: <cite>Babe</cite></h1>
      <p>A Mini-Review by Joe H. Moviefan</p>
    </div>
    <div class="opinion">
      <h2>The Best Movie <em>EVER</em></h2>
      <p>The movie <cite>Babe</cite> was the best family
         movie ever produced!  This great movie featured
         talking animals, a cantankerous old man, and
         subtle-yet-Oscar-winning special effects -- who
         could ask for more?  The clever writing and
         humorous touches make this all-ages movie great
         for children while still very enjoyable by
         adults. What a great movie!</p>
    </div>
    <div class="footer">
      <p>What did you think? Mail me at
         <a href="mailto:joe@example.com">Joe H.
         Moviefan.com!</a></p>
    </div>
  </body>
</html>
```

Descendant selectors define rules based on where a given tag appears within the page by combining together simple selectors, separated by spaces. For example, here's a rule to change the color of all `<cite>` tags contained within paragraphs:

```
p cite { color: white; background-color: black; }
```

You'll notice that I listed the outside tag first and then the inside. If you did it the other way around, you wouldn't match anything because no cite tags contain paragraph tags.

If this rule is added to the `<style>` element of the HTML page from Listing 5.3, the effect shown in Figure 5.2 is produced. Notice that the `<cite>` within the `<h1>` is not styled by this rule, only the `<cite>` inside the `<p>` element.

It's important to keep in mind that a descendant selector means any descendant, not just an immediate child. A descendant could be an element inside an element inside an element. This enables you to make rules that apply to any descendant element, no matter how deeply it's nested.

Movie Review: *Babe*

A Mini-Review by Joe H. Moviefan

The Best Movie *EVER*

The movie Babe was the best family movie ever produced! This great movie
featured talking animals, a cantankerous old man, and
subtle-yet-Oscar-winning special effects -- who could ask for more? The
clever writing and humorous touches make this all-ages movie great for
children while still very enjoyable by adults. What a great movie!

What did you think? Mail me at Joe H. Moviefan.com!

You can combine section styles (set via `class` and `<div>`) with element-based type
selectors, as well; for example, the following code changes the font face and colors
of `<p>` tags within the header section, but leaves the rest of the header alone—as
well as the other paragraph tags that aren't contained by something with the
`.header` class:

```
.header p { font-family: Verdana, sans-serif;
          color: white; background-color: black; }
```

The effects of this rule are shown in Figure 5.3.

Movie Review: *Babe*

A Mini-Review by Joe H. Moviefan

The Best Movie *EVER*

The movie *Babe* was the best family movie ever produced! This great movie
featured talking animals, a cantankerous old man, and
subtle-yet-Oscar-winning special effects -- who could ask for more? The
clever writing and humorous touches make this all-ages movie great for
children while still very enjoyable by adults. What a great movie!

What did you think? Mail me at Joe H. Moviefan.com!

A more complete style sheet that demonstrates how to set a number of different combined selectors is listed in Listing 5.4. To use this with my movie review page, I'll add the following to the <head> of the page:

```
<link type="text/css" rel="stylesheet" href="babe-5.4.css">
```

Figure 5.4 shows how Listing 5.3 looks with this style sheet applied.

LISTING 5.4   **A Variety of Selectors in a Single Style Sheet**

```
/* babe-5.4.css: Style sheet for Babe review        */

body
  { font-family: Arial, sans-serif;
    color: black;
    background-color: white; }

.header h1
  { font-family: "Courier New", monospace;
    color: silver;
    background-color: black; }

.header cite
  { font-family: Verdana, sans-serif;
    background-color: silver;
    color: black; }

.header p
  { font-family: Arial, monospace;
    color: black;
    font-size: x-large; }

.opinion h2
  { color: white;
    background-color: navy;
    font-family: Arial, sans-serif; }

em
  { font-size: larger; }

p cite
  { color: white;
    background-color: black; }

.footer
  { font-family: "Times New Roman", serif;
    font-size: small;
    color: white;
    background-color: gray; }

.footer a
  { color: white;
    background-color: black; }
```

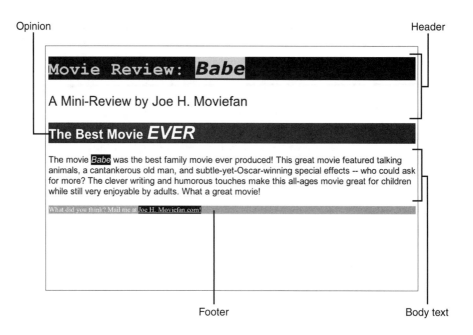

FIGURE 5.4
Displaying various selectors with separate styles.

Opinion

Header

Footer

Body text

▼ **Try it Yourself**

Experimenting with Simple Selectors

Why not try out these selectors yourself? You can use the example HTML files from this chapter.

1. Download either the accessibility tip in Listing 5.1 or the movie review in Listing 5.3 from the book's website.

2. Open the HTML file in a browser and view it without styles.

3. Create a style sheet. Add your own style rules based on the class and id attributes set in the HTML. Choose your own text colors, backgrounds, font sizes, and other properties.

4. Link your style sheet to the HTML file with the <link> element and view it in a browser. Are they styled the way you wanted? If not, try again until you're satisfied.

5. Add to the HTML files—rewrite the text, add more paragraphs, create new class and id attributes. Write new CSS rules based on these! Or even better, write your own pages from scratch and use your own content for testing out combined selectors.

▲

Pseudo-Classes and Pseudo-Elements

In addition to type selectors, id selectors, and `class` selectors, CSS also allows pseudo-class and pseudo-element selectors.

A *pseudo-class selector* is a selector based on a set of predefined qualities that an HTML element can possess. These qualities function in practice similar to a `class` attribute on the element, so in CSS terms, they are called *pseudo-classes*. No actual `class` attributes exist in the markup that corresponds to these pseudo-classes; instead, they represent some aspect of the element to which they're applied, or even the state of the browser's user interface relative to that element.

A *pseudo-element selector* identifies a virtual element, one that doesn't exist in the markup but can be deduced by the browser and used to apply a style. As with pseudo-classes, there is no markup that corresponds to the pseudo-element.

Simple Pseudo-Classes

The pseudo-classes in CSS are shown on Table 5.1. The `:active`, `:focus`, and `:hover` pseudo-classes are covered in Hour 12, "Styling Links."

TABLE 5.1 CSS Pseudo-Classes

Pseudo-class	Selects
`:active`	Elements that have been activated (such as active links)
`:first-child`	The first child of an element
`:focus`	Elements that have focus (such as form fields receiving input)
`:hover`	Elements that are pointed at (such as by a mouse)
`:lang()`	Styles for a specific language
`:link`	Unfollowed links
`:visited`	Previously visited links

Pseudo-classes can stand alone in a style rule, as classes can, but most commonly they're used with elements as a type selector, as follows:

```
:link      { color: red; }
a:link     { color: red; }
```

Both these rules are valid; the former applies to any element that happens to be a link, whereas the latter rule covers only <a> tags. In practice, these are the same things in HTML: Only the <a> elements are links, and so the rules mean the same thing.

You can combine pseudo-classes with real classes or even other pseudo-classes by putting them together with no spaces between, just the . and : indicators. For example, here's HTML with `class` attributes set on links:

```
<a href="search.html" class="nav">
  Search the Site
</a>
...
<a href="http://www.idyllmtn.com/" class="offsite">
  Idyll Mountain Internet
</a>
```

Here are rules to work with each of those links; note that the order of the `class` and the pseudo-class doesn't matter:

```
a:link.nav       { color: cyan; }
a.offsite:link   { color: green; }
```

The `:link` and `:visited` Pseudo-Classes

In HTML, you can use attributes on the `<body>` tag to determine the colors of links:

```
<body link="red" visited="gray">
```

CSS gives the same functionality through pseudo-classes, and by combining pseudo-class selectors with `class` or `id` selectors, you can put different link colors on different parts of the page as you'll see later in this hour.

The `:link` pseudo-class is the equivalent of the `<body>` attribute link in HTML: It defines a style for links that have yet to be followed. You usually set these on the `<a>` tag because `<a>` is the only visible linking element in HTML. Here's an example CSS rule using `:link`:

```
a:link     { color: red; }
```

Visited links are those that the user has already been to; the browser keeps track of a list of visited URLs and colors them differently. The `:visited` pseudo-class is used to write rules applying to those types of links, as follows:

```
a:visited  { color: gray; }
```

The `:link` and `:visited` pseudo-selectors are mutually exclusive; a given link is either one or the other at any given time and can't be both at once. However, you can write a rule that applies to both, such as

```
a:link,
a:visited  { color: blue; }
```

> Note that changing the :link and :visited colors to the same value can cause problems for users! Most users expect links to change to some color—anything other than the original, although usually from blue to purple—after they have been visited. Unless you've got a good reason for it, you'll probably want to supply different :link and :visited colors.

Unlike HTML, which lets you change only the colors of the links, CSS allows you to apply nearly any style to unvisited or visited links by using the :link and :visited pseudo-selectors. For example:

```
a:link      { color:            black;
              background-color: lime;
              font-family:      Arial, sans-serif; }
a:visited   { color:            gray;
              background-color: yellow;
              font-family:      "Times New Roman", serif; }
```

This puts your unvisited links in black text on a lime green background and puts the visited links in gray on a yellow background. Unvisited links are in Arial font, and visited links are in Times New Roman. Now, apart from an illustrative example, you never want to write rules like these; it doesn't make sense, for example, for the font face to change when you've clicked on a link and some of my color choices are just plain ugly. Background colors on links do help them stand out from rest of the page, though, and that's not such a bad thing. You'll learn more about the theory behind link styles in Hour 12.

To color links differently on different sections of the page, combine :link and :visited pseudo-selectors with section classes in a descendant selector, like this:

```
#breadcrumb           { background-color: black; color: white; }
#breadcrumb a:link    { color: cyan; font-size: large; }
#breadcrumb a:visited { font-size: small; color: fuchsia; }
```

This creates a black breadcrumb trail with unvisited links in large cyan letters (bright blue) and visited links in smaller, fuchsia (bright purple). If you add these styles to the style sheet in Listing 5.2, the accessibility tip page from Listing 5.1 will look like the page shown in Figure 5.5.

The :first-child **Pseudo-Class**

The :first-child pseudo-class is used to select an element that's the first child of another element. The first child is the first tag within some other element; if the first child matches the base type of the selector—the part before the :first-child pseudo-class—then the rule applies to that element.

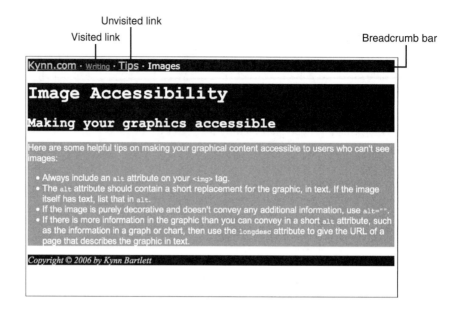

FIGURE 5.5
Pseudo-class selectors coloring links on a page.

Listing 5.5 shows the start of a short story. The style sheet in Listing 5.6 sets the first paragraph of the story to be larger than the rest, as well as gives it a silver background. The results are displayed in Figure 5.6.

LISTING 5.5   A Few Paragraphs in HTML

```
<!-- story-5.5.html -->
<html>
  <head>
    <title>Fortune of Reversal</title>
    <link type="text/css" rel="stylesheet"
        href="story-5.7.css">
  </head>
  <body>
    <h1 id="storytitle">Fortune of Reversal</h1>
    <div class="storybody">
      <p>They dined on heaping platters of Szechuan chicken, of
         spicy beef, of shrimp and vegetables in some exotic dish
         without a name. Bits of food were passed from chopsticks
         to chopsticks, violating all known laws of Chinese
         cuisine etiquette. The tea flowed hot and fast that night,
         until the meal finally concluded itself.</p>
      <p>"Thank you for dining here tonight," said the badgeless,
         anonymous waitress. She placed a small tray containing the
         check and two wrapped fortune cookies on the edge of the
         table, and hefted the empty plates one by one, forming a
         stack on the crook of her elbow.</p>
      <p>"Absolutely delicious," declared Oliver as he pulled a card
         from his wallet and flicked it onto the bill. He picked up
         the two cookies, an afterthought. "Fortune cookie, my
         love?" he asked Amanda.</p>
```

LISTING 5.5   Continued

```
    </div>
  </body>
</html>
```

LISTING 5.6   A Style Sheet Using `:first-child` Pseudo-Class Selector

```
/* story-5.6.css              */

#storytitle
  { font-family: Verdana; }

.storybody p
  { font-family: Arial; }

.storybody p:first-child
  { font-size: x-large;
    background-color: silver; }
```

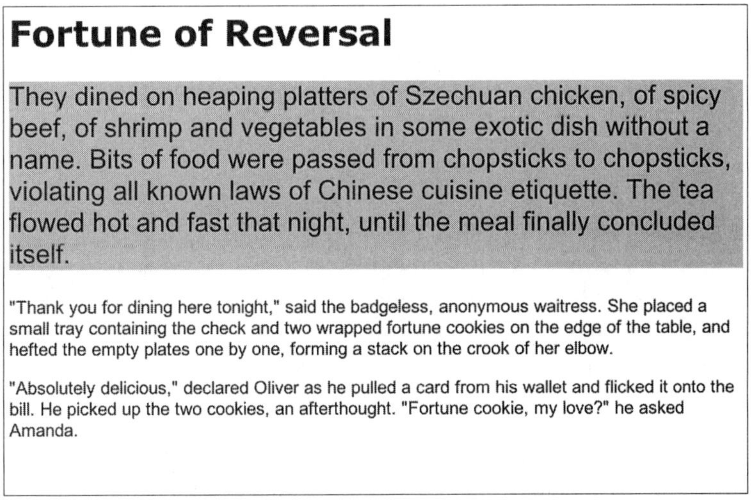

Fortune of Reversal

They dined on heaping platters of Szechuan chicken, of spicy beef, of shrimp and vegetables in some exotic dish without a name. Bits of food were passed from chopsticks to chopsticks, violating all known laws of Chinese cuisine etiquette. The tea flowed hot and fast that night, until the meal finally concluded itself.

"Thank you for dining here tonight," said the badgeless, anonymous waitress. She placed a small tray containing the check and two wrapped fortune cookies on the edge of the table, and hefted the empty plates one by one, forming a stack on the crook of her elbow.

"Absolutely delicious," declared Oliver as he pulled a card from his wallet and flicked it onto the bill. He picked up the two cookies, an afterthought. "Fortune cookie, my love?" he asked Amanda.

FIGURE 5.6
Firefox uses the `:first-child` selector to style the first paragraph.

Internet Explorer for Windows does not support the `:first-child` pseudo-element; rules with such selectors are ignored. For maximum compatibility, set a `class` attribute manually on your first child elements, such as `class="firstone"`, and then include that `class` as an additional selector in your rule. For example:

```
.storybody p:first-child, .storybody p.firstone
  { font-size: large; }
```

Watch Out!

> Of course, by doing so you've made the first half of the selector redundant—the other browsers understand the class-based workaround! So you may want to drop the use of `:first-child` entirely if you're going to add this workaround.

The `:lang()` Pseudo-Class

On the Web, languages are indicated by a two-letter code, sometimes followed by a dash and an additional country code for regional versions of a language. Some of these languages are shown on Table 5.2; for a complete list, see the book's website.

TABLE 5.2   **Several Language Codes**

Code	Language
de	German
en	English
en-ca	Canadian English
en-uk	British English
en-us	American English
fr	French
jp	Japanese
ru	Russian

The choice of language can dictate a number of factors, including the direction of the text, the fonts used, or even the dictionary for pronunciation used by a screen reader. The CSS language doesn't allow you to set the language, which must be done in the HTML or in an HTTP header, but it does let you create rules or style sheets that apply to only certain languages.

To set the language within an HTML document, you simply have to use the `lang` attribute on the `<html>` tag. Sections of a second language embedded within the document can be indicated with the `lang` attribute on a `<span>` or any other appropriate HTML element, such as `<blockquote>` or `<div>`.

The CSS specification defines a special pseudo-class, `:lang()`, for indicating rules that should be applied only to elements that match a certain language. Such a rule is written like the following:

```
:lang(en-uk) { background-color: #CCCCFF; }
```

This would display anything written in British English with a light blue background color. How does the browser know which parts of the text are written in British English? It needs to be set in the HTML, as in the following:

```
<p>He cried out in a bad Monty Python imitation,
  <span lang="en-uk">He's pinin' for the fjords!</span>
</p>
```

By itself, :lang() is not particularly useful, but when combined with other CSS rules and properties, it can be quite powerful.

Pseudo-Elements in CSS

Cascading Style Sheets defines four *pseudo-elements*—virtual elements created from their content in the document in relationship to a base element. These are shown in Table 5.3. The pseudo-elements :before and :after are used to insert generated content and are discussed in Hour 23, "User Interface and Generated Content."

TABLE 5.3 The Pseudo-Elements of CSS

Pseudo-Element	Selects
:before	Inserts something before an element
:after	Inserts something after an element
:first-letter	The first letter of a block element
:first-line	The first line of a block element

The pseudo-elements :first-line and :first-letter select portions of another element, and these portions operate as if they were separate inline elements; however, only certain properties can be applied to these pseudo-elements, as shown in Table 5.4.

TABLE 5.4 Recognized Properties for :first-line and :first-letter Selectors

Property or Category	:first-line	:first-letter	Hour Covered
Background properties	yes	yes	Hour 11
Border properties		yes	Hour 16
Color properties	yes	yes	Hour 10
Font properties	yes	yes	Hour 9
Margin properties		yes	Hour 16
Padding properties		yes	Hour 16
clear	yes	yes	Hour 15
float		yes	Hour 15
letter-spacing	yes		Hour 10

TABLE 5.4   Continued

Property or Category	:first-line	:first-letter	Hour Covered
line-height	yes	yes	Hour 10
text-decoration	yes	yes	Hour 10
text-shadow	yes	yes	Hour 10
text-transform	yes	yes	Hour 10
vertical-align	yes	yes	Hour 15
word-spacing	yes		Hour 10

The :first-line **Pseudo-Element**

The :first-line pseudo-element is a virtual element used to identify the first line of an element for adding specific styles that apply to only the first line. For example, you might want to put the first line of a news story in larger print to make it stand out. Such a rule would look like this:

```
p:first-line    { font-size: large; }
```

A :first-line pseudo-element creates a fictional tag set that is similar to a <span> or another inline element but whose content is determined when the page is rendered. As much as will fit on one line is included in the fictional tag. This will vary depending on the size of the user's browser window, the font size, and other factors, so there's no way to calculate it beforehand. This means that there aren't any viable workarounds for browsers that don't support :first-line because there's no way to know what will fit on one line. Fortunately, the current versions of modern browsers support :first-line.

The :first-letter **Pseudo-Element**

A :first-letter selector also references one of those imaginary, generated elements that doesn't appear in the source code but can be referenced by CSS rules. In this case, the imaginary tag is one surrounding the first letter of the element. The most common use for this is creating an initial capital letter that's larger than surrounding text.

Here's an example of a style sheet that uses both :first-letter and :first-line:

```
/* story-5.7.css */

#storytitle
  { font-family: Verdana, sans-serif; }

.storybody p
```

```
{ font-family: Arial, sans-serif; }

.storybody p:first-line
  { background-color: silver; }

.storybody p:first-letter
  { font-size: xx-large;
    color: white;
    background-color: black;
    font-family: Verdana, sans-serif; }
```

The result of applying this style sheet to the story sample from Listing 5.5 can be seen in Figure 5.7.

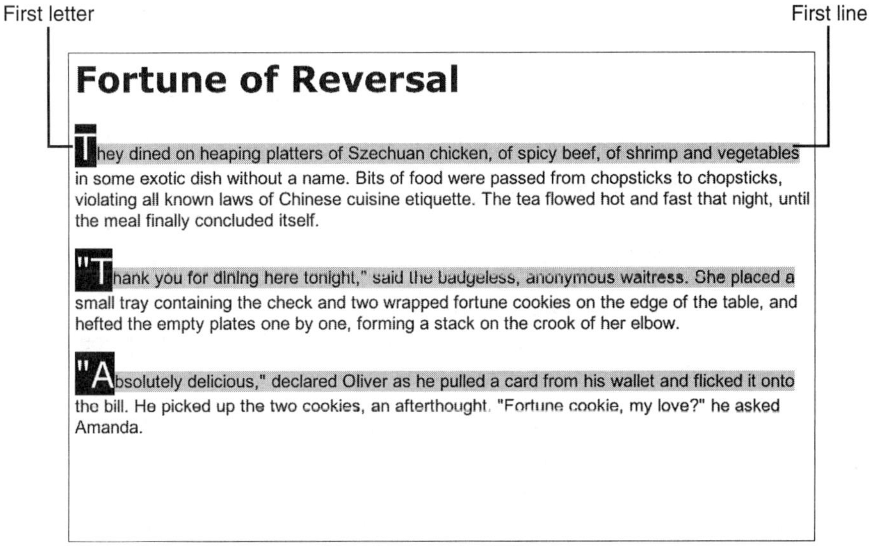

First letter   First line

Fortune of Reversal

They dined on heaping platters of Szechuan chicken, of spicy beef, of shrimp and vegetables in some exotic dish without a name. Bits of food were passed from chopsticks to chopsticks, violating all known laws of Chinese cuisine etiquette. The tea flowed hot and fast that night, until the meal finally concluded itself.

"Thank you for dining here tonight," said the badgeless, anonymous waitress. She placed a small tray containing the check and two wrapped fortune cookies on the edge of the table, and hefted the empty plates one by one, forming a stack on the crook of her elbow.

"Absolutely delicious," declared Oliver as he pulled a card from his wallet and flicked it onto the bill. He picked up the two cookies, an afterthought. "Fortune cookie, my love?" he asked Amanda.

FIGURE 5.7
A large initial capital letter styled by a `:first-letter` rule.

Try it Yourself ▼

Using `:first-letter` **with** `:first-child`

In Figure 5.7, each paragraph begins with a large capital letter, white on a black background. In many situations, however, only the first paragraph should have such a large initial capital letter. Make it so by doing the following:

1. Download both the HTML file in Listing 5.5 and the style sheet in Listing 5.6 from the book's website.

2. Edit the `.storybody p:first-letter` rule so that it looks like this:

   ```
   .storybody p:first-child:first-letter
     { font-size: xx-large;
   ```

▼

```
        color: white;
        background-color: black;
        font-family: Verdana, sans-serif; }
```

3. Open this in your browser. How does it look? If you aren't using Internet Explorer for Windows, you should see that only the first paragraph has a large initial capital letter.

4. How can you fix this to work in Internet Explorer? Recall the warning and work-around earlier this chapter.

5. Edit your HTML and CSS file to add a class and a style rule that will make your initial capital letter Internet Explorer-proof.

Summary

The selector is the part of the CSS rule that designates the recipient of the styles defined in the style declaration. Type selectors can be used to style specific types of HTML elements, and `class` and `id` selectors choose them according to attribute values. The universal selector sets a style on all elements.

You create a descendant selector by combining two or more simple selectors together to show the hierarchy of the elements on the page. Using this technique, you can apply different styles to different sections of the page.

Pseudo-element and pseudo-class selectors let you select parts of the page that aren't otherwise distinguished in the HTML. Rules with `:link` and `:visited` pseudo-class selectors can be used to style hypertext links. The `:lang()` pseudo-class can add styles to text in specific languages. The `:first-child`, `:first-letter`, and `:first-line` selectors are used for text formatting.

Workshop

The workshop contains a Q&A section, quiz questions, and an exercise to help reinforce what you've learned in this hour. If you get stuck, the answers to the quiz can be found after the questions.

Q&A

Q. *Are there other selectors that aren't covered here?*

A. Yes, and you'll learn about them in Hour 8, "Advanced Selectors." Some of these are not well supported by the browsers, however.

Q. *Can I string together as many selectors as I like?*

A. Certainly. You aren't limited to just two items in a descendant selector, for example. You could write a rule with a selector like the following, if you wanted:

```
body div #content p.special a:visited { color: green; }
```

Quiz

1. Which of the following selectors means "select any <em> tag that's both part of the class old and within a <p> tag?"

   a. `em.old p`

   b. `em.old, p`

   c. `p.old em`

   d. `p em.old`

2. What rules would you write to make all visited links red and all unvisited links lime, and to make both kinds of links display in Arial font?

3. Which pseudo-element or pseudo-class can't be duplicated by using a <span> tag with an appropriate class set, and why?

   a. `:first-child`

   b. `:first-line`

   c. `:first-letter`

Answers

1. The correct answer is (d), `p em.old`.

2. Here is one set of CSS rules to make unvisited links lime and visited links red, both in Arial font:

```
a:link { color: red; font-family: Arial, sans-serif; }
a:visited { color: lime; font-family: Arial, sans-serif; }
```

3. The `:first-line` cannot be duplicated by the <span> tag because the author of the web page doesn't know where the first line will end when displayed on the user's browser.

Exercise

In this hour, you saw several HTML pages and associated style sheets that used selectors to style the page. To further explore selectors, you can create additional style rules by selecting specific elements and styling them appropriately.

HOUR 6

The CSS Box Model

What You'll Learn in This Hour:

▶ How web content is displayed visually in CSS as boxes

▶ What categories of display elements are used and how you can affect an element's display type

▶ How CSS browsers interpret and display web pages

▶ How to set margins, borders, and padding on a box

This hour explores the core of Cascading Style Sheets—the part of the specification that defines how parts of a web page are displayed: as stacks of boxes. The visual presentation of CSS is defined as a series of boxes based on the structure of the original document.

Displaying Content in CSS

The *content* of a web page is the information encoded within the HTML page, found between the opening and closing tags of the HTML markup. These tags define the *structure* of the content, a framework that gives meaning to the content. For example, consider the following HTML:

```
<p>This is the <strong>tricky part</strong>,
   so pay attention!</p>
```

The content in this example is simply the sentence This is the tricky part, so pay attention! The tags embedded within (and surrounding) the content create the structure, which gives meaning to the content. Any browser that understands HTML knows that the whole thing is a paragraph (identified by the <p> tag) and that the phrase tricky part is strongly emphasized.

The presentation of the content, however, is not defined by the HTML; instead, it's determined by CSS rules. The browser has default rules for <p> and <strong> tags, which say that a <p> is shown visually as a paragraph on lines of its own, with leading and trailing space, and that the <strong> is shown as bold text within that paragraph.

Both the <p> and <strong> tags are shown as *display boxes*, which is how CSS browsers deal with HTML elements. Each HTML element corresponds to a display box, although not all elements are shown on the screen. A display box is a rectangular shape on the screen that can contain text content, images, form controls, or other display boxes.

The exact method by which HTML elements are shown as CSS display boxes is called the *visual formatting method*. The visual formatting method tells browsers how they should show HTML content on the screen.

Types of Elements

In the visual formatting model, markup elements are classified into two basic types—*block* and *inline*. The type of element determines how CSS browsers will display instances of that element.

The initial type of each HTML element is set by the HTML specification. For example, <p> tags are block elements, and <em> tags are inline elements. The full list is given in the HTML 4.01 Recommendation; each tag has an indication as to what type it is. You can change the type of a specific element with CSS, although often you won't need to.

Certain CSS properties can be set only on block or inline elements; for example, the text-indent property (which you'll learn about in Hour 15, "Alignment") applies only to block elements.

Block

A block element is one that is intended to be displayed as a distinct block of content, starting and ending with a new line. Besides the <p> tag, other block elements in HTML include <div>, <blockquote>, <table>, <br>, <ol>, and the <h1> to <h6> tags.

Block elements are listed one after each other, vertically down the page. They are as wide as they can be, which means that unless they're constrained in some way (by other block elements, by CSS properties, or by HTML markup), they'll stretch across the whole page.

One thing you'll notice when you start using CSS is that your headers (<h1> and friends) go all the way across the screen. Set the background-color property on an <h1> and you'll see how big it really is.

Inline

An inline element doesn't begin and end lines; instead, it is contained within the flow of the text. Examples of inline tags include <em>, <span>, <b>, <img>, <input>, and <a>.

Inline elements flow one after another in a line, with no line breaks, horizontally across the page until the end of the available space is used up; then they just continue where they left off on the next line down.

The display **Property**

You can change the type of an element by using the display property. This property can take several values; the ones we're primarily concerned with in this hour are block and inline. There's another important value for display that's called none; something that has the display property set to none does not display at all, nor is anything inside of it displayed.

Setting the display property to block or inline changes the type of that element to the specified type. For example, imagine that you want to make a navigation menu, and you want all your <a> elements within that menu to appear as block elements. The HTML code may look like this:

```
<div class="nav">
  <a href="friends.html">My Friends</a>
  <a href="cat.html">My Cat</a>
  <a href="friendscats.html">My Friends' Cats</a>
  <a href="catsfriends.html">My Cat's Friends</a>
</div>
```

The <a> element is an inline element according to the HTML 4.01 specification, so by default browsers display these links as a row all on the same line, or maybe wrapping around to the next line down if there is no more room. To display these <a> tags as block tags, use this rule:

```
.nav a { display: block; }
```

Figure 6.1 shows the effect of applying this rule; the first set of links is identical to the second, except that the previous rule and a silver background have been applied to it. The background illustrates that the block element goes all the way across the browser window and doesn't stop at the end of the text within it. Also, the links are clickable even on the far right side of the screen, not just on the blue underlined words.

FIGURE 6.1
Before and after
redefining the
<a> links as
block.

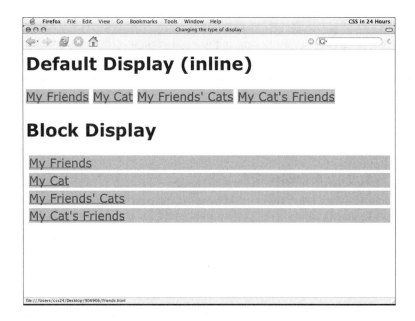

Understanding the Box Model

Within the visual formatting model, all elements generate specific types of boxes.
The method for displaying these boxes is called the *box model*, and understanding
the box model is crucial for understanding how Cascading Style Sheets will display
web pages.

The box model is defined in terms of elements, documents, trees, and of course,
boxes. Many of us are not used to thinking about web pages in terms of these elements unless we've done a lot with XML or SGML. So you first need to understand
the assumptions that CSS makes about web documents.

In formal W3C specifications, you rarely see terms such as *web page*; instead
everything talks about *documents*. Likewise, you don't see much about *tags* and
browsers, but instead *elements* and *user agents*. Although it may seem that this is
just semantic snobbishness—and to some degree it is!—there are actually some
valid reasons for drawing these distinctions when speaking formally. In this book, I
try to avoid writing text like you'd see in a W3C Recommendation; if you want one
of those, you can find it on the W3C site at http://www.w3.org/. However, terminology counts for this discussion, and my apologies if I sound formal.

Documents as Trees

Did you know that every web page is actually a tree of tags and content? If you didn't, that's okay; these types of trees are the same kind of data structures used in computer science, and most web developers aren't necessarily computer scientists.

A *tree* is a way of representing information in a hierarchy of elements. Think of it as somewhat similar to a family tree in genealogy—one that starts at a certain ancestor and goes down from there. Your great-grandmother may be at the top; her children (including your grandmother) in the second level down; your mother, her siblings, and her cousins in the third level down; and you and the other members of your generation in the fourth level.

In the same way, an HTML document can be thought of as a tree with the <html> element as the top. In this context, the <html> element is known as the *root element*.

The <html> element has two children: the <head> and the <body>. These are shown lower on the tree—the next levels down. The <head> has children too; <title> is one in every document, and <link> may be there to call in an external style sheet. The <body> element contains the content of the page; this could be anything from <h1> and <table> to <div> or <hr>. Some of those may have their own children, and some may not.

Each part of a tree is called a *node*. A node is either an element (possibly with children) or some text. *Text nodes* can't have children; they're just text.

Listing 6.1 shows a very simple web page, and Figure 6.2 shows a representation of a tree based on that page.

LISTING 6.1   The First Two Lines of a Poem About Trees

```
<html>
  <head>
    <title>Trees</title>
  </head>
  <body>
    <h1>Trees, by <i>Joyce Kilmer</i></h1>
    <p>
      I think that I shall never see
      <br>
      A poem as lovely as a tree.
    </p>
  </body>
</html>
```

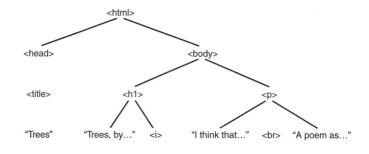

Documents as Boxes

After an HTML document has been defined as a data tree, it can then be *visually interpreted* as a series of boxes. This is probably an easier way for web developers to think of a page, but it's important to reach that understanding by first visualizing a tree because that's how a CSS browser considers the page.

You can think of these boxes as containers that hold other boxes or that hold text values. Each box in the CSS box model is held within another box, except for the box corresponding to the root node in the tree. The outer box is called the *containing box*. A block-containing box can hold other block boxes or inline boxes; an inline-containing box can hold only inline boxes.

In Figure 6.3, you can see the tree poem expressed as a series of nested boxes. You'll notice that some of these boxes don't have labels; a box exists, but no HTML tag! Those boxes are known as *anonymous boxes*. Anonymous boxes result whenever a tag contains mixed content—both text and some HTML tags. The text parts become anonymous boxes. An anonymous box is styled the same as its containing box.

Also notice that the <br> tag is an empty tag; it doesn't contain any content, but it still generates a box. The <head> box appears in Figure 6.3, but in HTML the <head> tag is defined as display: none;; this is why you never see the content of the <head> tag.

Box Display Properties

After a browser has established that a box exists by building a tree as shown earlier and then by filling in the box model; it displays that box, either according to its own internal rules for displaying HTML or according to the style properties on that box.

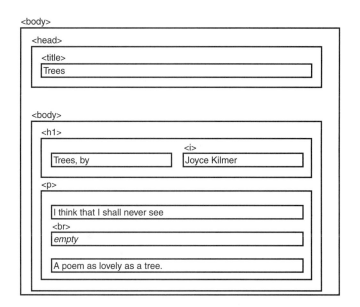

FIGURE 6.3
The tree poem as nested boxes.

In a way, all the CSS properties are box-display properties: They control how a box is displayed. However, three properties define the edges of that box: the `margin`, the `border`, and the `padding`.

The relationship between `margin`, `border`, `padding`, and the content itself is shown in Figure 6.4. In this example, the border color has been set to `gray` and the `background-color` to `silver`.

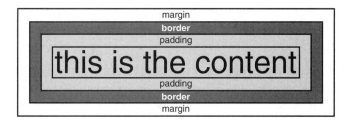

FIGURE 6.4
The `margin`, `border`, `padding`, and content of a box.

You'll learn more about the `margin`, `border`, and `padding` properties in Hour 16, "Borders and Boxes;" the current hour is a general introduction to the box model, and we'll get into more detail about other property values later in the book.

The margin **Property**

The margin is an invisible property that surrounds all CSS boxes; it dictates how far that box is from other boxes. The margin is the outermost property of the box and defines the far edge of the box. Nearly all of the visible HTML elements have margins, although for many the default margin is 0 pixels.

Values for margin can be expressed in a variety of units; the most common values are pixels or ems. A pixel is the width of a single dot on the screen; pixel values are written as a number followed by px, such as 4px or 12px. An em is unit of measure that refers to the size of the current font; if the font is 12 pixels, an em is a unit of measure equal to 12 pixels. You write ems by putting the word em after a number, such as 3em or 0.5em.

Pixels are absolute units; they do not scale with the user's preferences. Ems are relative units; relative units are calculated based on the current font. Other units you can use include points (pt), centimeters (cm), inches (in), and percentages.

To set a margin of 1 em around a specific box, such as an <h1>, you'd write a CSS rule like this:

```
h1 { margin: 1em; }
```

Margins are always transparent, meaning that whatever background color is set on the containing box shines through.

There's one more thing you need to know about margins, and that's *collapsing margins*. The vertical margins—those above and below the element—do something called collapsing, which means that only the largest value of the margins between two elements is used. Margins collapse only on block elements and only in a vertical direction, not horizontally.

One way to think of the collapse of margins is to imagine two motor homes parked next to each other. The owner of the motor home to the north says to the other, "Don't park within six feet of me." The owner of the southern motor home says, "Don't park within three feet of me." How close together can you park the motor homes, assuming you want to get them as close as you can? Obviously, you would park six feet away; that distance fits both requirements. That's what a margin value is like; you take the largest value of the two and use that as the vertical distance between two elements.

The border **Property**

The border property is used to draw a border around a box. All boxes have borders, even if the size of the border is 0 pixels or ems, which is the default for HTML elements.

Each border has three qualities associated with it, which can all be set with the border property: the size of the border, the style of the border, and the color of the border. A border declaration reads like this:

```
selector { border: size style color; }
```

The *size* of the border is measured the same way as the margin; pixels or ems are the most common units. Border *styles* include solid, dashed, and dotted; you'll use more border styles in Hour 16. The *color* of a border can be any CSS color name or RGB triplet.

So, to set a solid navy blue border that is 1/4 of the current font size around an <h1>, you would write a rule like this:

```
h1 { border: 0.25em solid navy; }
```

And here's a dashed three-pixel purple border around paragraphs:

```
p { border: 3px dashed #660099; }
```

You can set borders (and margins and padding) around inline elements as well as block elements. This sets a thin black border around <i> tags:

```
i { border: 1px solid black; }
```

The padding **Property**

The space surrounding the content is the padding; this could be thought of as white-space because there's nothing in it (no content or border), but keep in mind that it doesn't have to be white. The padding is always the same background color as the content itself, which means it is the color of the background-color set on the box.

Padding is measured in the same way as margins or borders; here's a three-pixel padding around <i> and a padding of 0.5 em around <h1>:

```
i { padding: 3px; }
h1 { padding: 0.5em; }
```

Want to see the result of all the examples discussed so far? Figure 6.5 shows what happens if you apply all the CSS rules named, including margin, border, and padding, to the poem from Listing 6.1. I added a <style> section in the <head> and included these rules as an embedded style sheet.

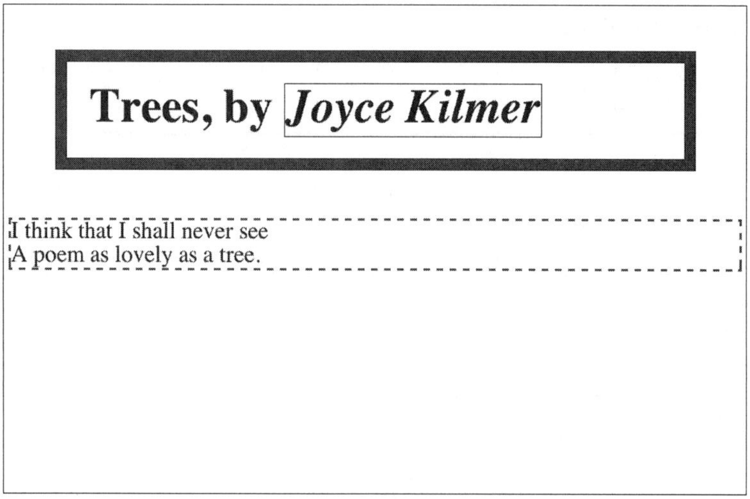

FIGURE 6.5
Applying various
box styles to
the tree poem,
as shown in
Firefox.

Summary

The visual formatting model of CSS describes how pages should be displayed. An HTML (or XML) element can be block or inline, and the `display` property can change how an element is displayed.

The box model views web pages as nested boxes based on a tree view of a web document. Web pages are displayed as CSS properties set on those boxes.

The `margin`, `border`, and `padding` properties define the outer edge of the box. Margins are transparent and surround the box, separating it from other boxes; vertical borders collapse to the largest value. Borders are in specified colors and styles and are within the box's margin. Padding is inside the border and is the same background color as the content.

Workshop

The workshop contains a Q&A section, quiz questions, and an exercise to help reinforce what you've learned in this hour. If you get stuck, the answers to the quiz can be found after the questions.

Q&A

Q. *What kind of element is a table cell? Is that block or inline?*

A. It's neither inline nor block. The display value for a table cell (`<td>`) is special; it's `table-cell`. An element that has been set `display: table-cell` is displayed like a table cell (of course). This is a special type of block element, although there are some limitations; a `table-cell` element can't have a `margin`, for example. You'll learn more about tables and CSS in Hour 17, "Styling Tables."

Q. *What is an em, anyway? Is it related to the size of a capital M?*

A. Not really, although that's where it gets the name from, historically. In CSS, an em is defined as a measure equal to the size of the font; it is a square that is as tall as the font size and as wide as it is tall. It's not related to letter M officially because some fonts—non-English fonts—don't have the letter M, and CSS needs to be able to function with all fonts around the world.

Q. *Okay, then what's a pixel? And a point? And how do percentages work?*

A. A pixel is basically one dot on a screen; if you've got 800×600 resolution displaying on your monitor, it is showing you 800 pixels across and 600 pixels down. A point is 1/72 of an inch in CSS. Percentages are based on the width of the containing block. You'll learn more about CSS's units of measurement in Hour 9, "Fonts and Font Families," and Hour 16.

Quiz

1. Is the `<hr>` element block or inline? How can you tell?

2. What is the correct order of the box model, from outside to inside?

    a. `border, margin, padding, content`

    b. `padding, border, margin, content`

    c. `margin, border, padding, content`

    d. `margin, padding, border, content`

3. Consider the following style rules:

```
body { background-color: red;
       color: white; }
h1 { color: black;
     padding: 1.5em;
     border: 5px solid green;
     background-color: yellow;
     margin: 0.5em; }
```

    What is the color of the margin around an `<h1>`? What is the color of the padding?

Answers

1. Because horizontal rules are on separate lines and don't occur inline, `<hr>` must be block. You can check by looking it up in the HTML 4.01 specification on the W3C's website, http://www.w3.org/.

2. (c). The outermost part of the box is the `margin`, then the `border`, and then the `padding` around the content.

3. The color of the `margin` would be the `background-color` of the containing box; assuming the `<body>` contains the `<h1>`, the color would be red. The `background-color` of the `<h1>` determines the color of the `padding`, so the padding color is yellow.

Exercise

Reading about margins and padding is one thing, but actually using them is how you'll learn to master them. Create a web page with some blocks to style—`<div>` or `<p>` work well for this, as do the `<h1>` through `<h6>` headings—and set various values of margin and padding on each.

Make sure that you know the difference between the margin and padding by setting the padding around a block to 1 em, then the margin. Add in a border and you'll be able to see even more clearly that padding is within the border line and margin is without.

HOUR 7

Cascading and Inheritance

What You'll Learn in This Hour:

▶ What the secret formula behind the cascade really is

▶ Which CSS rules have the highest weight, and how those relate to HTML attributes

▶ How you can override the order of the cascade when writing CSS rules

▶ How the user can supply her own style sheet to express her preferences for display, and how those are balanced with the author's desires

▶ How to include one style sheet's rules within another style sheet, and which set of rules takes priority

▶ Which property values are inherited, which are calculated, and what that means for your CSS designs

The cascade is one of the key concepts of Cascading Style Sheets—so important, in fact, that the language was named after it. The cascade defines how you combine rules, including rules from different sources—some provided by the web developer, some by the browser, and some from the user. When these are combined, values for properties on individual HTML tags are calculated. Some of these take their values directly from the CSS rules, whereas others are derived from other properties.

How the Cascade Works

The cascade is the set of directions that determine what rules apply to a given element on the page. Without a method for determining priority of conflicting rules, it would be impossible to figure out which styles should be used. Take, for example, the style sheet shown in Listing 7.1—different rules with a number of different selectors.

LISTING 7.1   A Colorful Style Sheet

```
/* colors-7.1.css */

body { background-color: white;
       color: black; }

h1 { background-color: blue;
     color: red; }

em { background-color: green;
     color: black; }

#serious { color: purple; }

.yahoo { color: black;
         background-color: yellow; }

#serious { color: maroon; }

h1 em { color: lime; }
```

Now you'll look at a page that uses the style sheet and also has its own embedded CSS rules within a `<style>` element in the `<head>`. Such a page is listed in Listing 7.2.

LISTING 7.2   An HTML Page with Tips on Color Use

```
<!-- tips-7.2.html -->
<html>
  <head>
    <title>Accessibility of Color</title>
    <link type="text/css" rel="stylesheet" href="colors-7.1.css">
    <style type="text/css">
      .yahoo { background-color: silver;
               color: white; }
      h1 { background-color: yellow; }
    </style>
  </head>
  <body>
    <h2>Accessibility Tip:</h2>
    <h1>Don't
       <em class="yahoo" id="serious"
           style="background-color: white;">Rely</em>
       on Color Alone</h1>
    <p> Some Web users may be unable to see color -- they may
       be blind (and use a screenreader program); they may
       be color-blind and unable to easily distinguish colors;
       or they could be using an access device, such as a cell
       phone, which does not display color. For this reason,
       the W3C's Web Accessibility Initiative recommends that
       you not <em>rely</em> upon color as the <em>only</em>
       way of conveying information.</p>
    <p style="color: navy;">This doesn't mean
       <em class="yahoo" style="color: red;">"don't use color"</em>
       -- on the contrary,
```

LISTING 7.2   **Continued**

```
      color is very useful to those who can see it, and will
      help make your page understandable.  What it does mean
      is that color (and other presentational effects) should
      not be the only way you make something special.  For
      example, rather than use a &lt;span&gt; and a color
      style to make something stand out, use the &lt;strong&gt;
      tag (which you can also style) so browsers that
      can't use the visual CSS color rule can at least know
      to emphasize that section -- perhaps by increasing the
      volume when reading the text out loud, for example.</p>
  </body>
</html>
```

Now concentrate on the second word in the headline, "Rely." This word is within an <em> element, which is part of an <h1>. It has a class of yahoo and an id of serious. What color will the text be, and what color background will it have? You have several choices from several sources; by using the cascade, you can figure out what a browser will do with your example.

In Table 7.1, I've listed the various sources from which the browser might find the background and foreground color for the word "Rely."

TABLE 7.1   CSS Rules Applying to the Word "Rely"

Color	Background	Selector	Source
black	white	body	Linked style sheet
red	blue	h1	Linked style sheet
black	green	em	Linked style sheet
purple		#serious	Linked style sheet
black	yellow	.yahoo	Linked style sheet
marooon		#serious	Linked style sheet
lime		h1 em	Linked style sheet
white	silver	.yahoo	Embedded style sheet
	yellow	h1	Embedded style sheet
	white	(implied)	Inline style element

Order of the Cascade

To be able to figure out which properties get applied to the <em> tag in your example, you need to think like a web browser. The first thing you need to do is to realize that many of your rules are combined rules. For example, take this rule:

```
.yahoo { color: black;
        background-color: yellow; }
```

The rule is actually two different rules, which happen to share a common selector, as follows:

```
.yahoo { color: black; }
.yahoo { background-color: yellow; }
```

This is important because each declaration (property name and value) could be overridden separately. A rule that changes the color might not change the background color at all, so the .yahoo background-color rule would continue to stay in effect even if the .yahoo color rule is superceded.

So you need to consider only those rules that are in conflict—in other words, those that designate different values for the same property name, such as those rules that affect the color property. When trying to analyze which rule takes priority, always break up rules in individual units as just shown.

How do you calculate which rule is applied? First, you sort these rules by their *origin*. In the cascade, the origin means one of the following: the *author* of the page, the *user*, or the *browser*. Author rules have priority over user rules, which have priority over the browser's default rules for how to display HTML elements. In this case, all of these rules have the same origin; they come from the author of the page.

Next you order the rules based on the selector and how specific it is. This *specificity* is calculated as follows:

1. An *inline style attribute* is the most specific type of rule. If there is an inline style rule for a specific CSS property, that rule "wins."

2. An id *selector* is the second most specific. If there is more than one id in the rule, the rule with greatest number of id selectors wins.

3. If there aren't any id selectors, or if there's the same number, count the number of *classes or pseudo-classes* in the rule. The rule with the most classes or pseudo-classes has the higher priority.

4. If there's the same number of classes (or no classes), compare the number of *elements*—the greater number of elements, the higher the specificity.

5. If the number of id values, classes, and elements are all the same, whichever was *declared most recently* has the highest priority. If two rules have the same selector and are in disagreement on the value of a specific CSS property, the one listed second is more specific.

If you ever encounter a tie, then move on to the next rule. For example, if you have a complex rule that has three id selectors, three class selectors, and two element selectors, and another with three id selectors, three class selectors, and one element selector, you have a tie for the id selectors, and a tie for the class selectors, so to resolve the cascade you need to move on to the number of elements to break the tie.

Applying these rules to your <em> text, you must consider the color property separately from the background-color property. The most specific rules that set the color property are the two rules with an id selector—the #serious rules. Of these, the second one takes priority, which means the text color will be maroon.

To figure out the background-color, you just have to determine the most specific rule as well. In this case, the most specific rule is the inline style attribute, so the background will be white.

Calculating the colors of the <h1> is also a useful illustration; you have two competing <h1> selectors: one in the linked style sheet and one in the embedded style sheet. Which one triumphs? The one declared most recently; because your <style> comes after your <link>, the background-color will be yellow. If the order of the <link> and <style> elements were reversed, the background would be blue.

Try it Yourself ▼

Pretend to Be a Web Browser

Here's your chance to show how good you are at imitating a web browser. In Listing 7.1, there's a section in the second paragraph that reads "don't use color."

1. Construct a table like Table 7.1. List the selector, the source, the color, and the background color of each rule that applies to that section of text.

2. For each rule, identify whether it comes from a style attribute, an id selector, a class (or pseudo-class) selector, an element selector, or a combination of these.

3. Rank each selector according to the specificity, as described this hour.

4. What color will the text be? Test it in your web browser to check your answer. ▲

Cascading and HTML Attributes

In addition to setting style, class, and id attributes, HTML also has presentational attributes that let you affect how the page looks. Examples include align, color, face, link, vlink, bgcolor, and background.

When these attributes conflict with a CSS rule, the HTML attribute is considered to be the least specific declaration possible. In other words, the HTML attribute always is overridden by a CSS rule. However, in many cases you may want to set an HTML presentation attribute in case CSS is disabled or not understood by an older browser. Keep in mind that HTML presentational attributes are ignored only if there is a corresponding CSS rule; if there's no rule setting the color of an item, for example, the HTML value is used.

> Remember, you generally can't use HTML presentation attributes with CSS if you are using the Strict variety of HTML. Use HTML 4.01 Transitional (or XHTML 1.0 Transitional) if you need to use HTML attributes along with your CSS styles.

Using `!important` in Rules

When necessary, an author of a style sheet can designate one rule as explicitly more important than others. To do this, the author adds `!important` after the specific property name and value declaration, like this:

```
em { color: blue !important; }
```

This overrides the normal order of the cascade by inserting a new requirement: Important rules come before rules that have not been designated as important. An `!important` rule, even one that is not very specific, always takes priority over a non-`!important` rule even if the latter is extremely specific.

The use of `!important` also changes one other part of the cascade: `!important` rules that originate with the user take priority over the author's rules. Normally, the author's rules have higher priority than the user's rules, but this allows users with special needs to define their own style sheets and designate their needs for access as more important than the author's desire for a certain style.

> Those of you who have done programming in a language such as C++ or Perl may find this particular part of CSS perplexing. In most programming languages, an exclamation point (!) means "not," so `!important` looks like it means "not important," which is the exact opposite of the true meaning. Don't be surprised if it takes a while to get used to reading `!important` as "very important."

User-Defined Style Sheets

A *user-defined style sheet* is one created by the user and stored on that person's local computer. The browser automatically loads this file and applies it to web pages that are viewed.

The purpose of a user-defined style sheet is to let the web surfer's preferences influence how he views the web. This is especially useful for certain specific groups of users, including those users with visual disabilities. For example, if you need a high-contrast display, your user style sheet could be set with a default black background, white text, and large font sizes.

In theory, user style sheets are quite beneficial; in practice, though, they require each web user to know how to write CSS to see the web the way she would like to see it! This is a rather high learning threshold for users who simply want to surf the web comfortably; you're learning CSS now because you want to design websites, not because you simply want to access information. Despite this, user style sheets are still incredibly functional for those who know how to use them, or for those who can download and install user style sheets written by others.

A user style sheet can have any kind of CSS rules that could normally be included in a style sheet, and the syntax is exactly the same; it's just another external style sheet, after all. However, there are certain types of rules that make less sense in a user style sheet, and several normal cautions can be relaxed.

In a user style sheet, you don't want to use any selectors that presume specific attribute values will be set, such as `class` or `id`, because you won't know what's in the HTML of each page.

Normally when creating a style sheet, you don't want to use absolute values in your font sizes, such as 9px or 2cm, because these don't take the user's preferences into account. A user with poor vision would have problems seeing a 9-pixel font size if you put this on a style sheet for the web. But because you *know* the exact properties of the final output medium when writing a user-defined style sheet for yourself, it's perfectly fine to use those values in your own user-defined style sheet.

Finally, you should declare these as `!important` to give them highest priority because, after all, it doesn't make sense to set your own preferences if the designer's style sheet can just overrule them.

An example of a user-defined style sheet is given in Listing 7.3. This style sheet is designed specifically for a user who needs large print and high contrast (white-on-black).

LISTING 7.3   A Sample User-Defined Style Sheet

```
/* user-7.3.css */
* { color: white !important;
    background-color: white !important;
    font-family: Verdana, sans-serif !important; }
body { font-size: 24pt !important; }
a:link { color: cyan !important; }
a:visited { color: violet !important; }
```

After you've created a user-defined style sheet and saved it on your hard drive (somewhere you can remember its location), you need to tell your browser to use it. How you do that depends on which browser you're using. In Internet Explorer, this is a preference under Accessibility. If you're using Firefox, you need to add your rules to the `user.css` file. In Opera, this is a preference under Document that lets you select a user-defined style sheet. It's an Advanced preference in Safari.

Importing CSS

To make style sheets that are more modular, you may want to *import* another style sheet. Importing, in this context, means that all the rules in the imported style sheet are included in the style sheet that is doing the importing. In this way, importing is like linking an external style sheet.

You can import another style sheet from an embedded style sheet, from a linked style sheet, or from a user style sheet. An imported style sheet can even import additional style sheets.

How do imported style sheets affect the cascade order? You might think that rules are included at the point where the importation is declared, but this actually isn't the case. Any imported style sheets are treated as if their rules had been declared before any of the rules in the importing style sheet.

You can think of the imported style sheet as being more distant, which means it is lower priority if there is a conflict. All other things being equal (same number of id attributes, classes, and elements), the importing style sheet's rules are considered more recently declared, even if the rule happens before the importation.

If you're designing a large website, and some CSS rules apply to the whole site, whereas others should be used only with certain sections of the site, you may want to write one site-wide style sheet and then import it into the style sheets you write for each part of the site.

The `@import` **Rule**

To import a file, you write as a complete rule (with no property declarations or curly braces) an @import statement that looks like this:

```
@import url("filename.css");
```

An alternate way to write the same rule is to leave out the `url()` function because everything you will @import will be a URL. So you can also write the rule like this:

```
@import "filename.css";
```

You can also give @import an extra parameter, which is a list of media types. Like the media attribute on the `<link>` attribute, the style sheet loads only if the media type is correct for the browser being used. For example:

```
@import "screenorprint.css" screen, print;
@import "allmedia.css" all;
```

Here's an example of @import in action. First, the importing style sheet:

```
h1 { color: red; }
h1, h2, h3, h4, h5, h6
  { font-family: sans-serif; }
@import "sitewide.css";
h2 { color: blue; }
```

And here's the imported style sheet:

```
/* sitewide.css */
h1, h2, h3, h4, h5, h6
  { color: green; }
body { background-color: silver; }
```

What color is an <h1>, <h2>, or <h3> on a page using the importing style sheet? The <h1> would be red and the <h2> would be blue because all the imported rules are considered to come before the original style sheet's rules. The <h3> would be green because that's the only rule setting its color.

The old, nearly extinct Netscape 4 browser didn't understand the @import rule; it simply wouldn't import other style sheets. This flaw actually got put to good use by web developers, to hide other rules that Netscape 4 couldn't understand. (It was a browser with lots of CSS problems.) All rules that were "Netscape 4 safe" could be put in the main CSS file, and then an additional style sheet could be @imported that contained style rules that would break in Netscape 4 but worked in other then-contemporary browsers.

This was the first browser filter ever developed. You'll learn more about filtering and other tricks in Hour 24, "Troubleshooting and Browser Hacks."

Inheritance

As you've already seen, some property values don't have to be explicitly set on each element if the value is already set on a parent element. For example, if you set a font-family property on the <body>, all other elements on the page will also have the same value unless it's changed by another rule. This is called *inheritance*; the page elements have inherited the property value from their parent element, <body>.

Not all properties inherit naturally; some simply don't make sense for inheritance. For example, the border, margin, and padding properties from Hour 6, "The CSS Box Model," don't inherit. Otherwise, whenever you'd draw a box, all elements inside it would have the same type of box around them. Each property, when it's defined in the CSS specifications, is designated as either inheriting or not inheriting, by default.

Inherited Values

An *inherited value* is passed along in most cases as if it had been set on the element itself. Thus, if you make an <h1> blue, you're making all its children blue because they'll inherit the color. Other rules—more specific or higher priority—could change this, of course.

Of the properties you've learned so far, font-family and color are inherited. The display, border, margin, and padding properties are not inherited. You might think that background-color is inherited, but actually it's not; the default when background-color is unset is actually the special value transparent, which means the color "underneath" can be seen, so it's not quite the same as inheriting the value.

Calculated Values

The font-size property works a little differently when it comes to inheritance. That's because you don't actually inherit the declaration; you inherit the *calculated value*. Some values are absolute values, such as 12px, but most will be relative values, such as smaller or 3em. When a relative value is inherited, the value is first calculated before being passed on to child element.

Specifying Inheritance

If you want a property to inherit from its parent, but it doesn't actually do so by default, you can use the special value of `inherit` in a rule you write. Say that you decide any `<div>` in the class `standout` should have a blue border and that any paragraphs inside it should have the same border. You could write these rules:

```
div.standout { border: 1px solid blue; }
div.standout p { border: inherit; }
```

Summary

In this hour, you learned about the cascade, user style sheets, importing style sheets, and inheritance.

The cascade first sorts rules based on source: Author style rules take priority over user style rules, which take priority over browser default styles. After that, the more specific a rule, the higher priority it's given. You can add `!important` to a rule to give it a higher priority.

User style sheets are a crucial part of the cascade that allows the user's preferences to blend with the author's desires. Users with disabilities can often benefit from specific style sheets tailored to their needs.

Not all values need to be explicitly set; values can be inherited from their parent element. Some properties inherit, and some don't; those that use relative values pass along the calculated value.

Workshop

The workshop contains a Q&A section, quiz questions, and activities to help reinforce what you've learned in this hour. If you get stuck, the answers to the quiz can be found after the questions.

Q&A

Q. *Why is it a big deal that calculated values are inherited, instead of relative values?*

A. Well, consider this example:

```
<div class="footer">
  <p>
    Questions?  Send me email at
    <a href="mailto:kynn@idyllmtn.com">
```

```
    kynn@idyllmtn.com
   </a>
  </p>
</div>
```

If the font on the page is 20 pixels, and the style rule is `div.footer {` `font-size: smaller; }`, text elements within the <div> inherit the calculated value 16 pixels, which is 20% smaller than 20 pixels. The elements within the <div> do not inherit the relative value `smaller`.

What if the text elements did inherit the relative value? Well, then the <p> would have to be 20% smaller than the size of the <div> (about 12.8 pixels). The <a> would inherit `smaller` from its parent and would shrink to 80% of the <p>, so the email address would be 10.24 pixels—incredible shrinking text! This is why calculated values are not inherited.

Q. *How did the order of the Cascade change between CSS Level One and CSS Level Two?*

A. When CSS Level One was published, the author's `!important` styles took precedence over the user's `!important` styles. This was found to be a problem because it meant that users with special needs had no way to insist that the browser meet their needs. In the CSS Level Two recommendation, this was changed so that the user's `!important` rules beat the author's `!important` rules. Note that this is a special case exception; in most cases, the author's styles override the user's styles, assuming the user's styles are not flagged as `!important`.

Quiz

1. Rank these CSS rules in order from least specific to most specific:

    a. `p { font-family: serif; }`

    b. `<p style="font-family: fantasy;">`

    c. `p#mocha { font-family: monospace; }`

    d. `tr td p { font-family: sans-serif; }`

    e. `td p.latte { font-family: cursive; }`

2. How would your answer to question 1 change if rule (a) were rewritten like this?

    a. `p { font-family: serif !important ; }`

Answers

1. The least specific is (a): It has no `id` selectors, no classes, and only one element. Rule (d) is more specific because it has three elements instead of one. Rule (e) is more specific than (d), even though it has only two elements, because (e) has one class and (d) has none. Rule (c) is less specific than Rule (b) because `id` selectors are less specific than inline styles. Therefore, a paragraph that was affected by all these rules would be in a `fantasy` font.

2. The addition of `!important` to rule (a) makes it more important than the others, and thus the `font-family` value would be `serif`. However, the specificity technically did not change; it is still less specific than the others, although it has higher priority. So it's a bit of a trick question; the priority would change, but because question 1 asked you about specificity, not priority, your answer should *not* change.

Exercise

One of the best ways to become familiar with the cascade is to set up your own user style sheet. Create your own style sheet, save it on your hard drive, and tell your browser to use it as a user style sheet. You can experiment with `!important` and other aspects of the cascade by changing your user style sheet.

HOUR 8

Advanced Selectors

What You'll Learn in This Hour:

▶ How to create CSS rules that select only those tags that have a specific attribute

▶ How to create rules based on the values of those attributes

▶ How to create rules that select direct children of another element and why you'd want to do that

▶ How to select an element that directly follows another element

Attribute Selectors

An *attribute selector* tests for the existence, and possibly the values, of any specific HTML attributes set on an element. You'd use an attribute selector if you wanted all elements with a certain attribute to be styled a certain way. For example, noshade is an HTML attribute for the <hr> tag; it means that there shouldn't be any shading effects applied to the tag. If you wanted all those <hr> tags to be colored silver, you'd use an attribute selector based on the noshade attribute. The simplest form of attribute selector is simply the attribute within square brackets, as follows:

```
element[attribute] { declaration; }
```

For example:

```
hr[noshade] { color: silver; }
```

This rule would declare that all <hr> elements with the noshade attribute should be colored silver.

You can write an attribute selector rule so that it selects all elements with the chosen attribute by using the universal selector (*). For example, you could set a specific rule for all tags that have a `title` attribute to indicate which parts of the page will pop up a tooltip when you move the mouse over them, as in the following:

```
*[title] { background-color: yellow; }
```

This marks with a `yellow` background all tags with `title` attributes. Because the universal selector is optional, you can also write the rule like this:

```
[title] { background-color: yellow; }
```

Internet Explorer (up to version 5.5) does not support attribute selectors. For compatibility with older Internet Explorer versions, you can use an explicit `class` attribute and `class` selector rule. For example, to make the two attribute selector examples work in Internet Explorer 5.5, you'll need to write your HTML like this:

```
<hr class="unshaded" noshade>
<a href="summer2001.html" class="hastooltip"
   title="What I Did for Summer Vacation">Summer 2001</a>
```

Your CSS rules would then look like this:

```
hr[noshade], hr.unshaded { color: silver; }
*[title], .hastooltip { background-color: yellow; }
```

Selecting by Attribute Value

In addition to checking for the existence of the attribute, you can also select by attribute value. There are three ways to do this:

```
element[attribute="value"]  { declaration; }
element[attribute~="value"] { declaration; }
element[attribute¦="value"] { declaration; }
```

The first version designates an exact match; it selects only those elements for which the attribute has the given value. The second registers a match if the value in the rule is one of several values given in the HTML, separated by spaces. The third matches the rule's value against the HTML's value and compares the characters before hyphens. (This is to allow matching of language groups, which are written as en-us, en-uk, en-au, and so on. See Hour 5, "Selectors," for a listing of some common language codes.) Table 8.1 shows several types of selectors and attribute values and indicates whether or not each selector would match the HTML.

TABLE 8.1 Testing Attribute Values

CSS Selector	HTML Snippet	Match?
table[summary="layout"]	<table summary="layout">	Yes
table[summary~="layout"]	<table summary="layout">	Yes
table[summary¦="layout"]	<table summary="layout">	Yes
div[class="bar"]	<div class="foo bar baz">	No
div[class~="bar"]	<div class="foo bar baz">	Yes
div[class¦="bar"]	<div class="foo bar baz">	No
*[lang="en"]	<span lang="en">	Yes
*[lang~="en"]	<span lang="en">	Yes
*[lang¦="en"]	<span lang="en">	Yes
*[lang="en"]	<span lang="en-us">	No
*[lang~="en"]	<span lang="en-us">	No
*[lang¦="en"]	<span lang="en-us">	Yes
*[lang="en"]	<span lang="english">	No
*[lang~="en"]	<span lang="english">	No
*[lang¦="en"]	<span lang="english">	No

Let's look at an example of attribute selectors in action. Listing 8.1 is an HTML page consisting of a table of departure times for airline flights. I've chosen to use the axis attribute on table cells to group similar types of flights. axis is an HTML 4.01 attribute that allows for groupings of related table cells. Those flights that fly through Saint Louis have been assigned an axis value of stlouis, whereas those going through Chicago are labeled with an axis value of ord.

LISTING 8.1 HTML Table Marked Up with the axis Attribute

```
<!-- flights-8.1.html -->
<html>
  <head>
    <title>Flights from Los Angeles to New York</title>
    <link type="text/css" rel="stylesheet"
          href="flights-8.2.css">
  </head>
  <body>
    <h1>Schedule of Flights</h1>
    <h2>Los Angeles to New York</h2>
    <table>
      <tr> <th>Monday</th> <th>Tuesday</th> <th>Wednesday</th>
           <th>Thursday</th> <th>Friday</th> </tr>
      <tr> <td axis="ord">09:13 (ORD)</td>
           <td axis="ord">09:13 (ORD)</td>
           <td>10:17 (direct)</td>
```

LISTING 8.1   Continued

```
              <td axis="ord">09:13 (ORD)</td>
              <td>10:17 (direct)</td> </tr>
       <tr> <td axis="stlouis">12:05 (STL)</td>
              <td axis="stlouis">12:05 (STL)</td>
              <td axis="stlouis">12:05 (STL)</td>
              <td axis="stlouis">12:05 (STL)</td>
              <td axis="stlouis">12:05 (STL)</td> </tr>
       <tr> <td axis="ord">17:15 (ORD)</td>
              <td axis="stlouis">13:44 (STL)</td>
              <td axis="ord">17:15 (ORD)</td>
              <td axis="stlouis">13:44 (STL)</td>
              <td>14:30 (direct)</td> </tr>
       <tr> <td></td>
              <td axis="ord">17:15 (ORD)</td>
              <td>19:20 (direct)</td>
              <td axis="ord">17:15 (ORD)</td>
              <td axis="ord">17:15 (ORD)</td> </tr>
    </table>
  </body>
</html>
```

The cascading style sheet for this example is shown in Listing 8.2; you'll use attribute selectors to set up rules on each flight type to show them with different background colors. This effect is shown in Figure 8.1.

LISTING 8.2   This Style Sheet Uses Rules Based on the `axis` Attribute Selector

```
/* flights-8.2.css */

body { font-family: Verdana, sans-serif; }

td { border: 1px solid black;
     padding: 0.25em;
     color: black;
     background-color: white; }

td[axis="stlouis"]
  { background-color: silver;
    color: black; }

td[axis="ord"]
  { background-color: black;
    color: white; }
```

You've been using shorthand versions of some attribute selectors for some time now; the class and id selectors are just special cases of an attribute value selector. The following pairs of rules are equivalent:

```
.apple              { color: green; }
*[class~="apple"]   { color: green; }
#banana             { color: yellow; }
*[id="banana"]      { color: yellow; }
```

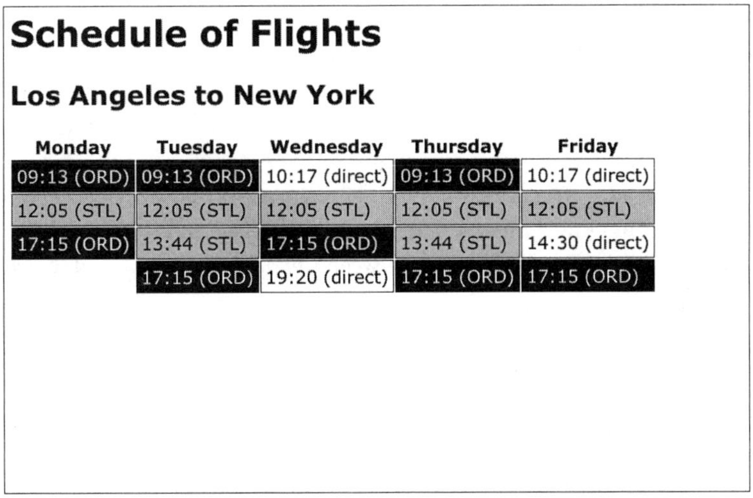

Schedule of Flights

Los Angeles to New York

Monday	Tuesday	Wednesday	Thursday	Friday
09:13 (ORD)	09:13 (ORD)	10:17 (direct)	09:13 (ORD)	10:17 (direct)
12:05 (STL)	12:05 (STL)	12:05 (STL)	12:05 (STL)	12:05 (STL)
17:15 (ORD)	13:44 (STL)	17:15 (ORD)	13:44 (STL)	14:30 (direct)
	17:15 (ORD)	19:20 (direct)	17:15 (ORD)	17:15 (ORD)

FIGURE 8.1
Using attribute selectors to make axis values visual.

You can combine multiple attribute values together by simply adding on another attribute test. Here's an example of a rule that selects all table cells that are right-aligned and vertically aligned to the bottom:

```
td[align="right"][valign="bottom"]
  { font-size: small; }
```

Did you Know?

You can use attribute selector rules with a user style sheet to create some very simple but powerful testing tools for web development. For example, to make anchors visible, create a style sheet, set it as your user style sheet in your browser, and add the following rule:

```
a[name], J     { border: 1px dotted red; }
```

This puts a dotted line around your anchors and anything else with the id attribute set. You can use this same trick to make table borders, form boundaries, field <label>s, and other block elements visible because they're outlined with a border. Here's a pair of rules to make it very clear which of your images don't have alt attributes on them:

```
img { border: 5px solid lime; }
img[alt] { border: none; }
```

Family Relationships

Family-based selectors in CSS choose elements based on the relationships between the HTML tags; these relationships are named after family relationships. You've already used one of the family relationship selectors: the descendant selector, which selects elements descended from another tag. Other relationship selectors include child and adjacent sibling selectors.

Child Selectors

A *child selector* is a special case of descendant selectors, which were covered in Hour 5. A child selector identifies only those elements that are immediate children of another element, not any "grandchildren" or other descendants. A child selector is indicated by a greater-than symbol (>) between the parent element and the child:

```
parent > child { declaration; }
```

For example, consider the following snippet of HTML:

```
<blockquote>
  <div class="opinion">
    <p>I'm voting Green next year.</p>
    <p>I'm wearing green, too!</p>
  </div>
</blockquote>
```

Here are some style rules, but only a few of these will be applied to the code sample:

```
blockquote p   { font-size:   large;               }
blockquote > p { font-family: Arial, sans-serif; }
.opinion > p   { font-color:  green;               }
```

The first rule is used on the quote; it's a normal descendant selector, and both of the paragraphs are within a <blockquote>. The second rule is not applied; there are no <p> tags that are direct children of a <blockquote> tag; both of them are direct children of the <div>. (They're *descendants* of the <blockquote>, of course, but only direct children, not grandchildren, count for child selectors.) The third rule is applied to the <p> text because both paragraphs are direct children of a tag with class="opinion". So the total effect will be two green paragraphs, both in the default font face.

Some older browsers, notably Internet Explorer 6 and earlier, don't recognize child selectors. For compatibility with these older browsers, use descendant selectors; if you're unable to get the effects you want with just descendants, use class selectors too. Here's how you would rewrite the green quote style sheet rules:

```
blockquote p   { font-size:   large; /* same */  }
blockquote p.childofblockquote
               { font-family: Arial, sans-serif; }
.opinion p     { font-color:  green;               }
```

You'll notice the additional class called childofblockquote; it has to be added to every <p> that is a direct child of a <blockquote>.

Internet Explorer's lack of support for child selectors has a silver lining. Because rules with child selectors are ignored, you're able to write styles that are understood by most other modern browsers but aren't displayed by Internet Explorer. This is an example of a *browser filter*; you'll learn more about those in Hour 24, "Troubleshooting and Browser Hacks."

Adjacent Sibling Selectors

Two HTML tags are *siblings* if they have the same parent; they are *adjacent siblings* if the second occurs directly after the first in the source code. Here's some HTML to illustrate a sibling relationship:

```
<ul>
  <li id="greg">Greg</li>
  <li id="peter">Peter</li>
  <li id="bobby">Bobby</li>
  <!-- id attributes are included for reference -->
</ul>
```

The `<li>` elements are all siblings of each other. The `greg` and `peter` `<li>` tags are adjacent siblings, and the `peter` and `bobby` `<li>` tags are adjacent as well. However, the `greg` and `bobby` tags are not adjacent.

An *adjacent sibling selector* makes a selection based on two adjacent siblings, but it applies the declared style only to *the second of the two*. This is very important to remember: You are not selecting the pair; you are selecting only the final one in the list.

You write an adjacent sibling rule by listing the first sibling, a plus sign (+), and then the second sibling. A rule such as the following turns only the Peter and Bobby names blue, because they're li elements that directly follow another li element:

```
li + li { color: blue; }
```

Like many other advanced selectors in CSS, the usefulness of adjacent sibling selectors has been crippled by a lack of browser support in Internet Explorer. Using the same techniques described previously in this hour, you can add a number of class attributes and selectors and approximate the behavior for those older browsers that don't support CSS Level 2 selectors. This isn't the best solution, but it's the only one that works now.

Adjacent sibling selectors are useful for adding or removing margins, padding, and borders when siblings are meant to flow together visually. An example of this is shown in Listing 8.3.

LISTING 8.3   A Definition List with Adjacent `<dt>` and `<dd>` Elements

```
<!-- acronyms-8.3.html -->
<html>
  <head>
    <title> Some Common Acronyms </title>
    <style type="text/css">
      body    { font-family: Verdana, sans-serif; }

      dt      { font-weight: bold; }

      dt + dt, dd + dt
              { margin-top: 1em;
                font-weight: bold;
                padding-top: 1em;
                border-top: 1px solid black; }
      /* These rules apply to any dt that follows
         another dt, or a dd. The only dt that
         would not match such a rule is the first
         one, which is a direct child of the dl. */

      dt + dd { margin-top: 0.5em; }
      /* This applies to any dd that immediately follows
         a dt. It doesn't apply to a dd that follows
         another dd. */

      dd + dd { font-size: small;
                border: 1px;
                padding: 0.1em; }
      /* This rule selects any dd that follows another
         dd, but not to a dd that follows a dt. */

    </style>
  </head>
<body>
  <h1>Common Acronyms</h1>

  <dl>
    <dt>CSS</dt>
    <dd>Cascading Style Sheets</dd>

    <dt>HTML</dt>
    <dd>Hypertext Markup Language</dd>
    <dd>See also: <cite>XHTML</cite></dd>

    <dt>WAI</dt>
    <dd>Web Accessibility Initiative</dd>
    <dd>See also: <cite>W3C</cite></dd>

    <dt>WCAG</dt>
    <dd>Web Content Accessibility Guidelines</dd>

    <dt>WWW</dt>
    <dd>World Wide Web</dd>

    <dt>WWWC -- see <cite>W3C</cite></dt>

    <dt>W3C</dt>
```

LISTING 8.3   Continued

```
      <dd>World Wide Wide Consortium</dd>
      <dd>See also: <cite>WAI</cite></dd>

      <dt>XHTML</dt>
      <dd>Extensible HTML</dd>
      <dd>See also: <cite>HTML</cite></dd>
    </dl>
  </body>
</html>
```

The embedded style sheet in Listing 8.3 uses styles based on adjacent-sibling rules applied to a definition list. In HTML, a definition list is declared by the <dl> element, which can only have <dt> (term) or <dd> (definition) elements as children; this is important for understanding why the adjacent-sibling rules work as shown in Figure 8.2.

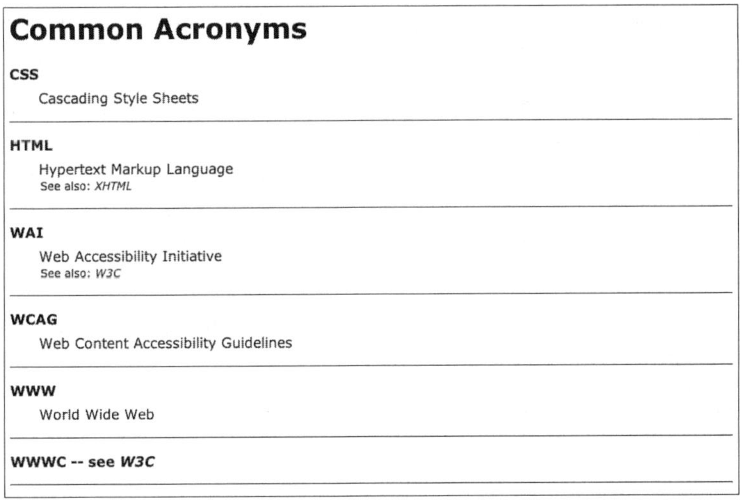

Common Acronyms

CSS
    Cascading Style Sheets

HTML
    Hypertext Markup Language
    See also: *XHTML*

WAI
    Web Accessibility Initiative
    See also: *W3C*

WCAG
    Web Content Accessibility Guidelines

WWW
    World Wide Web

WWWC -- see *W3C*

FIGURE 8.2
Adjacent sibling rules improve the look of a definition list.

Summary

Although unsupported by all but the newest browsers, advanced selectors add considerably to the CSS developer's toolbox. Attribute selectors allow styles to be set based on specific attribute values or even the existence of an attribute on the tag. Relationships between elements can be expressed in CSS by the child selector, which applies to direct children of a specific element, and by the adjacent sibling selector, which chooses the second of a pair of specified tags.

Workshop

The workshop contains a Q&A section, quiz questions, and activities to help reinforce what you've learned in this hour. If you get stuck, the answers to the quiz can be found after the questions.

Q&A

Q. *Can I do pattern matching in attribute values? Suppose I want to select all* <a> *tags that are* `mailto` *links. Can I use* `a[href="mailto:*"]` *as my selector?*

A. Nope. The CSS specifications don't define a way to do this type of pattern matching. Future versions of CSS based on XPath and XPointer might allow this, but for now there is no way to use pattern matching in CSS. To make your `mailto` links stand out, set a `class` attribute on them and use a `class` selector.

Q. *If I could use either a child selector or a descendant selector, which should I use? For example, if I want to select all* <img> *tags within* <a> *links.*

A. In theory, it's better to use a child selector if you know you're dealing with a direct child because it's quicker for the browser to calculate child selectors. It doesn't have to look over the full tree of the HTML document, just up one level. In practice, though, you are better off sticking with the descendant selector because of poor browser support; don't rely on a child selector alone. You can use both, if you like.

Q. *Can I combine advanced selectors with simple selectors or other advanced selectors?*

A. Certainly! This is a valid CSS rule:

```
.chap > th + td img[alt] { border: 2px solid green; }
```

What would match this? Basically, anything that meets the following criteria:

- ▶ An image element
- ▶ With an `alt` attribute set (to any value)
- ▶ Where that image is a descendant of a table cell
- ▶ Assuming that table cell has a table header cell as a sibling
- ▶ Which is a direct child of an element in the chap class

Quiz

1. What does the + symbol indicate, in a selector?

2. Which selector will select the HTML element `<h1 align="right">Welcome</h1>`, and why?

    a. `h1[align~="right"]`

    b. `*[align="right"]`

    c. `[align|="right"]`

    d. `h1[align]`

3. You're using Opera 8.5 and you want to write a rule in your user style sheet to hide banners that are 468 pixels across and 60 pixels high. How do you write that rule?

Answers

1. The + symbol designates a direct sibling selector.

2. It's kind of a trick question. All of them will select the `<h1>`. The first will select it because `right` is one of the values listed in the attribute (it's the only value, too). The second will select it because it's exactly the value (and the selector's type is universal). The third is also a universal selector, and it will compare values before a dash; because there is no dash, it will compare just `right` with `right`. The last matches because the `<h1>` tag has an `align` attribute, with any value.

3. Here's one way to zap away those annoying banners:

```
img[height="60"][width="468"] { display: none; }
```

Exercise

You'll master selectors gradually, as you work on other projects using CSS and write style sheets using these types of rules. To practice as you learn, make a "cheat sheet" to remind yourself which advanced selectors you can use, and keep that list handy as you read this book and create style sheets. Identify specific situations in which a complex rule might actually work better than simply adding `class` and `id` in HTML, which is an easy habit to fall into.

PART III

Styling Text with CSS

HOUR 9

Fonts and Font Families

What You'll Learn in This Hour:

▶ Which font properties specify bold, italic, and variant fonts

▶ How you can set a number of font properties at once using a shorthand property

▶ What the generic font families are and how to use them

▶ Which fonts are most commonly installed on browsers

One of the most effective changes you can make to a web page when using CSS is to simply alter the browser's default font. This can add a more professional look to your website immediately, as well as make it easier for users to read and find information.

Specifying Font Properties

In Hour 2, "Getting Started with CSS," you were introduced to two font properties: font-size and font-family. These enable you to specify the size and typeface of the font, respectively. In addition, a number of other properties can be used to further select fonts from within those families. These properties are font-weight, font-variant, font-style, font-stretch, and font-size-adjust.

To understand how these properties work, it's important to understand how CSS views fonts. A font in CSS is one specific instance of several properties: a specific typeface, size, weight, and other variables. So the font 12pt Arial bold italic is different from the font 10pt Arial. They are part of the same font family, of course. It's helpful to remember that when you declare a font family, you're actually selecting a group of fonts to be used. Other properties (or browser defaults) narrow down the specific font.

Font families generally include a number of variations on the base font—for example, an italic version of the font. In some cases, you will specify a font combination that simply isn't available as a distinct variant. The browser then has to create a variant on the fly by slanting the text to produce italic effects, for example, or by using the closest available equivalent in the font family.

The effects produced by various font settings are listed in Table 9.1 for reference; this is because it's not always clear which property controls which effect.

TABLE 9.1   Properties Affecting Font Display

Property	Effect
`font-family`	Selects the typeface family
`font-size`	Sets the size of the font
`font-weight`	Makes text bold or lighter
`font-variant`	Creates "small caps" effect
`font-style`	Sets italic font
`text-decoration` (Hour 10)	Underlines text
`color` (Hour 10)	Changes the color of text
`line-height` (Hour 15)	The height of the line (but not the text height)
`font`	Sets `font-family`, `font-size`, `font-weight`, `font-variant`, `font-style`, and `line-height`

The `font-weight` Property

The `font-weight` property controls how heavy a font appears—in other words, the thickness of the lines used to draw that font, relative to the size of the font. The weight of a font is measured in numbers that range from `100` to `900`, in steps of `100`. The higher the number, the bolder the font; normal text has a weight of `400` and bold text (as created by the HTML <b> tag) has a weight of `700`.

Not all font families have specific fonts at all values; in such a situation, the browser usually uses the closest match. For example, if there's no weight `800` variant for a font, the browser may substitute weight `700`.

Many browsers support only two to four `font-weight` values. Figure 9.1 shows how Safari displays each `font-weight` value of Verdana, whereas Figure 9.2 is from Firefox. Notice that they differ on whether weight `600` should be weighted like `500`, `700`, or somewhere in between. Keep this in mind; it will be important later on.

In addition to numeric values, the `font-weight` property can take named values, as shown on Table 9.2. The `font-weight` value is inherited from the containing box if any is set. The default value is `normal` (`400`) for most HTML tags; some, such as <b>, <strong>, <h1> to <h6>, and <th>, default to `bold` (`700`).

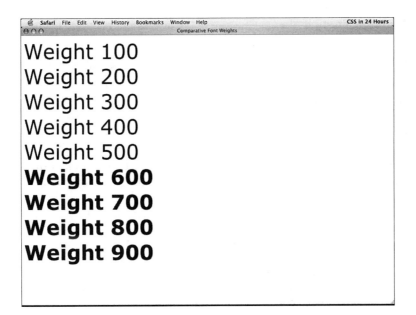

TABLE 9.2   Values for the font-weight **Property**

Value	Effect
100 to 900	Lightest (100) to heaviest (900) font weight
bold	Same as 700

TABLE 9.2   Continued

Value	Effect
bolder	One step (+100) heavier than the containing box's `font-weight`
lighter	One step (-100) lighter than the containing box's `font-weight`
normal	Same as 400
inherit	The value of the containing box's `font-weight` property

If a font's weight is already at 900, the value bolder won't make it any heavier; likewise, if the font-weight is 100, lighter has no additional effect.

Comparing Figure 9.1 and Figure 9.2, it's clear that browsers aren't consistent about how heavy they make in-between values such as 500 or 600. Because bolder and lighter move up or down in steps of 100, it's possible that a bolder (or lighter) rule may have no effect. If the default is 400, and the browser does not render 500 as 700 but as 400, an increase of 100 is meaningless. For this reason it's better to use either explicit numeric values (400 or 700) or the keyword bold for cross-browser consistency.

The font-variant **Property**

Only one type of variant font can be set with the font-variant property, a variant where lowercase letters are represented with smaller versions of capital letters. The three possible values for font-variant are shown in Table 9.3; the default value is normal, and if there is a value set on the containing box, it will be inherited.

TABLE 9.3   Values for the font-variant **Property**

Value	Effect
normal	Use normal lowercase letters
small-caps	Use small capitals instead of lowercase letters
inherit	Use the value of the containing box's font-variant property

An example of font-variant is shown in Figure 9.3; the rule used is

```
#a { font-family: Optima, sans-serif;
     font-variant: small-caps; }
```

The font-style **Property**

To set something in an italic or oblique font, you can use the font-style property; font-style is not used for anything else, although the name seems deceptively general. The values for font-style are shown in Table 9.4. If a font-style property is set on the containing box, it is inherited. Otherwise, the default is usually normal, although some HTML properties, such as <i>, <em>, and <address>, are normally italicized by web browsers.

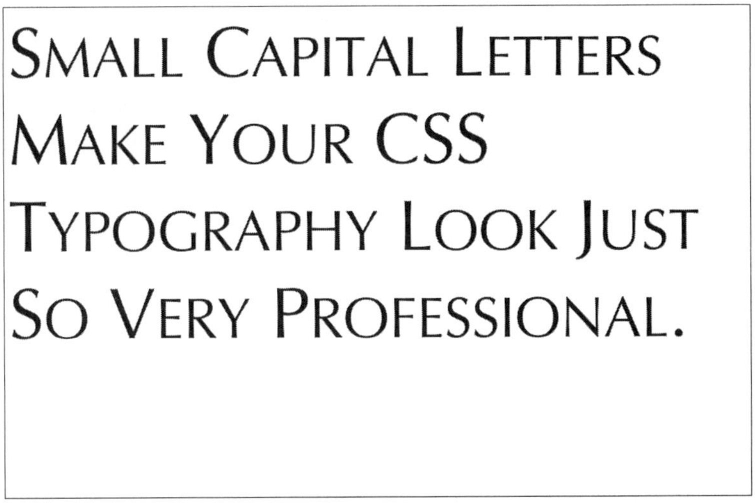

SMALL CAPITAL LETTERS MAKE YOUR CSS TYPOGRAPHY LOOK JUST SO VERY PROFESSIONAL.

FIGURE 9.3
Using font-variant: small-caps.

TABLE 9.4   Values for the font-style **Property**

Value	Effect
italic	Use an italic font.
normal	Use a non-oblique, non-italic font.
oblique	Use an oblique or slanted font.
inherit	Use the value of the containing box's font-style property.

Did you Know?

What is oblique? Although it's a less common term than italic, it's a related concept.

Most fonts we see are called *Roman fonts*; these are not slanted, and they correspond to the CSS value of normal. An *italic font* is created by making slanted, slightly curly alternate versions of the letters in a Roman font; each letter has been redesigned so that it's essentially a new set of characters within the same font family.

An *oblique font*, on the other hand, is created by just tilting the Roman font's characters at an angle. This doesn't always require font redesign and can be done automatically by a computer, but often the results are not nearly as nice looking. Many typography books explicitly discourage the use of computer-created obliques.

Browsers treat italic and oblique property values the same because they don't really know the difference most of the time. The CSS specification allows for italic fonts to be displayed as oblique (even oblique fonts generated automatically) if a matching italic font is not available. You'll probably want to simply use italic; don't worry about the difference unless you are a professional typographer, in which case you don't need me to explain the difference between oblique and italic.

Figure 9.4 shows the lack of difference between oblique and italic by current browsers; they're both rendered the same, in slanted text. This is unfortunate for typographers, but for most of us it won't be a major problem. The code used in this screenshot is

```
<div style="font-style: normal;">
  This is normal text.
</div>
<div style="font-style: italic;">
  This text is italic.
</div>
<div style="font-style: oblique;">
  This text is oblique.
</div>
```

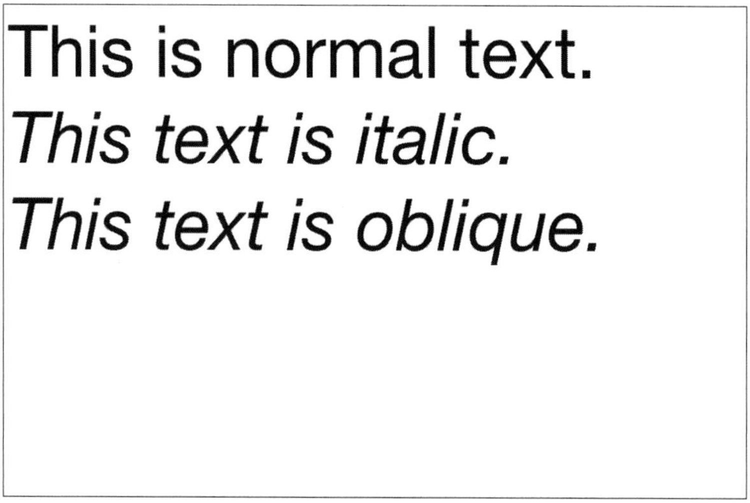

FIGURE 9.4
Oblique versus italic. In practice, there's no difference.

This is normal text.
This text is italic.
This text is oblique.

The font **Shorthand Property**

As you've probably noticed this hour, quite a few properties define a font. Rather than typing out each property, the font property enables you to set these values at one time.

The font property is a *shorthand property* in CSS terminology. A shorthand value has two effects: It sets all affected properties to their default values, and it assigns designated values to the appropriate properties. The font property is shorthand for the font-family, font-size, font-weight, font-variant, font-style, and line-height properties. (You'll learn about line-height and how to use it with font in Hour 15, "Alignment.") The font property doesn't let you set values for font-stretch or font-size-adjust; these need to be set in separate rules.

<table>
<tr>
<td>

Don't overlook that first function, resetting to default values! You can easily spend hours trying to debug your style sheet if you don't remember that shorthand properties set all values, even those not shown. In addition to anything else a font rule does, it also is roughly equivalent to the following declarations:

```
font-family: serif; /* or the default browser font */
font-size: medium;
font-weight: normal;
font-variant: normal;
font-style: normal;
line-height: 100%;
```

</td>
<td>

Watch Out!

</td>
</tr>
</table>

A font rule looks like this:

```
selector { font: style variant weight size family; }
```

The values for *weight*, *size*, and *family* must be specified in that exact order, but other than that the values can appear in any order. Any values that aren't listed are set to their default values. Here are some examples of font shorthand rules:

```
body { font: 12pt normal "Times New Roman"; }
h1 { font: 20pt Arial italic small-caps; }
blockquote { font: bold "Courier New", sans-serif; }
```

When using font it's important to keep in mind that the first function of this property is to reset values to their defaults; this means that priority order counts. For example, consider these two pairs of rules:

```
#a { font-weight: 700;
     font: large Verdana, sans-serif; }

#b { font: large Verdana, sans-serif;
     font-weight: 700; }
```

In the #a rules, the font-weight gets set to 700 by the font-weight property, but then the font property resets it to the default, so the weight is back to 400. The #b rules are in the correct order to make the text bold; first the font rule sets everything to default values, and then the specific rule for font-weight overrides the default.

The font property can also take values based on the user's operating system fonts; these are discussed in detail in Hour 23, "User Interface and Generated Content."

▼ **Try it Yourself**

Setting Font Properties

The best way to understand how the font properties and font shorthand work is to try it yourself. Follow these steps:

1. Create an HTML page with various types of text for styling. Include <h1> and <p> elements, plus other types of text such as <blockquote>.

2. For each type of text, write a series of separate CSS rules, using font-family, font-weight, font-style, font-size, and font-variant. For example:

```
h1 { font-family: Verdana, sans-serif;
     font-weight: normal;
     font-size: 200%;
     font-style: italic;
     font-variant: small-caps; }
```

3. Give different rules for your headlines and your body text. Set aside quotes with <blockquote> rules. Choose fonts and font sizes that complement the different types of text. Do your headlines have to be bold?

4. Now combine your style rules together into one font rule, being mindful of the default values set by a shorthand property. For example, you could write

```
h1 { font: italic small-caps 200% Verdana, sans-serif; }
```

▲

Font Families

As you learned in Hour 2, the font-family property is used to select the family of font faces. A font-family rule can be written like this:

```
selector { font-family: font1, font2, font3, ...
           generic; }
```

You can give as many alternate fonts as you want; the browser looks through its own list (from the computer's operating system) and locates the closest match. After it finds one, it displays the text with that font face. For example, consider this rule:

```
h1 { font-family: "MS Sans Serif", Palatino, Helvetica,
     "Bookman Old Style", "Times New Roman", Times,
     Garamond, Chicago, Arial, Geneva, Verdana,
     cursive; }
```

The browser starts looking through the list of fonts, and if it finds a match, it uses that font. So on my Windows computer, it might find "MS Sans Serif" and display the <h1> in that font; on my Apple iBook, it won't find "MS Sans Serif" and will go on to the next one. If the iBook has Palatino (which it does), that's the font family that will be used.

Remember to include quotes around font names that are more than one word!

The Generic Font Families

In the long rule you just saw, I included a generic font family name at the end— cursive. In case the browser can't find any of the 11 named fonts, it will use the browser's cursive font. The exact value of the cursive font varies a lot from operating system to operating system; also, modern browsers (such as Firefox or Opera) enable the user to set specific fonts tied to the generic families. So on my Firefox browser, cursive might mean "Apple Chancery", whereas on yours it may be the "Lucida Handwriting" font.

The five generic font families in CSS are serif, sans-serif, cursive, fantasy, and monospace. To show you how different browsers (on two different operating systems) will display the generic font families, I've taken some screen shots. Your browser may display these differently as well; in most browsers you can reconfigure your generic font families depending on which fonts are installed on your system.

Listing 9.1 is a simple HTML file with embedded style attribute rules that use the generic font families.

LISTING 9.1 Styling with Generic Font Families

```
<!-- generic-9.1.html -->
<html>
  <head>
    <title>Generic Font Families</title>
  </head>
  <body>
    <h1 style="font-family: serif;">Serif Family</h1>
    <h1 style="font-family: sans-serif;">Sans-Serif Family</h1>
    <h1 style="font-family: monospace;">Monospace Family</h1>
    <h1 style="font-family: fantasy;">Fantasy Family</h1>
    <h1 style="font-family: cursive;">Cursive Family</h1>
  </body>
</html>
```

In Figure 9.5, you can see the generic font families from Listing 9.1 as shown in Firefox, running on my iBook Macintosh laptop.

FIGURE 9.5
Generic font
families in
Firefox (Mac
OS X).

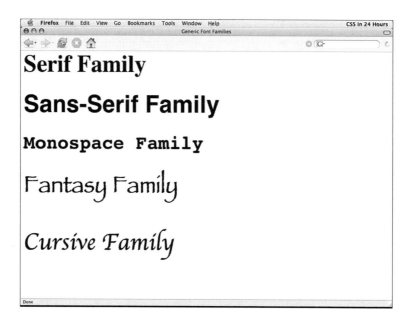

Figure 9.6 shows you what the generic font families look like in Firefox running on my Windows desktop computer. Notice that the serif, sans-serif, and monospace families are consistent with the iBook's families, but the cursive and fantasy families are very different. In fact, the fantasy font family seems to be unsupported in this particular browser configuration, as it uses a plain looking sans-serif font. Especially for the fantasy and cursive families, the choice of font for generic families depends a lot on which browser and operating system are used, and which fonts are installed—even when the browser versions are identical.

What about Internet Explorer's generic fonts? Figure 9.7 shows how Internet Explorer on Windows handles the fonts. In this example as well, there is no special font for the fantasy family; it may well be that whatever font Internet Explorer is looking for is not installed on the computer in question. You can't rely on having any given font on a user's machine, or even rely on the generic fantasy and cursive families being either fantastic or cursive. They may just be plain fonts, as these examples show.

As described in Hour 3, "Browser Support for CSS," Internet Explorer for Macintosh is an entirely different piece of software than Internet Explorer on Windows. This is evident in the generic font families, as shown in Figure 9.8.

FIGURE 9.6
Generic font families in Firefox (Windows XP).

FIGURE 9.7
Generic font families in Internet Explorer (Windows XP).

Figure 9.9 shows the generic font families as displayed by Opera 8.5 on the Macintosh. There are several things to note here: The first is that Opera isn't displaying Arial for the sans-serif family, as you see with the other browsers. The second is that the MS Comic Sans font, used as a `cursive` font by Internet Explorer and Firefox on Windows, appears here as a `fantasy` font!

FIGURE 9.8
Generic font families in Internet Explorer (Mac OS X).

FIGURE 9.9
Generic font families in Opera 8.5 (Mac OS X).

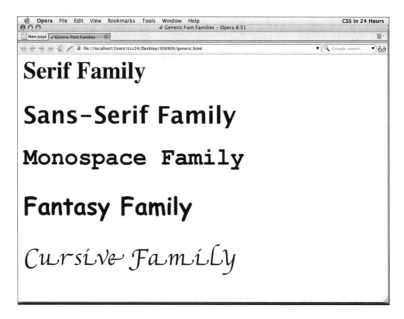

Finally, Figure 9.10 shows how Safari displays the font families. In short, it doesn't
bother with the cursive and fantasy fonts; instead, they're shown as plain, ordinary
sans-serif Arial.

FIGURE 9.10
Generic font
families in
Safari (Mac
OS X).

Generic font families are good for fallback; without them, your font face will be the
single default of the browser, usually something like `"Times New Roman"`. Though
as you can see, they're not very consistent. They are still better than the basic
default, however, and you will want to include a generic family in each
`font-family` property value (or `font` shorthand property value).

Serif

In font terminology, *serifs* are defined as the little feet or curved bits added to the
ends of the straight lines that constitute a letter. These help to make the characters
easier to distinguish when reading, especially when reading print. A serif font makes
it much easier to distinguish among the number 1, the lowercase letter l, and the
uppercase letter I, as shown in Figure 9.11.

Serif fonts are often used for normal body text in web browsers. The default test font
is commonly `"Times New Roman"`, which is usually the generic `serif` family font as
well. However, serif fonts tend to display poorly on the screen compared with print,
especially at smaller font sizes. Many web developers will immediately change the
`font-family` to a sans-serif font as the first rule of their style sheets.

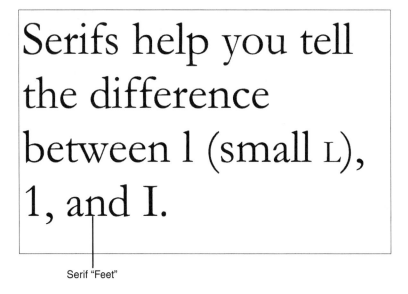

Serif "Feet"

Other examples of serif fonts include "Bookman Old Style", "Book Antiqua", "Century Schoolbook", Garamond, "Goudy Old Style", Palatino, and Sonoma. The font Times is similar to "Times New Roman", and it's often useful to specify both of those fonts together, like this:

```
blockquote { font-family: "Times New Roman",
             Times, serif; }
```

Sans-serif

The prefix *sans* means "without," so a sans-serif font is one that does not have serifs. Sans-serif fonts look cleaner and more streamlined than serif fonts, and they often fit better on most web pages. (Not all web designs are the same, though, and you can many times find uses of both serif and sans-serif fonts, often within the same style sheet.) A sans-serif font is shown in Figure 9.12.

The most common sans-serif font is Arial; its near relatives are Helvetica and Geneva. Another important font is Verdana, which was specifically developed for on-screen display; it is wider than Arial and easier to read, especially at smaller sizes. Other examples of sans-serif fonts are "Century Gothic", Chicago, Futura, and Tahoma.

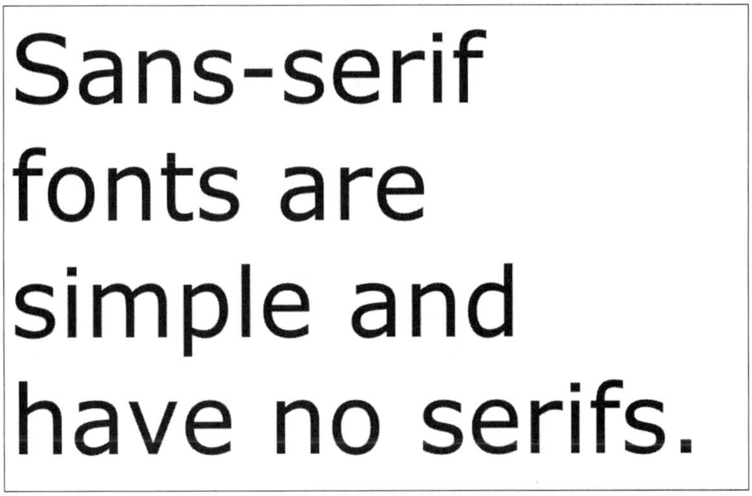

Sans-serif
fonts are
simple and
have no serifs.

FIGURE 9.12
Sans-serif fonts
have a more
modern look
than serif fonts.

Monospace

The term *monospace* means that each letter is displayed in the same amount of space; columns of text line up by character, for example, so that the 15th character from the left on each line is always at the same location. This is rather like an old typewriter. (Do people still use typewriters in the 21st century?) The code samples in this book are set in a monospace font, as is any word meant to be typed, such as property values and the names of properties and selectors. Figure 9.13 is an example of the monospace generic family.

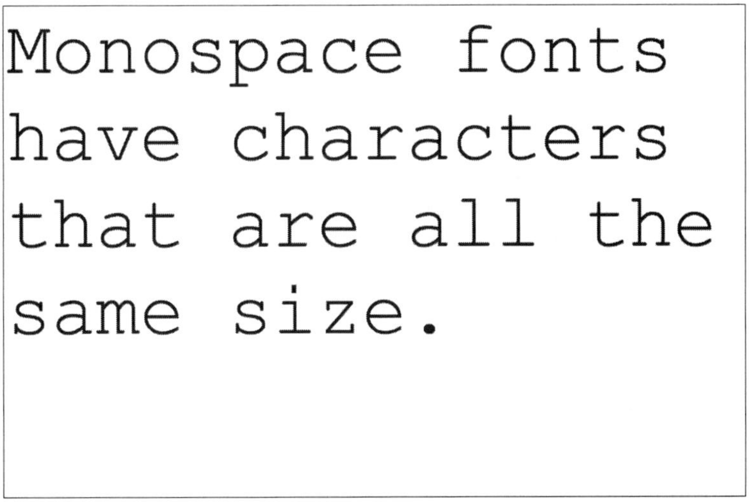

```
Monospace fonts
have characters
that are all the
same size.
```

FIGURE 9.13
The letters of monospace fonts line up in columns.

The most common monospace font family is "Courier New", and this is the default monospace value on pretty much every browser. Courier is an older version of "Courier New"; you may want to list both of these to ensure a greater likelihood of a font match.

Other monospace fonts include "Andale Mono", VT102, and Mishiwaka.

Fantasy

The fantasy generic family is even more of a grab bag than the cursive family; any irregular, somewhat-whimsical font falls into this category. Some are old woodcut-style ornate letters; some are bizarre squiggles; some look like animals; and some look like letters cut from newspapers for a ransom note. Figure 9.14 has an example of a font from the fantasy generic family.

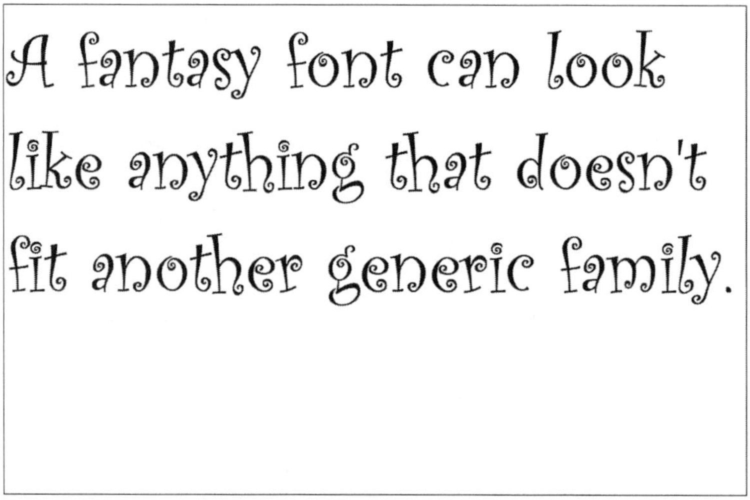

FIGURE 9.14
One of many possible fantasy fonts.

A fantasy font can look like anything that doesn't fit another generic family.

Because the fantasy generic family is so loosely defined and because browsers have interpreted this as a catchall for any strange fonts that may come along, a declaration of fantasy could produce text that looks like anything. For example, on my browser it may display in a comic book print font, but on yours it could appear in an old English woodcut font. Because this kind of irregularity makes it hard to design effectively, you'll probably want to avoid using this family.

Cursive

The cursive generic family is very variable; it refers to any font that was based on the way people handwrite text. As with fantasy, there are no real standards on what the default cursive family should be, which is why it is different from computer to computer and even from browser to browser. Examples include `"Script MT Bold"`, `"Apple Chancery"`, `Swing`, `"MS Sans Serif"`, and `"Lucida Handwriting"`. In Figure 9.15, you can see one example of a cursive font.

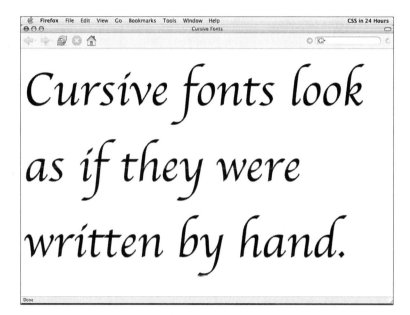

FIGURE 9.15
One browser's cursive font (Firefox running on Mac OS X).

Cursive fonts tend to be very difficult to read onscreen and probably should be avoided unless you have a very specific reason to use one, such as the writer's name after a formal letter, styled to represent a written signature.

Commonly Installed Fonts

Because there's so much variance among computers, you may not be able to know with certainty whether or not a given font will appear on a user's computer. She might indeed be using Internet Explorer 6 on Windows, but she also could have decided to delete Arial entirely! (Why someone would do this, I'm not quite sure.)

However, it's possible to devise a list of relatively safe fonts—those that are found on most operating systems and browsers. You should continue to use generic families as fallbacks, but these are relatively safe.

The common fonts are `"Times New Roman"`, `Times`, `Arial`, `Helvetica`, `Geneva`, `Verdana`, `"Courier New"`, and `Courier`. Other fonts are less reliable, such as `"MS Comic Sans"`, `Papyrus`, and `Optima`.

▼   **Try it Yourself**

Font Families in Action

Let's look at what fonts you have installed on your computer which are used by your browser. Do the following:

1. Create an HTML file with various types of text to style. You can download Listing 9.1 from the book's website, or make up your own page.

2. Try out the generic fonts. Set a rule like this to make all the text on your page the same font family:

   ```
   body { font-family: sans-serif; }
   ```

3. Then try setting different fonts for the headline elements and the body text; combine them together to get the best appearance.

   ```
   h1, h2, h3, h4, h5, h6 { font-family: fantasy; }
   p { font-family: cursive; }
   ```

4. Now view the page in a different browser. How does your page change, or does it?

5. Try using the common fonts such as Arial or Verdana. These are nearly ubiquitous on the Web, but what about Papyrus or Optima?

   ```
   h1 { font-family: Verdana, sans-serif; }
   blockquote { font-family: Papyrus, fantasy; }
   ```

▲

Summary

When you specify a font, you're actually selecting a font from a set maintained by the user's browser and operating system. Browsers use the various font properties, such as font-weight, font-variant, font-style, and font-size, to narrow down the fonts within a specific font-family and select the right one to use. All these properties can be specified with the font shorthand property.

Five generic font families—serif, sans-serif, cursive, fantasy, and monospace—are used if the user's computer doesn't contain a font you specify. A short list of common fonts is available on all browsers. CSS describes a method for downloading fonts on demand, but unfortunately neither of the two competing methods for downloading fonts is very reliable.

Workshop

The workshop contains a Q&A section, quiz questions, and an exercise to help reinforce what you've learned in this hour. If you get stuck, the answers to the quiz can be found after the questions.

Q&A

Q. *I need to have specific fonts on my page, even if the user doesn't have them on his computer. What can I do?*

A. If you want specific fonts for headers or navigation buttons, you can create graphics containing your text, using a graphics editing program to choose the exact fonts required. The problem with text-as-graphics is that the images don't scale at all with the user's preferences, which may make it harder for some users with visual disabilities. In any case, you need to remember to set the `alt` attribute on the HTML `<img>` tag to a value equal to the text on the graphic. For more on this, see Hour 22, "Accessibility and Print Media," and Hour 24, "Troubleshooting and Browser Hacks."

Quiz

1. Consider the following HTML:

```
<div style="font-weight: bold;">
  That's <span style="font-weight: bolder;">heavy</a>,
  man.
</div>
```

What numeric value (`100` to `900`) is the equivalent of the font weight on the word heavy?

2. How do you write the following properties with the `font` shorthand property?

```
.double { font-weight: 700;
          color: navy;
          font-family: Verdana, sans-serif;
          font-size: x-large;
          font-style: oblique;
          font-variant: small-caps; }
```

3. What are the generic font families that are closest to each of these fonts?

   a. Verdana

   b. Times New Roman

   c. Lucida Handwriting

   d. Helvetica

   e. Courier New

Answers

1. The value bold is inherited from the containing box, and it has a value of 700. The bolder property value increases the inherited value by 100, so the total is 800.

2. Here's one way to write that rule with the font property:

```
.double { font: oblique small-caps 700
                 x-large Verdana sans-serif;
          color: navy; }
```

Because color isn't included in the font shorthand property, it has to be declared separately. Note that the order of *weight*, *size*, and *family* is used; hopefully, you remembered that the order does matter for those values.

3. The generic families for each font are

   a. sans-serif

   b. serif

   c. cursive

   d. sans-serif

   e. monospace

Exercise

Explore the use of fonts in CSS with this optional project. Create a web page with a style sheet that uses a number of different fonts for headers, paragraphs, navigation, footers, tables, and anything else. Go overboard with your font choices—make up dozens of styles, a different font for each type of content—and then start decreasing the variety of fonts you use. Discover at what point "a lot" is "too many," and discover how many fonts you really need to make a web page look right. (My preference? No more than two or three.)

HOUR 10

Text Colors and Effects

Use of Cascading Style Sheets can transform a plain, boring page of text into a visual treat, without even any graphics. The CSS specifications define ways to enhance your textual content visually, from changing the colors to adding strikethrough lines. In addition, you can change the spaces between letters, words, and lines, as well as the points at which browsers wrap lines, by using simple CSS properties.

Text Colors

Colors are a key part of conveying information in a visual medium. Giving distinct colors to certain types of information on a page can emphasize or de-emphasize the importance; for example, new content can be marked with a bright, vivid color, and outdated content may be presented in a more muted hue.

As you already know, using the color property is the primary method for setting the foreground color. You can set the background color with the background-color property, which is covered in detail next hour.

The foreground color is also used by other properties as a default color value if none is specified. For example, if a color value is omitted for the border property, the foreground color will be used.

Specifying Color Values

CSS provides two ways to define a color. The first is to use a color name, such as green or black; the second is to use a set of three RGB values, corresponding to the amount of red, green, and blue desired. RGB colors were introduced in Hour 2, "Getting Started with CSS," and in this hour we'll tell you other ways to specify a set of RGB values.

Color Names

Back in Hour 2, you learned about the 17 colors recognized by the CSS specifications. These color names—aqua, black, blue, fuchsia, gray, green, lime, maroon, navy, olive, orange, purple, red, silver, teal, white, and yellow—are well-supported by the browsers.

Most browsers accept other color names as well, such as pink, cyan, and violet. However, until a future version of CSS adds those colors to the official specification, it's probably best to avoid using such nonstandard colors. There's no guarantee that a browser will support them, so you're safer with RGB values.

Some other colors are accepted by browsers as well; those are based on the user's operating system preferences and are called *system colors*. In Hour 23, "User Interface and Generated Content," you'll learn more about system colors and how to use them in your web design.

RGB Color Values

To specify a color in RGB notation, you need to know how much red, green, and blue is contained in that color. Web colors are a bit strange at first if you're not used to them; they're not at all like mixing paints as a child. For example, when you're blending paint colors, you mix red and yellow to make orange. When you're making RGB colors, you mix red and green to make yellow! If you did that with paint, you'd get some ugly, muddy gray-brown shade.

Paints (and ink, as well as most other physical objects you look at) have color because they selectively reflect light; something that actually emits light, as your monitor does, creates colors by adding together portions of colored light. It's a bit confusing, but you'll get used to it after you've worked with RGB values.

Even more confusing is the way RGB colors are written. All RGB colors are measured based on a scale from 0 to 255. They're usually counted in hexadecimal, which means a base-16 number system where the digits are 0, 1, 2, 3, 4, 5, 6, 7, 8, 9, A, B, C, D, E, and F. The number 32 is written as 20 (two sixteens and zero ones), and the number 111 is 6F (six sixteens and 15 ones).

CSS offers four ways to present RGB values. The first uses straightforward *hexadecimal notation*, as a six-digit number:

```
body { color: #CC66FF; }
```

This means the foreground color should have a red value of CC (204 out of 255, or 80%); 66 green, which is 102 (40%); and FF blue, or 255 (100%). What does this color look like? Kind of a light lavender. The closer you are to white (#FFFFFF) the more pastel the colors, and when you mix large amounts of blue and red, you get a purple effect.

You can also write this in *short hex notation*. This is a three-digit hexadecimal number; to convert a three digit RGB code to a six-digit one, simply double each letter. So the same rule can be written like this:

```
body { color: #C6F; }
```

The rgb() function provides two more ways to set colors, especially if you don't know hexadecimal numbers well. One of those is to provide a triplet of RGB numbers, rated from 0 to 255, separated by commas. The other is to give percentages. Here's how the lavender rule can be written:

```
body { color: rgb(204, 102, 255); }
body { color: rgb(80%, 40%, 100%); }
```

You can use these color values when setting any color in CSS, not just the color property. For example, you can set a background-color or a border with any of these types of values.

To design effectively with color, you need a color chart, or else you have to be very willing to experiment with RGB values! I recommend getting a color chart; either a printed one you can keep by your computer or an electronic file you can refer to, or both. A great site for web color information is VisiBone, http://www.visibone. com/, which has a hex color chart arranged by hue.

Using Color Effectively

When you're designing a web page and adding color by using CSS, it is always helpful to put some thought into the process. The theory and practice of employing color is a topic that could fill an entire book or several books, as not everyone seems to agree! However, here are some pointers that can help you use color more effectively in your designs; most of these are common sense, but it's amazing how many web designs don't seem to have taken these into account.

▶ Use colors to visually emphasize important differences among types of content. The presentation of your content should be derived from the meaning of that information. Color your navigation bar differently from your main content. Set sidebars apart visually with background colors that fit well with the rest of the page. Change the color of headings to make them more visible.

▶ Change colors for a reason, not on a whim. I've seen many websites where the developers appear to have discovered color just the day before and changed the color for no reason. Be able to justify your color choices.

▶ Bright colors draw attention; faded colors hide unimportant material. As an example, if some content is more important or changes often, give it a vibrant, bright color, such as yellow (on a dark background) or red, to make it stand out.

▶ Too many colors will make your page seem confusing and unprofessional; a restricted set of hues often works better. If you don't have any experience with graphic design, pick up a good book on color and design, and notice that many great designs have a limited palette.

▶ You don't have to change the color of everything. Black on white is not the enemy. Web users are accustomed to the default colors, and often it's easier to read text if there's high contrast, such as black on white (or white on black).

▶ If you're designing for a whole site, use a consistent look across your pages. Consistency helps users recognize that they're still at your site and helps establish a feeling of familiarity. If you change your site too often, regular users may be disoriented.

▶ If there are identifiable subsites, consider assigning each one a color scheme. Don't create a brand new design for each; it can be disorienting if each section looks like a brand new website. Instead, add color that complements the primary site design.

▶ Make sure your color choices look good together and contrast well. Subtle shades of difference, such as medium blue on dark blue, may not come across well and content could be lost.

▶ Use colors that complement any images or graphics on your page. You can derive color schemes from your graphical content, or choose graphics that fit your chosen colors. The more coordinated your colors, the better your site will look.

▶ Test your colors in several browsers and computers; your monitor's settings may be different than someone else's. Try testing with 256 colors instead of thousands, millions, or billions; if you can, try your site in black and white.

▶ Don't employ color as the only way of conveying information; visually impaired users might miss important context. It's fine to use color, but make sure that important distinctions among content are reflected in the markup as well. In Hour 22, "Accessibility and Print Media," you'll learn more about designing to enable access for people with disabilities.

Special Text Effects

In addition to changing the colors of the text and the font properties from Hour 9, "Fonts and Font Families," Cascading Style Sheets can be used to produce text effects ranging from decorations to drop shadows. These can be used only on CSS elements that actually contain text; on anything else, they have no effect. For example, a text-shadow property set on an <img> tag doesn't produce a shadow under the displayed image.

The text-decoration Property

CSS uses the term *text decoration* to refer to a specific set of effects that can be applied to text: lines through, under, or around the text, and blinking text. The types of values that can be set for the text-decoration property are shown in Table 10.1. The default value for text-decoration is usually none, although most browsers automatically use text-decoration: underline for hypertext links.

TABLE 10.1   Values for the text-decoration Property

Value	Effect
blink	The text blinks off and on.
line-through	Draws a line through the middle of the text.

TABLE 10.1   Continued

Value	Effect
overline	Draws a line over the top of the text.
underline	Draws a line under the bottom of the text.
none	None of the effects listed here.
inherit	Uses the value of text-decoration on the containing box.

**Watch
Out!**

> The blink property value is not very popular, primarily because of serious abuse of the `<blink>` tag by designers when it was first introduced by Netscape. The `<blink>` tag is nonstandard in HTML and highly discouraged. Therefore, `text-decoration: blink` is specifically stated to be an optional part of the CSS specification; browsers don't have to support it, and in fact, most of them do not.

The value of text-decoration technically is not inherited, although if it is set on a block element, the decoration should be applied to all text within that block.

The color of the text-decoration—the line through, over, or under the text—is the same as that of the text itself, and so can be set with the color property. The lines drawn are thin, and the exact thickness is up to the browser; you can't change the line thickness with CSS.

The most common value for text-decoration in style sheets is none; the property is mainly used to turn off underlines rather than add them or any other text decorations. Why is this so? Because you can use text-decoration to turn off the underlines on links by writing a:link and a:visited rules. Many designers find underlined links to be annoyingly ugly and much less elegant than links without underlines.

However, there are some problems with that approach: Namely, it makes it harder for the user to know what's a link and what's not. If you're going to remove one of the user's primary cues to find clickable links, you need to make sure that the links are obvious. Color typically isn't enough by itself, even though web developers like to think it should be.

If you're using inline links—those within paragraphs of text—then you should probably leave the underlines alone. An alternative approach is to set obvious borders or background colors on your inline links.

Navigation bars are a different case; even without underlines, users can tell they're supposed to click on things that look like buttons or a list of options. Removing underlines from navigation bars is acceptable and won't cause problems.

The other side of the link-underlining coin is this: Users think that anything that is underlined is clickable. If you put text-decoration: underline on your <h2> tag, people will try to click it. And they'll get annoyed when it doesn't click. Therefore, you should avoid using underlines nearly all the time. If you need to call attention to something, use the <em> or <strong> tags, font effects such as font-weight or font-style, or colors. For more about styling links, see Hour 12, "Styling Links."

Listing 10.1 is an HTML file with an embedded style sheet that demonstrates text-decoration in action; you can see the results displayed in Figure 10.1.

LISTING 10.1 Text Decorations in an Embedded Style Sheet

```
<!-- decorate-10.1.html -->
<html>
  <head>
    <title>I love to decorate</title>
    <style type="text/css">
      body      { font-family: Verdana, sans-serif; }
      h1 em     { text-decoration: underline; }
      .nav      { border: 0.3em solid black; }
      .nav a:link, .nav a:visited
                { text-decoration: none; }
      .oops     { text-decoration: line-through; }
      .eg       { border: 1px solid black;
                  margin: 2em; padding: 1em; }
      #a        { text-decoration: underline; }
      #b        { text-decoration: line-through; }
      #c        { text-decoration: overline; }
      #d        { text-decoration: blink; }
    </style>
  </head>
  <body>
    <table class="nav" border="0" align="right">
      <tr><th><a href="home.html">Home</a></th></tr>
      <tr><th><a href="info.html">Info</a></th></tr>
      <tr><th><a href="help.html">Help</a></th></tr>
      <tr><th><a href="news.html">News</a></th></tr>
    </table>
    <h1>I <em>love</em> to decorate!</h1>
    <p> I think that decorating
        <span class="oops">cakes</span>HTML is lots
        of fun. Here are some of my favorites: </p>
    <div class="eg">
      <p id="a">Underlined text (don't you want to
                click here?) </p>
      <p id="b">Line-through text</p>
      <p id="c">Overlined text</p>
      <p id="d"> Blinking text (this is hard to show
                  in print!) </p>
    </div>
  </body>
</html>
```

FIGURE 10.1
A variety of text
decoration
effects.

The text-transform **Property**

You can change the case of text from upper- to lowercase, or vice versa, by using the text-transform property. Well, you're actually not changing the text itself, but rather how a CSS-enabled browser displays it. The values you can set for this property are shown in Table 10.2; the default is none, although if a text-transform property is set on the containing box, that value will be inherited.

TABLE 10.2   Values for the text-transform **Property**

Value	Effect
capitalize	Capitalizes the first letter of each word.
lowercase	Changes all uppercase letters to lowercase.
uppercase	Changes all lowercase letters to uppercase.
none	Doesn't change anything.
inherit	Uses the value on the containing box.

This property is dependent upon the language and character set being used; if a language doesn't have upper- or lowercase letters, nothing is changed.

Listing 10.2 is an HTML file with an embedded style sheet that contains text-transform examples.

LISTING 10.2   Text Transforms in an Embedded Style Sheet

```
<!-- transform-10.2.html -->
<html>
  <head>
    <title>Text Transformations</title>
    <style type="text/css">
      body      { font-family: Verdana, sans-serif; }
      div.eg    { margin: 1em; padding: 1em;
                  font-family: Arial, sans-serif;
                  border: 1px solid black; }

      /*
      #nav      { text-transform: lowercase; }
      #header h3 { text-transform: capitalize; }
      #header h4 { text-transform: uppercase; }
      #lion p:first-child:first-line
                 { text-transform: uppercase; }
      */
    </style>
  </head>
  <body>
    <h3>Navigation Bar:</h3>
    <div class="eg" id="nav">
      <a href="index.html">Teach Yourself CSS</a> &middot;
      <a href="about.html">About</a> &middot;
      <a href="author.html">Author</a> &middot;
      <a href="downloads.html">Downloads</a> &middot;
      <a href="contact.html">Contact</a>
    </div>
    <h3>Subheading:</h3>
    <div class="eg" id="header">
      <h3>george l. mountainlion</h3>
      <h4>Born February 1952<br>Died March 8, 1955</h4>
    </div>
    <h3>First Line:</h3>
    <div class="eg" id="lion">
      <p>I freely give all signs and sounds of nature I
         have known to those who have the grace to enjoy
         not man-made materialism but God-made beauty.</p>
      <p>The magnificent Arizona sunsets I have watched
         from my enclosure, I bequeath to all who see
         not only with their eyes but with their hearts.</p>
    </div>
  </body>
</html>
```

As listed, the style sheet doesn't actually display any transformations because the style rules that use text-transform are commented out. This enables you to see the "before" view as shown in Figure 10.2.

By removing the lines containing the /* and */ markers (but not the rules between them), you can turn the transformations on, and the results are shown in Figure 10.3. The style examples used here are commonly found on the Web—many web designers enjoy putting navigation elements in all lowercase or uppercase text, and news sites frequently use all capital letters for sub-headlines and the first line of a story.

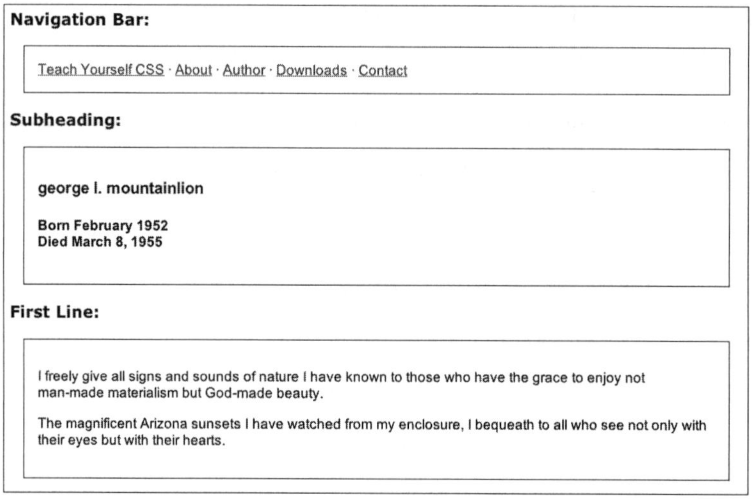

FIGURE 10.2
Example page
before text-
transform
rules are
applied.

Navigation Bar:

Teach Yourself CSS · About · Author · Downloads · Contact

Subheading:

george l. mountainlion

Born February 1952
Died March 8, 1955

First Line:

I freely give all signs and sounds of nature I have known to those who have the grace to enjoy not man-made materialism but God-made beauty.

The magnificent Arizona sunsets I have watched from my enclosure, I bequeath to all who see not only with their eyes but with their hearts.

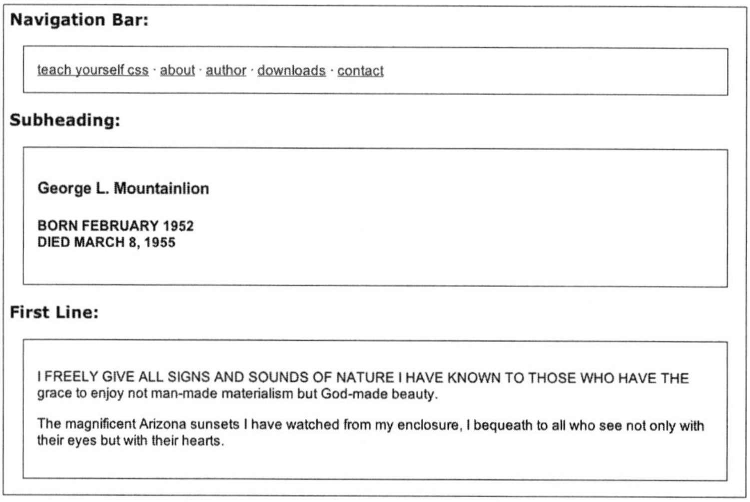

FIGURE 10.3
Example page
after text-
transform
rules are
applied.

Navigation Bar:

teach yourself css · about · author · downloads · contact

Subheading:

George L. Mountainlion

BORN FEBRUARY 1952
DIED MARCH 8, 1955

First Line:

I FREELY GIVE ALL SIGNS AND SOUNDS OF NATURE I HAVE KNOWN TO THOSE WHO HAVE THE grace to enjoy not man-made materialism but God-made beauty.

The magnificent Arizona sunsets I have watched from my enclosure, I bequeath to all who see not only with their eyes but with their hearts.

▼

Try it Yourself

Transform Text to Uppercase and Lowercase

It's one thing to look at a pair of screenshots, but another to actually see the effects of style rules yourself. Try out text-transform by doing the following steps:

1. Download a copy of the HTML file in Listing 10.2 from the book's website.

2. View the untransformed text in your web browser.

▼

3. Edit the file to remove the comments and reload, noting the changes.

4. Start changing the style rules. Make the headers all follow `text-transform: capitalize`. Change the navigation to uppercase.

5. Capitalize everything except the first letter of every #lion paragraph with rules that use `:first-letter` (from Hour 5, "Selectors") like this:

```
#lion { text-transform: uppercase; }
#lion p:first-letter { text-transform: lowercase; }
```

6. Get creative! View your page in your web browser to see how text-transform works. How can you incorporate text-transform into your own site designs?

Controlling Text Spacing

The display characteristics of the text can be controlled by a number of properties that affect the spaces between characters and words. These properties are less useful than many others, such as the font properties, but if you ever need to fine-tune your text display, these are the properties you will use.

The `letter-spacing` Property

All browsers use default spacing between letters; if there wasn't such a space, the letters would touch up against each other and would be nearly impossible to read. The `letter-spacing` property lets you adjust this space by increasing or decreasing the value of the default spacing. Values for `letter-spacing` are listed in Table 10.3; the default value is `normal`. If the letter-spacing property is set on the containing box, the value is inherited.

In typography, the space between letters is known as the *kerning*. Professionally typeset text often contains very subtle but important kerning effects. For example, the letters in most logos are not evenly spaced; varying the kerning can make text look a lot better. Usually this doesn't matter too much on the Web, but sometimes it is vitally important, especially to professional typesetters.

TABLE 10.3   Values for the `letter-spacing` Property

Value	Effect
normal	Don't insert extra spacing between letters.
measurement	Insert extra letter spacing.
negative measurement	Reduce spacing between letters.
inherit	Use the value of `letter-spacing` from the containing box.

The text-align property can also affect the letter-spacing; if text-align is set to justify, the browser automatically adjusts the space between letters so that the text can be justified. If the letter-spacing property is set to a measurement, such as 0.1em or 2px, the browser isn't allowed to change that space, even if it is justifying text.

The word-spacing **Property**

The word-spacing property is similar to the letter-spacing property, except, of course, that it controls the space between words. Browsers convert any whitespace (spaces, tabs, line breaks) to a single space and then display that space as a gap between words. The size of the space depends on the browser and the font; the word-spacing property adjusts from that initial size.

Values for word-spacing are shown in Table 10.4. If there is a value on a containing box, that will be inherited; otherwise, the default value is normal. Like letter-spacing, if a word-spacing value is set, the browser is not allowed to change the spacing even when the text-align value is justify.

TABLE 10.4   Values for the word-spacing **Property**

Value	Effect
normal	Don't insert extra spacing between words.
measurement	Insert extra word spacing.
negative measurement	Reduce spacing between words.
inherit	Use the value of word-spacing from the containing box.

Keep in mind that both letter-spacing and word-spacing add or subtract from the default browser spacing; they don't set it to that value. So if a browser normally has a space of 0.5 em between words, a word-spacing value of 0.3em will make the total gap 0.8 em, not 0.3 em. Examples of letter-spacing and word-spacing rules are shown in Listing 10.3.

LISTING 10.3   Styles Affecting Letter and Word Spacing

```
<!-- spacing-10.3.html -->
<html>
  <head>
    <title>Tips on Color Use</title>
    <style type="text/css">
      body { font-family: Verdana, sans-serif; }
      li { margin: 0.5em; }
      h1 { letter-spacing: 0.25em;
          word-spacing: 0.5em;
```

LISTING 10.3   Continued

```
        }
    li#a { word-spacing: 1.5em; }
    li#b { letter-spacing: 8px; }
    li#c { letter-spacing: -0.1em; }
    li#d { word-spacing: -0.3em; }
    </style>
  </head>
  <body>
    <h1>Tips on Color Use</h1>
    <ul>
      <li id="a">
        Use colors to visually emphasize important differences
        among types of content. The presentation of your
        content should be derived from the meaning of that
        information. Color your navigation bar differently
        from your main content. </li>
      <li id="b">
        Change colors for a reason, not on a whim. I've seen
        many websites where the developers appear to have
        discovered color just the day before and changed the
        color for no reason. Be able to justify your color
        choices.</li>
      <li id="c">
        Bright colors draw attention; faded colors hide
        unimportant material. As an example, if some content
        is more important or changes often, give it a
        vibrant, bright color, such as yellow or red, to make
        it stand out.</li>
      <li id="d">
        Too many colors will make your page seem confusing
        and unprofessional; a restricted set of hues often
        works better. If you don't have any experience with
        graphic design, pick up a good book on color and
        design, and notice that many great designs have a
        limited palette.</li>
    </ul>
  </body>
</html>
```

Each list item in this example has a different style for the word or letter spacing but the same font size, as shown in Figure 10.4.

The white-space Property

When displaying a web page, browsers condense all whitespace in the source and consider it as if there's only one space. This is *whitespace condensation*. If the content exceeds the width of the box allocated to that content, the browser simply moves down to the next line and continues with the rest of the text. This is called *word wrapping* because the new lines occur immediately before a new word.

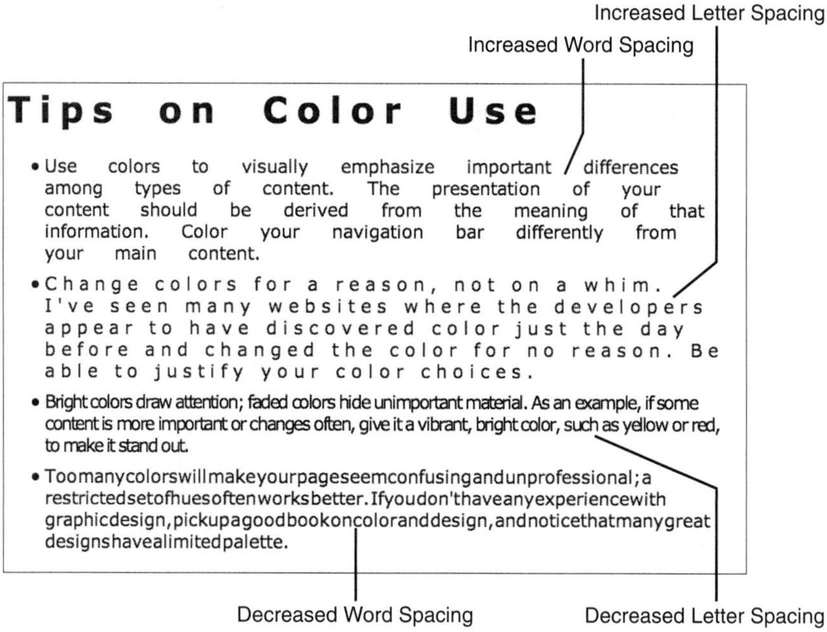

Increased Letter Spacing

Increased Word Spacing

FIGURE 10.4
Letter and word
spacing can
make a differ-
ence.

Tips   on   Color   Use

- Use colors to visually emphasize important / differences among types of content. The presentation of your content should be derived from the meaning of that information. Color your navigation bar differently from your main content.

- Change colors for a reason, not on a whim. / I've seen many websites where the developers appear to have discovered color just the day before and changed the color for no reason. Be able to justify your color choices.

- Bright colors draw attention; faded colors hide unimportant material. As an example, if some content is more important or changes often, give it a vibrant, bright color, such as yellow or red, to make it stand out.

- Toomanycolorswillmakeyourpageseemconfusingandunprofessional;a restrictedsetofhuesoftenworksbetter.Ifyoudon'thaveanyexperiencewith graphicdesign,pickupagoodbookoncoloranddesign,andnoticethatmanygreat designshavealimitedpalette.

Decreased Word Spacing   Decreased Letter Spacing

The white-space property enables you to control both the condensation of white-space and the word wrapping by setting the values shown in Table 10.5. The value of this property is inherited if it is set on a containing box; otherwise the default is normal.

TABLE 10.5   Values for the white-space **Property**

Value	Effect
normal	Do normal word wrapping and whitespace condensing.
nowrap	Condense whitespace, but don't wrap lines.
pre	Don't condense whitespace, and wrap lines as in the source markup.
pre-line	Don't condense whitespace, and wrap lines where there are line breaks in the source or at the end of the line.
pre-wrap	Condense whitespace, and wrap lines where there are line breaks in the source or at the end of a line.
inherit	Use the value of white-space from the containing box.

A value of nowrap means that the text won't have automatic lines inserted, and that can lead very long lines that force the browser to display horizontal scroll bars. The nowrap value is similar to the old <nobr> element, which was a nonstandard

HTML tag introduced by Netscape to prevent lines from breaking in the wrong place. The <nobr> tag was never adopted as an official part of the HTML standard; if you need that same effect, use a white-space: nowrap rule instead.

The value pre produces an effect quite similar to the <pre> tag in HTML, except that <pre> also sets the font to a monospace font. The white-space: pre declaration doesn't change the font-family unless you explicitly write a rule to that effect.

> The pre-line and pre-wrap values were introduced in the CSS 2.1 specification and aren't supported uniformly by the browsers, with the exception of Opera—which recognizes pre-wrap (but not pre-line).

Watch Out!

The HTML file in Listing 10.4 includes an embedded style sheet with white-space declarations.

LISTING 10.4   A Demonstration of white-space Values

```
<!-- white-space-10.4.html -->
<html>
  <head>
    <title>White-Space in Action</title>
    <style type="text/css">
      h1 { font-family: Verdana, sans-serif; }
      h2 { font-family: "Courier New", monospace; }
      p#a { white-space: nowrap; }
      p#b { white-space: pre;
            font-family: Verdana, sans-serif; }
    </style>
  </head>
  <body>
    <h1>White-Space in Action</h1>
    <h2>nowrap</h2>
    <p id="a">A value of <tt>nowrap</tt> means that the
       text won't have automatic lines inserted, and that
       can lead very long lines that force the browser
       to display horizontal scroll bars. </p>
    <h2>pre</h2>
    <p>You can use <tt>white-space: pre</tt> to display
       code samples. Unlike <tt>&lt;pre&gt;</tt>, the font
       isn't automatically monospaced.<p>
<p id="b">&lt;html&gt;
  &lt;head&gt;
    &lt;title&gt;Simple HTML Page&lt;/title&gt;
  &lt;/head&gt;
  &lt;body&gt;
    &lt;h1&gt;Simple HTML Page&lt;/h1&gt;
    &lt;p&gt;This is a basic HTML web page.&lt;/p&gt;
  &lt;/body&gt;
&lt;/html&gt;</p>
  </body>
</html>
```

Figure 10.5 shows how this page is displayed by a web browser. Notice that the nowrap value has caused the first paragraph to scroll off the screen to the right, creating a horizontal scrollbar.

FIGURE 10.5
The effects of the white-space property.

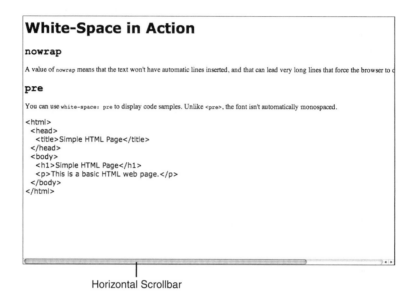

Horizontal Scrollbar

The line-height **Property**

The *line height* of a line of text is determined initially by the font-size property's value. Usually the line height is either the same as the font-size or a little larger, depending on the browser's internal rules for the line height.

The line-height property enables you to adjust the height of the line by using a value listed in Table 10.6. The value normal means that the the browser's usual methods should be used to calculate the line height; this is the default value. Usually browsers calculate line-height as equal to the font size times 1 or 1.2. A font that is 12pt tall will have a line height of 12pt to 14pt in most browsers.

TABLE 10.6   Values for the line-height Property

Value	Effect
normal	Use the default line height.
measurement	Set the line height to a particular value.
multiplier	Set the line height based on the font-size.
percentage	Set the line height based on the font-size.
inherit	Use the value of line-height from the containing box.

A *multiplier* is a normal number without any units, such as 1.5 or 3, which is multiplied by the font-size value. A multiplier of 1.5 means the same thing as a percentage of 150%, and is also the same as 1.5em.

The value of line-height is inherited from a containing box if the property is set; in most cases, the calculated value is inherited. For example, if the font-size is 18pt and the value of line-height is 200%, the calculated value 36pt will be inherited by children boxes. However, if a multiplier value such as 2 is set, that multiplier is passed on directly, and not the calculated value.

> Because the specification allows a browser some latitude in determining the default line height, you may not get identical line spacing across all browsers. You can force a specific line height by setting the line-height property, thus taking the decision out of the hands of the browser's default style sheet.

Did you Know?

Listing 10.5 is a set of style rules that can be applied to the HTML file in Listing 10.3 to change the line height of the list items; in Figure 10.6, this is displayed by a browser. Setting the line-height to a value based on the font-size, such as 2 or 200%, has the effect of spacing out the lines equally, assuming the font-size doesn't change; 200% is double-spacing. To double-space text that contains several different font sizes, you need to use an absolute measurement, such as 32px.

LISTING 10.5 Making Space with line-height

```
body { font-family: Verdana, sans-serif; }
li { margin: 0.5em; }
h1 { letter-spacing: 0.25em;
     word-spacing: 0.5em;
   }
li#a { line-height: 1.2; }
li#b { line-height: 0.8em; }
li#c { line-height: 2; }
li#d { line-height: 200%; }
```

You can also set the line-height value as part of the font property, which you learned about in Hour 9. When setting the font with the font shorthand property, include a slash after the font-size and indicate the desired line-height value. For example, to set a paragraph font that's 12-point Verdana with a line height of 200%, you'd write the following rule:

```
p { font: 12pt/200% Verdana, sans-serif; }
```

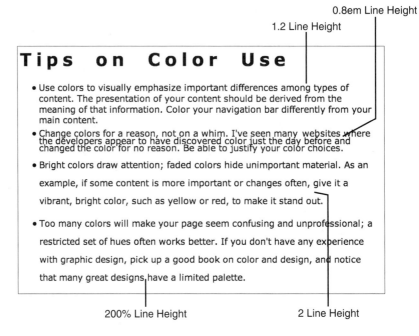

FIGURE 10.6
Spacing out
lines.

Summary

The foreground color of text can be set with the `color` property, as you've seen in previous hours. You can set the color value in several ways, including color names, long or short hexadecimal values, and the `rgb()` function.

Color is a powerful tool for visual communication, but you also need to take care to use it effectively. Consistency and simplicity will help your websites convey information better and produce a more professional look.

Other effects you can apply to your text include decorations such as underlines and strikethroughs using the `text-decoration` property and changes of case with `text-transform`.

Using the `letter-spacing` and `word-spacing` properties, you can fine-tune the display of your text, increasing or decreasing the gaps between letters and words. The `white-space` property controls both the condensation of whitespace and word wrapping. The `line-height` property can be used to double-space text or otherwise control the distance between each line.

Workshop

The workshop contains a Q&A section, quiz questions, and activities to help reinforce what you've learned in this hour. If you get stuck, the answers to the quiz can be found after the questions.

Q&A

Q. *I've heard someone mention "browser-safe colors" before. What is that?*

A. When web browsers were first created, they couldn't handle the full range of colors available. Instead, they displayed only a limited subset of specific colors—216 colors to be precise. Any other colors were displayed poorly, making some backgrounds and images look quite bad. These days, browsers can support a full range of color choices, so the browser-safe color list isn't as important, although you may want to look into it if you are supporting older hardware or software. For more information, see the VisiBone site at http://www.visibone.com/.

Q. *I really want to use* `text-decoration: blink`. *Can I?*

A. No.

Q. *Are you serious?*

A. Well, if you *have* to, you can use it. Keep in mind that blinking text is very hard to read and very distracting. Use it only if that's the only way you can get an effect; remember, though, that most browsers don't support it.

Q. *How can I set an exact value for* `letter-spacing` *or* `word-spacing`?

A. You can't; you can adjust it only from what the browser uses as a default. Fortunately, most browsers use sensible defaults, but there's no way to set an absolute value for letter or word spacing.

Quiz

1. Consider the color #FFFF00. How do you write this color in the following ways?

    a. Short hexadecimal

    b. RGB percentages

    c. RGB values

    d. Color names

2. You want to transform this text so that the first line is in uppercase, the second line is mixed case but with each letter capitalized, and the third is in lowercase. What CSS rules do you write?

```
<div id="a">CSS is fun.</div>
<div id="b">I use CSS each day.</div>
<div id="c">Do you like it too?</div>
```

3. The default word spacing in a hypothetical browser is 0.5 ems, and you'd like to put a full em between each word. Which of these declarations accomplishes that?

   a. word-spacing: 0.5em;

   b. word-spacing: 1em;

   c. word-spacing: 200%;

4. You want to space out each line of <p> text evenly so they are double-spaced, 16-point Arial font. How do you write this with a line-height rule, and how do you write it without using line-height?

Answers

1. Here are the alternate ways to write #FFFF00:

   a. #FF0

   b. rgb(100%, 100%, 0%)

   c. rgb(255, 255, 0)

   d. yellow

2. Here's how you transform that text:

```
#a { text-transform: uppercase; }
#b { text-transform: capitalize; }
#c { text-transform: lowercase; }
```

3. Declaration (a) produces a total word spacing of 1 em if the browser's default is 0.5 em, but remember that you can't set the exact value. If the browser's default is 0.75 em, (a) results in a gap of 1.25 em, and (b) produces a 1.75 em gap. Percentages, such as (c), aren't valid values for word-spacing.

4. Here's one way to write the line-height rule:

```
p { line-height: 200%; }
```

You could also write the same rule with a line-height value of 2, 2em, or even 32pt. Without using line-height, you'd use the font property:

```
p { font: 16pt/32pt Arial, sans-serif; }
```

Exercises

To get your hands dirty with text colors and formats, try these exercises; you'll know whether you've succeeded because you'll be able to see the desired effect.

1. Make a page with headings that contrast in color with the text. What color combinations work best?

2. See whether you can specify each color in more than one way; first try it with words, and then RGB values. Which approach is easier, and which is more flexible?

3. Turn off underlining of links on a page. Have someone else try to use it; is it easier or harder to use? Then try overlines.

4. Convert text to upper- or lowercase, using text-transform. In what circumstances would it be easier to simply change the text in the HTML rather than using CSS? You will discover that in some situations, text-transform is more convenient, and in others it's easier to just edit the source.

HOUR 11

Backgrounds and Background Colors

What You'll Learn in This Hour:

▶ More using about the `background-color` property
▶ How to use background and foreground colors together effectively
▶ How to set a background image and how to control the display of that background
▶ Which types of images you can use as backgrounds

In Hour 2, "Getting Started with CSS," you learned how to use the `background-color` property to change the appearance of HTML elements. Background colors can be used to good effect in web design to group related items together, or to highlight important parts of the page. In addition to pure colors, you can also use images as backgrounds for the whole page or for any element on the page.

Setting Background Color

As you've learned already, the `background-color` property is used to set the background of an HTML element and is written like this:

```
selector { background-color: color; }
```

This property is similar to the bgcolor attribute in HTML. The CSS version of background colors is a lot more useful, if just because it can be applied to anything. The bgcolor attribute can be set only on <body>, <table>, <tr>, <th>, and <td> tags. CSS selectors, such as class selectors, id selectors, and :link and :visited pseudo-class selectors, let you change the background colors for specific parts of the page.

The background-color **Property**

Like the foreground colors discussed in Hour 10, "Text Colors and Effects," a background-color can be specified in a number of ways: color name, RGB codes, triplets of numbers, or triplets of percentages. Here are some examples of background color declarations:

```
h1 { background-color: white; }
h2 { background-color: #FFFFFF; }
h3 { background-color: #FFF; }
h4 { background-color: rgb(255, 255, 255); }
h5 { background-color: rgb(100%, 100%, 100%); }
```

In addition to color values, background-color can take two other values: transparent and inherit.

The transparent value is actually the default for all elements; transparent means that whatever background already exists will be shown. So if a background-color of blue is set on the <body>, all elements that don't have a background-color setting are transparent and thus are blue. This actually isn't the same as inheriting the value because background-color doesn't naturally get inherited from the containing block.

If you really need the background-color property to inherit, you can use the value inherit. In practice, transparent and inherit almost always have the same effect, although there are a few cases when you'd need to use inherit instead of transparent. Remember that inherit is the same as setting a value equal to that of the containing block's value, whereas transparent just makes the background so that it can be seen through. It is the difference between painting the ceiling blue and installing a window on the roof. If the sky is blue anyway, they'll look about the same.

Backgrounds and Foregrounds

When you're setting background and foreground colors in CSS, it's very important to make sure that your color choices will be usable by your audience. You'll need to worry about both the *contrast* of your color choices and the *completeness* of your color declarations.

Lack of contrast between your foreground and background colors can make your page difficult for a variety of users to use. Those who have poor vision will struggle to see the letters, and users of limited or black-and-white displays may be left out as well. Printed pages can also suffer from contrast problems.

When considering contrast, you also have to take the needs of users with color blindness into account; if someone can't distinguish between red and green, they may not be able to make out your green heading on a red background.

It's not just users with specific disabilities who have problems with low contrast text; many people find text or images that have poor contrast to be harder to read. High contrast between foreground and background makes your site more useable by everyone, not just users with specific needs.

An excellent site for color advice is Bob Stein's VisiBone website at http://www.visibone.com/. Bob offers color charts as well as suggestions on testing your site for use by color-blind users. You can also check how users with color vision deficiencies view websites by visiting http://www.vischeck.com/.

In addition to contrast, you also have to consider completeness. By this I mean that if you specify a foreground color, you also need to specify a background color. Don't assume that all users have the same initial background and foreground colors that you do!

For example, let's say you write the following rule:

```
h1 { color: black;
     font-family: Verdana, sans-serif; }
```

Looks harmless, until you consider that the user's browser settings or style sheet may have set text to be white on a black background. Your <h1> becomes invisible black-on-black by this rule!

So if you want it to be visible, you have to set the background color explicitly whenever you set the foreground color—something like this:

```
h1 { color: black;
     background-color: white;
     font-family: Verdana, sans-serif; }
```

Using Background Images

In addition to using solid colors as your background, you can also use images. This is similar to using the background attribute of HTML; the background attribute can be set only on the <body> tag, but CSS allows you to set a background image on any element.

A background image can be of any type understood by the browser, which means most background images are GIFs or JPEGs (a few browsers also support PNG background images). Background images are more versatile than a solid color; for example, by using an image with a gradient, you can introduce fades and blends into your backgrounds. Photographic images used as backgrounds can often have a striking affect that can't be achieved with a solid RGB color. However, complex back-grounds also have their price: It is much harder to find text colors that will contrast well with a background image.

The `background-image` property is used to set a background image on an element. The browser loads the image and then displays it behind the foreground content as specified by the CSS properties `background-repeat`, `background-position`, and `background-attachment`. Transparent parts of the background image show the background color of the element (if any) or the background of the containing element.

In most cases, a background image *tiles*, which means that it repeats both horizon-tally and vertically across the box containing that element. A background image fills only the area inside the border (if any), which means the padding and the con-tent itself, as defined by the box model.

> Remember that to set a background image for the entire page, you just need to write a CSS rule for the <body> tag.

A good background image intended to tile both across and down should be created so that it doesn't have visible edges and seems to flow smoothly between one tile and another. If you're going to position text over the graphic, you should also make sure that it's not too busy; you should still be able to read text after that text is placed over the background.

For the examples in this hour, I created a very simple background graphic—a star field. I created a 100 pixel by 100 pixel black square, made a few dots in various colors, and saved it as `stars.gif`. The background image is shown in Figure 11.1.

I also created a simple HTML page with some content, so you can see the effects of using this background image behind text; the page contains the first few lines of the U.S. national anthem, the Star Spangled Banner; apologies to my non-American readers—it just seemed appropriate given the background graphic! Listing 11.1 shows this sample HTML page, which will be used for applying styles learned this chapter. You can download the full HTML listing from the book's website.

LISTING 11.1   The Sample HTML Page

```
<!-- anthem-11.1.html -->
<html>
  <head>
    <title> The Star Spangled Banner </title>
    <style type="text/css">
      /* insert style rules here */
    </style>
  </head>
```

LISTING 11.1 Continued

```
<body>
  <h1>The Star Spangled Banner</h1>
  <h2>By Francis Scott Key</h2>
  <h3>HTML markup by <a href="http://kynn.com/">Kynn Bartlett</a></h3>
  <p>
    Oh say, can you see, by the dawn's early light, <br>
    <!-- rest of the lines omitted here -->
  </p>
</body>
</html>
```

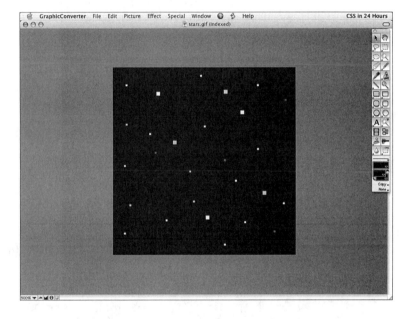

FIGURE 11.1
A star-spangled background image, enlarged for editing.

The background-image **Property**

Values for the background-image property are an image address URL, none, or inherit. URLs are indicated by the url() function around the address of the image. Quotes around the URL are optional and can be either single or double quotes (but they have to match); the following rules are all identical:

```
selector { background-image: url(image.gif); }
selector { background-image: url('image.gif'); }
selector { background-image: url("image.gif"); }
```

The URL is calculated relative to wherever the rule appears, not necessarily to the web page. For example, the page URL might be http://www.css24.com/author/index.php, and it links in an external style sheet located at http://www.css24.com/styles/site.css. A value in that style sheet, such as url("bg.gif"), refers to

something in the /styles/ directory, not the /author/ directory, because the url()
style rule is located in a file in /styles/.

However, if the same rule were part of an embedded style sheet or an inline style
attribute on the index.php page, it would reference something in the /author/
directory because it's all relative to the file that contains the rule.

When you set the background-image, you should set the foreground colors so that
they contrast with the background, just as you do when setting the
background-color. You should also designate a background-color that is roughly
equal to most of the background-image or at least one that contrasts well with the
foreground color. If the background-image can't be loaded, the background-color
is displayed instead. If you have a cloudy, sky-blue background-image, set your
color property to black (because that contrasts well with the light background) and
the background-color to something like #CCCCFF (light blue).

For example, here's a rule to set the stars.gif image as the background-image of
the page, along with the appropriate colors:

```
body       { background-image: url("stars.gif");
             background-color: black;
             color:            white; }
a:link     { color:            yellow; }
a:visited { color:            lime; }
```

You'll notice I set the a:link and a:visited colors as well; otherwise, my links
might not be visible against the dark background if they were left as the browser's
default (blue and purple, respectively). You can see these style rules applied to the
Star Spangled Banner page in Figure 11.2.

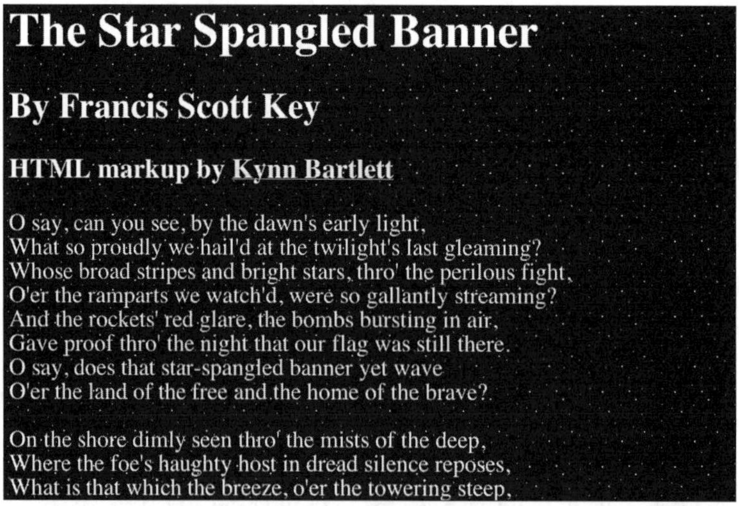

FIGURE 11.2
Oh say, can you
see the
stars.gif
background?

The Star Spangled Banner

By Francis Scott Key

HTML markup by Kynn Bartlett

O say, can you see, by the dawn's early light,
What so proudly we hail'd at the twilight's last gleaming?
Whose broad stripes and bright stars, thro' the perilous fight,
O'er the ramparts we watch'd, were so gallantly streaming?
And the rockets' red glare, the bombs bursting in air,
Gave proof thro' the night that our flag was still there.
O say, does that star-spangled banner yet wave
O'er the land of the free and the home of the brave?

On the shore dimly seen thro' the mists of the deep,
Where the foe's haughty host in dread silence reposes,
What is that which the breeze, o'er the towering steep,

As you can see, the image was tiled across and down the page and looks like it fills up the entire page with a star field.

As noted earlier, you can set background images on any element, not just the <body>. This lets you set a background on paragraphs, <div> tags, or any other HTML tags. For example, these rules set the background-image on headline elements:

```
body       { background-color: white;
                    color:            black; }
    h1, h2, h3 { background-image: url("stars.gif");
                    background-color: black;
                    color:            white; }
    h1         { padding: 0.5em; }
    h2, h3     { padding: 0.25em; }
    a:link     { color:            yellow; }
    a:visited  { color:            lime; }
```

I've added padding here to make it easier to see the effects of the background behind the text. Apply these rules and you get a different look to the page, as shown in Figure 11.3.

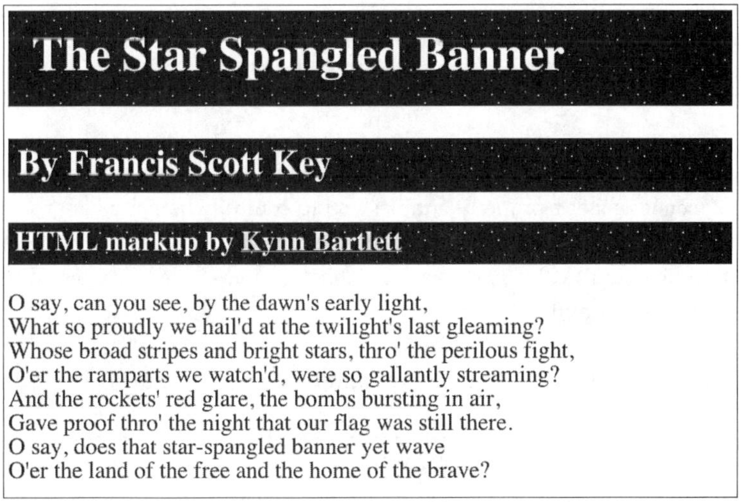

FIGURE 11.3
Background
images behind
<h1>, <h2>, and
<h3>.

Inline elements as well as block elements can have backgrounds; here's a set of rules that just make the star field appear behind links:

```
body       { background-color: white;
             color:            black; }
a:link     { background-image: url("stars.gif");
             background-color: black;
             padding:          0.5em;
             color:            cyan; }
```

```
a:visited { background-image: url("stars.gif");
            background-color: black;
            padding:          0.5em;
            color:            violet; }
```

You can see these styles at work in Figure 11.4.

FIGURE 11.4
Inline background image.

The Star Spangled Banner

By Francis Scott Key

HTML markup by Kynn Bartlett

O say, can you see, by the dawn's early light,
What so proudly we hail'd at the twilight's last gleaming?
Whose broad stripes and bright stars, thro' the perilous fight,
O'er the ramparts we watch'd, were so gallantly streaming?
And the rockets' red glare, the bombs bursting in air,
Gave proof thro' the night that our flag was still there.
O say, does that star-spangled banner yet wave
O'er the land of the free and the home of the brave?

On the shore dimly seen thro' the mists of the deep,
Where the foe's haughty host in dread silence reposes,
What is that which the breeze, o'er the towering steep,

The background-repeat Property

The background-repeat property enables you to control whether or not the background image tiles across the screen. Values for background-repeat are shown in Table 11.1; the default value is repeat, and background-repeat values do not inherit from the containing block.

TABLE 11.1   Values for the background-repeat Property

Value	Effect
repeat	Tile horizontally and vertically
repeat-x	Tile only horizontally (along the X-axis)
repeat-y	Tile only vertically (along the Y-axis)
no-repeat	Display the image only once, with no tiling
inherit	Inherit the background-repeat value of the containing block

It's easier to demonstrate these in action rather than explain them in text, so let's look at how you use background-repeat. Listing 11.2 is a style sheet that sets a horizontally repeating background on the <body>, which puts a band of stars across the top of the page.

LISTING 11.2 A repeat-x Background Image

```
/* stars-11.2.css */
    body { background-color: gray;
           background-image: url("stars.gif");
           color: white;
           background-repeat: repeat-x; }
```

In this example, you'll notice I set the background color to gray; this makes it easier to see where the black image starts and stops. I had to choose a color that would be dark enough to show the white text, but light enough to contrast with the black of the starfield. Figure 11.5 shows this style sheet applied to the HTML page in Listing 11.1.

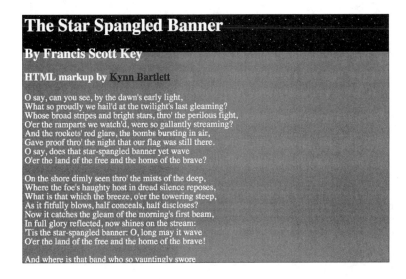

FIGURE 11.5
Horizontal tiling of the background image.

To tile the figure vertically, you use the background-repeat value of repeat-y, as in Listing 11.3.

LISTING 11.3 A repeat-y Background Image

```
/* stars-11.3.css */
    body { background-color: gray;
           background-image: url("stars.gif");
           color: white;
           background-repeat: repeat-y; }
```

This creates a stripe down the left side, as shown in Figure 11.6. In the next section of this hour, you'll learn how you can use the background-position property to move the stripes created by repeat-x and repeat-y.

FIGURE 11.6
Vertical tiling of
the background
image.

The Star Spangled Banner

By Francis Scott Key

HTML markup by Kynn Bartlett

O say, can you see, by the dawn's early light,
What so proudly we hail'd at the twilight's last gleaming?
Whose broad stripes and bright stars, thro' the perilous fight,
O'er the ramparts we watch'd, were so gallantly streaming?
And the rockets' red glare, the bombs bursting in air,
Gave proof thro' the night that our flag was still there.
O say, does that star-spangled banner yet wave
O'er the land of the free and the home of the brave?

On the shore dimly seen thro' the mists of the deep,
Where the foe's haughty host in dread silence reposes,
What is that which the breeze, o'er the towering steep,

If you don't want the image to repeat at all, use the background-repeat value of
no-repeat, as in Listing 11.4. You use this value whenever you want a single placement of an image, such as a watermark or a very large background that shouldn't
be repeated. See Figure 11.7.

LISTING 11.4   A Nonrepeating Background Image

```
/* stars-11.4.css */
    body { background-color: gray;
           background-image: url("stars.gif");
           color: white;
           background-repeat: no-repeat; }
```

Did you Know?

When an image doesn't repeat or repeats only in one direction, you can worry less
about the sides of the image matching up properly when it tiles. A no-repeat
image doesn't wrap around, so there's no need to blend the top and bottom, or
the left and right, into each other smoothly.

The background-position **Property**

As you can see in Figure 11.7, a background image is placed in the upper-left corner
of the element box it is styling. If tiling occurs, either by default or because of the
background-repeat property setting, the image reproduces itself to the left and
right horizontally, or up and down vertically—or both—from that starting position.

You can change the location of the initial image by using the
background-position property. A background-position value consists of two size
values or percentages: one indicating the horizontal position and the second indicating the vertical. If only one value is given, it sets the horizontal position.

FIGURE 11.7
The background
image without
tiling.

A size value for background-position is a number and a unit, such as 30px or 4em;
this tells where the initial image's upper-left corner is to be placed.

A percentage value indicates how far over the image should be aligned; 50% means
that the center of the image (horizontally or vertically) aligns with the center of the
element being styled. A pair of values, such as 75% 25%, means the spot on the
image that's 75% over from the left horizontally and 25% down from the top should
be matched with the corresponding location in the element's box.

In addition to sizes and percentages, word values can be used for background-position; these are shown in Table 11.2. Values can be combined together; right
center means 100% 50%, for example. However, if only one word value is given, the
second value is assumed to be center. Word values can be listed in either order, so
bottom left is the same as left bottom.

You can use the background-position property to place repeating stripes across
or down your page in conjunction with the background-repeat property. A single
faint image can be used as a watermark with the background-repeat value of
no-repeat and the background-position of center center.

The default value of this property is top left, which is the same as 0% 0%. Like background-repeat, this property's value is not inherited from the containing block.

TABLE 11.2   Values for the background-position **Property**

Value	Effect
size size	Place the image at the specified location
percent% percent%	Place the image proportionally
top	Corresponds to 50% 0%
left	Corresponds to 0% 50%
right	Corresponds to 100% 50%
bottom	Corresponds to 50% 100%
center	Corresponds to 50% 50%
top left	Corresponds to 0% 0%
top center	Same as top (50% 0%)
top right	Corresponds to 100% 0%
left center	Same as left (0% 50%)
center center	Same as center (50% 50%)
right center	Same as right (100% 50%)
bottom left	Corresponds to 0% 100%
bottom center	Same as bottom (50% 100%)
bottom right	Corresponds to 100% 100%

Listing 11.5 uses the background-position property to place an image that is set to tile horizontally.

LISTING 11.5   A Positioned, Repeating Background Image

```
/* stars-11.5.css */
    body { background-color: gray;
           background-image: url("stars.gif");
           color: white;
           background-repeat: repeat-x;
           background-position: 0% 33%; }
```

As shown in Figure 11.8, when this style sheet is applied to Listing 11.1's HTML page, the effect is a stripe across the page.

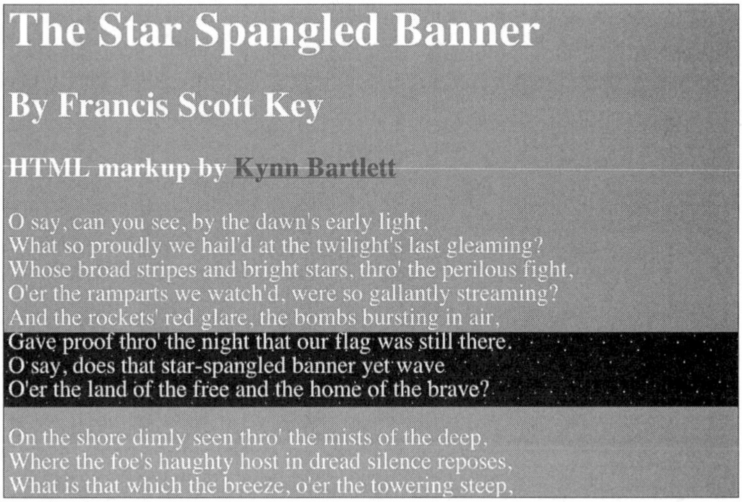

The Star Spangled Banner

By Francis Scott Key

HTML markup by Kynn Bartlett

O say, can you see, by the dawn's early light,
What so proudly we hail'd at the twilight's last gleaming?
Whose broad stripes and bright stars, thro' the perilous fight,
O'er the ramparts we watch'd, were so gallantly streaming?
And the rockets' red glare, the bombs bursting in air,
Gave proof thro' the night that our flag was still there.
O say, does that star-spangled banner yet wave
O'er the land of the free and the home of the brave?

On the shore dimly seen thro' the mists of the deep,
Where the foe's haughty host in dread silence reposes,
What is that which the breeze, o'er the towering steep,

FIGURE 11.8
Placing an image with background-position.

The background-attachment **Property**

Normally, images scroll with the rest of the page; however, you can change that by using the background attachment property. This property can take three values: scroll, fixed, or inherit. The default value is scroll, and the property's value is not inherited from the containing block unless the value is explicitly set to inherit.

A background-attachment value of fixed means that the image doesn't move relative to the original position of the page, even if this means it might not be displayed because the element being styled is not on the screen or is not within the region where the background image could be seen (as determined from the background-repeat and background-attachment properties). If the value of background-attachment is fixed, the location of the image is placed relative to the whole page, not to the element being styled.

You can see an example of using a fixed background image in Listing 11.6. This is a repeating stripe across the top of the page, which won't move even when the page is scrolled up or down.

LISTING 11.6 Style Sheet for a Fixed Background

```
/* stars-11.6.css */
    body { background-color: gray;
          background-image: url("stars.gif");
          color: white;
          background-repeat: repeat-x;
          background-position: top left;
          background-attachment: fixed; }
```

In Figure 11.9, I've scrolled down a little with the scrollbar, but the background image remains at the top of the page where I placed it. You can test this yourself by viewing the page at the book's website; you can also download the HTML page, style sheet, and image, for local viewing.

FIGURE 11.9
A fixed background doesn't scroll from its original position even when you scroll the page.

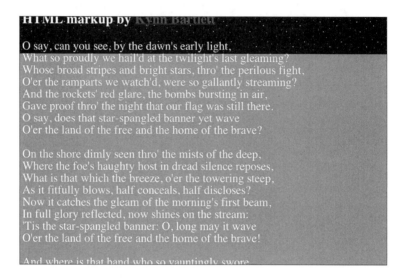

Watch Out!

Fixed backgrounds are supposed to be placed relative to the page even when set on boxes within the page; however, Internet Explorer positions them relative to the box of the element being styled. For this reason, it's usually best to set the style rules for watermarks or other fixed background images on the <body> tag, or another HTML element that's the same size as the whole page (such as an outermost <div>).

The background **Shorthand Property**

Like the font property, background is a shorthand property that enables you to set several properties at once. By using background, you can set the background-color, the background-image, the background-repeat, the background-position, and the background-attachment. Simply list the values you want (in any order) as the value for background; any values you don't set are set to their default values.

The CSS rules used to create Figure 11.9 can be rewritten like this:

```
body { color: white;
       background: url("stars.gif") repeat-x
                   fixed top left gray; }
```

Create a Web Page Watermark

Let's put together everything you've learned in this chapter and create a practical example: A transparent, fixed position watermark for a web page.

1. Create a watermark image, using a graphics program. This should be something light enough that your text can be seen over it. Figure 11.10 shows a rather tongue-in-cheek light blue watermark I created.

FIGURE 11.10
Surely you can do better than this.

2. Write a style sheet, using the image you created in step one. Set the image as a background using a rule like this:

```
background-image: url("watermark.gif");
```

3. Center it on your page with this kind of style rule:

```
background-position: center center;
```

4. Make sure it doesn't repeat:

```
background-repeat: no-repeat;
```

▼

5. Prevent it from scrolling:

   ```
   background-attachment: fixed;
   ```

6. Set the background for the rest of the page:

   ```
   background-color: white;
   ```

7. Now, show off by replacing all those rules with a single background shorthand property rule!

Summary

The background of any element can be set with the background-color and background-image properties. When using backgrounds, make sure there is contrast between the colors you're using (including image colors), and also ensure that you've set the foreground colors as well.

The tiling, position, and scrolling of the background image can be set with the background-repeat, background-position, and background-attachment properties. All the background properties can be set at once with the background shorthand property.

Workshop

The workshop contains a Q&A section, quiz questions, and exercises to help reinforce what you've learned in this hour. If you get stuck, the answers to the quiz can be found after the questions.

Q&A

Q. *What if I want a graphic to tile across the page horizontally and vertically, forming a "T" or "L" shape instead of filling the whole page? Can that be done?*

A. Yes, but it's kind of tricky. Here's how you do it: Add a <div> tag just inside the <body> of your page; have it contain all the content you'd normally put in <body> and give it an id attribute. Then use the transparent value for background-color, like this:

```
body { background: gray url("stars.gif") repeat-x;
       padding: 0px;
       margin: 0px; }
div#mydiv { background: transparent url("stars.gif")
```

```
                    center repeat-y;
          color: white;
          padding: 0.5em; }
```

This makes a T-shaped star background. The `padding` and `margin` adjustments are necessary to remove the default padding and margin the browsers put on `<body>` and add them back in for the `<div>`.

Q. *Why doesn't the order matter for the* `background` *shorthand property? That seems confusing. Shouldn't they be in some specific order?*

A. Nope. Because the properties set by the shorthand property all have completely different types of values that can be assigned to them, it's pretty easy for a browser to figure out that, for example, the value `green` must go with `background-color` and the value `url("stars.gif")` with `background-image`.

Quiz

1. Which of these values for `background-position` places the background image at the middle and bottom of the styled element's display box?

    a. `bottom center`

    b. `center bottom`

    c. `bottom`

    d. `50% 100%`

2. You have an image named `skyblue.jpg`; it's a graphic that looks like a blue sky with a few wispy clouds. The color is closest to `rgb(75%, 75%, 100%)`. You want it to tile down the right side of the page, and the background image shouldn't scroll when the page scrolls. The rest of the page will be white; all your text will be black or other colors that contrast against the background. What CSS rule would you write, using the `background` shorthand property?

Answers

1. Trick question! They all do; they're all the same value.

2. Because you want the rest of the page to be white, the RGB values of the sky don't matter that much; your black text will contrast nicely with either white or light blue. Therefore, the rule can be written like this:

```
body { background: url("skyblue.jpg") white
                   right top repeat-y fixed; }
```

Exercises

The best way to understand background colors and images is to get some hands-on practice. Create yourself a test page, an image or two, and a style sheet. Try the following exercises:

1. Position the graphic in each corner of the page.

2. Tile the graphic along each edge of the page.

3. Set backgrounds on inline and block elements besides just <body>. Make them scroll or tile!

HOUR 12

Styling Links

What You'll Learn in This Hour:

▶ What pseudo-selectors let you designate effects for active links, mouse hovers, and an element focus

▶ Which order pseudo-classes follow for link styling and inheritance

▶ How to create some of the most common link effects, including replacing the attributes on the <body> tag, removing underlines, and creating dynamic mouseovers

The capability to make hyperlinks is what enables the interconnectedness of the Web; HTML itself is named for the hypertext links. Cascading Style Sheets can be used to style these links beyond the default blue-underlined-text. You've already learned how to use :link and :visited pseudo-classes to create CSS rules for link presentation in Hour 5, "Selectors," and this hour expands on that knowledge and gives you additional types of selectors and style rules to use with links.

CSS for Link Styling

The style rules you write to affect hypertext links are much the same as other CSS rules: You identify the elements to be styled by using a selector, and you write property declarations describing how you want the elements to appear. So why spend a whole hour on links?

One reason is that rules for hypertext links require extensive use of pseudo-selectors, whereas most other rules don't. You can't just use the element name alone and get full functionality; you need to write your rules with a:link and a:visited selectors. In this hour, you'll learn about three more pseudo-classes, as well—:active, :hover, and :focus.

Link styles are very dependent upon the state of the user interface; what the user is doing and has done is at least as important as the content. That's not the case with most styles. You don't have to worry about your paragraph text changing state after the styles have been applied to it. Links require dynamic reapplication of the cascade and inheritance rules as the page is used.

One more reason that links are set off with their own hour is that questions about them are among those most commonly asked by people learning CSS. Underlines, mouseovers, and special effects on links are some of the coolest simple style effects you can add to a site, along with colors and fonts. Links are active styles, and the pseudo-classes used with them can add unexpected pleasant touches to a page, if done properly.

The `:link` and `:visited` **Pseudo-Classes**

Although you learned about a:link and a:visited selectors in Hour 5, we revisit them briefly here. The :link state and the :visited state are *mutually exclusive*, which means that either one or the other applies, but not both. Neither inherits property values from the other; if you set a style property on a:link, the same property isn't set on a:visited. You'd need to write two rules (or one rule with a combined selector).

A rule based on the <a> tag is applied to <a> links, visited or unvisited. They also are used on anchors set with the <a name="anchor"> syntax. So if you want your links to all have a yellow background, you're better off with a rule based on a:link and a:visited instead of a by itself, or else your anchor points will be yellow, too.

Other styles set on the box holding the <a> tag are inherited normally if those properties usually inherit. So the font-family and font-size properties, for example, are inherited from whatever element contains the link tag.

One exception is the default styling on links. Unless explicitly set by a CSS rule to something else, your links will look like whatever the browser thinks they should look like. At least, that's true when it comes to two specific properties: color and text-decoration. The accepted practice is to make unvisited links blue, visited links purple, and both kinds of links underlined. Effectively, browsers have a built-in set of style rules that look like this (although user preferences can change the specifics):

```
a:link             { color: blue; }
a:visited          { color: purple; }
a:link, a:visited { font-decoration: underline; }
```

To change these default styles, you need to override these style rules explicitly with more specific ones of your own. Remember that the cascade counts pseudo-classes as classes, and it gives priority to author styles over browser default styles; that means that your a:link rule will win out.

The `:active` Pseudo-Class

An *active link* is a link that's in the process of being activated by the user in some way. How this activation occurs is dependent on the type of input and output media used. Usually this means that a mouse pointer has clicked on the link and the page is about to be replaced by a new one reached by following the link. This corresponds to the HTML attribute `alink`, which can be set on the `<body>` tag (although `alink` can change only the color, whereas a CSS rule can do far more). Browsers usually display this as if the following rule were in its default style sheet:

```
a:active { color: red; }
```

The `:active` state is not mutually exclusive with `:link` or `:visited`. In fact, any link that is `:active` is undoubtedly going to be one or the other: visited or unvisited. Property values set on the `:link` or `:visited` state are inherited by the `:active` element, as appropriate for each value. For example, if you've already declared that there should be no underlines in your `a:link` and `a:visited` rules, you don't need to worry about declaring `text-decoration: none;` in the `a:active` rule if you want active links to continue to be underlined.

Cascading is also a consideration. If there's a property value conflict between an `a:link` and `a:active` rule, which one wins according to the cascade order? Well, they have the same origin (your style sheet), the same number of `id` attributes (none, presumably), the same number of classes or pseudo-classes, and the same number of elements, which means it's a tie. Therefore, the winner is whichever one is declared last, according to the source code. In practice, this means that you should put your `a:active` rule after your `a:link` and `a:visited` links.

You can combine together two or more pseudo-class selectors by simply chaining them together without spaces, like this:

```
a:link              { color: blue;
                      background-color: white; }
a:link:active       { color: white;
                      background-color: blue; }
a:visited           { color: purple;
                      background-color: white; }
a:visited:active    { color: white;
                      background-color: purple; }
```

These rules display unvisited and visited links in blue or purple as usual, but when the link is clicked, the colors invert while the page is loading. Combined selectors let you make sure the colors are kept straight. If you didn't write a rule with two pseudo-classes, you'd have to choose either blue or purple as the color you'd use, like this:

```
a:active { color: white; background-color: purple; }
```

The :hover **Pseudo-Class**

Hovering means that the mouse pointer has been positioned over a particular element, but the user has not necessarily clicked a button to activate it. In HTML, this state triggers a mouseover event, which can invoke JavaScript functions set on the onMouseOver attribute; when the mouse is no longer hovering, that's an onMouseOut event.

The CSS approach is to add the state of :hover to any other states currently on the element (such as :link or :visited) and apply an appropriate style. You can change the color, of course, but you can also change the background properties, border, font-family, font-size, or anything else you like. Some of these changes may cause the dimensions of displayed boxes to change, which can be distracting because the page has to redraw itself and shift about as someone moves the mouse, so you probably should avoid major changes such as padding or display.

Here's an example of the :hover rule in action. I want to make my links change color and background-color when the user moves the mouse. This points out which link will be followed if the user clicks—a typical mouseover function. Listing 12.1 has an embedded style sheet in the HTML for this example.

LISTING 12.1   **A Simple Question that Hovers Ominously**

```
<!-- game-12.1.html -->
<html>
  <head>
    <title>Want to play a game?</title>
    <style type="text/css">
      body {
        background-color: black;
        color:           lime;
        font:            xx-large Verdana, sans-serif; }
      a:link, a:visited {
        color:           lime;
        text-decoration: none; }
      a:hover {
        background-color: white;
        color:            black; }
    </style>
  </head>
  <body>
    <h1>Want to play a game?</h1>
    <h1>
      <a href="yes.html">yes</a> /
      <a href="no.html">no</a>
    </h1>
  </body>
</html>
```

Figure 12.1 shows what this looks like in a browser; unlike most of the screenshots in this book, I've included the mouse pointer so you can see where it is. The no option is in black-on-white text when the mouse is over it, and when the mouse is elsewhere, it turns back to lime-on-black.

The CSS specifications are very vague on which HTML tags must be able to take on the :hover state. Can you set a rule with a selector like h1:hover and then change the styling on the <h1> tag whenever the mouse is moved over it? Good question. At the present time, you can't; only items that can be clicked can enter the :hover state in current browsers.

If you want to add mouseover effects to other items, you can use the HTML event attributes and JavaScript. For example, the following bit of HTML code creates an <h1> tag that changes color when the mouse moves over it:

```
<h1 onmouseover="style.color = 'blue';"
    onmouseout="style.color = 'red';"
    style="color: red; background-color: white;"
    >Superman</h1>
```

Did you Know?

The :focus **Pseudo-Class**

If you can type something into an HTML element, that element is said to have the *focus*. Focus is an indication of something that's been selected but not necessarily activated. The focus is often indicated by a light dashed line or by a colored glow around part of the page.

Being able to identify the current focus is important for keyboard access to the Web. Web surfers who aren't able to use a mouse use the tab key to move from link to link or to <form> field tags, such as <input> and <textarea>. The HTML tabindex attribute can affect the order of tabbing.

When an element receives the focus, it enters the :focus state and applicable styles are applied. In the example from Listing 12.1, the background and foreground colors don't change if someone tabs through the links; they change only if the mouse is used. Because you want to serve all your web users—not just those with mice!—you need to add the following rules to the style sheet:

```
a:focus {
  background-color: white;
  color:           black; }
```

> Not all browsers support the :focus pseudo-class. You can use the same JavaScript techniques as already described for :hover, but you should use the onFocus attribute when the element comes into focus and the onBlur attribute when it loses focus.

It's possible for an element to be in a state of :active, :hover, and :focus all at the same time; none of them are mutually exclusive. An <a> link is either :link or :visited as well. You should put your :active, :hover, and :focus rules after the :link and :visited rules because of the order of the cascade and inheritance.

Common Link-Styling Techniques

The rest of this hour, I'll show you how to do some of the most common tasks related to styling links. Think of this section as a small cookbook with some key recipes. Armed with these and with your growing knowledge of CSS, you can improvise on your own sites, creating your own style sheet culinary masterpieces.

Replacing HTML <body> Attributes

The <body> tag in HTML lets you set a number of attributes that affect the appearance of the entire page. Now you can replace those with CSS rules and go further than the capabilities of HTML because you can fine-tune parts of the page separately by using selectors and by having better control over backgrounds and link styles.

Here's a typical <body> tag:

```
<body background="mybg.jpg" bgcolor="#FFFFCC"
      text="#000066" link="red" vlink="#999999"
      alink="#FFCC99">
```

As you can see, this uses presentational HTML attributes—the `background`, `bgcolor`, `text`, `link`, `vlink`, and `alink` attributes—to control the colors and background image on the page. This works in current browsers, but from a CSS point of view, it's a poor idea because the presentation is mixed in with the markup, and that always makes things harder, not easier. For example, if you want to change the appearance of the entire site at once, you need to go into every single HTML file and edit the attributes, but if you are using a linked style sheet, it's just a minor tweak to a single style sheet file.

So, how do you write the `<body>` tag with Cascading Style Sheets rules? Something like this would work:

```
body { background: #FFFFCC url("mybg.jpg");
       color: #000066; }
a:link { color: red; }
a:visited { color: #999999; }
a:active { color: #FFCC99; }
```

Removing Underlines

This seems to be one of the first questions web developers want to know: How do I turn off the underlines? If you've been reading this book straight through from beginning to end, you learned about the `text-decoration` property in Hour 10, "Text Colors and Effects." However, in case you jumped directly to this chapter, we'll review and summarize here.

You remove underlines by using the `text-decoration` property with a value of `none`. Here's an example:

```
.navbar a:link,
.navbar a:visited
  { text-decoration: none; }
```

> **By the Way**
>
> Several important cautions were mentioned in Hour 10 about the effect on usability if you remove link underlines; you may want to go back and read that section if it's not fresh in your mind.

Removing underlines from links can be relatively easy. The bigger question is how will you replace them? The reason that links were underlined in the first place was to make them stand out so the web user doesn't have to randomly guess what can be clicked and what can't. Here are some ideas, which can be used separately or in combination:

▶ Use very bright colors, set with the `color` property, to make links that much more visible. Links should stand out from the rest of the page and should be easily seen.

▶ Put borders around the links by using the `border` property so that the links are in boxes. Boxes can draw attention, as color does.

▶ Employ the `font-weight` property to make your links stand out better. Bold links likewise catch the eye; I have used `font-weight: bold` for unvisited links and `font-weight: normal` for visited links when designing styles for certain sites.

▶ Make all links italic (or oblique) by using `font-style`, or put them in small caps with `text-transform`. Be careful about readability, though; excessive use of this technique can make your navigation hard to use.

▶ Add a background color to your links with the `background-color` property. This can often give an effect similar to a highlighter pen; make sure your background stands out against both the visited and unvisited link colors.

▶ Utilize `class` or `id` selectors to give different styles to different kinds of links; for example, style offsite links differently from local links. Likewise, use different styles for inline links in the body of your text and for navigation links located in a sidebar.

Mouseover Effects

A mouseover effect can be as simple as swapping the colors, as you've seen earlier in this hour, or as subtle as adding the underline back on a mouseover, as follows:

```
a:link, a:visited { text-decoration: none; }
a:hover { text-decoration: underline; }
```

You can also head for the other extreme and get pretty complex. Here's an example of making buttons with CSS and making those buttons change when the mouse rolls over them, all without using JavaScript. Listing 12.2 is the HTML file to be styled, and Listing 12.3 is the style sheet. In this example, I'm using tables for layout, but in Hour 20, "Page Layout in CSS," you'll learn how to lay out a page with pure CSS.

LISTING 12.2   An HTML Page with a Navigation Bar

```
<!-- buttons-12.2.html -->
<html>
  <head>
    <title>About the Local Writers Group</title>
    <link type="text/css" rel="stylesheet"
        href="buttons-12.3.css">
  </head>
  <body>
    <table width="100%" border="0">
      <tr><td valign="top" align="center" width="150">
        <div class="navbar">
```

LISTING 12.2   Continued

```
          <a href="/">Home</a>
          <a href="about.html">About Us</a>
          <a href="writers.html">Writers</a>
          <a href="links.html">Links</a>
          <a href="map.html">Map</a>
          <a href="calendar.html">Calendar</a>
          <a href="contact.html">Contact</a>
        </div>
      </td><td valign="top">
        <h1>About Us</h1>
        <p>The Local Writers Group is an informal group of
          writers who meet <a href="calendar.html">every other
          Wednesday evening</a> from 7:30 to 9:00, at the
          bookstore near the mall.</p>
        <p>If you'd like to attend, just stop by for the next
          meeting, or <a href="contact.html">drop a note via
          email</a> to one of our members.</p>
    </td></tr></table>
  </body>
</html>
```

LISTING 12.3   Style Sheet with Mouseover Effects

```
/* buttons-12.3.css */

body    { font-family: Verdana, sans-serif;
          color: black; background-color: white; }
h1      { color: navy; }

/* link colors */
.nav a:link    { color: yellow; }
.nav a:visited { color: lime; }

/* link buttons */
.nav a:link, .nav a:visited
      { font: bold 12pt Verdana, sans-serif;
        padding: 0.5em; margin: 0.5em;
        display: block; text-decoration: none;
        background: url("button.gif") transparent 50% 50% no-repeat; }

/* change the button on hover and focus */
.nav a:hover, .nav a:focus
      { background-image: url("button_yellow.gif");
        color: black; }
.nav a:visited:hover, .nav a:visited:focus
      { background-image: url("button_green.gif");
        color: black; }
```

The three button images used are shown in Figure 12.2, and the final effect can be seen in Figure 12.3. When the mouse is moved over the navigation bar, the glow graphic is used. You'll notice that I used an a:hover:visited rule, as well, so that visited links glow lime green instead of yellow.

FIGURE 12.2
Background
graphics for
making buttons.

FIGURE 12.3
Mouseovers in
action, with the
mouse over
"Map."

▼

Try it Yourself

Link Buttons in CSS

The technique shown here can be used to make buttons quickly and easily, without
having to create each one in a graphics program. Try this:

▼

1. Make a default blank button in a graphics program, or download one from the Web.

2. Using the file from Listing 12.2 or your own web page, employ styles to use the blank button in your navigation menu. Use Listing 12.3 as an example.

3. Try changing the font size of the text links. What happens if the text is too big for a button?

4. Create (or download) a button with a mouseover effect, such as a glow or outline.

5. Change the colors of your links text. How does it contrast with your button you've chosen? Make sure your links are readable when moused over, when visited, and when the page is newly loaded.

Summary

CSS rules for styling hypertext links use the same properties as other style rules but extensively utilize pseudo-class selectors. These pseudo-class selectors track the state of various qualities—:link and :visited depend on web browsing history; :active, :hover, and :focus depend on the user's interaction with the page.

Link styles can be used to replace the <body> attributes in HTML, remove links, and even create complex mouseover effects without requiring JavaScript. Armed with your growing knowledge of CSS, you can now confidently apply styles to your hypertext links.

Workshop

The workshop contains a Q&A section, quiz questions, and activities to help reinforce what you've learned in this hour. If you get stuck, the answers to the quiz can be found after the questions.

Q&A

Q. *Now that I know CSS, I can throw away all those* <body> *attributes, such as* vlink *and* bgcolor, *right?*

A. Well, probably. If you are using the Strict versions of HTML or XHTML, you have to remove them for your markup to be valid anyway. On the other hand, there are a few old browsers still out there that understand only the <body> attributes, and it probably can't hurt to include presentation markup.

Q. *What about those annoying blue borders around image links? How do I get rid of those?*

A. How about this?

```
a:link img, a:visited img { border: 0px; }
```

Quiz

1. Which of these rules makes the text bold when the user tabs to a link with the keyboard?

    a. `a:visited { font-weight: 700; }`

    b. `a:hover { font-weight: 700; }`

    c. `a:active { font-weight: 700; }`

    d. `a:focus { font-weight: 700; }`

    e. `a:active:hover { font-weight: 700; }`

2. How would you rewrite this <body> tag as CSS rules?

```
<body text="white" background="stars.gif"
      bgcolor="black" link="#00FFFF"
      vlink="#FF00FF" alink="#FFFF00">
```

Answers

1. d. The `a:focus` selector activates whenever a link has the keyboard focus.

2. Here's one way to rewrite the <body> attributes in CSS:

```
body { color: white;
       background: url("stars.gif") black; }
   a:link { color: #00FFFF; }
   a:visited { color: #FF00FF; }
   a:active { color: #FFFF00; }
```

Exercises

What makes for good link styles and for bad? Experimenting is the best way to figure out what works for the needs of each website. Here are some ideas you can try:

▶ Eliminate underlines from your inline links, but replace them with another style that makes them stand out. Which works best, in your opinion—background colors, font weight, italics, or something else?

▶ Build a navigation menu that uses backgrounds, borders, and fonts instead of images. Is it easier to maintain CSS-styled text links than graphical navigation bars?

Lists

What You'll Learn in This Hour:

▶ How lists are formatted in CSS

▶ What the different types of lists are, and how they're coded in HTML

▶ How other elements can be displayed as lists

▶ Which CSS properties change the shape and appearance of bullets

▶ How to set the counting methods of numbered lists

Not all information is organized into paragraphs of text. Many types of web content are actually lists of information, including navigation menus, product feature lists, glossaries, and step-by-step instructions. Because of the way information is read on the Web, the use of lists can be one of the most effective and direct methods of conveying information to an audience. Styling lists attractively can also enhance their usefulness.

List Formatting

Before I discuss how CSS browsers display lists, I need to define some terms that will be important this hour.

A *list* is just a set of information that has been organized into discrete pieces called *list items*. A list can be *ordered*, which means that the order in which the items are presented is important, or it can be *unordered*, indicating that there isn't any specific order to the items or that order isn't important. A third type of list is the *definition list* (also called a *dictionary list*); these consist of pairs of shorter terms and longer explanations.

Types of HTML Lists

Lists in HTML are usually indicated by appropriate list markup, which means they usually include a list tag such as <ol>, <ul>, or <dl>, and then list items marked up with <li> or <dt>, and <dd> for definition lists. It's also possible to create a list using non–list tags, such as <div> or <a>, and use CSS to convert them into lists.

Within a CSS context, an element is a list item if it has the display property value list-item. When that value is set, the element is treated as an <li> tag by the browser, no matter what the tag really is. The list-item value designates the element as a block element, except that it also allows for a *list marker*. A list marker is a symbol before each list item that indicates it's a list.

In Listing 13.1, you can see each of the three types of HTML lists, along with a fourth "list" done without using HTML list markup.

LISTING 13.1   Four Lists in HTML

```
<!-- lists-13.1.html -->
<html>
  <head><title>List-O-Rama</title></head>
  <body>
    <table border="0" width="100%">
      <tr><td valign="top" width="50%">
          <h2>Ordered List: Tallest Mountains</h2>
          <ol><li>Everest</li>        <li>K2</li>
              <li>Kangchenjunga</li>  <li>Lhotse</li>
              <li>Makalu</li>         <li>Cho Oyu</li>
              <li>Dhaulagiri</li>
          </ol></td>
          <td valign="top" width="50%">
            <h2>Unordered List: Flavors of Soda</h2>
            <ul><li>Peach</li>
                <li>Berry:
                  <ul><li>Raspberry</li>
                      <li>Blackberry</li>
                      <li>Boysenberry</li>
                  </ul></li>
                <li>Orange</li> <li>Kiwi</li>
            </ul></td>
      </tr>
      <tr><td valign="top" width="50%">
          <h2>Definition List: Common Abbreviations</h2>
          <dl> <!-- definition list -->
            <dt>CSS</dt>   <dd>Cascading Style Sheets</dd>
            <dt>HTML</dt> <dd>Hypertext Markup Language</dd>
            <dt>W3C</dt>   <dd>World Wide Web Consortium</dd>
          </dl></td>
          <td valign="top" width="50%">
            <h2>Non-List: Links</h2>
            <div id="nav"> <!-- not done with list markup -->
```

LISTING 13.1   Continued

```
          <a href="/">Home</a>
          <a href="info/">Info</a>
          <a href="shop/">Shop</a>
          <a href="map/">Map</a>
          <a href="contact/">Contact</a>
        </div></td>
    </tr>
</table></body></html>
```

The four lists are shown in a browser in Figure 13.1; this HTML file will be used in the examples later this hour to illustrate how CSS can be used to style lists.

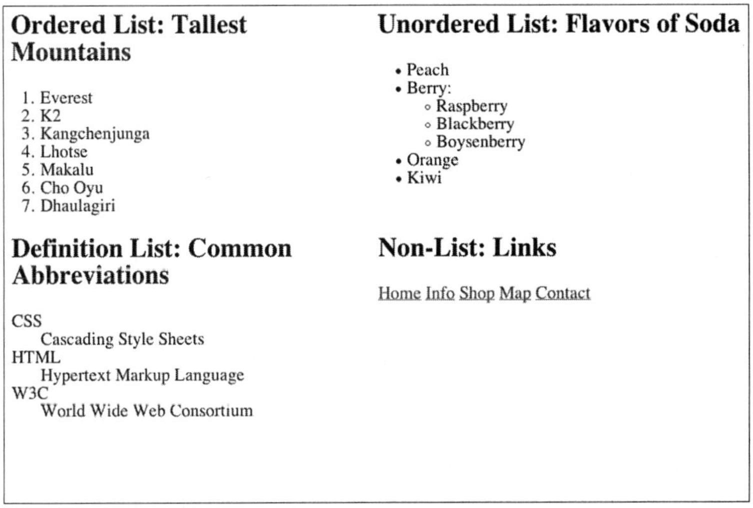

Ordered List: Tallest Mountains

1. Everest
2. K2
3. Kangchenjunga
4. Lhotse
5. Makalu
6. Cho Oyu
7. Dhaulagiri

Definition List: Common Abbreviations

CSS
    Cascading Style Sheets
HTML
    Hypertext Markup Language
W3C
    World Wide Web Consortium

Unordered List: Flavors of Soda

- Peach
- Berry:
  - Raspberry
  - Blackberry
  - Boysenberry
- Orange
- Kiwi

Non-List: Links

Home Info Shop Map Contact

FIGURE 13.1
Four different lists displayed by Firefox.

Ordered (Numbered) Lists

Browsers display an ordered list by putting a *number marker* of some kind before the list items. Usually number markers are ordinary numbers, such as 1, 2, 3, and so on, but later in this hour you'll learn to change those to other counting methods.

Examples of ordered lists include the top ten best-seller list at a bookstore or a set of instructions for making a cake. In both cases, the specific order of the list items is significant.

Ordered lists in HTML are created by the `<ol>` element, which contains `<li>` tags for each list item.

> Users with visual disabilities often find ordered lists easier to navigate than unordered lists because they have a better sense of context; the numbers can be used to keep track of location in a list. Using ordered lists on your page is very helpful to these users.

Unordered (Bulleted) Lists

An unordered list is commonly displayed with a bullet marker. This is a symbol placed before each item of the list; it most often looks like a solid circle. During this hour you'll learn how to change the list bullet to other shapes or replace it with an image.

Unordered list examples include a list of toppings you could order on a pizza or a roster of students in a class. Even though the class roster may have an order—usually alphabetical by last name—the order probably isn't significant; it's arbitrary. For example, the list isn't ordered by the tallest or the shortest in the class. In most cases, the significance of a list's order depends on how the list is meant to be used. A list's order may not matter in one case but might in another.

To create an unordered list in HTML, you use the <ul> element, and each bullet point gets an <li> tag. Two other HTML tags create bulleted lists, <dir> and <menu>, but these are deprecated in HTML 4.01, which means that you should use the <ul> tag instead; newer browsers may not support the deprecated tags.

Definition Lists

Definition lists consist of pairs of content—a shorter *term* and a longer *definition*. The term is displayed first, and then the definition is displayed on a new line with an indented left margin. A definition list in HTML is created with the <dl> element, with several <dt> and <dd> tags inside it.

A definition list doesn't have to be a glossary. Although that's a common use, it could be anything from a listing of features in a car to a menu of desserts that describes each treat. A definition list can be used whenever you have pairs of shorter text and longer explanations or descriptions of that text.

Unlike the <li> tags in <ol> or <ul> elements, the <dt> and <dd> tags do not have the property display set to list-item. Instead, they have the display value of block, although the <dd> tag usually has an extra margin-left value of 1.33em.

Sometimes web developers use the <ol>, <ul>, or <dl> tags to create indented texts or margins. Using structural tags, such as the list elements, for presentational effects such as margins reduces the separation of content from presentation. To create margin effects, use the CSS properties in Hour 16, "Borders and Boxes," not list markup.

Changing List Type with display

Using the CSS display property, you can override the default presentation of a tag and create a list from nonlist elements or change a list into a nonlist.

If you change the value of the display property, it changes only how it's presented— block or inline—and in the case of the list-item value, it sets aside space for a marker. Changing the display property doesn't affect any other values, such as the inherent margin-left on <ol> or <dd>.

Examples of setting display properties can be seen in Listing 13.2, a style sheet to change the appearance of your HTML lists. Notice that I set margin-left values to remove the left margins when changing the display value to block, and I add margin-left when setting display: list-item.

LISTING 13.2   Several Lists with Type Changed

```
/* lists-13.2.css */
ul li { display: inline; }

ol { margin-left: 0px; }
ol li { display: block; }

dt { display: list-item;
     margin-left: 1em; }

dd { display: list-item;
     margin-left: 2em; }

div#nav a { text-decoration: none;
            margin-left: 2em;
            display: list-item; }
```

The effects of this style sheet can be seen in Figure 13.2, which applies the style sheet to the HTML lists from Listing 13.1. The Unordered List is jumbled, there are no number markers for the Ordered List, and there are new list markers before the Definition List and Non-List items. Because the type of list marker is not set, the exact marker used varies from browser to browser, depending on what the browser chooses to use for a default; your browser may show some of the lists differently than in Figure 13.2. To ensure consistency across browsers, you should set the list item properties described later this hour whenever you change the `display` of an element to `list-item`.

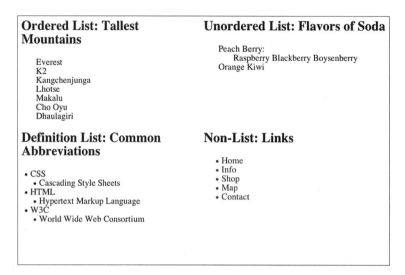

FIGURE 13.2
Displaying alternate list formatting.

Ordered List: Tallest Mountains

Everest
K2
Kangchenjunga
Lhotse
Makalu
Cho Oyu
Dhaulagiri

Unordered List: Flavors of Soda

Peach Berry:
    Raspberry Blackberry Boysenberry
    Orange Kiwi

Definition List: Common Abbreviations

• CSS
    • Cascading Style Sheets
• HTML
    • Hypertext Markup Language
• W3C
    • World Wide Web Consortium

Non-List: Links

• Home
• Info
• Shop
• Map
• Contact

The `list-style-type` Property

You can change the type of list marker by using the `list-style-type` property. This property is used only on elements that have the `display` value of `list-item`, but it can be set on any tag, and the value is inherited by children that are list items. Most commonly, it's set on the `<ol>` or `<ul>` tags that enclose the `<li>` list items; this way you can set different styles for each list.

The most common values for `list-style-type` are shown in Table 13.1. The default value for `<ol>` is `decimal`, for `<ul>` is `disc`, and for lists created with `display: list-item` it is `disc` as well.

TABLE 13.1   Values for the `list-style-type` Property

Value	Effect
circle	A hollow circle bullet
decimal	Decimal number markers (1, 2, 3, ...)
decimal-leading-zero	Decimal number markers with leading zeros (01, 02, 03, ...)
disc	A solid circle bullet
lower-alpha	Lowercase alphanumeric markers (a, b, c, ...)
lower-roman	Lowercase roman number markers (i, ii, iii, ...)

TABLE 13.1   Continued

Value	Effect
none	Don't display any marker before the list
square	A square bullet
upper-alpha	Uppercase alphanumeric markers (A, B, C, ...)
upper-roman	Uppercase roman number markers (I, II, III, ...)
inherit	Use the value of list-style-type from the containing box

There are two types of values: those that set bullet markers and those that set number markers. It is possible to set a bullet list-style-type for ordered lists or to set a number marker on unordered list, but generally speaking, this should be avoided. As a rule of thumb, you should use number markers only with ordered lists, and bullet markers only with unordered lists.

One list contained within another list is called a *nested list*. Most browsers display nested, unordered lists by changing the bullet type from disc, to circle, and then to square. Using list-style-type, you can control the marker with appropriate descendant rules. Topical outlines created using <ol> tags can be styled as well, like the following:

```
ol { list-style-type: upper-roman; }
ol ol { list-style-type: upper-alpha; }
ol ol ol { list-style-type: decimal; }
ol ol ol ol { list-style-type: lower-alpha; }
ol ol ol ol ol { list-style-type: lower-roman; }
```

A style sheet that changes list markers is shown in Listing 13.3.

LISTING 13.3   Setting the list-style-type in CSS

```
/* lists-13.3.css */

ol { list-style-type: upper-roman; }

ul { list-style-type: square; }
ul ul { list-style-type: circle; }

#nav a { display: list-item;
         margin-left: 2em;
         list-style-type: square; }
```

The results of applying this style sheet to your sample lists are shown in Figure 13.3.

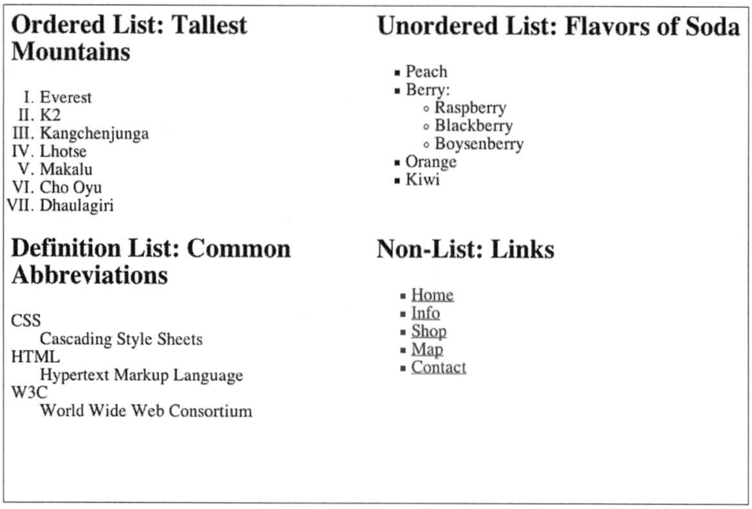

FIGURE 13.3
Lists with different marker types.

Ordered List: Tallest Mountains

   I. Everest
   II. K2
   III. Kangchenjunga
   IV. Lhotse
   V. Makalu
   VI. Cho Oyu
   VII. Dhaulagiri

Unordered List: Flavors of Soda

- Peach
- Berry:
  - Raspberry
  - Blackberry
  - Boysenberry
- Orange
- Kiwi

Definition List: Common Abbreviations

CSS
   Cascading Style Sheets
HTML
   Hypertext Markup Language
W3C
   World Wide Web Consortium

Non-List: Links

- Home
- Info
- Shop
- Map
- Contact

By the Way

Markers (bullet or number) are displayed with the same font characteristic as the list item. If you want to change a property—for example, the color—set the property on the list item, and then use a <span> or other inline element to change the text, as in the following:

```
<ol>
  <li><span class="person">Nick Mamatas</span></li>
</ol>
```

To change the color of the list marker but not the list text, write rules like these, which put the number in red:

```
ol { color: black; }
ol li { color: red; }
ol li span.person { color: black; }
```

International List Markers

You can set the list marker to count using Roman numerals, numbers, or letters, but what about languages that don't use the same alphabet? A list of additional values for the list-style-type property is shown in Table 13.2.

TABLE 13.2   International Values for the list-style-type Property

Value	Effect
armenian	Traditional Armenian numbers
cjk-ideographic	Ideographic numbers (Asian languages)
georgian	Traditional Georgian numbers

TABLE 13.2 Continued

Value	Effect
hebrew	Traditional Hebrew numbers
hiragana	Japanese hiragana numbers
hiragana-iroha	Japanese hiragana-iroha numbers
katakana	Japanese katakana numbers
katakana-iroha	Japanese katakana-iroha numbers
lower-greek	Lowercase Greek letters

The :lang() pseudo-selector, described in Hour 8, "Advanced Selectors," can be used in conjunction with these list-style-type values; or you could use a normal element selector, a class or id selector, or anything else that fits your markup. Here are two examples:

```
li:lang(jp) { list-style-type: hiragana; }
ul.alphabeta { list-style-type: lower-greek; }
```

> These are supported only for those browsers and operating systems that support these character sets and appropriate fonts. This is highly dependent upon the specific version and language support on each computer. Although you should feel free to use these with content in the appropriate language, you should also expect that browsers without support for such a given language will display these as list-style-type: decimal.

Try it Yourself ▼

Styling Your To-Do List

If you're like many people, you probably keep a list of what you need to get done. You can organize your life and practice your new CSS skills by following along:

1. First, create a list in an HTML page of the items you need to complete. Use standard list markup—the <ol> tag is probably most appropriate, so that you can prioritize your list.

2. Add a style rule, on a linked style sheet or in a <style> section of the <head>, that sets the list-style-type property.

3. Experiment with different list types. Does your list look better with letters, numbers, or Roman numerals?

▼

▲

4. Try it with a circle, disk, and square as list markers. Which is best for checking off completed items when you print out the list?

The list-style-image **Property**

You aren't restricted to bullets that are circles or squares; you can actually use any image you like by using the list-style-image property. Naturally, you'll want to use only small images that can function as bullets for this purpose; images that are too large overwhelm the text. As an approximate rule, you should use bullets that are between 12 and 20 pixels in size.

I created a simple one-bullet image in a graphics program by first creating a 16-pixel by 16-pixel blank image, then drawing a black circle, and then adding a yellow plus sign in the middle of it; this is shown in Figure 13.4.

FIGURE 13.4
Creating a simple list bullet image.

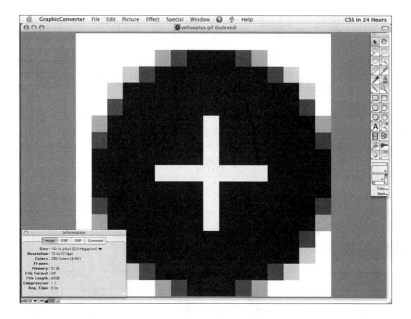

To use this image as a bullet, I simply need to set the list-style-image property in a rule, as in the following:

```
selector { list-style-image: url("graphic");
```

An example of a style sheet that uses bullet images is shown in Listing 13.4. Notice that I also set the list-style-type property to circle; if the image can't be loaded for any reason, the circle is displayed instead.

LISTING 13.4 Setting a `list-style-image`

```
/* lists-13.4.css */

ol { list-style-type: upper-roman; }

ul { list-style-type: square;
     list-style-image: url("yellowplus.gif"); }
ul ul { list-style-type: circle; }
       /* This will inherit the list-style-image above */

#nav a { display: list-item;
         margin-left: 2em;
         list-style-type: square;
         list-style-image: url("yellowplus.gif"); }
```

Applying this style sheet to the sample lists gives the results in Figure 13.5.

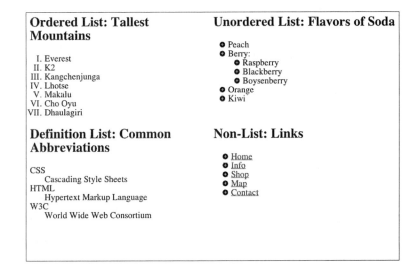

FIGURE 13.5
Bullet images marking lists.

The `list-style-position` Property

When a bullet or number marker is placed, it's normally located outside the main content to the left of the list element's box. A *virtual marker box* is created; the box inherits the text properties of the list item, although the background is always transparent.

The browser determines the placement of this virtual marker box; as a web developer, you can't affect the exact placement of the marker. You can control one thing, though: You can move the marker box inside the list element's box, so it functions as an inline box instead. You do this by setting the `list-style-position` property.

Three values are possible for list-style-position: outside (the default), inside, and inherit. Any value set on a containing box is inherited, so you can set it on <ol> or <ul> selectors and it will apply to list items within them.

The effects of list-style-position are clarified in Listing 13.5; border properties have been added to make the list item display boxes clear.

LISTING 13.5   Setting the Position of the List Bullet or Number

```
/* lists-13.5.css */

ol { list-style-type: upper-roman;
     list-style-position: inside; }

li { border: 1px solid black; margin: 2px; }
ul { list-style-type: square;
     list-style-image: url("yellowplus.gif");
     list-style-position: outside; }
ul ul { list-style-type: circle;
        list-style-position: inside; }

#nav a { display: list-item;
         list-style-position: inside;
         list-style-type: square;
         list-style-image: url("yellowplus.gif");
         border: 1px solid black; margin: 2px; }
```

The repositioned markers are shown in Figure 13.6.

FIGURE 13.6
List positioning shown by out-line boxes.

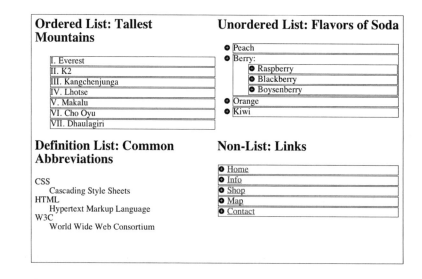

The `list-style` **Shorthand Property**

Like other shorthand properties, the `list-style` property lets you set multiple CSS properties at once. A `list-style` rule is written like the following:

```
selector { list-style: type position image; }
```

The values for `type`, `position`, and `image` can appear in any order; any values that aren't specified are set to their default values. For example, to set the image to `yellowplus.gif`, the bullet type to `square`, and the position to `inside`, you can use the following rule:

```
ul li {
  list-style: url("yellowplus.gif") square inside;
}
```

Try it Yourself ▼

Further To-Do List Styling

Let's apply what you've learned to further enhance your list of items that need to be done:

1. If you haven't done so already, create an HTML file with your to-do list in an ordered list (`<ol>`).

2. For each item, set a `class` attribute—either pending or done.

3. Create two separate graphics, or download them from the Web, to represent pending and done. I like a simple empty square box for `pending`, and the same box with a check mark for done.

4. Set a `list-style` rule that uses your graphics. Be sure to include default values for the marker type if the graphic isn't available, and adjust the location if you need to.

5. Load your HTML page in a web browser and change the style rules until you're happy. You can add additional rules that aren't related to `list-style` properties, of course: Do you want to put pending items in bold, or use a strikethrough text effect on completed items? It's your to-do list—style it the way you'd like!

▲

Summary

HTML defines three types of lists: ordered lists, unordered lists, and definition lists. Ordered and unordered lists contain `list-item` elements, which are a special type of `block` content.

Any HTML element with the CSS property display set to `list-item`—including `<li>` tags, thanks to browsers' default style sheets—will generate a virtual marker box. This marker box contains a marker of some kind; ordered lists have number markers and unordered lists have bullets.

The type of marker can be set with the `list-style-type` property; a variety of number schemes and bullet types are available. Bullet images can also be used with the `list-style-image` property. The location of the marker box is set with the `list-style-location` property. All these properties can be set at once with the `list-style` shorthand property.

Workshop

The workshop contains a Q&A section, quiz questions, and activities to help reinforce what you've learned in this hour. If you get stuck, the answers to the quiz can be found after the questions.

Q&A

Q. *How do I set styles on definition lists? You've mostly talked about* `<ol>` *and* `<ul>`, *not* `<dl>`.

A. That's because from the CSS perspective, definition lists aren't lists at all! They're simply `block` content, not `list-item` elements. That means that you can just create style rules for `<dl>`, `<dt>`, and `<dd>` normally, as you would for any block elements. I personally like to do the following:

```
dt { font-weight: bold; }
```

Q. *How do I use CSS to set the starting values for ordered lists?*

A. Unfortunately, you can't set those with CSS. To set specific number values for ordered lists, you need to use the HTML `start` attribute on the `<ol>` element or the `value` attribute on `<li>`. Both these values are deprecated in HTML 4.01, which means you can't use them in Strict HTML documents.

Quiz

1. Which of these rules will make an ordered list count in lower-case letters?

    a. `ol { list-style-type: alphabet; }`

    b. `ol { list-style-type: lower-case; }`

    c. `ol { list-style-type: lower-letters; }`

    d. `ol { list-style-type: lower-alpha; }`

2. Assuming the following style rules, what color will the numbers before a list item be?

```
ol { color: green; }
ol li { color: blue; }
li { color: black; }
ol li span { color: red; }
```

3. You want your bullet list items to be marked by a graphic, `bullet01.jpg`, which looks like a small box. You also want the graphic to be placed inside the list item's display box. How do you write this with the `list-style` short-hand property?

Answers

1. The correct answer is (d); the `lower-alpha` value orders list items with a, b, c, and so on.

2. The numbers will be the same color as the `<li>`; in this case, that color is `blue`. (If you think it's `black`, you're forgetting that the second rule is more specific than the first in cascade order.)

3. Here's one way to write such a rule:

```
ul { list-style: square inside url("bullet01.jpg"); }
```

Exercises

Some projects you can undertake to investigate list styles on your own include the following:

▶ Build an outline using `<ol>` and `list-style-type` properties. Adjust the margins and padding to suit taste.

▶ Design several list bullet graphics for your web pages, and add these using the `list-style-image` property. Which kinds of bullets are best at capturing the user's attention?

▶ Create a navigation bar on a web page, consisting of <a> links not grouped in a list. Use `display: list-item` to change the <a> links to a list, then add two types of list bullets—one for unvisited links, one for visited links.

HOUR 14

Forms

What You'll Learn in This Hour:

▶ The structure of HTML forms and how they interact with CSS rules

▶ How to style labels, field sets, and legends

▶ How to style text input fields

▶ How to style Submit and Reset buttons

▶ How to style check boxes and radio buttons

▶ How to style pull-down selectors and selection lists

▶ Which style properties are supported for HTML form elements

The HTML language provides a <form> element that can be used to gather information interactively from the user, either for submission to the web server or for processing with JavaScript. These forms can be styled with CSS rules, although variable browser support makes it an uncertain proposition. In this hour, you'll learn about which types of styles are supported for forms and which are not.

Styling Form Controls

You create a form in HTML by using the <form> element. Between the <form> and </form> tags, you put the HTML that will comprise the form. This consists of normal markup and content, plus form controls and other HTML tags used specifically for creating forms.

Form controls are the interactive portions of the form that let the user enter data for processing on the server or in the browser via JavaScript (or another browser-side language). Examples include text input boxes, check boxes, Submit buttons, and pull-down menus. Other tags that are used with forms designate labels for form elements or group them together in identified sets. Such labels are beneficial for users with disabilities who employ assistive technologies for web access, as well as make your forms easier for everyone to use.

If you aren't familiar with the HTML tags for forms, you can learn more by reading *Sams Teach Yourself Web Publishing with HTML and CSS in One Hour a Day*; ISBN: 0672328860, 5th Edition.

The full list of form controls and markup for labels is shown in Table 14.1. The <input> tag alone can be used to create 10 different types of form controls; the specific control created depends on the type attribute.

TABLE 14.1 Form Controls and Label Markup

HTML Tag	Function
<button>	Creates a Reset, Submit, or other programmable pushbutton
<fieldset>	Groups related form controls
<input type="button">	Creates a programmable push button
<input type="checkbox">	Creates a check box
<input type="file">	Selects a file from the user's computer system for uploading
<input type="hidden">	Creates a hidden field
<input type="image">	Creates a Submit button from an image
<input type="password">	Creates a single-line text field with obscured input
<input type="radio">	Creates one in a set of radio buttons
<input type="reset">	Creates a Reset button
<input type="submit">	Creates a Submit button
<input type="text">	Creates a single-line text field
<label>	Provides a text label for a form control
<legend>	Provides a text label for a <fieldset>
<optgroup>	Groups related <option> elements together
<option>	Designates one choice in a <select> menu
<select>	Creates a pull-down menu or scrollable section menu
<textarea>	Creates a multi-line text input box

Listing 14.1 is an example of an HTML form that shows off a number of different form controls. This is part of a hypothetical e-commerce system that enables the user to add a note card to what she's bought from the site. As with most examples, this is a bit contrived, but the purpose is to demonstrate how styles can be applied to HTML forms.

LISTING 14.1   An HTML Form

```
<!-- form-14.1.html -->
<html>
  <head>
    <title>Include a Note Card</title>
  </head>
  <body>
    <h1>Include a Note Card</h1>
    <form method="post" action="placeholder.php">
      <p><label><input type="checkbox" id="gift" name="gift"
              value="1">
         Check this box if your order is a gift</label></p>
      <p><label for="sendername">Sender's Name:</label>
         <input type="text" name="sendername"
                value="Your Name Here"
                size="40"  id="sendername"></p>
      <fieldset id="papercolorfieldset">
        <legend>Color of Paper:</legend>
        <label><input type="radio" name="papercolor"
                   id="papercolorblue" value="blue">
            Blue</label>
        <label><input type="radio" name="papercolor"
                   id="papercolorpink" value="pink">
            Pink</label>
        <label><input type="radio" name="papercolor"
                   checked="checked"
                   id="papercolorwhite" value="white">
            White</label>
      </fieldset>
      <p><label for="inkcolor">Ink Color:</label>
         <select name="inkcolor" id="inkcolor">
           <option selected value="black">Black</option>
           <option value="navy">Navy Blue</option>
           <option value="maroon">Maroon</option>
           <option value="green">Green</option>
           <option value="gray">Gray</option>
           <option value="red">Red</option>
         </select></p>
      <p><label for="message">Card Message:
         </label>
         <textarea id="message" name="message" rows="4"
           cols="40">Type your message here.</textarea></p>
      <p><label for="font">Choose a Font:</label>
         <select name="font" id="font" size="4">
           <option selected value="TimesNewRoman">
              Times New Roman</option>
           <option value="Optima">Optima</option>
           <option value="Verdana">Verdana</option>
           <option value="Papyrus">Papyrus</option>
```

LISTING 14.1   Continued

```
            <option value="MarkerFelt">Marker Felt</option>
            <option value="Arial">Arial</option>
            <option value="CourierNew">Courier New</option>
        </select></p>
    <p><button type="button" id="backbutton"
            name="backbutton">&lArr; Go Back</button>
        <input type="submit" id="submitbutton"
            name="submitbutton" value="Submit Form">
        <input type="reset" id="resetbutton"
            name="resetbutton" value="Reset Form"></p>
    </form>
  </body>
</html>
```

Without styles, this is a rather boring form, as shown in Figure 14.1. Have no fear; it can be improved with CSS.

FIGURE 14.1
Firefox displays the HTML form with default styles.

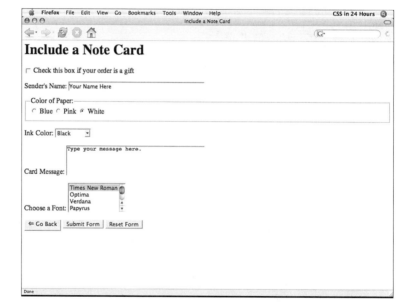

Labels, Fieldsets, and Legends

The labels for form elements are the easiest to style; they're not even form controls, just normal HTML blocks. The `<label>` tag, for labeling individual form controls, is an inline element and can be styled like any other inline element. The `<fieldset>` tag is a block element, used to group together related elements (such as a group of radio buttons), and the `<legend>` element serves as a label for a `<fieldset>`. These are shown by example in Listing 14.1. As shown in Figure 14.1, the `<fieldset>` tag creates a border around the form controls it encloses, and <legend> is set as an introductory header. This styling convention isn't specified in the standards, but is ubiquitous in modern browsers.

Listing 14.2 is a style sheet that adds rules specifically to style the <label>, <fieldset>, and <legend> elements, as well as adding a border and font to the entire <form>.

> This hour's style sheets demonstrate some style properties that you haven't learned yet, if you're reading this book in sequential order. You'll learn about float in Hour 15, "Alignment"; padding, margin, and border properties in Hour 16, "Borders and Boxes"; and width and height in Hour 18, "Box Sizing and Offset."

By the Way

LISTING 14.2 A Style Sheet for Form Labels

```
/* labels-14.2.css */

form { padding:0 0.5em;
       margin: 0 0.5em;
       border: 1px solid black;
       font-family: Arial, sans-serif; }

label { border: 1px dotted gray;
        background-color: silver; }
label[for] { border: none; background-color: inherit;
             float: left;  width: 25%; }

fieldset { margin-left: 25%; width: 60%; padding: 0; }
legend { color: white; background-color: black; }
```

> The style sheet in Listing 14.2, and the rest of the style sheets in this hour, use attribute value selectors, which were introduced in Hour 8, "Advanced Selectors." Internet Explorer version 6.0 (and earlier) does not support attribute value selectors; to support these styles in Internet Explorer, you need to add additional class or id selectors. The examples in this hour omit these additional selectors to make it clear which form controls are being styled. You can download the versions that work with Internet Explorer 6 from the book's website.

Watch Out!

Linking the style sheet in Listing 14.2 to the HTML file in Listing 14.1 produces the effect shown in Figure 14.2. You can use any styles with <form>, <label>, <fieldset>, or <legend> that you can use with any normal box elements in HTML, and this is well supported by the web browsers.

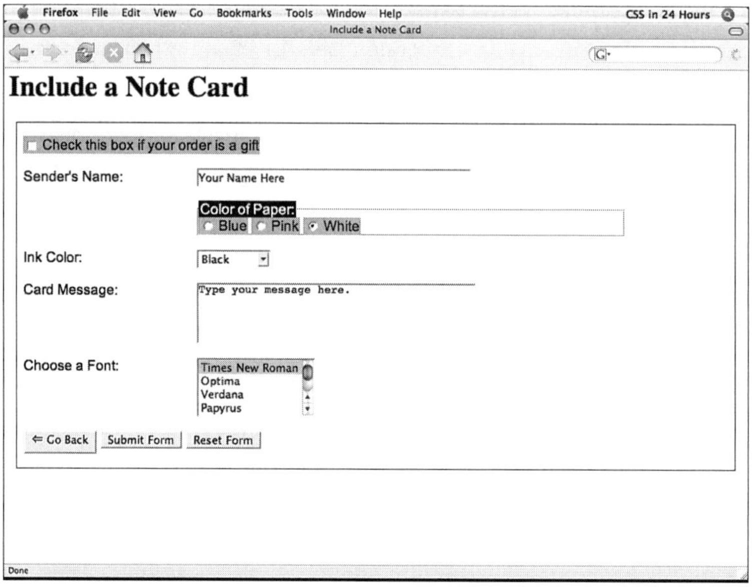

FIGURE 14.2
Borders, mar-
gins, and back-
grounds are
added to form
labels.

Text Input Fields

Text boxes are created by the `<input type="text">` tag or by the `<textarea>` tag.
The `<input type="password">` tag creates a text box as well; any letters typed in it
are shown as asterisks but are stored by the browser as data.

You can set the font, text color, and background color on a text box. Most browsers
default to a white background with black text for text boxes, with `<input
type="text">` displaying in a serif font, and `<textarea>` in monospace (as shown
in Figure 14.1), but there are no hard and fast rules. Your CSS rules can override
these browser defaults.

Listing 14.3 is a style sheet with rules for text fields.

LISTING 14.3   Style Rules for Text Input Fields

```
/* textboxes-14.3.css */

input[type="text"]
     { font-size: x-large; background-color: yellow;
       font-variant: small-caps;
       color: maroon; width: 60%;
       padding-left: 1em; padding-right: 1em;
       font-family: "Courier New", monospace; }

textarea { font-family: cursive; width: 60%;
           color: white; background-color: navy; }
```

The style sheet also sets the `padding` and the text box `width` in one rule. In general, dimensions can be set reliably, but other box values (`padding`, `margin`, and `border`) are less reliable because of browser differences.

The results of applying this style sheet to the form in Listing 14.1 are shown in Figure 14.3. The label style sheet from Listing 14.2 was also applied, because it makes the form look a little more tidy.

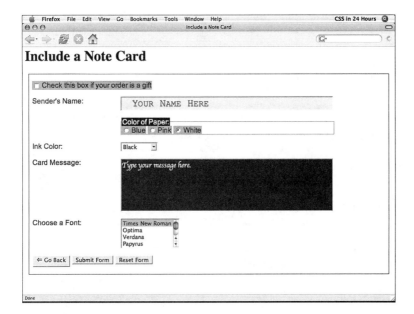

FIGURE 14.3
Colors and fonts can be set on text input fields.

Buttons

A button in an HTML form does one of three things: submits, resets, or is a programmable button called a "push" button. A Submit button, when clicked by the user, sends the form data to the server. A Reset button restores the form to its original state, with fields that are either blank or preset to a default value by the form designer. A pushbutton has no predefined action associated with it; a JavaScript action needs to be attached to make the button do anything. See Bonus Web Hour 1, "CSS and JavaScript," for more on the JavaScript language.

A button is created by the `<input>` tag or the `<button>` tag. There are three buttons in Listing 14.1, one of each type: Submit, Reset, and a programmable push button—the "Go Back" button which, on a real form, could be tied to a JavaScript function. The style sheet in Listing 14.4 sets CSS values on these buttons.

LISTING 14.4   Rules for Styling Form Buttons

```
/* buttons-14.4.css */

input[type="submit"]
    { font-style: oblique;
      background-color: navy; color: white;
      padding-left: 2em; padding-right: 2em; }

input[type="reset"]
    { font-family: cursive; background-color: white;
      border: 3px solid blue; color: red;
      margin-left: 25%; width: 300px; }

button { border-style: inset;
         border-color: green;
         padding: 10px; color: green; }
```

Figure 14.4 shows the style sheet from Listing 14.4 applied to the HTML form in Listing 14.1, as well as the label styles from Listing 14.2.

FIGURE 14.4
Each button has been styled separately.

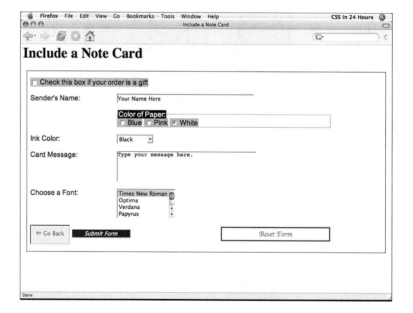

Check Boxes

A check box in HTML is created by the `<input type="checkbox">` tag, and is a simple binary switch: It is either off or on, like a light switch. Browsers display check boxes as square boxes that can be clicked, and when clicked, an "X" or a check mark appears in the box.

A radio button is one of a set of form controls that share the same name attribute, created by <input type="radio">. Only one radio button in a set can be checked at a time; selecting a new value deselects the previous setting. This is analogous to old-time analog car radios, which had push buttons that caused the tuner to jump to a new value. Browsers display radio buttons as circles with a dark dot in the selected value.

The <label> tag is used to provide a label for each type of check box. It can be either wrapped around a check box by containing the <input> tag that defines the check box, or set next to it with a for attribute designating which form control it labels. A set of radio buttons can be wrapped in a <fieldset> tag to group the <input> tags with an appropriate <legend> label.

Listing 14.5 is a style sheet that provides some style rules for the HTML form's check boxes.

LISTING 14.5 A Style Sheet That Styles Check Boxes

```
/* checkradio-14.5.css */

input[type="checkbox"]
  { background-color: blue;
    color: yellow;
    font-size: xx-large;
    width: 50px; border-style: solid; }

input[type="radio"]
  { background-color: lime;
    color: orange;
    font-size: small; }

input[checked]
  { color: black; background-color: silver;
    width: 50px; }
```

You can see the results of linking this style sheet (and the label styles from Listing 14.2) to the HTML form in Listing 14.1 in Figure 14.5. As you can see, most of the rules, such as the font-size and the color rules, have had almost no effect. The width rule has stretched out the check box and radio button, however. As you'll see later in this hour, Firefox is the only browser that does this; other browsers reserve more room for the check box, but leave the actual check box the same.

Directly styling a check box or radio button is not very useful because most browsers ignore such attempts. It is better to apply styles to the labels surrounding the check boxes.

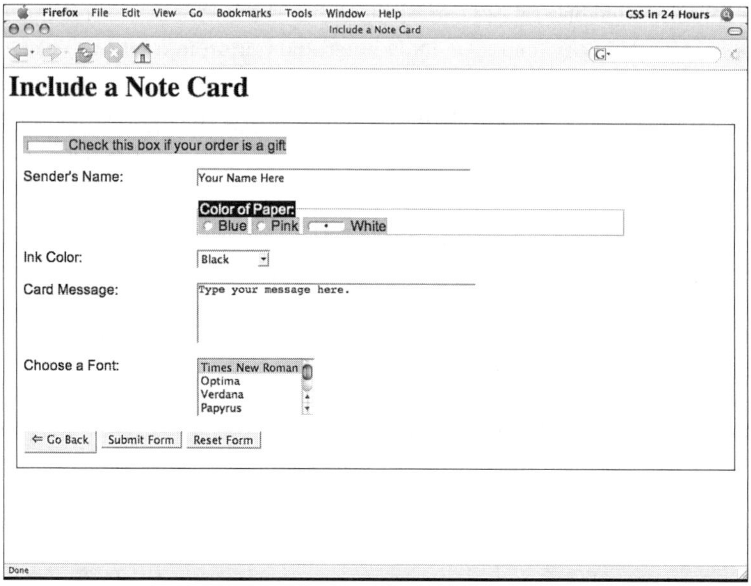

FIGURE 14.5
The effects of
styling a check
box are mini-
mal, as seen in
Firefox.

Selection Lists

You form a selection list by wrapping the `<select>` tag around one or more
`<option>` tags. If no `size` property is given, the selection list will be a pull-down list;
if a `size` value is given, it will be a scrollable list showing as many lines as indicated by the `size`.

Listing 14.6 is a style sheet that gives a width to the two `<select>` tags in the example form, as well as setting various properties on the `<option>` elements.

LISTING 14.6   Style Rules for Changing Selection List Options

```css
/* select-14.6.css */

select { width: 60%; }

#inkcolor option { color: white; }
option[value="black"]  { background-color: black;   }
option[value="navy"]   { background-color: navy;    }
option[value="maroon"] { background-color: maroon;  }
option[value="green"]  { background-color: green;   }
option[value="gray"]   { background-color: gray;    }
option[value="red"]    { background-color: red;     }

#font { border: none; background-color: silver;
        padding: 1em 15%; height: 100px; }
#font option
      { text-align: center; border: 1px solid black;
        margin: 3px 0; font-size: large;
```

LISTING 14.6 Continued

```
        background-color: white; }
option[value="TimesNewRoman"]
    { font-family: "Times New Roman", serif; }
option[value="Optima"]
    { font-family: Optima, sans-serif; }
option[value="Verdana"]
    { font-family: Verdana, sans-serif; }
option[value="Papyrus"]
    { font-family: Papyrus, fantasy; }
option[value="MarkerFelt"]
    { font-family: "Marker Felt", cursive; }
option[value="Arial"]
    { font-famiy: Arial, sans-serif; }
option[value="CourierNew"]
    { font-family: "Courier New", sans-serif; }
```

Figure 14.6 shows Listing 14.6 (and Listing 14.2) applied to the HTML form in Listing 14.1. As you can see, the fonts and colors specified are used, as well as the box properties (padding, margins, borders) in the second <select> that sets the font choices.

Although this is a very neat effect, don't get too excited about it. Figure 14.6 was created with Firefox, which is the only browser to support restyling selection lists in this manner, as you'll see later this hour. Applying styles to <option> elements is fun, but not reliable.

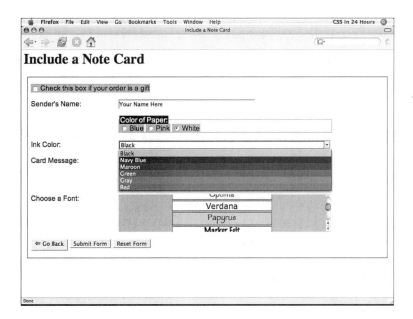

FIGURE 14.6
The selection options appear in different colors and fonts.

▼   **Try it Yourself**

Styling a Simple Email Form

Create your own form to apply style rules and find out which your browsers fully support. Follow these steps:

1. Create an HTML file in your text editor or web development software.

2. Add a form tag like this, but with your own email address:

   ```
   <form action="mailto:kynn@example.com">
   ```

3. Create a text input field in which the user can enter her email address, a pull-down menu for choosing a subject category, and a text area for a message. Make sure you include `<label>` tags for the field labels as well.

4. Include a button for submitting the form, and don't forget to close the form with a `</form>` tag.

5. Now create a style sheet for the form. Set your default styles such as the font and colors first.

6. Add styles for the text input field. Select colors and fonts that are pleasing.

7. Similarly, write style rules for the text area; add a background color and change the font if you wish.

8. Provide style rules for the pull-down menu as well. Not all browsers support these rules, so don't be too disappointed if they don't show up.

9. View the form in your web browser, with the style sheet unlinked, then link it in. How does it look to you?

▲

Browser Support for Form Styles

As noted earlier in this hour, browsers don't reliably style form elements in the same way, making certain styles—especially on check boxes and selection lists—very hit-and-miss in actual practice. Why is this?

The CSS specifications themselves are conspicuously silent on the issue of styling form controls. Form controls are considered part of the browser's user interface (UI), not actual content for manipulation by CSS rules. The way buttons, check boxes, and pull-down lists are displayed depends on the browser's UI scheme, which is based on the operating system's user interface. For example, the figures in this chapter were primarily shot on a computer running Mac OS X. If you are using a

Windows computer, the appearance, shape, and size of your Submit button will look appropriate for your system, and not like those in the book.

This means that form controls fall into a no-man's-land in the specification; it is up to the browser programmers to decide to what extent the form controls can be reshaped with CSS. Each browser company has chosen a different solution, which makes form element styling inconsistent from browser to browser.

Firefox

Firefox (and any other Gecko-based browser) supports styling for most form controls, as seen earlier in this hour, with the exception of check boxes, which are minimally styled. Figure 14.7 shows the results of applying all five style sheets in this hour to Listing 14.1.

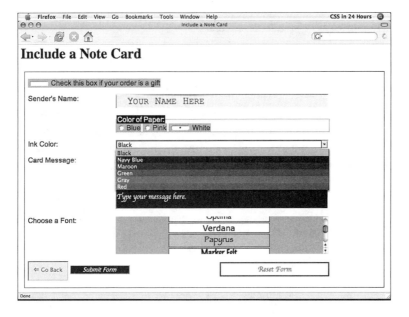

FIGURE 14.7
Firefox displaying all form styles.

Opera

Opera is the only browser to allow extensive styling of check boxes; the color, background-color, and border properties are applied correctly, and the check box is not stretched out. However, Opera (as of version 8.5) doesn't allow restyling of selection boxes. Figure 14.8 shows all five style sheets linked to Listing 14.1. Compare this with Figure 14.7; the font-variant and padding properties for the text input box aren't respected. (The <textarea> box is styled correctly, though, even though you can't see it in Figure 14.8 because of the pull-down menu.)

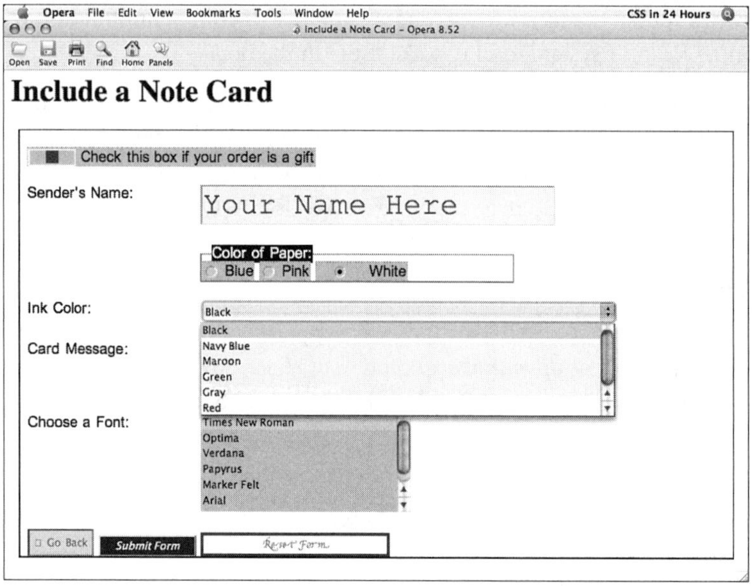

FIGURE 14.8
All form style sheets, shown by Opera.

Safari

Safari's take on the five style sheets is shown in Figure 14.9. Space is reserved for check boxes with `width` set, but they're not stretched as in Firefox. Note that only the button created with `<button>` is styled; the submit and reset button are unchanged. As with Opera, neither `<select>` menu is styled.

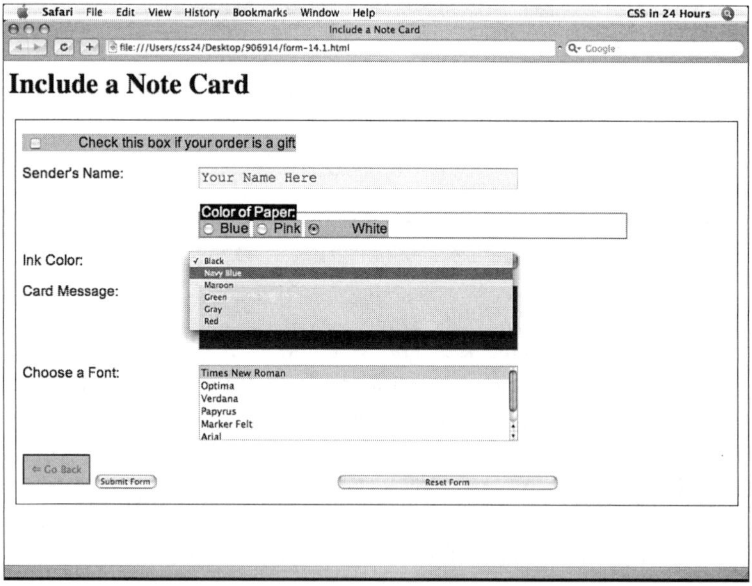

FIGURE 14.9
Form styles displayed by Safari.

Internet Explorer

Internet Explorer 6 applies the fewest style rules from the five style sheets, as you can see in Figure 14.10. Style rules are applied to the <textarea> box, but not the simple text box created by <input>. The width properties on the check boxes are ignored, and the styles for <select> menus aren't used. You can't add many styles to your forms in Internet Explorer 6.

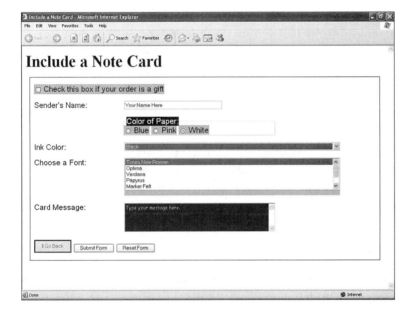

FIGURE 14.10
Internet Explorer attempts to display form styles.

The screenshot in Figure 14.10 was taken after ID values were added to the HTML in Listing 14.1, and additional ID selectors in the five style sheets given this hour, as noted earlier.

By the Way

You can use CSS rules to produce some very extensive changes in the appearance of form controls. On browsers supporting specific form styles, you can drastically change the appearance of Submit buttons, of selection lists, and other aspects of the HTML form elements. Figure 14.10 is vivid example of this.

But just because you can do something, that doesn't mean you should do it. Your web page visitors are used to standard forms, with the Submit and Reset buttons at the bottom of the form and the text input fields displayed in a standard font. The more changes you make with CSS rules to the appearance of your form, the

Watch Out!

more likely you are to throw off your users. When styling your form elements, don't confuse your users by going against their expectations unnecessarily. Use moderation and care when styling forms, and try to avoid making your form look anything like the demonstration form in Figure 14.10!

Summary

CSS rules can be written to style form elements, but the results of these rules are very browser dependent. Some browsers allow extensive restyling of form elements, whereas others are very restrictive.

Form labels can be styled easily because they are treated like any other HTML box element. Text input elements can be styled in most browsers; all modern browsers support fonts, colors, and background colors for `<textarea>`.

Buttons created with the `<button>` tag can be styled in all browsers; however, Submit and Reset buttons created with `<input>` are less consistent. Check box styles are ignored by most browsers, and only Firefox allows restyling of selection menu options.

Workshop

The workshop contains a Q&A section, quiz questions, and activities to help reinforce what you've learned in this hour. If you get stuck, the answers to the quiz can be found after the questions.

Q&A

Q. *Listing 14.5 has a style rule for a checked radio button. Does this change the style dynamically if you select another radio button?*

A. Nope. Browsers unfortunately don't work that way with HTML forms and CSS. To get that type of dynamic effect, try using JavaScript, as described in Bonus Web Hour 1.

Q. *What's a* `&lArr;` *anyway? You use it in Listing 14.1 but it shows up as a little rectangle in half the browsers.*

A. The double left arrow symbol is represented in HTML by the `&lArr;` entity, and is part of HTML 4.01. A few browsers don't fully support all HTML entities, because they are naughty, naughty browsers. You can use the `&larr;` (left arrow) entity, which is better supported, or just leave it out of your web designs.

Quiz

1. Which of the following tags does not create a submit button?

   a. `<submit value="Send it!">`

   b. `<input type="submit" value=Sent it!">`

   c. `<input type="image" src="submit.gif" alt="Send it!">`

   d. `<button type="submit">Send it!</button>`

2. You want to put a dotted, silver line under all form labels that enclose their associated form controls. You don't want any underlines on form labels that use `for` attributes to associate the label with the form control. How do you write this rule?

3. Which statements about browser support for form styling are true?

   a. Only one browser lets you style selection list values separately.

   b. Internet Explorer 6 has good support for form styles.

   c. Most browsers ignore style rules relating to check boxes.

   d. Labels and legends are hard to style in CSS.

Answers

1. (a). There is no `<submit>` tag in HTML. The others all create Submit buttons.

2. Here is one way you could do this, using two rules:

```
label { border-bottom: 1px dotted silver;}
label[for] { border-bottom: none; }
```

Remember that this won't work in Internet Explorer 6, which doesn't recognize attribute value selectors. All your labels will be underlined in Internet Explorer.

3. Statements (a) and (c) are true, and statements (b) and (d) are false.

Exercise

You are now able to add styles to your HTML forms. To get a better grasp on the browser support issues, create several different types of forms, and add styles to the labels, the text areas, and the form controls such as buttons and check boxes. Which styles not covered in this hour work reliably with each of these types of form elements? Build your forms in a way that the CSS enhances the usefulness for your website visitors.

PART IV

Layout with CSS

HOUR 15

Alignment

What You'll Learn in This Hour:

▶ How to align, justify, and center content with CSS

▶ How to indent paragraphs and other HTML elements

▶ How to make text that rises above or sinks below the rest of the text, such as subscripts or superscripts

▶ How to float an element on the right or left side so that subsequent content wraps around it

Control over text formatting enables you to replace many HTML tags with CSS rules. Effects that were previously available only as presentational markup attributes are part of the Cascading Style Sheets specification and can help you separate presentation from content.

Aligning and Indenting Text

The *alignment* of text defines the way in which the text lines up with the left or right margins. Most things you read (including this book) are left aligned; left-aligned text is generally easier to read. Centered text is often used on headlines, but it is rarely used on blocks of text because both margins are irregular and jagged, and experienced designers usually reserve right-aligned text for special text effects.

An *indent* is the extra space at the start of a line that lets you know you're on a new paragraph. In web design, new paragraphs are more commonly indicated by extra spacing than by indented text, although you are free to combine both if it suits your needs.

CSS properties enable you to control both the alignment and the indentation, setting them to whatever values you like on HTML block elements.

The text-align **Property**

Alignment of text inside a block property is controlled by the text-align property. This property has meaning only on block boxes; the content of inline boxes has no alignment, although the inline boxes themselves are aligned within the surrounding box. The block box itself is not actually positioned; only the content inside the box is aligned. To position the box itself, rather than its content, use either the margin properties you'll learn in Hour 16, "Borders and Boxes," or the positioning properties you'll learn in Hour 19, "Absolute and Fixed Positioning."

Table 15.1 shows the values you can assign to the text-align property; the default value is left. The text-align property is inherited, so you can use a single <div> or even a rule on the <body> to center an entire page. There's one exception; for backwards compatibility, browsers usually have a default rule that sets text-align: left for <td> tags and text-align: center for <th> tags. Keep this in mind when using tables, especially if you use them for layout.

TABLE 15.1   Values for the text-align **Property**

Value	Effect
center	Center the content.
justify	Justify text on both sides.
left	Align content on the left.
right	Align content on the right.
inherit	Use the value of text-align from the containing box.

Text that is *justified* is printed so that both the left and right sides line up; browsers accomplish this by adding extra spaces between words and letters. The last line of a justified paragraph is usually left aligned, if it's too short to fill an entire line by itself.

A simple HTML page with embedded style sheet that uses text-align is shown in Listing 15.1; the style rules result in the effects shown in Figure 15.1. Borders have been added to the paragraph boxes to make it easier to see how the text aligns with the edges of the boxes.

LISTING 15.1   CSS for Alignment

```
<!-- imgtip-15.1.html -->
<html>
  <head>
    <title>Image Accessibility</title>
    <style type="text/css">
      body { font-family: Arial, sans-serif; }
```

LISTING 15.1 Continued

```
    p     { border: 1px solid #333333;
            padding: 0.5em; }
    p#a  { text-align: left; }
    p#b  { text-align: justify; }
    p#c  { text-align: center; }
    p#d  { text-align: right; }
  </style>
</head>
<body>
  <p id="a">
    Always include an <tt>alt</tt> attribute on your
    <tt>&lt;img&gt;</tt> tag.
    The <tt>alt</tt> attribute should contain a short
    replacement for the graphic, in text. If the image
    itself has text, list that in <tt>alt</tt>.
    If the image is purely decorative and doesn't convey
    any additional information, use <tt>alt=""</tt>.
    If there is more information in the graphic than you
    can convey in a short <tt>alt</tt> attribute, such
    as the information in a graph or chart, then use
    the <tt>longdesc</tt> attribute to give the URL of
    a page that describes the graphic in text.
  </p>
  <p id="b">
    ...
    <!-- repeat of the previous paragraph -->
  </p>
  <p id="c">
    ...
  </p>
  <p id="d">
    ...
  </p>
  </body>
</html>
```

The `text-indent` Property

Although it's most commonly used on <p> tags, the `text-indent` property can be
set on any block element in HTML. (It has no effect if applied to an inline tag.) The
effect produced by this property is indentation of the first line of the element, resulting from an added blank space. This blank space is treated similarly to the `padding`
of the displayed box: It is inside the `margin` and `border` of the box, and it is colored
with the same `background-color` as the element content.

The values for `text-indent` are shown on Table 15.2; in summary, you can either
give a measurement value, such as `3em` and `10px`, or a percentage value based on
the size of the containing box. The default indentation is `0px`. The value of
`text-indent` is inherited by all children elements, but keep in mind that it has no
effect on inline elements, only block elements that inherit the value.

FIGURE 15.1
Lining up margins with CSS.

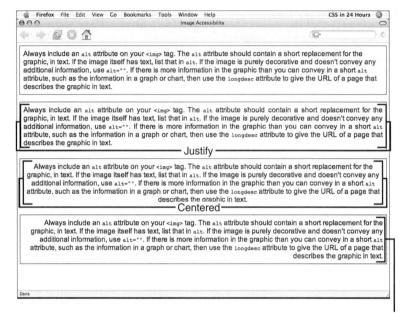

TABLE 15.2   Values for the `text-indent` Property

Value	Effect
measurement	Sets an indent.
negative measurement	Sets a hanging indent.
percentage	Sets an indent based on a fraction of the containing box.
`inherit`	Use the value of `text-indent` from the containing box.

The simplest indentations are the most straightforward; here's a rule to indent all paragraphs by 3ems:

```
p { text-indent: 3em; }
```

It gets a little trickier if you want to make a hanging indent—one where the first line is not actually indented but the other lines of the text *are* indented. To do this, you can give a negative measurement, but it then flows off the left side of the element's box, which means it may not be visible or may overwrite other content.

The best solution is to add a `margin` to the box, which indents all the text except for that initial line, which subtracts its value from the `margin`. Here's an example, which creates a `2.8em` hanging indent:

```
p { text-indent: -2.8em;
    margin-left: 3em; }
```

> This example used the `margin-left` property, which sets the `margin` for just the left side of the box. You'll learn about this and other properties that affect only one side of the box in Hour 16.

By the
Way

The style sheet in Listing 15.2 uses several different ways to set indents. Replacing the embedded style sheet in Listing 15.1 with the style sheet in this listing produces the effects shown in Figure 15.2. The border on the fourth box shows how the hanging indent actually extends outside the paragraph element's display box. In practice, when using hanging indents you should avoid using borders or backgrounds on those elements; wrap them in a `<div>` and style instead to get the appropriate border or background effect.

LISTING 15.2   Style Sheet with Several Different `text-indent` Values

```
body { font-family: Arial, sans-serif; }
p    { border: 1px solid #333333;
         padding: 0.5em; }
p#a { text-indent: 25px; }
p#b { text-indent: 75%; }
p#c { text-indent: 3em; }
p#d { text-indent: -3em;
         margin-left: 3em; }
```

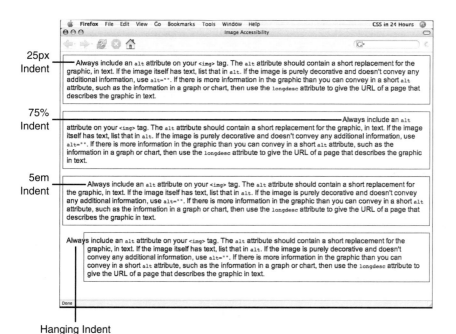

FIGURE 15.2
Various types of indentations.

There is no value none for `text-indent`; `text-indent` only takes measurements (or `inherit`) as values. To set indentation to "none" use `text-indent: 0`.

The `vertical-align` **Property**

The property `vertical-align` is used to adjust vertical alignment within an inline box. This can be used to make text appear higher or lower compared with the rest of the text on the line; it's most useful for creating superscripts or subscripts. *Superscripts* are bits of text with the baseline above the surrounding text; *subscripts* have baselines lower than the surrounding text.

Except for table cells, only inline elements use the `vertical-align` property. The use of `vertical-align` with table cells is covered in Hour 17, "Styling Tables."

The types of values that can be set for the `vertical-align` property are shown in Table 15.3. The default value is `baseline`, and any values set on containing boxes are not inherited.

TABLE 15.3   Values for the `vertical-align` **Property**

Value	Effect
baseline	Align with the surrounding text.
bottom	Align the bottom with bottom of line.
middle	Align with the middle of the surrounding text.
sub	Lower to subscript level.
super	Raise to superscript level.
text-top	Align with the top of surrounding text.
text-bottom	Align with the bottom of surrounding text.
top	Align the top with top of line.
measurement	Raise above surrounding text.
negative measurement	Lower below surrounding text.
percentage	Raise as a percentage of the `line-height`.
negative percentage	Lower as a percentage of the `line-height`.

Several of these values require further explanation. The `middle` value aligns the middle of the text with a height that's `0.5ex` above the baseline of the surrounding text. An ex is a unit of measure equal to the height of a lowercase letter, usually about half the font-size. Percentages are based on the value of the line-height, which is usually equal to the font-size. The top and bottom values align with the highest and lowest parts of the line, whereas text-top and text-bottom are based only on the containing box's font-size values.

> Browser implementation of vertical-align is highly variable and is dependent upon factors such as font-size, ex calculation, and others. The safest values for consistency's sake are sub, super, measurements, and percentages; fortunately, the others are not particularly useful most of the time, anyway.

Watch Out!

To create superscripts or subscripts, you use the vertical-align property, probably in combination with font-size; the vertical-align property doesn't affect the size of text, but most subscripts or superscripts are smaller than the surrounding text. Here are some example rules:

```
.atoms { vertical-align: -0.4em;
         font-size: smaller; }
.power { vertical-align: super;
         font-size: smaller; }
```

You'd use these style rules in HTML by setting class attributes, like this.

```
H<span class="atoms">2</span>0
x<span class="power">2</span> - 1 = 63
```

The effects of these styles can be seen in Figure 15.3. You could also use the HTML Transitional elements <sub> and <sup> for the same effects, but CSS affords you more control over the specific presentation details.

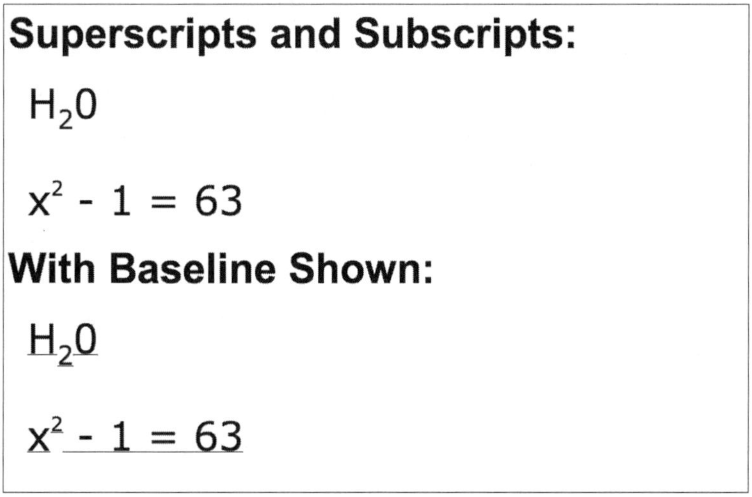

Superscripts and Subscripts:

$H_2 0$

$x^2 - 1 = 63$

With Baseline Shown:

$H_2 0$

$x^2 - 1 = 63$

FIGURE 15.3
Superscripts and subscripts in CSS.

Floating Content

Another way to align content is to *float* it. Floating boxes move to one side or another according to the value of the `float` property, and any following content flows around them in a liquid fashion. The `clear` property can be used to indicate when the rest of the content should stop flowing around the floating box.

This effect should be familiar to experienced HTML developers who have used the `align` attribute on `<img>` or `<table>` tags to position floating content on either side of the page layout. The `clear` attribute on the `<br>` tag has been used to control when the floating should end. The CSS properties `float` and `clear` can be used on any HTML elements and therefore greatly extend the types of content that can be set to float or to stop flowing.

An example of floating content can be seen in Figure 15.4; the pull quote is positioned on the left, and the subsequent text content wraps around it on the right side and then flows back out to the full width when the quote ends.

FIGURE 15.4
Floating content to the left.

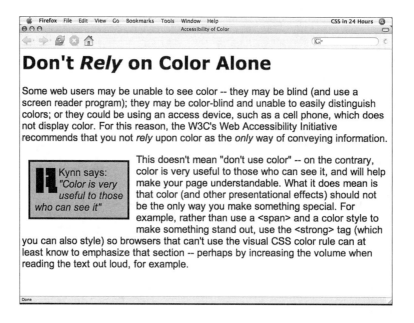

Floating content is especially useful for pictures (with or without captions), pull quotes, and sidebar text.

The `float` **Property**

The values for the `float` property are shown in Table 15.4; the default value is none, meaning that the box and subsequent content are laid out according to the normal flow.

TABLE 15.4 Values for the `float` **Property**

Value	Effect
left	The box moves to the left, and text flows around the right side.
none	The box doesn't move, and text is not flowed around it.
right	The box moves to the right, and text flows around the left side.
inherit	Use the `float` value of the containing box.

When a box is floated, it is positioned within its containing box's content section. The floating box remains within the margin, border, and padding of its containing box; it simply moves to the right or left side as appropriate. Any subsequent content is placed alongside the floating box for the length of that box.

The source for the page in Figure 15.4 is shown in Listing 15.3.

LISTING 15.3 An HTML File with a Pull Quote That Will Be Floated

```
<!-- pullquote-15.3.html -->
<html>
  <head>
    <title>Accessibility of Color</title>
    <style type="text/css">
      h1 { font-family: Verdana, sans-serif; }
      p  { font-size: large;
           font-family: Arial, sans-serif;
           line-spacing: 1.25; }
      .pullquote
        { float: left;
          font-family: Verdana, sans-serif;
          text-indent: 0;
          border: 5px solid black;
          padding: 0.5em;
          margin: 0.75em;
          background-color: silver; }
      .pullquote p
        { margin: 0; padding: 0; }
      .pullquote blockquote
        { font-style: italic;
          padding: 0; margin: 0; }
      .pullquote img { float: left; }
    </style>
  </head>
  <body>
    <h1>Don't <em>Rely</em> on Color Alone</h1>
```

LISTING 15.3   Continued

```
<p> Some web users may be unable to see color -- they may
   be blind (and use a screen reader program); they may
   be color-blind and unable to easily distinguish colors;
   or they could be using an access device, such as a cell
   phone, which does not display color. For this reason,
   the W3C's Web Accessibility Initiative recommends that
   you not <em>rely</em> upon color as the <em>only</em>
   way of conveying information.</p>
<div class="pullquote">
   <img src="k.gif" alt=""> <!-- decorative only -->
   <p>Kynn says:</p>
   <blockquote>
      <p>"Color is very<br>
      useful to those<br>
      who can see it"</p>
   </blockquote>
</div>
<p> This doesn't mean "don't use color" -- on the contrary,
   color is very useful to those who can see it, and will
   help make your page understandable.  What it does mean
   is that color (and other presentational effects) should
   not be the only way you make something special.  For
   example, rather than use a &lt;span&gt; and a color
   style to make something stand out, use the &lt;strong&gt;
   tag (which you can also style) so browsers that
   can't use the visual CSS color rule can at least know
   to emphasize that section -- perhaps by increasing the
   volume when reading the text out loud, for example.</p>
</body>
</html>
```

The rule that makes the content move to the side is float: left. To place the pull-quote on the right side of the text, you can simply change that rule to read float: right instead. This is shown in Figure 15.5.

Did you Know?

> Other properties can be set on floated elements, of course, and some of the most useful are the margin properties, which can be used to affect how close subsequent content will flow. For example, margin-left on a right-floating element keeps the flowing text at a respectable distance. The example in Listing 15.3 also sets a background on the pull quote, as well as increases the size and adds italics.

In addition to the pull quote itself, there's an additional piece of floating content in this example—the graphic symbol within the pull-quote is also floating. This was set by the following rule in the embedded style sheet:

```
.pullquote img { float: left; }
```

Notice that this rule moves the image within its own containing box—the pull quote <div>—and doesn't move it to the edge of the entire page.

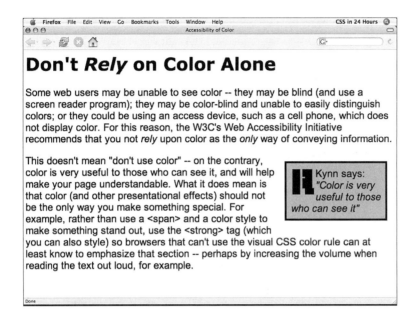

FIGURE 15.5
Floating the content to the right.

The clear Property

To stop subsequent text from flowing around a floating element, you can set the clear property on the first element you don't want to flow. This moves that element down far enough so that it doesn't wrap around the floating box. This effectively increases the top margin of the element with the clear property on it by an amount calculated by the browser to provide enough space to reach past the floating box.

The values for clear are shown in Table 15.5; naturally, the default value is none. Other values specify whether the content should stop the flow around all floating boxes or only boxes on either the left or right side.

TABLE 15.5 Values for the clear Property

Value	Effect
both	Move this box down enough so it doesn't flow around floating boxes.
left	Move this box down enough so it doesn't flow around left-floating boxes.
none	Don't move this box; allow it to flow normally.
right	Move this box down enough so it doesn't flow around right-floating boxes.
inherit	Use the clear value of the containing box.

To use this property with the pull quote example from Listing 15.3 requires only adding a rule such as this to the embedded style sheet:

```
blockquote { clear: left; }
```

This rule says that when a `<blockquote>` element is found, stop flowing the text around floated elements, and move down far enough to get past any that are present.

The `<blockquote>` in Listing 15.3 would normally flow around the floating image next to "Kynn says:", but as shown in Figure 15.6, the `clear` rule stops the flow of text.

FIGURE 15.6
Clearing the float at the blockquote.

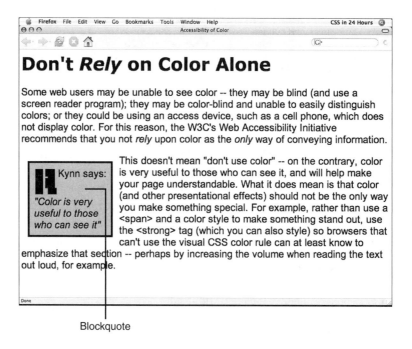

Blockquote

Sometimes, if you float multiple boxes of content, you get a staggered effect down the page, where one box is positioned against the lower right corner of another. This happens because floated content tries to locate itself as high as possible, in addition to moving to the left or right. To avoid this problem, set a `clear` property on your floating content, like this:

```
div#sidebar { float: right; clear: right; }
```

Thumbnail Galleries

A common use for the float property is in creating a gallery of thumbnail images
that link to larger pictures, for displaying photographs or artwork on a website.
Listing 15.4 is an HTML page with embedded style sheet that employs float in this
manner.

LISTING 15.4   A Simple Photo Gallery Page

```
<!-- gallery-15.4.html -->
<html>
  <head>
    <title>Desert Museum Pictures</title>
    <style type="text/css">
      body { font-family: Verdana, sans-serif; }
      #gallery
        { border: 3px solid gray;
          margin: 1em;
          padding: 0.75em; }
      #gallery h2 { margin: 0; }
      #gallery div
        { border: 1px solid black;
          margin: 10px;
          padding: 10px;
          width: 100px;
          font-size: small;
          float: left;
          text-align: center; }
      #gallery h2
        { clear: left; }
      #credits { clear: both; }
    </style>
  </head>
  <body>
    <h1>Desert Museum</h1>
    <p>Here are some pictures I took at the
      Arizona-Sonora Desert Museum in Tucson:</p>
    <div id="gallery">
      <h2>Mammals:</h2>
      <div>
        <a href="pics/coyote-001.jpg"><img
          src="pics/thumb/coyote-001_thumb.jpg"
          border="Thumbnail"></a><br>
        A Coyote
      </div>
      <div>
        <a href="pics/coyote-002.jpg"><img
          src="pics/thumb/coyote-002_thumb.jpg"
          border="Thumbnail"></a><br>
        Another Coyote
      </div>
      ... <!-- more like these -->
      <h2>Birds:</h2>
      ...
      <p id="credits">
        Pictures taken by
```

LISTING 15.4   A Simple Photo Gallery Page

```
        <a href="http://kynn.com/">Kynn Bartlett</a>.
      </p>
    </div>
  </body>
</html>
```

The picture gallery here uses the `width` property, which you'll learn about in Hour 18, "Box Sizing and Offset." The `width` property forces all the images and their captions to take up the same horizontal space.

Figure 15.7 shows the results of displaying this page in a browser. When the browser window changes—because of different screen resolution or simply shrinking the size of the browser application's window—the pictures continue to line up. The extra pictures just get pushed down to the next available space.

FIGURE 15.7
Thumbnail gallery displayed in a browser.

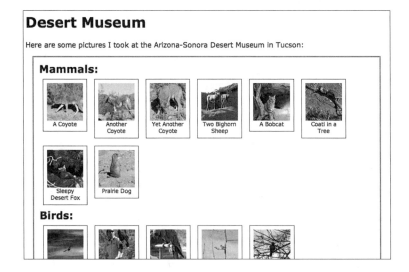

Try it Yourself

Create an Image Gallery

Use CSS to display your own pictures as in this example. Follow these steps:

1. Get a number of pictures together, perhaps some you've taken on a family vacation or at a friend's birthday party. Save these all in one web directory.

2. Using a graphics program, create smaller versions of these pictures that are no more than 100 pixels wide. Save these in a "thumb" directory.

3. Create an HTML page similar to that in Listing 15.4, which has a `<div>` around each picture and its caption. Each picture should be a link to the full-size version of the picture.

4. Write a CSS rule using `float` to line up these `<div>`s so that they line up across the page and continue down to the next line when they're out of room.

5. View your gallery in your web browser. What other styles would you like to add to your gallery to enhance its appearance? Some font choices perhaps?

Summary

Several CSS properties allow you to adjust the appearance of text when displayed by the browsers, altering the alignment, indentation, and flow of content.

The `text-align` property specifies whether the text should be lined up on the left side, the right side, or both sides, or in the center. The `text-indent` property lets you set a paragraph indent or other indent, although hanging indents are somewhat unreliable across browsers. The `vertical-align` property lets you specify how text is aligned within an inline box and can create subscripts or superscripts.

The normal flow of the page can be affected by the `float` property, which positions a display box on either the right or left side of its containing box's content area. Subsequent text then flows around the floating box, wrapping around the outer margin. The `clear` property can be used to move content down the page until it no longer flows.

Workshop

The workshop contains a Q&A section, quiz questions, and exercises to help reinforce what you've learned in this hour. If you get stuck, the answers to the quiz can be found after the questions.

Q&A

Q. *The `text-align` property works only on inline content. So how do I align a block element?*

A. You can align a block element in two ways: with margin properties and float. To place a block element on the left side of its containing block, use the `margin-right` property with a value of `auto`, and to align it on the right, use a `margin-left` value of `auto`. To center it, set both `margin-left` and `margin-right` to `auto`. You'll learn more about the right and left margins in Hour 16.

Quiz

1. Which of these rules sets a paragraph indent equal to 300% of the font-size?

    a. p { text-indent: 300%; }

    b. p { text-indent: 30px; }

    c. p { text-indent: 3em; }

2. Part of your web page consists of an image followed by text; the next section begins with an <h3> tag. You want the image to be located on the left and the text to flow around it, but you don't want the next section's header to be placed next to the image. What CSS rules would you write to do this?

Answers

1. Rule (c) is the correct answer. 1em equals the font-size measurement; if the font-size is 12pt, 3em is 36 points. Percentages in text-indent, such as rule (a), are based on the containing block's size; so text-indent: 300% means to have a first line indent that is three times larger than the box holding the paragraph! A more reasonable value would be between 0% and 50%.

2. Here's an example of the type of rules you would write; in practice you'd probably use class or id selectors to make these more specific:

```
img { float: left; }
h3 { clear: left; }
```

Exercises

Your own experiments with the properties in this hour will help you master how to use them to style your text and float content. Try the following to expand your understanding:

- ▶ Using vertical-align: super, create some links that are anchors to footnotes at the bottom of the page. What makes a good-looking footnote reference? Experiment with smaller font size and adding or removing underlines.

- ▶ Try some text styles for your paragraphs, including line spacing (from Hour 10, "Text Colors and Effects") coupled with text-indent. Printed text has often used indentation for paragraph text, whereas web browsers simply use vertical space (created by margins) between paragraphs. Test it out yourself to see how indenting paragraphs changes the feel of your page.

▶ The `float` property can be used to position menus on the sides of your web pages. Create some pages that use `float` to provide simple layout. You'll learn more about using `float` in layout in Hour 20, "Page Layout in CSS," but for now you have a useful tool for styling your pages.

HOUR 16

Borders and Boxes

What You'll Learn in This Hour:

▶ What the four sides of each box are called, and how to refer to them in CSS rules

▶ How to use the margin shorthand property to specify margins for specific sides of a box

▶ Which margin values to set to center boxes horizontally

▶ How to set the padding on each side of a box

▶ Which width, color, and line styles can be used on box borders

▶ How to set borders for specific sides of the box

▶ Which properties and values enable you to hide the display of a box and its contents

Within the CSS visual formatting model, all HTML elements are displayed as either inline boxes or block boxes. Property values in CSS rules affect the way these boxes are displayed by applying the styles to the content of each box.

You learned about the box model in Hour 6, "The CSS Box Model," and how you can use the margin, padding, and border properties to affect how a box is displayed. Those core properties enable you to manipulate the edges of the box itself, from the space around the content, to the border around the box, and finally to the space surrounding the content of the box.

Adjusting Boxes

As you've seen before, CSS browsers view all web pages as a series of nested boxes. Block boxes contain inline boxes or other block boxes; inline boxes contain content, usually text. Styles are applied on a box-by-box basis, using selectors that identify boxes or groups of boxes.

Each of these boxes consists of the inside of the box, which is where you can find the content or any child boxes, and the edge—the margin, border, and padding. As you learned in Hour 6, you can adjust these by using properties known as the *edge properties.* You use the `margin` property to set the blank space just within the limits of the box; the `border` property to set a line surrounding the content, within the margin; and the `padding` property to add spacing between the content and the other edge properties.

Changing these properties lets you affect the appearance and placement of a display box so that you can better control how your content is shown to the web user.

In Hour 6 when I introduced the `margin`, `padding`, and `border` properties, I didn't mention that they are actually shorthand properties, as are the `font` and `background` properties. A shorthand property is one that sets several properties at once, first resetting them to their default values (as defined by the W3C specification) and then setting individual values as given in the declaration. Each of the edge shorthand properties sets the edge characteristics of all four sides of the box.

A box in the CSS has four sides: top, bottom, left, and right. The edge properties for each side are displayed in Figure 16.1.

FIGURE 16.1
The edge properties surrounding the content in the box model, on four sides.

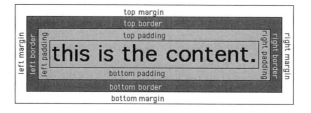

Edge properties for each side enable you either to set the margin, padding, and border separately for every side or to set several at once with a shorthand property. When using a shorthand property, you can specify between one and four values; the results of these values are shown on Table 16.1.

TABLE 16.1 Shorthand Values for Edge Properties

Shorthand Values	Effect
value	Sets all four properties to the same value
value1 value2	Set the top and bottom properties to *value1* and the right and left properties to *value2*
value1 value2 value3	Set the top property to *value1*, the right and left properties to *value2*, and the bottom property to *value3*
value1 value2 value3 value4	Set properties in clockwise order: top, right, bottom, left

Values can also be set with individual properties, such as `margin-left` or `padding-bottom`. A shorthand value always sets all appropriate values; no sides are left unset, even if less than four values are specified.

Setting the Margins

Take a look at setting the margins first. You can set all the margins to a single value with the `margin` property, like this:

```
#content p { margin: 3em; }
```

This would put a margin space of 3 ems around any paragraphs identified by this selector. Remember that vertical margins collapse, so the nearest vertical content will be 3 ems away, unless the other content has a greater margin.

When collapsing margins, you compare the bottom margin of the first box to the top margin of the second. If both are positive, the distance is the greater of the two; if one is negative, the distance is the difference between them. If both vertical margins are negative, the distance between the boxes is the largest negative value. Negative distances mean overlapping display boxes, which is allowable in CSS, albeit often confusing.

Imagine that you want to set just the horizontal margins. Here are four ways to do that:

```
#content p { margin-left: 3em;
             margin-right: 3em; }
#content p { margin: 0em 3em; }
#content p { margin: 0em 3em 0em; }
#content p { margin: 0em 3em 0em 3em; }
```

All these rules are identical in effect; they set the right and left margins to 3 ems.

> Nearly any displayed element box has margins that can be adjusted; the exceptions are table cells. Table cells, represented by <td> or <th> in HTML, don't have margins. See the discussion of table styling in Hour 17, "Styling Tables," for more about this.

Margin values are not inherited; unless otherwise set, a box's margin will be zero. The types of values you can set for margins are shown in Table 16.2.

TABLE 16.2   Values for the `margin` Properties

Value	Effect
measurement	Set the margin(s) to a specified size.
negative measurement	Reduce the margin(s) of touching boxes by a specified size.
percentage	Set the margin(s) to a percentage of the containing box's width.
auto	Automatically calculate the margin(s).
inherit	Use the margin value(s) of the containing box.

> Note that percentages are always based on the width of the containing block, even vertical margins. You'd expect them to be determined relative to the height of the containing box, but this just isn't the case in CSS.

The value auto requires some explanation. If it is set on an inline element's margins, the value is calculated to 0. If set on a box element's left margin or right margin, the margin is set to be all remaining space within the containing box; this will move the box with the margin to one side or another. If both the left and right margins are set to auto, the box will be centered within its containing box. A value of auto for a top or bottom margin has no effect.

Did you Know?

> Actually, a value of auto for any margin can mean more than what I've described here, but only when you're using CSS to position content on the screen. You'll learn more about auto margins in Hour 19, "Absolute and Fixed Positioning," in the discussion on CSS positioning.

Setting the Padding

Setting values for padding in CSS is simpler than setting margin values because there are no auto values and no negative measurements. The only values for padding are measurements and percentages.

Percentage values for padding, such as margin percentages, are based on the containing box's width, even for the top and bottom padding properties.

Here are four different ways to set the top padding to 4 pixels, the left and right padding to 0 pixels, and the bottom padding to 8 pixels:

```
#content p { padding-top: 4px;
             padding-bottom: 8px; }
#content p { padding: 4px 0px 8px; }
#content p { padding: 4px 0px 8px 0px; }
#content p { padding: 4px 0px;
             padding-bottom: 8px; }
```

Note that in the last rule, the padding-bottom was set twice, once as part of the padding shorthand rule, to 4px, and later separately to 8px. Because the second rule comes later (and all other priority factors are the same), the bottom padding will be 8 pixels.

Setting the Border

Borders in CSS have three distinct values associated with them: the width, or thickness of the border; the color of the border; and the style, or type of line drawn. With four sides, that means that there are actually 12 properties associated with the borders: the width, color, and style for top, bottom, left, and right. Each is written as border-*side*-*property*, such as border-left-style or border-bottom-color.

The border shorthand property sets all 12 of these properties at once. Using the border property, you'd write a rule like this:

```
#nav div { border: solid purple 3px; }
```

This defines the border as a solid purple line that is 3 pixels wide. This is the same as the following rule:

```
#nav div { border-top-style: solid;
           border-top-color: purple;
           border-top-width: 3px;
           border-right-style: solid;
           border-right-color: purple;
           border-right-width: 3px;
           border-bottom-style: solid;
           border-bottom-color: purple;
           border-bottom-width: 3px;
           border-left-style: solid;
           border-left-color: purple;
           border-left-width: 3px; }
```

Unlike margin and width, you can't set one to four different values for each side's border using the border shorthand property; instead, you can use one shorthand property per side, as in the following:

```
#nav div { border-left: 1em solid green;
           border-right: 2em dashed blue;
           border-top: 1.5em dotted red;
           border-bottom: 0.5em solid purple; }
```

Alternately, you can use other shorthand properties to set all the border-width, border-color, and border-style values at once. You also can set the 12 border-style properties individually or combine these approaches, using normal CSS cascading rules to resolve priorities.

Border Width

The thickness of the border is set by a border-width value; possible values are shown on Table 16.3. If no border-width value is specified in a shorthand property, the default is medium. For a border to be displayed at all, the border-width value for each side must be set to something, even if it's simply set to the default with a shorthand property.

TABLE 16.3   Values for the border-width **Properties**

Value	Effect
medium	Sets a medium thickness border
thick	Sets a thick border
thin	Sets a thin border
measurement	Sets a border as wide as the specified measurement
inherit	Uses the inherited border-width value of the containing box

The values thin, medium, and thick are relative values whose exact measurements are left up to the browser. The browser can determine the precise thickness however it likes, though within certain constraints; thin can't be thicker than medium, thick can't be thinner than medium, and when displaying a page, all borders of a given thickness must be the same width. One browser's interpretation of these values is shown in Figure 16.2.

The thickness of each side's border doesn't have to be the same; each can be set to a different value if you like. To set different thicknesses, you can either use multiple values with the border-width shorthand property, or use the border-width property for each side. Here are some examples:

```
#nav div { border-width: 3px 2px 3px 4px; }
#nav div { border-top-width: 3px;
           border-right-width: 2px;
           border-bottom-width: 3px;
           border-left-width: 4px; }
#nav div { border-width: 3px 4px;
           border-right: 2px; }
```

These all set the same effect: a top border of 3 pixels, a right border of 2 pixels, a bottom border of 3 pixels, and a left border of 4 pixels.

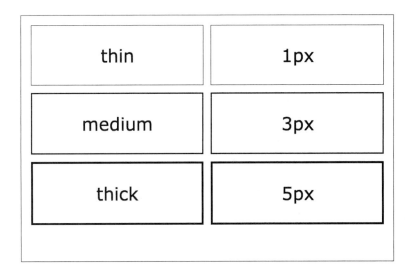

FIGURE 16.2
Each border-
width value dis-
played in
Firefox.

Border values that are measurements based on ems are calculated based on the size of the text for that box. For example, if you have the following rules in your style sheet:

```
body { font-size: 30px; }
.sidebar { font-size: 50%; border: 0.2em; }
```

The text within the .sidebar will be 50% of 30px, or 15px, and the border will be 0.2em at that current size, or 3px wide. It won't be 6px, which is what it would be based on the size of the body text, not the .sidebar text. If there were no font-size rule for .sidebar, then the border would be 6px wide. This also applies to margins and padding, so when you change the size of the text in a box, you may also change relative units as well, which are based on that font size.

Did you *Know?*

Border Color

The color of all borders can be set at once with the border-color shorthand property or set individually with the border-top-color, border-right-color, border-bottom-color, and border-left-color properties. If no color is specified, the default color value will be the foreground text color set by the color attribute.

You can specify the border color as you would any other colors in CSS: by RGB hex values, numeric values, or percentages, or by color name. Examples of setting border color are

```
#nav div { border-color: red white blue; }
#nav div { border-top-color: red;
           border-right-color: white;
           border-bottom-color: blue;
           border-left-color: white; }
```

Border Style

The line appearance of the border is determined by the border-style properties: border-top-style, border-right-style, border-bottom-style, and border-left-style. These can be set with the border shorthand property or with the border-style shorthand property that sets the style for all four of the borders.

Valid border types are shown on Table 16.4. Hour 6 introduced the solid, dashed, and dotted values. This hour adds the three-dimensional border values groove, ridge, inset, and outset, as well as the hidden and double values.

TABLE 16.4   Values for the border-style **Properties**

Value	Effect
dashed	A dashed border
dotted	A dotted border
double	A solid double line border
groove	The border appears to be carved into the page
hidden	No border displayed; borders collapsed in tables
inset	The entire box appears to be carved into the page
none	No border displayed
outset	The entire box appears to rise up from the page
ridge	The border appears to rise up from the page
solid	A solid single line border
inherit	Use the value of the border-style from the containing box

The none and hidden values are identical—no border is displayed—except in table styles. In Hour 17 you'll learn more about collapsing borders for table cells.

The exact rendition of each border style is left up to the browser implementation, constrained by the definitions of each style; obviously, a dashed border should be made up of dashed lines. Examples of each type of border are shown in Figure 16.3.

Not all browsers support all border styles; in fact, the CSS specifications explicitly allow them to opt out certain border styles. Browsers that don't display all border styles can instead choose to show them as solid. However, the styles listed here are currently supported by all modern browsers.

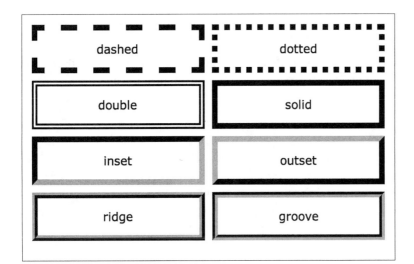

FIGURE 16.3
Each border-style value displayed in Firefox.

Displaying Boxes

In addition to changing the properties of the box edge, you can also set certain boxes to not be displayed at all or to display differently. The properties controlling this are the display and visibility properties.

Why wouldn't you want a box to display? Well, in most cases you'll want them to show up; this is why they're in the page content, after all. However, you may want to hide a display box if that content is inappropriate for the type of output medium being used. For example, a navigation bar may not make sense on the printed page because you obviously can't click on paper. The display and visibility properties are also useful with JavaScript to produce Dynamic HTML effects.

> You'll learn more about style sheets for printers in Hour 22, "Accessibility and Print Media." Bonus Web Hour 1, "CSS and JavaScript" (on the book's website), can fill you in on Dynamic HTML.

By the Way

The display **Property**

As you've seen before, you can use the display property to change a box from a block element to an inline element or vice versa; you can also use it to make something display as a list item. In general, you'll want to avoid overriding the default display rules for HTML in browsers; there are too many things that can get confused if you do this, such as the default margins on certain elements. However, setting the `display` property is very useful when you're dealing with XML, as you'll learn in Bonus Web Hour 2, "CSS and XML" (on the book's website).

There are going to be some times when you're going to want to use the `display` property with HTML, especially if you need to hide some content. The values you can assign to `display` are shown in Table 16.5.

TABLE 16.5   Values for the `display` Property

Value	Effect
`block`	Display as a block box
`inline`	Display as an inline box
`inline-block`	Display inline, as an inline box, but with the box's content displayed as if it were a block box
`list-item`	Display as a list item with list item marker
`none`	Don't display the box or its children boxes
`run-in`	Display as a run-in box
`inherit`	Use the display value of the containing box

In addition to the values listed here, there are several values for display that apply only to tables, such as `inline-table` or `table-row-group`; these are covered in Hour 17.

The `inline-block` property was introduced in CSS Level 2.1, and is a compromise between an `inline` box and a `block` box. For purposes of placing the `inline-block` box, it is treated as an `inline` element. However, `inline` elements usually contain only other `inline` boxes; the `inline-block` element contains block-level boxes.

Boxes with the `display` value `run-in` are displayed as either block or inline depending on context. A `run-in` box displays as a block element unless there's another block element (which isn't positioned with CSS positioning) after it as a sibling element, in which case it will become the first inline block of that subsequent block element.

> The `run-in` value for the `display` property isn't supported by Firefox. However, `run-in` boxes are rather complex for the actual benefit they provide; you can likely get the same effect with other properties, values, and markup, rather than try to use `run-in`.

Hiding Boxes with `display: none`

The value *none* means that any selected elements aren't displayed; their boxes (and the boxes of their children) don't even appear. This value technically isn't inherited, but if you set one box to `display: none` and then try to set one of its children to `display: block` (or `display: inline`), the inner box still doesn't appear.

Did you Know?

The `display` property is a handy way to include messages for users with browsers that don't support CSS, such as Lynx. For example, if you're using a specific color to mark new entries, you can add some text explanations with `display: none`. Here is an example:

```
New books are marked in red<span class="hidden">
or with the word New</span>:
<ul>
  <li><span class="hidden">New:</span>
      <span class="new">Teach Yourself CSS in 24 Hours</span>
  </li>
</ul>
```

You'd then write CSS rules to support those classes, like this:

```
.hidden { display: none; }
.new { color: red; }
```

Watch Out!

You might guess you'd be able to use the `display` trick to hide or reveal content selectively for users with visual disabilities who use screen readers, perhaps in combination with a media type. If you thought that, you wouldn't be alone (a lot of experienced web developers have assumed it would work that way), but unfortunately it's not true in practice. Screen readers take their presentation from what's displayed on the screen by a browser such as Internet Explorer, and if you hide accessibility information with a `display: none` rule, the browser won't see it— and neither will the screen reader. For some interesting attempts at work-arounds, see Hour 24, "Troubleshooting and Browser Hacks."

Styling Navigation Lists

A navigation bar on a web page is simply a list of links—a list in the normal English sense of the word *list*, not the HTML meaning with <ul> and <li> tags. Or is it?

Most navigation bars don't need list markers, such as bullets or numbers. Furthermore, many navigation bars are horizontal, whereas lists are vertical. So at first glance, an HTML list built with <ul> would seem inappropriate for navigation.

However, you can use the `display` property to change the way these lists are displayed. Consider the following HTML, which contains a navigation list:

```
<ul id="nav">
  <li><a href="/">Home</a></li>
  <li><a href="/author.html">The Author</a></li>
  <li><a href="/downloads.html">Downloads</a></li>
  <li><a href="/contact.html">Contact</a></li>
</ul>
```

Normally this is displayed by a browser as a list of bullet items. Using CSS, you can style this to be either a vertical navigation bar or a horizontal one.

To create a vertical navigation bar, simply use these simple style rules:

```
#nav li { display: block; }
#nav { padding: 0; margin: 0; }
```

This changes the list items from `display` type `list-item` to `block`, and remove the padding and margins inserted by `<ul>` lists.

To create a horizontal navigation bar, you can do the same, but change the list items to inline blocks:

```
#nav li { display: inline; padding-right: 1em; padding-left: 1em; }
```

Some `padding` was added to provide some extra space. Of course, you can use CSS to set background colors, borders, and any other appropriate properties you wish on the `<ul>` and `<li>` elements. Figure 16.4 displays the same navigation list three times—the identical HTML, but styled to be a vertical navigation bar and a horizontal navigation bar.

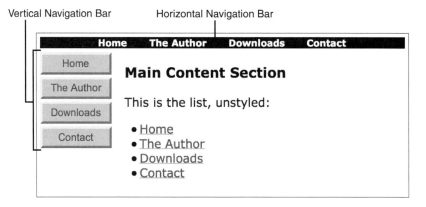

FIGURE 16.4
A navigation list restyled to navigation bars.

Try it Yourself   ▼

Create Graphics-Free Navigation Buttons

The border properties can be used in conjunction with color, background-color, and font properties to create "buttons" that look like graphics but are really HTML tags with styles applied. Here are some ideas you could try for practice:

1. Use a simple HTML list to create a menu bar. Add this to a web page as a navigation bar, using either tables for layout or CSS-based layouts (described in Hour 20, "Page Layout in CSS").

2. Add style rules to change the navigation bar to be either vertical or horizontal, as fits your page. If you have two navigation bars—and many pages will—then style one as horizontal and one as vertical.

3. Set the font characteristics and size, the foreground and background colors, and the text-decoration on any links present.

4. Draw a border around each list item, using an inset or outset border-style. This will make your button appear to stand out (or sink into) the page.

5. Finally, change the border style to solid and try setting your own colors on each border to give a different three-dimensional effect. If you set the colors explicitly, you have more control over the resulting button's appearance. To make a button stand out from the page, use a light color on the top and left and a darker color on the right and bottom.   ▲

The visibility **Property**

Both the visibility and display properties affect whether or not the element's display box is shown. The difference between the two is that visibility sets aside a place on the page for an undisplayed box, whereas display does not. The place where the box (and its contents) would normally be displayed is instead shown as a transparent box of the same size. The values for visibility are shown on Table 16.6.

TABLE 16.6   Values for the visibility **Property**

Value	Effect
collapse	Collapse only table cells; see Hour 17
hidden	Don't display the box, but reserve the space in the layout
visible	Display the box normally
inherit	Use the visibility value of the containing box

The `visibility` property is most useful in dynamic HTML and JavaScript, where you can interactively change the `visibility` of a box in response to user actions. For more on this, see Bonus Web Hour 1 on the book's website.

Summary

Each side of a display box is named: top, right, bottom, and left. You can set the margins and padding space for each, using shorthand properties or individual properties. If you use shorthand properties and specify one value, it applies to all sides; two values assign the top/bottom and left/right; three designate top, left/right, and bottom; and four values set the properties in clockwise order.

There are also 12 properties that control the borders, and a number of shorthand properties exist to set them all in various combinations. The width, color, and line style of the borders can be set all at once, or they can be set individually for each side.

You can also control whether or not a box is displayed at all. To hide a box entirely, use the `display: none` value. If you want to reserve space for the box, but not actually show it or its content, use the `visibility` property with a value of `hidden`.

Workshop

The workshop contains a Q&A section, quiz questions, and an exercise to help reinforce what you've learned in this hour. If you get stuck, the answers to the quiz can be found after the questions.

Q&A

Q. *How can I align a box with* `margin` *properties?*

A. Here's how it works. First, don't use `text-align` unless you want the content of the box to be aligned. Instead, use `margin-left` and `margin-right` properties as shown here:

```
.left   { margin-right: auto; }    /* align left */
.right  { margin-left:  auto; }    /* align right */
.center { margin-right: auto;
          margin-left:  auto; }    /* center */
```

Q. *I tried setting a black border that should be* `inset, groove, outset,` *or* `ridge,` *and it showed up as* `solid`*! What gives?*

A. When you set a border with those three-dimensional border types, you add the third dimension by adjusting the base color. The edges "facing the light" are colored lighter, and the edges "in shadow" are darker. The CSS specification doesn't say how to derive those colors, so browsers are free to use their own methods. If a browser decides that the light color is 20% brighter and the dark color is 20% darker, that works unless your color is less than 20% dark to begin with, like black (#000000)—you can't actually make a darker version of #000000. If you want to be certain that your border colors appear properly three-dimensional, you should set the border style to solid and manually choose your own lighter and darker side colors, setting them individually on each side border.

Quiz

1. These two shorthand properties set the margin and padding. What are equivalent declarations that don't use shorthand properties, and instead use properties such as margin-left?

   ```
   #demo { margin: 0em 1em 1.5em;
           padding: 5px 7px; }
   ```

2. Likewise, these border shorthand properties can be written as 12 separate property value declarations. What are they?

   ```
   #demo2 { border: 3px groove black;
            border-style: dashed dotted double solid;
            border-left: medium inset green; }
   ```

3. A box that looks like it's depressed into the page has been styled with which border line style?

   a. border-style: emboss;

   b. border-style: groove;

   c. border-style: inset;

   d. border-style: sunken;

4. What's the difference between these two rules?

   ```
   .hide1 { visibility: hidden; }
   .hide2 { display: none; }
   ```

Answers

1. The equivalent declarations are

```
#demo { margin-top: 0em;
        margin-right: 1em;
        margin-bottom: 1.5em;
        margin-left: 1em;
        padding-top: 5px;
        padding-right: 7px;
        padding-bottom: 5px;
        padding-left: 7px; }
```

2. Here's how to write those rules as separate properties:

```
#demo2 { border-top-width: 3px;
         border-top-color: black;
         border-top-style: dashed
         border-right-width: 3px;
         border-right-color: black;
         border-right-style: dotted;
         border-bottom-width: 3px;
         border-bottom-color: black;
         border-bottom-style: double;
         border-left-width: medium;
         border-left-color: green;
         border-left-style: inset; }
```

Aren't shorthand properties nicer?

3. The correct answer is (c), inset. The groove value makes the line appear carved but not the box itself, and there are no such values as emboss or sunken for border styles.

4. With the first rule, empty (transparent) space is reserved for the box, but with the second, no space is reserved and the box won't be displayed at all.

Exercise

Give yourself some practice with the box properties by experimenting with the appearance of padding, margin, and borders. The <blockquote> element is a good subject for such experimentation: It is used to identify sections of text that are quoted from another source. Special margins, padding, and borders are therefore useful for identifying these.

The default styles in web browsers for <blockquote> set margins on the left and right side. Try writing rules that style these quotes differently. For example, your block quotes could have a solid, thin black line on the top and bottom (with an attractive bit of padding added), or a thick dotted line on the left side with no extra margins added. Find something you like—and don't neglect changing the font, the color, and the background color to suit your tastes.

HOUR 17

Styling Tables

What You'll Learn in This Hour:

▶ What the HTML table model is, and how it is used with CSS
▶ How tables are laid out on the screen
▶ What the layers of a table are, and how CSS rules can be used to affect cells in those layers
▶ How the borders, padding, and spacing of table cells can be affected by CSS
▶ How to use other CSS properties with table layout

Tables in HTML are a staple of web development and are used for everything from schedules and calendars to page layout. Although CSS offers the capability to replace tables for visual design of the page, it's a more common scenario to find tables and CSS styles used together for best effect.

Table Formatting

Tables are ubiquitous on the Web and constitute the primary way of formatting output visually; they were intended originally for pure data but have evolved to serve as a rudimentary page-layout sublanguage within HTML.

In Hour 20, "Page Layout in CSS," I show you how you can eliminate tables entirely from your web designs and use pure CSS for the positioning of page elements. In this hour, I'm going to assume that you are using tables either for data or layout; the properties here can be used for either. The examples given are for data tables but apply equally well to layout tables.

HTML Table Model

The way HTML browsers display tables should be familiar to anyone who has done web development work. Tables are employed not only for displaying columns of tabular data, but also for graphically laying out entire pages on the screen.

To do any serious web development, you need to know how tables are used in HTML. This same knowledge will serve you well in CSS because the CSS table model is based on the HTML table model. You have probably worked with tables before, and this explanation will be a review for you.

An HTML table is defined by the `<table>` element. Within the opening and closing tags of the `<table>` can be found a number of table rows, designated by the `<tr>` tag. Each row is composed of one or more table cells. A table cell can be either table data, `<td>`, or a table header, `<th>`. Table headers are generally assumed to convey some sort of information about the corresponding table data cells; at least, if the markup is used properly, this will be true.

More complex tables can be built by collecting table rows into groups, using the `<thead>`, `<tbody>`, and `<tfoot>` elements. Each of these tags defines a container that holds one or more table rows and identifies them as a group. The `<thead>` tag is used to designate table header rows; if a printed table spans more than one sheet of paper, the `<thead>` should be repeated on the top of each page. The `<tfoot>` is the complement of the table header rows; it is a group of rows that serves as a footer and should also be repeated if the table spans multiple pages. Table body sections, marked with `<tbody>` tags, group together related rows; a table can have one or more `<tbody>` sections.

An example of a data table built with table row groups can be seen in Listing 17.1; this is an HTML file that contains a weekly listing of scheduled events. In fact, it's my current schedule, as I'm writing this book; you can assume that all other time is taken up with either writing or sleeping, and often with very little of the latter!

LISTING 17.1   A Simple HTML Table

```
<!-- schedule-17.1.html -->
<html>
  <head>
    <title>Weekly Schedule</title>
  </head>
  <body>
    <table>
      <caption>My Schedule</caption>
      <thead>
        <tr>
          <th></th>
          <th>Mon</th>
          <th>Tue</th>
```

LISTING 17.1 Continued

```
          <th>Wed</th>
          <th>Thu</th>
          <th>Fri</th>
        </tr>
      </thead>
      <tbody>
        <tr>
          <th>Morning</th>
          <td>Class</td>
          <td></td>
          <td>Class</td>
          <td></td>
          <td></td>
        </tr>
        <tr>
          <th>Afternoon</th>
          <td></td>
          <td>Online Gaming</td>
          <td></td>
          <td></td>
          <td></td>
        </tr>
        <tr>
          <th>Evening</th>
          <td></td>
          <td>Class</td>
          <td></td>
          <td>Game Night</td>
          <td></td>
        </tr>
      </tbody>
    </table>
  </body>
</html>
 </html>
```

This sample table also contains a <caption> tag; the caption is used to provide a label for the table. You could have specified table columns, as well, by using the <colgroup> and <col> tags, but for now, this table will serve as an effective example for your table-related style properties. Later in this hour, I'll cover columns and column groups.

A web browser displays tables with default styling based on the browser's understanding of table markup. Borders typically aren't drawn between cells or around the table; table data cells are left-justified in normal text; table header cells are center-justified and set in bold font; and captions are centered over the table. This can be seen in Figure 17.1, which shows the default styles Firefox uses to display a table.

FIGURE 17.1
Schedule table
with default
HTML styling in
Firefox.

My Schedule				
Mon	**Tue**	**Wed**	**Thu**	**Fri**
Morning Class		Class		
Afternoon	Online Gaming			
Evening	Class		Game Night	

CSS Table Layout

The Cascading Style Sheets model for tables is based on the HTML model; CSS was specifically built to be compatible with HTML as used on the web. Style sheets can be used in conjunction with HTML markup to style and present columns and rows of information or to lay out the whole page on the screen.

> Just because you can do something, that doesn't mean you always should. HTML tables were not originally designed for page layout; in Hour 20 you'll learn how you can use CSS positioning properties to create powerful and flexible layouts without using `<table>` tags. You may still want to use layout tables for backward compatibility with older browsers, but you should also be aware that tables, as a visual way of conveying information, may sometimes leave behind people who have vision-related disabilities. For more on users with disabilities, see Hour 22, "Accessibility and Print Media."

The link between the HTML and CSS table models is the `display` property in CSS. Each table tag corresponds to a value for `display`; the default style sheet within a CSS-based browser specifies how each item should be shown to the user. The list of additional `display` values is shown in Table 17.1.

TABLE 17.1   Table-Related Values for the `display` Property

Value	Effect
`inline-table`	As `<table>`; displayed as an inline box.
`table`	As `<table>`; displayed as a block box.
`table-caption`	As `<caption>`; displayed before, after, or beside the table.
`table-cell`	As `<td>` or `<th>`; an individual table cell.
`table-column`	As `<col>`; not displayed but can be used for formatting.
`table-column-group`	As `<colgroup>`; not displayed but can be used for formatting.
`table-footer-group`	As `<tfoot>`; designates a group of footer rows.

TABLE 17.1 Continued

Value	Effect
table-header-group	As <thead>; designates a group of header rows.
table-row	As <tr>; a row of table cells.
table-row-group	As <tbody>; designates a group of rows.

Because these values are built into the browser, you won't ever actually need to change the display property to work with tables, but it is useful to know how CSS considers each. For example, CSS classifies <td> and <th> as the same type of display property.

Table cells in CSS are treated as block boxes; they can contain inline or block content and are contained by table-row block boxes. Table rows and groups of table rows are used primarily for grouping. Usually, styles can't be applied to them directly, although properties that are inherited can be set on rows or groups of rows and will apply to cells (<td> or <th>) within those rows.

In general, applying styles to table cells is straightforward and follows all the normal rules of cascade and inheritance; nearly any CSS properties can be set on table cells. There are a few exceptions, however, so before you go on, I'll spend some time looking at how CSS styles interact with HTML tables.

Layers and Inheritance

One key way in which tables differ from other block boxes is the introduction of table layers into the inheritance method. Each cell is considered to be a descendant of several other layers of markup, as shown on Table 17.2.

TABLE 17.2 Table Layers, in Order from Most Specific to Most General

Layer	Equivalent HTML
cells	<td>, <th>
rows	<tr>
row groups	<thead>, <tbody>, <tfoot>
columns	<col>
column groups	<colgroup>
table	<table>

The most surprising thing about table layers is that they exist even if the actual tags do not! For example, all cells are part of a row group, even if there are no <thead>, <tbody>, or <tfoot> tags in the document. It is assumed that there is an unstated, invisible `<tbody>` surrounding all table rows that aren't already within a row group. Likewise, all cells are part of columns and column groups.

When considering the appearance of a table cell, you need to take into account the effects of these table layers. For example, the `background-color` property is normally transparent unless otherwise specified. This means that the background of the containing box of the `<table>` is visible. If `background-color` is set on a `<tbody>`, that is the cell's background color, unless the property is set on a `<tr>` or a table cell, which are more specific, according to the table layers model.

Automatic and Fixed Layouts

The browser usually automatically determines the dimensions of the table's box and of the box sizes of each cell within it. Browsers generally follow the same method of calculating the size, but this is not a requirement, and in fact the CSS Level 2.1 specification allows browsers to use whatever method they like to size a table and its cells. This is called an *automatic layout*.

However, in many cases you need more control over the dimensions of the table. At those times, you'll want to use a *fixed layout*, one where the width and cells of the table are specified in the CSS rules. To tell the browser you're working with a fixed layout, use the `table-layout` property. Values for `table-layout` are shown in Table 17.3; the default is `auto`. This property can be set only on table elements.

TABLE 17.3   Values for the `table-layout` Property

Value	Effect
`auto`	Let the browser determine the dimensions of the table and table cells.
`fixed`	Explicitly designate the width of each table cell.
`inherit`	Use the value of `table-layout` set on the containing block.

After you have informed the browser that you're using a fixed layout, you then need to define the widths of each column. You do this by setting the `width` property on the table and on each table cell. The value of the `width` property can be either a measurement, such as `300px` or `6em`, or a percentage value.

Did you Know?

The `width` property can be used with other block elements, as well; you'll learn more about this useful property in Hour 18, "Box Sizing and Offset."

The style sheet in Listing 17.2 sets the `table-layout` property to `fixed` and provides width values for the table and for each table cell. A border is drawn around each cell to make the widths more apparent.

LISTING 17.2 Style Sheet with Fixed Layout

```
/* schedule-17.2.css */

table { table-layout: fixed;
        width: 90%; }
td, th { width: 15%;
        border: 2px solid gray; }
```

Applying this style sheet to the schedule table from Listing 17.1 produces the effects shown in Figure 17.2. The primary advantage of a fixed layout is that it displays faster because the browser doesn't have to calculate the column widths.

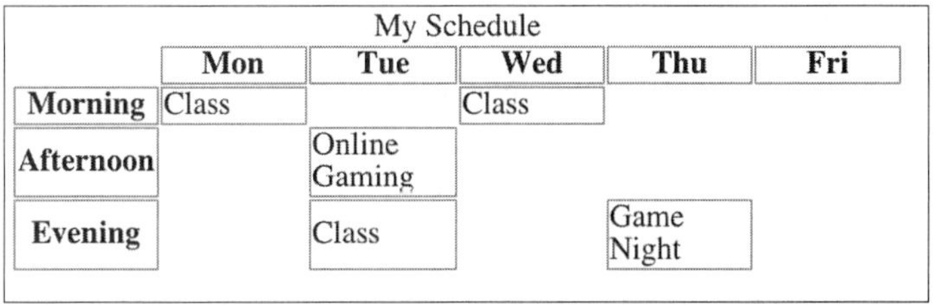

FIGURE 17.2
Firefox displays a schedule with a fixed layout.

Table Borders, Padding, and Spacing

Like other block display boxes in CSS, table cells can be surrounded by borders and can have internal padding. Unlike other block boxes, though, a table cell never has a margin on any side. Instead, table styles are used to control spacing around table cells.

The appearance of a table cell's borders is affected by several properties that determine which cells display borders and how adjacent borders interact with each other.

Displaying or Hiding Empty Cells

If you looked carefully at Figure 17.2, you might have noticed something unusual: Only cells that contained content had borders drawn around them. This can be an effective way of presenting information in some circumstances, but in others you are going to want a border drawn around all table cells, even those that are empty. You can control the display of borders around table cells by using the `empty-cells` property.

The empty-cells property can be set only on table elements, and the valid values for this property are shown in Table 17.4. The default is hide, which means borders aren't shown for empty cells.

TABLE 17.4   Values for the empty-cells **Property**

Value	Effect
hide	Don't display borders for empty cells.
show	Display appropriate borders for empty cells.
inherit	Use the value of empty-cells set on the containing box.

By setting empty-cells to show, you are telling the browser that if a cell is empty, it can go ahead and apply whatever border style would be used if the cell contained content. If there is no applicable border to use, the cell isn't displayed. Setting only the empty-cells property without the appropriate border properties (or the border shorthand property) is ineffective.

Listing 17.3 contains rules for several styles of borders, along with an empty-cells: show declaration on the table.

LISTING 17.3   Turning on Borders Around Empty Cells Via the empty-cells **Property**

```
/* schedule-17.3.css */

table { table-layout: auto; width: 90%;
        font-size: large;
        empty-cells: show; }
td, th { width: 15%; }
thead th { border: 0.20em dashed gray; }
tbody th { border: 0.25em solid black; }
td { border: 0.10em solid gray; }
```

In Figure 17.3, you can see the results of applying this style sheet to Listing 17.1; a border surrounds every table cell, in contrast to Figure 17.2.

Collapsing Borders

Within CSS you can have two options for how you want table cell borders to be handled: They can either collapse or remain separate. You can choose which of these two display models to use by setting a value for border-collapse on your <table> element; appropriate values are shown in Table 17.5.

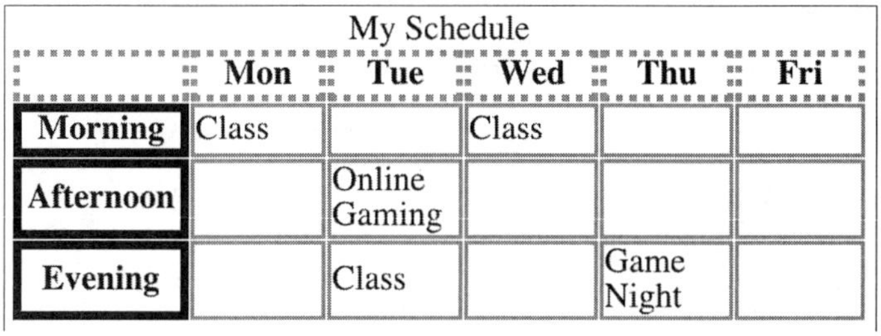

My Schedule					
	Mon	Tue	Wed	Thu	Fri
Morning	Class		Class		
Afternoon		Online Gaming			
Evening		Class		Game Night	

FIGURE 17.3
Empty cells become visible, as shown by Firefox.

TABLE 17.5   Values for the `border-collapse` Property

Value	Effect
collapse	Collapse adjacent borders together.
separate	Keep adjacent borders separated.
inherit	Use the value of `border-collapse` set on the containing box.

In the *collapsed border model*, two cells that are adjacent, horizontally or vertically, share a single, common border line between them. There is no space between the cells; one ends where the other begins. You'd use this to produce a clean, simple table presentation where the cells aren't separated within distinct boxes. This is a style choice you'd make based on how you envision the final look of the table.

If two adjacent cells have different border properties set on them, the border is based on the most visible border of the two. A wider border takes precedence over a narrow border. If two borders are the same width, the border-style determines which one is chosen; in order from most important to least important, a border-style value of double takes precedence over solid, dashed, dotted, ridge, outset, groove, and inset. If two border declarations have the same width and style and differ only in color, a rule set on a more specific layer takes precedence; a style on a table cell beats a row, row group, column, column group, or table rule. Otherwise, normal CSS cascading order is followed.

An example of collapsed borders is shown in Listing 17.4. This table has different border values for <td> and <th> elements in the table heading and body.

LISTING 17.4   Style Sheet to Collapse Borders Between Cells

```
/* schedule-17.4.css */

table      { table-layout: auto; width: 90%;
             border-collapse: collapse;
             font-size: large; empty-cells: show; }
td, th     { width: 15%; }
thead th   { border: 0.20em dotted gray; }
```

LISTING 17.4   Continued

```
tbody th    { border: 0.25em solid black; }
td          { border: 0.10em solid gray; }
```

The effect of collapsing these borders can be seen in Figure 17.4.

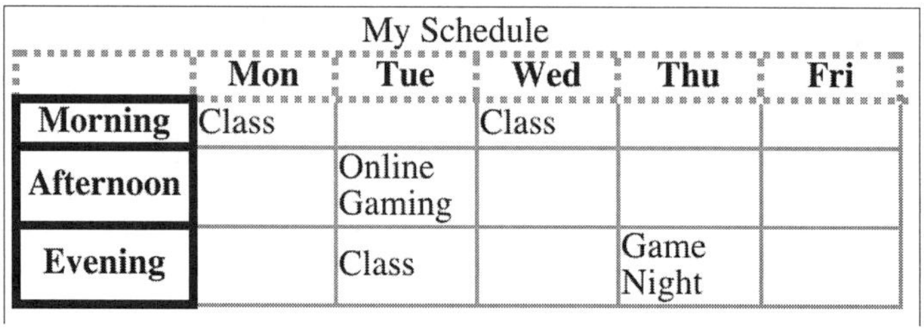

FIGURE 17.4
Collapsed cell borders displayed by Firefox.

Separated Borders

Table cells can also be displayed with space between them. This is known as the *separated borders model* and is selected by a rule on the <table> cell setting the border-collapse property to separate. You'd choose this stylistic approach if you want cells presented as a distinct box, with a background surrounding each one. For example, a table meant to look like a telephone keypad would use separated borders.

In HTML, the spacing between cells is set by the cellspacing attribute; in CSS the same effect is accomplished by the border-spacing property. The border-spacing property sets the distance between the outer edge of adjacent cells—in other words, the spacing between each border. Table 17.6 indicates the possible values for border-spacing; if one value is given, that sets both the horizontal and vertical border-spacing; if two are supplied, the first is the horizontal spacing and the second is the vertical. The space between cells displays the background of the table.

TABLE 17.6   Values for the border-spacing **Property**

Value	Effect
measurement	Set the horizontal and vertical cell-spacing to the same value
measurement measurement	Set the horizontal and vertical cell-spacing, respectively
inherit	Use the value(s) for border-spacing set on the containing box.

Current versions of Internet Explorer do not support the `border-spacing` property.

Listing 17.5 is a style sheet that you can apply to the schedule from Listing 17.1; it displays the cells with a horizontal spacing of `0.45em` and a vertical spacing of `1em`.

LISTING 17.5 Increasing the Spacing Between Cells Using the `border-spacing` **Property**

```
/* schedule-17.5.css */

table      { table-layout: auto; width: 90%;
             border-collapse: separate;
             font-size: large; empty-cells: show;
             border-spacing: 0.45em 1em; }
td, th     { width: 15%; }
thead th   { border: 0.20em dotted gray; }
tbody th   { border: 0.25em solid black; }
td         { border: 0.10em solid gray; }
```

As you can see from Figure 17.5, the applied style sheet spaces out the cells appropriately in the schedule.

My Schedule					
	Mon	Tue	Wed	Thu	Fri
Morning	Class		Class		
Afternoon		Online Gaming			
Evening		Class		Game Night	

FIGURE 17.5
Firefox displays spacing between cells.

Try it Yourself ▼

Styling Your Weekly Calendar

To get your hands dirty with table styles, why not make your own weekly schedule?

1. Create an HTML table containing your weekly schedule.

2. You can break it down into the hours of each day, and then group morning, afternoon, and evening rows, using <tbody> elements.

▼

3. Set specific styles for the `<th>` and `<thead>` elements that are the headers for your columns and rows.

4. Select border styles that fit your personal preferences. Try both the separated and collapsed border models, and see which one you like best. Do you want to display borders around empty cells?

Table Captions

The HTML `<caption>` tag gives the *caption*, which is a label for a table. This appears within the `<table>` element as the first child, and it is usually presented before the table. The display box containing the `<caption>` is as wide as the table itself.

The location of the caption isn't fixed; the CSS `caption-side` property can be used to place the caption on a different side of the table box. The values for `caption-side` are shown in Table 17.7. This property can be set only on `<caption>` elements, and the default value is `top`.

TABLE 17.7   **Values for the `caption-side` Property**

Value	Effect
bottom	Caption appears after the table.
top	Caption appears before the table.
inherit	Uses the value of `caption-side` set on the containing box.

Internet Explorer does not support the `caption-side` property. Your caption always appears before the table rows in Internet Explorer.

The style sheet in Listing 17.6 moves the caption from the top to the bottom and sets specific font and box properties on the caption, as well. The default styling for `<caption>` in most browsers is the default font, centered above the table.

LISTING 17.6   **Style Sheet to Move the Caption to the Bottom of the Table**

```
/* schedule-17.6.css */

table     { table-layout: auto;       width: 90%;
            border-collapse: separate; font-size: large;
            border: 6px double black;
            padding: 1em;
            margin-bottom: 0.5em; }
td, th    { width: 15%; }
```

LISTING 17.6   Continued

```
thead th { border: 0.10em solid black; }
tbody th { border: 0.10em solid black; }
     td { border: 0.10em solid gray; }

caption  { caption-side: bottom;
           font-size: x-large;       font-style: italic;
           border: 6px double black;  padding: 0.5em; }
```

The results of applying this style sheet to the schedule from Listing 17.1 can be seen in Figure 17.6; notice that the widths of the table and the caption are the same.

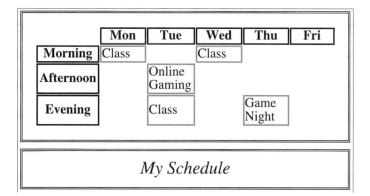

FIGURE 17.6
The caption displayed after the table, by Firefox.

Styling Columns

As noted before, each cell in a table is part of a column in addition to being in a row. Cascading Style Sheets can be used to affect the presentation of columns, but only within certain parameters. If you need to apply a set of style rules to a specific column, such as making the third column of cells have a black background, there are two approaches. The first way to do this is to set the third cell of every row to the same class and then to write a class selector. The second is to write selectors based on columns.

To designate a column or a group of columns, you use the <col> and <colgroup> tags. These can be given class or id attributes to be used in selectors, or they can have style attributes for inline styles.

You'll extend your schedule markup by adding the <colgroup> and <col> tags in your example. Add the following lines to the HTML file from Listing 17.1 immediately after the <caption> tag to define the columns:

```
<colgroup>
  <col id="time">
```

```
</colgroup>
<colgroup id="days">
  <col id="mon">
  <col id="tue">
  <col id="wed">
  <col id="thu">
  <col id="fri">
</colgroup>
```

These tags define specific identifiers for columns, which you can use in your CSS rules with id selectors. Listing 17.7 contains several examples of these types of selectors.

LISTING 17.7   A Style Sheet Based on Columns

```
/* schedule-17.7.css */

table    { table-layout: auto;        width: 90%;
           empty-cells: show;         font-size: large; }
td, th   { width: 15%; }
tbody th { border-top: 2px solid black; }
tbody td { border-top: 2px solid black; }
caption  { caption-side: top;         text-align: right;
           font-size: x-large;        font-style: italic; }
col#mon { background-color: silver; }
col#tue { background-color: black;
          color: white;     /* Note: color rule is ignored! */ }
col#wed { background-color: violet; }
col#thu { background-color: yellow; }
col#fri { background-color: lime; }
```

Only certain types of properties are allowed in column or column group rules; other properties are ignored. The appropriate properties are background and related properties; width; visibility; and the border properties. The visibility property can take the value of collapse to hide an entire column; the border properties are respected only if the collapsing border model has been chosen with the border-collapse property.

Opera and Safari do not support the use of columns and column groups in selectors. To set styles on specific columns in these browsers, you will need to set class attributes on specific table cells and use appropriate class-based selectors.

The effects of applying the style sheet from Listing 17.7 to the modified HTML page, with added column markup, can be seen in Figure 17.7. Note that the rule setting text color on Tuesday is ignored because only background, width, visibility, and border can be set on columns, but the background-color rule was still applied. This leads to black-on-black text, which is unreadable. Be careful that you aren't hiding text like this accidentally.

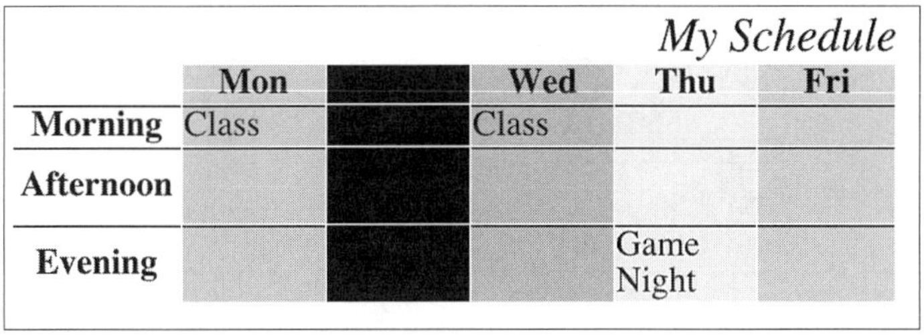

FIGURE 17.7
The effects of applying the columnar style.

Applying Other Styles to Tables

Nearly any other styles that can be applied to block elements can be applied to tables or table cells; the primary exception is that table cells never have margin properties. To set the spaces between table cells, you would instead use a separated-borders model, as described earlier, and set the border-spacing property on the table. The effect is the same as setting the margin between the cells.

Horizontal Alignment

As with other block boxes, the alignment of inline elements inside a table cell can be set with the text-align property. Use of text-align can easily make tables more readable, lining up columns to the left, right, or center as appropriate. Because <th> cells are center-aligned and <td> cells are left-aligned, columns can look a bit disorganized; text-align rules can correct this. For example, if you have a table listing movie show dates, you'd want to align the columns to the right, so that the times line up.

A sample style sheet using text-align is shown in Listing 17.8.

LISTING 17.8   Setting the Horizontal Alignment of Table Cells

```
/* schedule-17.8.css */

table     { table-layout: auto;          width: 90%;
            border-collapse: separate; border-spacing: 0.25em;
            empty-cells: hide;           font-size: small;
            margin-left: auto;           margin-right: auto; }
td, th    { width: 15%; }
th        { border: 2px solid black; }
td        { border: 2px solid gray; }
caption   { caption-side: top;          text-align: left;
            font-size: x-large;         font-style: italic; }

tbody th { text-align: right; }
tbody td { text-align: center; }
```

Applying this style sheet to the HTML file from Listing 17.1 gives the effects shown in Figure 17.8. For this screenshot, I've decreased the font size so that you can see the text alignment effects easily in each cell.

FIGURE 17.8
Aligning cells
horizontally.

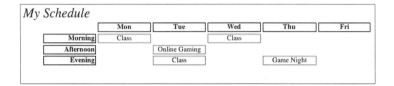

Vertical Alignment

The vertical-align property in CSS is the equivalent of the HTML valign property; browsers often align table cells to the vertical middle, and this can make cell contents look clumsy if the text wraps. Most of the time you are going to want to align data cells vertically so that the first line of each row is lined up on the top. Column header cells may look better aligned along the bottom. You can use the vertical-align property to affect these styles.

By the
Way

> The vertical-align property was introduced in Hour 15, "Alignment."

Listing 17.9 is a style sheet that aligns the content of each <td> cell with the bottom of that cell—see Tuesday evening for an example. It also vertically centers each <th> cell with the middle value for vertical-align.

LISTING 17.9 Setting the Vertical Alignment of Table Cells

```
/* schedule-17.9.css */

table     { table-layout: auto;          width: 90%;
            border-collapse: separate;  border-spacing: 0.25em;
            empty-cells: hide;          font-size: medium;
            margin-left: auto;          margin-right: auto; }
td, th    { width: 15%; }
th        { border: 2px solid black; }
td        { border: 2px solid gray; }
tbody th  { text-align: right; }
tbody td  { text-align: center; }
caption   { caption-side: top;          text-align: right;
            font-size: x-large;         font-style: italic; }

td        { vertical-align: bottom; }
th        { vertical-align: middle; }
```

The results of this style sheet, when applied to the HTML file from Listing 17.1, are shown in Figure 17.9.

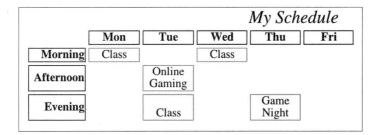

FIGURE 17.9
Aligning cells vertically.

Try it Yourself
Further Styles for Your Calendar

You can add to your calendar additional styles based on what you've learned this hour.

1. Add <col> and <colgroup> elements to your HTML, and a <caption> to title your calendar.

2. Move the <caption> to before or after the calendar table, based on what you think looks best.

3. Set the backgrounds of each day by using column-based selectors.

4. Adjust the alignment, colors, and fonts of your table to suit your taste, and now you've got your own calendar!

Summary

CSS rules can be used in conjunction with HTML tables to create a pleasing presentation of columnar data or layout tables. CSS browsers conceptualize tables as a series of layers: In order from most specific to least, those are the table cells, the table rows, the groups of table rows, the table columns, the groups of table columns, and the table itself. Inheritance follows these layers, as can be seen in background property effects.

Nearly any CSS property can be applied to table elements, although table cells don't have margins. Borders are of special importance when dealing with tables, and CSS offers two models for displaying tables: collapsed and separated. Both are set via the border-collapse property.

Table cells in the collapsed border model share a common border, whereas in the separated border model, a distance defined by the border-spacing property separates all cells from each other. In both models, the empty-cells property defines whether or not borders around empty table cells are displayed.

The caption, a label for the content of the table, can be located on any side of the table and styled separately. Rules can also be set by column rather than by row or cell if you use the <col> and <colgroup> tags, although the types of properties available for column styling are limited. You can improve the appearance and usability of a table by adjusting the text-align and vertical-align properties of the cells.

Workshop

The workshop contains a Q&A section, quiz questions, and activities to help reinforce what you've learned in this hour. If you get stuck, the answers to the quiz can be found after the questions.

Q&A

Q. *When would I ever want to change the* display *property value of a tag to a different type of table element?*

A. When using HTML, you pretty much don't ever want to do that. The browsers all understand what the default display values for each table element are supposed to be, and they often ignore attempts to change those values. The table-related display values are intended for use with XML, which doesn't have specific tags that are shown as tables. Using the display property, you can make XML elements show up as tables with rows, columns, and cells.

Quiz

1. All the following rules apply to a certain cell in a table. What color will the background of that cell be?

```
tbody { background-color: green; }
table { background-color: blue; }
tr    { background-color: transparent; }
col   { background-color: yellow; }
```

2. You want to set the spacing between table cells to 10 pixels in both the horizontal and vertical directions. Which of the following CSS rules accomplishes that?

   a. `table { cell-spacing: 10px; table-layout: separate; }`

   b. `table { cell-spacing: 10px; border-collapse: collapse; }`

   c. `table { border-spacing: 10px; border-collapse: separate; }`

   d. `table { cell-spacing: 10px; border-collapse: separate; }`

3. How would you write a rule to make the caption appear after the table in a smaller, italic font with a thin black border around it?

Answers

1. The background color will be green. In order from most specific to least specific, the selectors are `<tr>`, `<tbody>`, `<col>`, and `<table>`. Because the background color of the table row is `transparent`, the next selector's `background-color` shows through, and that is the green of the `<tbody>`.

2. The correct answer is (c). There is no `cell-spacing` property; the correct name is `border-spacing`.

3. Here is one such rule:

```
caption { caption-side: bottom;
          font-size: smaller;
          font-style: italic;
          border: thin solid black; }
```

Exercise

Tables are all around us, and not just for page layout. Any time in which you're building a grid that conveys information based on position in that grid, you're dealing with a table.

Write up some tables based on what you encounter around you—a bus schedule, a campus phone and office directory, columns of weights and measures, accounting records, or whatever else strikes your fancy.

Use the HTML tags and style rules presented in this hour to create data tables. Get creative—how can you best present this tabular data in a clear, straightforward manner where the styles enhance the tables?

HOUR 18

Box Sizing and Offset

What You'll Learn in This Hour:

- ▶ How browsers calculate the width and height dimensions of a display box
- ▶ Which properties can control the dimensions of a box
- ▶ What browsers will do if a box's content exceeds the dimensions of the box, and how you can control the result with CSS
- ▶ How to reposition a box from its original location, using relative positioning and the four offset properties

Sizing Content

When laying out a page, it's not always enough to specify only where content should be placed, as you can do with the `float` property (or the positioning properties, which you'll learn about in this hour and the next). To create effective layouts, you need to set the size of display boxes. In HTML, this is done with the `height` and `width` attributes; unsurprisingly, those are the names of the CSS properties that control a content box's dimensions.

To illustrate the use of the `width` and `height` attributes, I've created a sample HTML page that is used use for most of this hour. You can see this in Listing 18.1, or you can download it from the book's website.

LISTING 18.1   This HTML Page Has Unsized Boxes

```
<!-- sizes-18.1.html -->
<html>
  <head>
    <title>Tucson Valley News</title>
    <style type="text/css">
      body { font-family: Verdana, sans-serif; }
      h3 { font-style: oblique;
          font-weight: normal; }
```

LISTING 18.1   Continued

```
    #nav { float: right; }
    #nav ul { padding-left: 0; }
    #nav li { display: block; }

    div { border: 1px solid black; margin: 1em; }
  </style>
</head>
<body>
  <div id="banner">
    <h1>Tucson Valley News</h1>
  </div>
  <div id="nav">
    <h4>Tucson Valley News Quick Navigation
        Links</h4>
    <ul>
      <li><a href="/breaking/">Breaking
          News</a></li>
      <li><a href="/current/">Current
          Issue</a></li>
      <li><a href="/editorial/">Editorial
          Page</a></li>
      <li><a href="/subscribe/">Subscriptions
          </a></li>
    </ul>
  </div>
  <div id="main">
    <h2>Desert Museum hires webmaster</h2>
    <h3>Congrats to Liz Bartlett</h3>
    <p>The <a href="http://www.desertmuseum.org/">
       Arizona-Sonora Desert Museum</a> has hired
       <a href="http://www.khyri.com/">Liz
       Bartlett</a> to be their new webmaster.</p>
    <p>Founded in 1952 by William Carr and Arthur
       Pack, the Desert Museum is a private, nonprofit
       organization dedicated to the conservation
       of the Sonoran Desert.</p>
    <p>Liz Bartlett has over 11 years' experience in
       web design, and was a founder of Idyll
       Mountain Internet in 1995. She now lives in
       Tucson with her husband Kynn.</p>
  </div>
</body>
</html>
```

The intent of the embedded style sheet within Listing 18.1 is to create a very simple "newspaper" layout, with a headline at the top, a navigation menu at the right, and an article to the left and middle. To help you keep track of the display boxes involved, CSS rules add borders and margins to each <div>.

When a browser displays this page, it determines the layout based on the space available and how large the content is. You can see this in Figure 18.1—note how the <h4> headline in the navigation bar expands that box out to fill the available space. It's not the best design, especially because the <h4> isn't line-wrapping nicely.

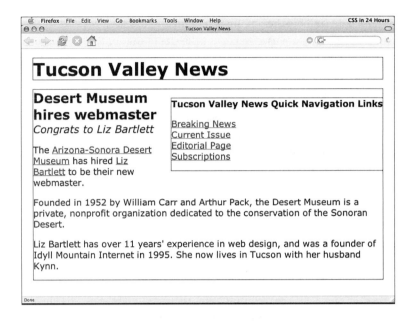

The width **and** height **Properties**

To correct the problems displayed in Figure 18.1, you need to use the width and height properties. Hour 17, "Styling Tables," briefly introduced width, and in this hour you'll learn to use it with all block content, as well as with its fraternal twin, height.

A CSS display box actually has two widths: the content width and the box width. The *content width* is, as you might imagine, the width of the box's content area; it is the area where the box's content exists, within the padding, the border, and the margin; this is what's set by the width property. The *box width* is the width of the entire box, including the left and right padding, the left and right border, and the left and right margin, as well as the content width. You can see this visually displayed in Figure 18.2.

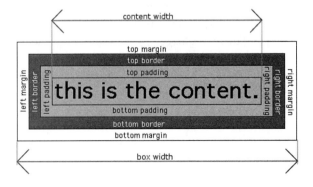

FIGURE 18.2
Content width and box width.

The content height and box height are determined in the same way. The CSS properties width and height are used to control the size of the content width; the box width and box height can't be set directly. Instead, you can control the box width and height by setting appropriate padding, border, and margin values that add to the content width and height.

Values for width and height can be measurements, such as 3em or 5px. They can also be percentage values, such as 20%. The percentage is based on the height or width of the parent box's content area. Listing 18.2 shows a style sheet that fixes the text wrap problem from Figure 18.1 by using height and width properties to help lay out the page.

LISTING 18.2   Setting height and width Values via CSS

```
#banner { width: 80%; height: 4em; }
#nav { width: 20%; }
#nav { height: 15em; }
#main { width: 60%; }
```

This sets a height and width on the banner, making it at least 4ems tall, and with a width of 80% of the available screen space. The navigation bar is 20% wide, and the height is 10ems. The main article space is 60% wide.

In Figure 18.3, you can see the result of applying this style sheet to the HTML page of Listing 18.1. Because a width has been set on the navigation bar, the text is forced to wrap. Also, there is extra white space at the bottom of the navigation bar; the height has been set, and the space is reserved even if the content does not fill that space. There is no height for the #main <div>, so the box ends when the text ends.

You should notice one more thing here. The #banner element is 80% wide, and the #nav element is 20% wide. You'd think they'd line up, right? But look carefully at Figure 18.3. If the two boxes were right on top of each other, they'd intersect. Why is that?

The width property sets only the content width, not the actual size taken up by the box. The true box width includes the margin (which is 1em in this example), the border (which is 1px) and any margins set. So the #banner's content width may be 80%, but the box width is 80% + 2em + 2px—remember to add in both the left and right sides!—whereas the #nav element is 20% + 2em + 2px. Together they add up to 100% of the screen, plus 4em, plus 4px. Oops.

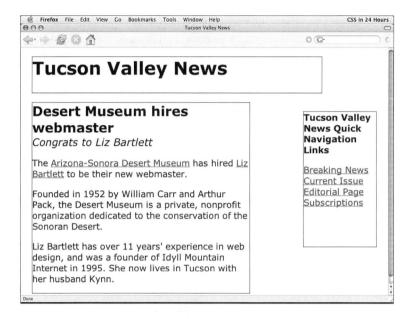

FIGURE 18.3
Boxes set to specific heights and widths.

The Internet Explorer width Bug

Unfortunately, previous versions of Internet Explorer for both Windows and Macintosh have a bug that miscalculates content width. Internet Explorer prior to version 6 doesn't consider the content width to be just the width of the content area of a box; instead, it includes the padding and the border width, as well. This is shown in Figure 18.4.

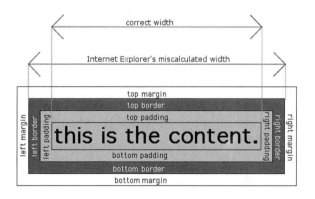

FIGURE 18.4
How Internet Explorer 5.5 (and earlier) improperly calculates widths.

This leads to a problem where Internet Explorer miscalculates the size of a display box, throwing off the display of your web page. Fortunately, there is a workaround for this bug. The trick is to create two <div> elements instead of just one, thus using two boxes. The first <div> box has width and margin properties set on it. The second box is located inside the first and has border and padding properties. Boxes nested in this way display properly in Internet Explorer, as well as in properly compliant browsers, such as Firefox, Opera, and Safari.

This bug was fixed in Internet Explorer 6; however, to get correct width calculations, you need to use a correct DOCTYPE statement at the beginning of your document. If you don't use a DOCTYPE statement, IE 6 displays the page using a backward-compatible method identical to IE 5, which means the buggy version. For more on DOCTYPE switching, see http://msdn.microsoft.com/library/default.asp?url=/library /en-us/dnie60/html/cssenhancements.asp. Keep in mind that some Internet Explorer users are still using Internet Explorer 5.0 or 5.5, so the type of workaround described in this hour may still be necessary on your site even if you use the correct DOCTYPE.

Minimum and Maximum Dimensions

Sometimes you might not want to set specific sizes for dimensions; instead, you might want more flexible designs that allow something to range in size between two values. A *constraint* is a value beyond which a box isn't allowed to grow or shrink; if the size is smaller than the minimum constraint, the size is that minimum, and if it's larger than the maximum constraint, the size is that maximum value.

For example, you might want a navigation bar to be as wide as 20% of the screen most of the time, but if the browser's window is only 500 pixels across, this may be too small to display your navigation links. A minimum size of 10em would therefore be a constraint placed on the width.

The constraints for width are set with the min-width and max-width properties; for height, the values are min-height and max-height. Listing 18.3 is a style sheet that sets constraints on the boxes in Listing 18.1.

LISTING 18.3   A Style Sheet to Constrain the Maximum and Minimum Sizes of Display Boxes

```
/* sizes-18.3.css  */
#banner { width: 60%;
          min-width: 500px;
          min-height: 5em;}
#nav { width: 30%; min-width: 200px; }
#nav { max-height: 15em; }
```

LISTING 18.3 Continued

```
#main { min-width: 300px;
        width: 50%;
        max-width: 600px; }
```

You can see the results of using this style sheet in Figure 18.5.

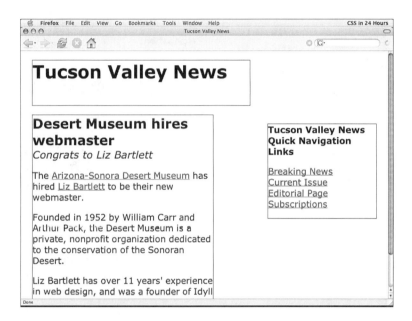

FIGURE 18.5
Setting box
size with
constraints.

This style sheet gives the navigation menu a width of 30%, which works decently enough unless the browser window is small. In such cases, the minimum width is set to 200px. The #banner is 60% of the space available, or a minumum of 500 pixels wide; it is also a minimum height of 5em, although there is no extra content to fill in that space, which is just left blank. The #main section varies between 300 and 600 pixels, based on the width of the browser window. If the browser display space is less than 600 pixels, #main is 300px (the min-width value); between 600 and 1200 pixels wide, #main is 50% of the display space; and if the browser's display area is more than 1200 pixels wide, the max-width constrains it to 600px and no more.

Figure 18.6 demonstrates what happens when the display area changes—in this case, the browser window has been decreased to about two thirds of the screen, and the minimum values are being used for each window.

FIGURE 18.6
Shrinking the browser window brings constraints into play.

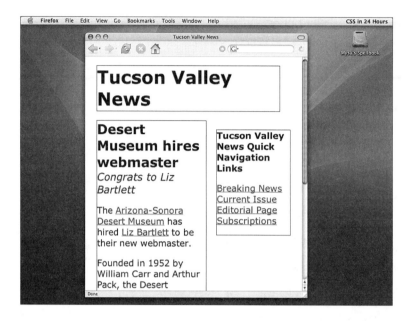

Content Overflow

If a display box's height hasn't been set by the `height` property, the height is calculated automatically to take up enough room for all the content. But what happens if a `height` property has been set that doesn't allow enough space for all the content? This creates a situation called *overflow*. Listing 18.4 is a style sheet specifically designed to create overflow.

LISTING 18.4   A Style Sheet Where the Size of the Content Exceeds the Height

```
/* sizes-18.4.css   */
#banner { width: 80%; height: 1.5em; }
#nav { width: 20%; }
#nav { height: 8em; }
#main { width: 500px; height: 450px; }
```

As shown in Figure 18.7, the content of the columns simply spills out the bottom of the box because there's not enough room. This is the default behavior for overflow, but you can change it by using the `overflow` property.

The `overflow` Property

To change what happens when a box's content overflows, you can set the `overflow` property to one of the values shown in Table 18.1. The default value is `visible`, which has the effect shown in Figure 18.7.

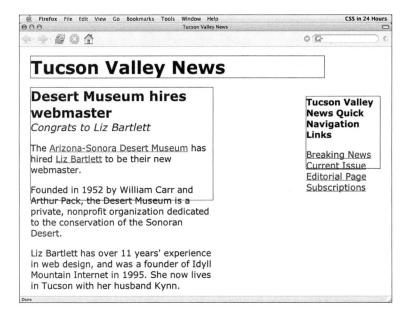

FIGURE 18.7
Sometimes content just won't fit inside a box, and it overflows.

TABLE 18.1   Values for the `overflow` Property

Value	Effect
`auto`	The browser determines what to do with overflowing content, choosing either `scroll` or `visible`.
`hidden`	Overflowing content is clipped and not displayed.
`scroll`	A scrollable box is used to provide access to all content.
`visible`	The overflowing content spills out of the box.
`inherit`	Use the value of `overflow` set on the containing box.

The `scroll` value provides scrollbars at the edges of the display box that let the user access all the content. The `hidden` value prevents that content from being displayed, so it should be used with care. A value of `auto` leaves the decision up to the browser; because this can vary from browser to browser, I advise against relying on it.

Two examples of the `overflow` property are shown in Listing 18.5, a style sheet that sets one column to `scroll`, and the other to `hidden`.

LISTING 18.5   A Style Sheet Using the `overflow` Property

```
/* sizes-18.5.css */
#banner { width: 80%; }
#nav { width: 20%; }
#nav { height: 8em;
```

LISTING 18.5   Continued

```
        overflow: scroll; }
#main { width: 500px; height: 300px;
        overflow: hidden; }
```

As you can see in Figure 18.8, a scrollbar gives access to the content in the menu bar. How do you see the content in the left column? You don't. Only the content that fits in the box is visible. This is known as *clipping,* a term that refers to cutting away (and not displaying) all the extra content that won't fit. To prevent your content from being lost to clipping, you can avoid using overflow: hidden and instead set overflow: scroll on elements that might exceed the space you've allocated.

FIGURE 18.8
Overflowing content can scroll or be clipped.

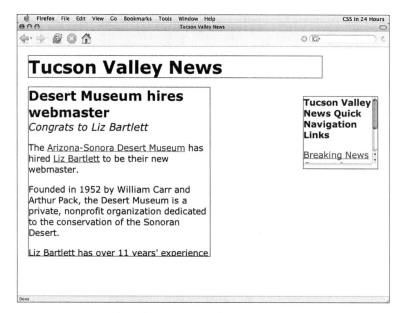

Try it Yourself

Create Scrollable Panels with CSS

One of the more controversial HTML tags has historically been <frame>, which enables you to make distinct panels for content, which can be scrolled separately from the rest of the page. The <frame> tag (and its sibling <iframe>) is considered harmful by some web development gurus because of accessibility problems and other perceived flaws. Using what you learned this hour, you can now make separately scrollable sections of your web page without using <frame> or <iframe>. Follow these steps:

1. Make a web page with a reasonably large amount of text to read—perhaps a letter, a short story, or even a style sheet listing. (If it's a style sheet, try setting the white-space property to pre, as described in Hour 10, "Text Colors and Effects.")

2. Enclose the text within a <div> and give that <div> a class such as scrollable.

3. Set a width and height for the .scrollable class in a style sheet, and link to or embed that style sheet in the HTML page. Give it a border as well, so you know where the content starts to overflow.

4. Test the page now—you will see something similar to Figure 18.7, with text overflowing the boundaries of the box.

5. Add a rule for your .scrollable box that sets the overflow property to scroll.

6. Try it out in your browser—you should now have a scrollable text window!

Relative Positioning

CSS offers several ways to position boxes on the screen. You've already learned about the float property in Hour 15, "Alignment." You can also use the position property to designate a box's location on the screen.

A box that has been placed according to *relative positioning* has been located relative to the position in which that box would normally appear, modified by an *offset*. This offset is designated by the top, left, right, and bottom properties.

You declare a box to be relatively placed by setting the position property on it with a value of relative. The possible values for position are shown in Table 18.2.

TABLE 18.2 Values for the position Property

Value	Effect
absolute	Position the box relative to the containing box.
fixed	Position the box relative to the containing box, and don't move it even if the page scrolls.
relative	Position the box relative to its normal position.
static	Position the box where it should normally be placed.
inherit	Use the position value of the containing box.

You'll learn about the position values absolute and fixed in Hour 19, "Absolute and Fixed Positioning." The value static simply tells the browser to not apply any special positioning and to ignore the four offset values.

Listing 18.6 is an HTML page with an embedded style sheet to relatively position one of the boxes outside of its normal position.

LISTING 18.6   Relative Positioning Shown via a Style Sheet

```
<!-- relative-18.6.html -->
<html>
  <head>
    <title>Three Boxes in a Row</title>
    <style type="text/css">
      .demobox {
        border: 3px solid black; width: 8em;
        font-family: Verdana, sans-serif;
        background-color: white;
        padding: 1em; margin: 0.5em; }
      #mars { position: relative;
             left: 5em; top: 2em; }
    </style>
  </head>
  <body>
    <div class="demobox" id="earth">
      Earth</div>
    <div class="demobox" id="mars">
      Mars</div>
    <div class="demobox" id="jupiter">
      Jupiter</div>
  </body>
</html>
```

As shown in Figure 18.9, the space that would normally be taken up by the box has still been set aside for it, although the box itself is now located 5 ems to the right and 2 ems down from where it would normally be.

The top, right, bottom, and left Properties

As shown in the previous example, the top and left properties can be used to set the distance by which a relatively positioned box is placed, with respect to the static position. The bottom and right properties also can be used to designate offsets. The types of values that can be given to these offset properties are shown in Table 18.3. The default value is auto, which means that it is up to the browser to determine where something should be placed—which is to say it places the box where it belongs according to normal (static) flow.

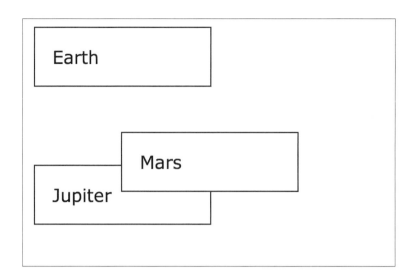

FIGURE 18.9
One of the planets is out of position.

TABLE 18.3   Values for the Offset Properties

Value	Effect
measurement	Offset the box by some amount, toward the "inside."
negative-measurement	Offset the box by some amount, toward the "outside."
percentage	Offset the box by a percentage, toward the "inside."
negative-percentage	Offset the box by a percentage, toward the "outside."
auto	Calculate the offset automatically.
inherit	Use the value of the offset property from the containing box.

Because positive values are toward the center point of the context box, some of these offsets can seem backward in effect from what you'd expect. For example, setting a left value of 4em actually moves the box to the right; a right value of 4em moves the box to the left; and a top value of -4em moves the box up, not down. You need to remember this when placing boxes. Positive values are toward the middle of the box, and negative are away from the middle.

You can also use negative values to move a box away from the center of its normal location. Listing 18.7 is a style sheet that can be used to position the planet-named boxes from Listing 18.6.

LISTING 18.7   Moving Boxes with Relative Positioning

```
.demobox {
  border: 3px solid black; width: 8em;
  font-family: Verdana, sans-serif;
  background-color: white;
  padding: 1em; margin: 0.5em; }
#earth {
  position: relative;
  top: -2em; right: -5em; }
#mars {
  left: 5em; top: 2em; }
#jupiter {
  position: relative;
  left: 10em; }
```

The effects of applying Listing 18.7 to the HTML page of Listing 18.6 are shown in Figure 18.10. The Earth box has been moved up and right; in fact, the top of the box is off the screen entirely. Likewise, the Jupiter box has moved far to the right—remember that the `left` value moves the box to the right when positive. A horizontal scroll bar has appeared for Jupiter; you can scroll to the right to see the whole box, even though you can't scroll up to see the Earth box.

FIGURE 18.10
Boxes placed with relative offsets, shown in Firefox.

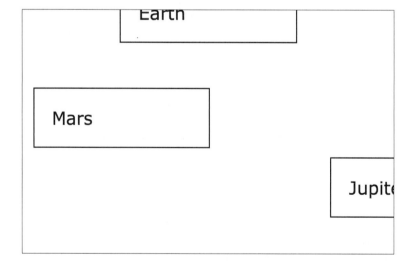

The Mars box didn't move this time. Why not? Because there is no `position` property for `#mars` in this style sheet, the `left` and `top` values are ignored. The default value for `position` is `static`, and unless you set `position: relative`, the box isn't offset.

Summary

The CSS language provides a number of properties for fine-tuning your layout, giving functionality that actually exceeds that of HTML layout tables, such as scrollable display boxes.

These properties include the width and height properties for setting a box's dimensions, as well as the min-width, min-height, max-width, and max-height properties that constrain a box's dimensions.

Content that naturally exceeds the dimensions of its display box is said to have overflowed. The overflow property can be used to determine whether the excess content is shown, clipped, or shown with a scrollbar.

In addition to sizing boxes, you can also move them from their original positions with relative positioning. Setting the position property to relative turns on relative positioning for that box, and the four offset properties—top, right, bottom, and left—can be used to adjust the box's location.

Workshop

The workshop contains a Q&A section, quiz questions, and an exercise to help reinforce what you've learned in this hour. If you get stuck, the answers to the quiz can be found after the questions.

Q&A

Q. *What's the difference between relative positioning, absolute positioning, and fixed positioning?*

A. Giving a position rule to a box is the way to set all these types of positioning initially, but each is very different in practice. Relative positioning always involves moving a box from its original location, and always reserves the space for that box in the layout. Absolute and fixed positioning, which you'll learn about in Hour 19, place the box relative to a containing block, not the original position of the box, and neither of these types of positioning reserves the space where the box would normally appear.

Q. *When would I use relative positioning instead of absolute or fixed positioning?*

A. Relative positioning is useful if you need to make small changes in the location of a box, such as moving a header a little to the left or adjusting the vertical position of a box. You can also use a position: relative rule without any offset properties to establish a containing box for absolute positioning, as you'll learn in Hour 19. In fact, this is probably the most common use for the `relative` value for `position`. It's rare to create style sheets that actually use relative positioning for offsets.

Q. *You wrote that there's a bug in Internet Explorer 5 related to box dimensions. Do I really need to worry about that in this day and age?*

A. Yes! At least, as of early 2006, Internet Explorer versions 5 and 5.5 are still used by a decent portion of the web-navigating population. You wouldn't want one user in twenty to experience problems on your site, would you? As described in Hour 3, "Browser Support for CSS," IE 5 and 5.5 are quirky browsers, and require special considerations. The method described in this hour—using two `<div>`s to set box properties—is one such approach, and using a browser filter is another. You'll learn about browser filters in Hour 24, "Troubleshooting and Browser Hacks."

Quiz

1. The browser's display window is 500 pixels wide. How wide will an `<h1>` be, assuming it's the first element of the `<body>` and that the following CSS rule applies to it?

```
h1 { width: 20%; min-width: 125px;
     max-width: 200px; }
```

2. Which of these rules will make scrollbars on a `blockquote`?

    a. `blockquote { height: 175px; scroll: auto; }`

    b. `blockquote { overflow: scroll; }`

    c. `blockquote { scroll: overflow; }`

    d. `blockquote { height: 175px; overflow: scroll; }`

3. Which of the following best describes relative positioning?

    a. Subsequent text is flowed around the positioned box, relative to the box's new left or right location.

    b. The box is held in a location relative to where it is located, even if the page is scrolled.

    c. Relative to the box's original location, the box is offset by a certain distance.

    d. The box is placed relative to its containing box.

4. Which of these offset declarations moves a display box 20 pixels to the right?

    a. `right: 20px;`

    b. `left: 20px;`

    c. `left: -20px;`

    d. `right: -20px;`

Answers

1. The `<h1>` tag will be 125 pixels wide, the minimum width. The calculated width, 100 pixels (20% of 500), is smaller than the `min-width` value, so it is increased to the value of `min-width`. Because it is not larger than the `max-width` value of `200px`, the final size is 125 pixels.

2. The correct answer is (d). There is no CSS property named `scroll`, and the `height` property is necessary or else the content doesn't overflow.

3. Choice (c) is a description of relative positioning, (a) describes floating content (from Hour 15), (b) describes fixed positioning, and (d) defines absolute positioning. (You'll learn about those latter two in Hour 19.)

4. Both (b) and (d) shift a box to the right. Remember that positive offsets are toward the middle of the box, and negative offsets are away from it.

Exercise

One of the trickier things to understand about relative positioning is that box properties offset in a funny direction. If you want to move something to the right, you set a positive `left` value, or a negative `right` value. To move something down, you set the `top` value. To get a grasp on the way that box offsets always point toward the middle of the box, create a web page with a relatively positioned box and then play with the various options for offset properties. This will be good practice for Hour 19 because offset properties are also used with the other possible values for the `position` property.

HOUR 19

Absolute and Fixed Positioning

What You'll Learn in This Hour:

▶ The types of positioning schemes available for placing a display box on the screen

▶ How to place an HTML element in relation to its containing block

▶ How to use CSS positioning to create a simple cartoon combining a photograph, text, and graphics

▶ How to control clipped content that is larger than the size allotted to a display box

▶ How to create rounded corners for boxes and position them with CSS

▶ How to designate which items should appear in front or back when content is layered over other content

▶ How to fix an HTML element on the screen, even if the page scrolls

Positioning Content

Whenever you include an HTML element on a page, it generates a display box, as you learned in Hour 6, "The CSS Box Model." Normally, these boxes are placed one after another or within another box, based on the structure of the document and whether the box is an inline or block box. This is known as *normal flow* in the CSS specifications. Whenever you move an element's display box to a new location, you are disrupting the normal flow to create a new layout.

One way to disrupt the normal flow of content is by using the float (and clear) properties, which you learned about in Hour 15, "Alignment." Floating content moves out of the normal order to one side or the other, and subsequent content flows around it.

Relative positioning preserves the normal content flow by reserving the appropriate amount of space for the relatively positioned element, and then moving it relative to that location.

There are two other types of positioning techniques you can use, called *absolute* and *fixed* positioning. These methods also use the `position` property and the four offset properties—`top`, `right`, `bottom`, and `left`—introduced in Hour 18, "Box Sizing and Offset," but the exact meanings of these properties are different from how they're used in relative positioning.

The first way to lay out the page with CSS is to use styles that position an element relative to a specific context on the page. The `position` property is used to choose that context. Positioned content is offset from the context by a specific amount that you can set with the `top`, `right`, `bottom`, or `left` properties.

> As a historical footnote, the positioning properties in CSS were originally introduced in a draft produced between the CSS Level 1 and CSS Level 2 recommendations and were called CSS-P, for CSS Positioning. CSS-P properties were partially implemented by the browsers and were formally added to the CSS language when CSS Level 2 was released.

The Containing Block

To properly place a display box by using positioning styles, you must establish the context of that position. You accomplish this by using the `position` property, which defines how a box should be positioned. The values for the `position` property were listed in Table 18.2 in Hour 18; the two we're concerned with in this hour are `position: absolute` and `position: fixed`.

When you set the `position` property to `absolute`, you are taking the element out of the normal flow of text and locating it relative to another box. This is called the *containing block*. The positioned element is placed relative to this containing block based on the offset properties `top`, `right`, `bottom`, and `left`.

The containing block is one of the parent boxes that contains the box being displayed—but it's not necessarily the immediate parent. The containing block is defined as the nearest ancestor to that box that has a `position` property value set on it (to something besides `static`). If none of the box's ancestors has a `position` property set, then the containing block is the display box of the <body> tag.

The easiest way to force a box to become a containing block for everything within it—and thus change the context in which those elements are positioned—is to set the position property of that box to relative. This tells the browser to reserve the space that the box would normally take up, and then move the box by the measurements given by the top, right, bottom, and left properties. If you don't set any values for the offsets, however, they default to 0—and the box doesn't move. The effect of using position: relative without offsets is to simply create a new containing block context.

Did you Know?

Absolute Positioning

In *absolute positioning*, the display box is placed in relation to the containing block, offset by a certain amount. The box is removed from the normal flow, and in fact the space normally taken up by the absolutely positioned box isn't even allocated for it. Instead, it appears somewhere else, possibly even overlaying existing content.

The containing block in absolute positioning is initially set to be the box of the <body> tag, and absolutely positioned elements are placed relative to the rest of the page. However, if an ancestor box of an element is positioned (with absolute, relative, or fixed positioning), that positioned box becomes the new containing block for absolute positioning.

Listing 19.1 is a web page with embedded style sheet that sets the inner <div> to use absolute positioning, and specifies an offset of 4em on the left and top from the outer box, which has been set to position: relative to make it the new containing block for its children.

LISTING 19.1 A Web Page Demonstrating Absolute Positioning

```
<!-- absolute-19.1.html -->
<html>
  <head>
    <title>Three Boxes in a Row</title>
    <style type="text/css">
      .demobox {
        border: 3px solid black; width: 8em;
        font-family: Verdana, sans-serif;
        background-color: white;
        padding: 1em; margin: 0.5em; }
      #mars  { position: absolute;
              right: 2em; top: 6em; }
    </style>
  </head>
  <body>
    <div class="demobox" id="earth">
      Earth</div>
    <div class="demobox" id="mars">
```

LISTING 19.1   Continued

```
    Mars</div>
  <div class="demobox" id="jupiter">
    Jupiter</div>
 </body>
</html>
```

So what effect does the embedded style sheet have? Figure 19.1 shows absolute positioning at work. The middle box, Mars, has been removed entirely from its position in the normal flow of layout; unlike relative positioning, absolute positioning does not leave the appropriate space for the positioned object in its original position.

FIGURE 19.1
Absolute positioning is based on the containing block.

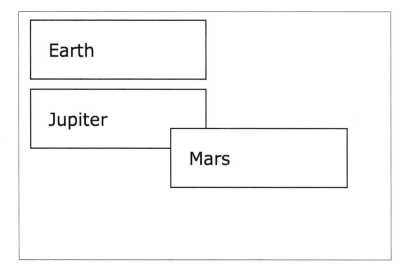

Offset Properties in Absolute Positioning

The #mars box in Figure 19.1 has been positioned at right: 2em and top: 6em—this is not relative to the original position, but to the containing block of the #mars box. In this case, there are no ancestors to #mars that have a position property, so the containing block is the <body> element of HTML. Thus, the right side of the box is placed 2 ems in from the right side of the browser's display area, and the top side of the box is placed 6 ems down from the top.

The top, right, bottom, and left properties have different meanings when used with absolute positioning than their meanings under relative positioning. Table 19.1 is a summary of these values and their effects; contrast this with Table 18.3 in the last hour.

TABLE 19.1 Absolute Positioning Values for the Offset Properties

Value	Effect
measurement	Position the edge of the box toward the "inside" of the containing block
negative-measurement	Position the edge of the box toward the "outside" of the containing block
percentage	Position the edge of the box toward the "inside" of the containing block, as a percentage of the containing block's dimension
negative-percentage	Position the edge of the box toward the "outside" of the containing block, as a percentage of the containing block's dimension

Listing 19.2 is a style sheet that can replace the embedded style sheet in Listing 19.1 with one that uses percentages. (To make it more clear where the boxes meet, the margin property has been removed.)

LISTING 19.2 Percentages for Absolute Positioning

```
/* absolute-19.2.css */
.demobox {
  border: 3px solid black; width: 8em;
  font-family: Verdana, sans-serif;
  background-color: white;
  padding: 1em; }
#mars   { position: absolute;
        right: 50%; bottom: 50%; }
#earth { position: absolute;
        left: 50%; top: 50%;}
#jupiter { position: absolute;
          left: -50%; bottom: 100%; }
```

Figure 19.2 is the result of applying the style sheet in Listing 19.2 to the HTML page in 19.1.

Notice that the Mars and Earth boxes almost touch in the center. This is because they have values of 50% set for their right and left values, and 50% for their top and bottom values. However, the effects of these rules are not the same; 50% right and 50% left are two different positions. The right property lines up the right edge of the box along that halfway line, and the left property positions the left edge of the box at the same line.

There are three boxes in the HTML source code, but only two boxes in Figure 19.2. Where's Jupiter? The rule of -50% left moved the left side of the box half a screen's width off to the left of the display window. The `bottom: 100%` rule moved the bottom of the box a full screen's height up, so it's off the top of the screen. The Jupiter box is located off to the upper left, where we can't see it.

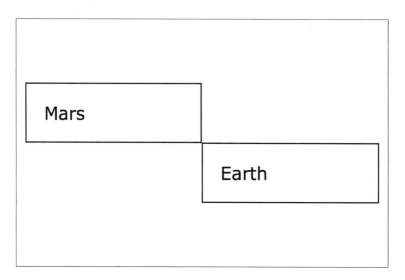

FIGURE 19.2
Percentages used to place boxes absolutely.

Watch Out!

> It's entirely possible to position a box off the visible part of the page. For example, if you use a value of `-1000px` for `left` and `-800px` for `top`, the box will probably be displaced completely off the page. Such a box still "exists," but just won't be seen. In some cases, this may be exactly what you want—in Hour 24, "Troubleshooting and Browser Hacks," you'll learn how this type of technique can be used to hide content from certain browsers, with varying degrees of success.

You can also use the `top`, `right`, `bottom`, and `left` properties to place content atop existing content when you use absolute positioning. Listing 19.3 is an HTML file that contains four elements to position: a picture of a coyote, a bit of text, a graphic of a triangle, and a picture credit.

LISTING 19.3 Parts of a Cartoon to Be Positioned

```
<!-- cartoon-19.3.html -->
<html>
  <head>
    <title>Coyote Cartoon</title>
    <style type="text/css">
      body { font-family: Verdana, sans-serif; }
      a:link, a:visited { text-decoration: none;
                color: inherit; font-weight: bold; }
      #cartoon { padding: 16px; margin: 10px auto;
                border: 1px solid black; }
```

LISTING 19.3   Continued

```
    #bubble { font-size: 24px;
              text-align: center;
              border: 1px solid black;
              background-color: white; color: black;
              width: 250px; padding: 2px; }
    #credits { font-size: 14px;
               bottom:  16px; right: 20px; }
  </style>
</head>
<body>
  <div id="cartoon">
    <img src="coyote.jpg" alt="Coyote">
    <div id="bubble">
      Hey! I can see my house from here!
    </div>
    <img src="balloontail.png" id="tail" alt="">
    <div id="credits">
      Picture by
      <a href="http://kynn.com/">Kynn Bartlett</a>
    </div>
  </div>
</body>
</html>
```

The balloontail.png image is a simple black and white triangle made with a transparent section. Figure 19.3 is a screen capture of the image creation process, with the transparent section shown in a gray checkerboard pattern.

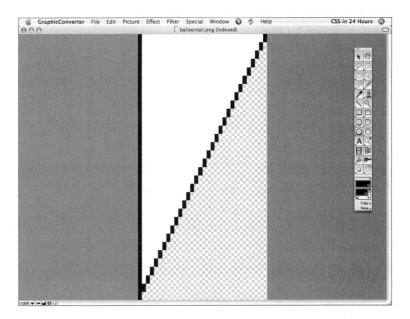

FIGURE 19.3
Creating an image with a transparent section.

Without any positioning properties, the cartoon appears as shown in Figure 19.4.

FIGURE 19.4
Not very much
of a cartoon, is
it?

Listing 19.4 is a style sheet that can be embedded in Listing 19.3 (or linked from it) to position each of the elements absolutely on top of the coyote's picture and assemble the cartoon properly.

LISTING 19.4   Style Sheet to Lay Out the Cartoon

```
/* cartoon-19.4.css */
#cartoon { position: relative;
           width: 600px; }
           /* sets the containing block */

#bubble  { position: absolute;
           bottom: 340px; left: 215px; }
#tail    { position: absolute;
           bottom: 277px; left: 240px; }
#credits { position: absolute;
           bottom:  16px; right: 20px; }
```

You can see the results of this style sheet in Figure 19.5. The box is over the coyote's head, and the triangular wedge serves to show that the coyote is "speaking." The transparent section of the triangle graphic lets the coyote image show through the transparent area.

The 1px border of the word bubble is missing where it touches the `balloontail.png` graphic. This isn't a CSS trick; the graphic is simply positioned so that it overlaps, and thus covers, the border at that point. You'll learn more about controlling overlap of layered content later this hour.

FIGURE 19.5
A cartoon built
with CSS. Can
you do better?

Try it Yourself ▼

Use Absolute Positioning to Create a Cartoon

This is your chance to express the budding cartoonist within you.

1. Find a photograph you like. Maybe it's one you've taken, maybe it's one of you. Create an HTML page with that picture.

2. Write some dialogue for the picture and add it to the HTML page. Set a `class` or `id` on the dialogue so you can position it.

3. Create a "tail" graphic for your word balloon, or use a simple one like the one above (available from the book's website). Add a `class` or `id` here as well.

4. Add a wrapper `<div>` around your cartoon, with a `class` or `id` property. This is important so that you can set the containing box in your CSS rules.

5. Write the style sheet. The first thing you'll want to do is define the containing box by setting `position: relative` on your wrapper `<div>`; also give it a width and a border.

6. Position the dialogue, using `position: absolute` and the offset properties (`top`, `right`, `bottom`, and `left`). Reload the page in your browser as you make changes; it could take several tries to position the box right where you want it to be.

7. Put your word balloon "tail" in place. Again, this may require fine adjustments, possibly pixel-by-pixel, as you line it up just right. ▼

▲

8. View the cartoon in your web browser. If it looks good, you're ready to share this with your friends, who will delight in your wonderful sense of humor and thrill to your CSS positioning skills!

The `clip` Property

In Hour 18, you learned how you can clip content that extends out of the display box by using the `overflow` value of `hidden`.

Normally, only content that extends outside the display box is clipped. However, the `clip` property enables you to define a *clipping area* within an absolutely positioned box that defines where the content will be clipped. The types of values that can be set for the `clip` property are shown in Table 19.2. The `clip` property is used only if the box's `overflow` value is not `visible`, and if the `position` value is `absolute`.

TABLE 19.2   Values for the `clip` Property

Value	Effect
`auto`	The clipping area is defined by the box's edges.
`rect(top, right, bottom, left)`	The clipping area is a rectangle defined by four measurements.
`inherit`	Use the value of `clip` set on the containing block.

When using the `rect()` function to define a clipping area, you're defining a sub-box relative to the display box. The values *top*, *right*, *bottom*, and *left* are measurements (which can be ems, pixels, percentages, or other types of CSS measurement) which define where the box is clipped—relative to the upper-left corner of the box.

The easiest way to think of these values is to consider them a pair of points, the first in the upper-right corner and the second in the lower-left, which define the clipping area. For example, let's say you're using clipping on a box that is 400 pixels wide and 300 across, and you have written a rule such as this:

```
#box { overflow: hidden;
       clip: rect(0px, 300px, 200px, 100px);
```

This defines a clip area where one corner is at 400px to the right, 0px down, and the other corner is at 300px down, and 100px to the right. Thus the displayed area would be from 100px to 300px horizontally, and 0px to 200px vertically.

Figure 19.6 shows this rule in action, clipping text content down to size. Note that even the border is clipped; this clips the entire element box.

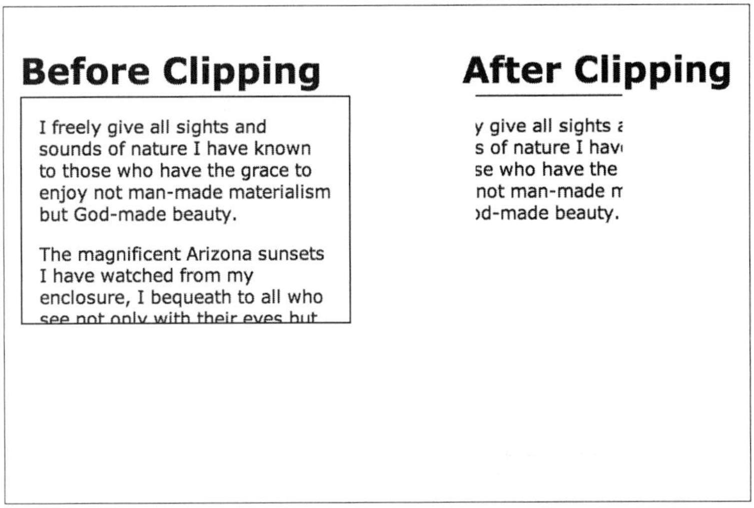

FIGURE 19.6
Clipped content, before and after.

You can use clipped content with absolute positioning for some interesting effects. Listing 19.5 is an HTML page with one graphic that will be placed in each corner of the content box.

LISTING 19.5 A Text Box with Corner Graphics

```
<!-- corners-19.5.html -->
<html>
  <head>
    <title>Rounded corners</title>
    <style type="text/css">
      /* basic formatting styles */
      body { font-family: Optima, Geneva, serif;
           color: white; background-color: black; }
      .section { margin: 2em; padding: 1em 2em;
               color: black; background-color: white; }
      h1, h2 { text-align: center; margin: 0;
             font-variant: small-caps; }
      p { text-indent: 3em; text-transform: uppercase; }
    </style>
  </head>
  <body>
    <div class="section">
      <img src="corners.png" alt=""
          class="corner" id="topleft">
      <img src="corners.png" alt=""
          class="corner" id="topright">
      <img src="corners.png" alt=""
          class="corner" id="bottomleft">
      <img src="corners.png" alt=""
```

LISTING 19.5   Continued

```
                class="corner" id="bottomright">
      <h1>George L. Mountainlion</h1>
      <h2>Born February 1952</h2><h2>Died March 8, 1955</h2>
      <p>I freely give all sights and sounds of nature I
          have known to those who have the grace to enjoy
          not man-made materialism but God-made beauty.</p>
      <p>The magnificent Arizona sunsets I have watched
          from my enclosure, I bequeath to all who see not
          only with their eyes but with their hearts.</p>
      <!-- ... -->
    </div>
  </body>
</html>
```

The corner graphic is simply a circle on a square black background, 32 pixels by 32 pixels. Figure 19.7 shows the image being created in a simple graphics program.

FIGURE 19.7
Creating a graphic for rounded corners.

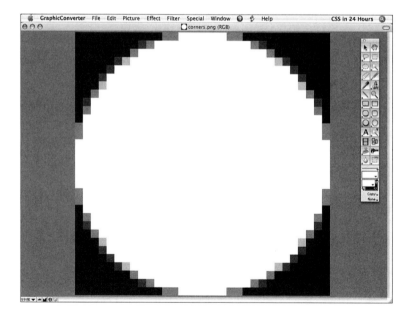

Displayed without positioning and clipping properties added, the HTML page in Listing 19.5 looks passable, but the corner images aren't in the corners, as shown in Figure 19.8.

Listing 19.6 is a style sheet that uses absolute positioning to position the graphic, and then clips off everything except the appropriate corner of the circle.

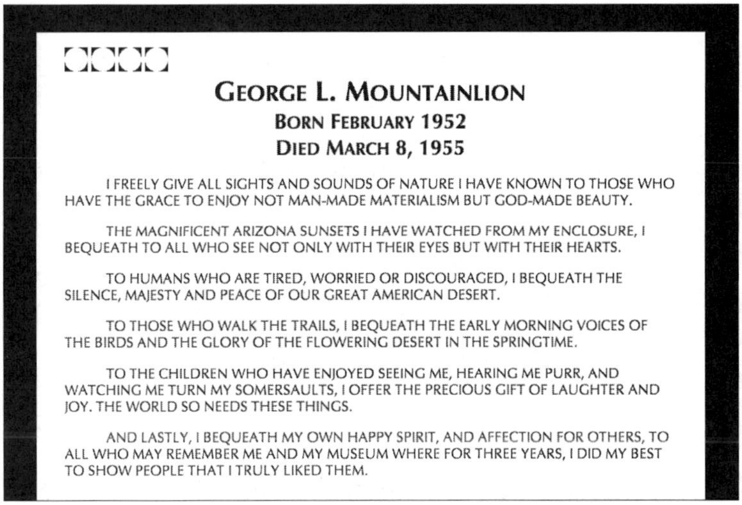

FIGURE 19.8
Unpositioned
and unclipped
corners.

LISTING 19.6 Positioning and Clipping Round Corners

```
/* corners-19.6.css */
.section { position: relative; }
.corner { position: absolute; }
#topleft     { top: 0px; left: 0px;
               overflow: hidden;
               clip: rect(0px, 16px, 16px, 0px); }
#topright    { top: 0px; right: 0px;
               overflow: hidden;
               clip: rect(0px, 32px, 16px, 16px); }
#bottomleft  { bottom: 0px; left: 0px;
               overflow: hidden;
               clip: rect(16px, 16px, 32px, 0px); }
#bottomright { bottom: 0px; right: 0px;
               overflow: hidden;
               clip: rect(16px, 32px, 32px, 16px); }
```

You can see the properly positioned and clipped corner graphics in Figure 19.9.

Layered Content

As you've seen in the coyote cartoon example, content can be positioned into a location already occupied by something else through the use of absolute (or relative) positioning. Each of the overlapping display boxes can be thought of as existing in a third dimension, as if it were printed on a piece of clear plastic. This is commonly referred to as a *layer*.

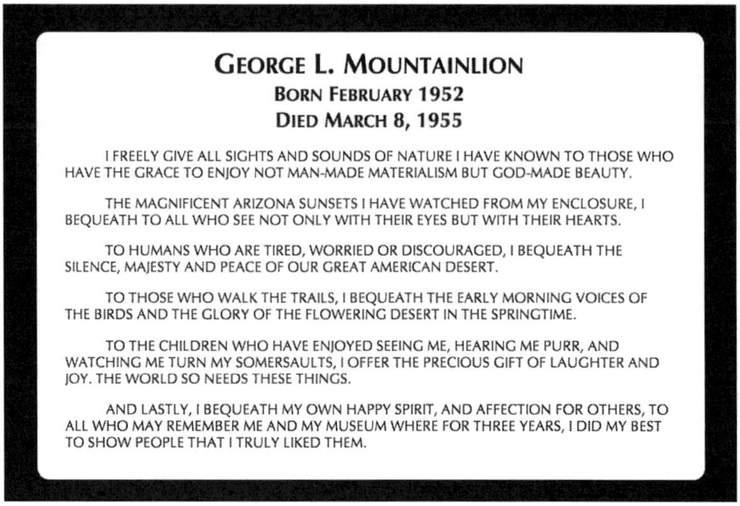

FIGURE 19.9
Rounded cor-
ners, positioned
and clipped.

FIGURE 19.9
Rounded cor-
ners, positioned
and clipped.

> **By the Way**
>
> Netscape 4 also used the term *layer* to refer to the nonstandard `<layer>` tag. The `<layer>` tag should be avoided because it is not part of the HTML specification and is not widely supported by browsers. In this book, *layering* refers to creating distinct, overlapping boxes with CSS and does not refer to the `<layer>` tag.

Listing 19.7 is a simple logo designed in HTML and CSS. The intent is to create a box with "Pie Walkers of Tucson" in the foreground, and a large pi (π) symbol in the background.

LISTING 19.7   Content to Be Displayed in Overlapping Layers

```
<!-- layers-19.7.html -->
<html>
  <head>
    <title>Pie Walkers of Tucson</title>
    <style type="text/css">
      body { font-family: Arial, sans-serif; }
      .pwlogo { position: relative; overflow: hidden;
               height: 175px; width: 350px;
               border: 2px solid black;
               margin: 10em auto; }
      .pwlogo span { display: block; }
      .pwlogo .pi { font: 360px bold Verdana, sans-serif;
               position: absolute; color: silver;
               left: 40px; top: -165px; }
      .pwlogo .pw { font: 60px "Times New Roman", serif;
               position: absolute;
               font-variant: small-caps;
               left:  10px; top: 10px; }
      .pwlogo .of { font: 70px oblique bold Papyrus, cursive;
               position: absolute; color: gray;
```

LISTING 19.7 Continued

```
                    left: 150px; top: 30px; }
      .pwlogo .tucson { font: 60pt bold Verdana, sans-serif;
                        position: absolute;
                        text-transform: uppercase;
                        bottom: 5px; right:  5px; }
    </style>
  </head>
  <body>
    <div class="pwlogo">
      <span class="pw">Pie Walkers</span>
      <span class="of">of</span>
      <span class="tucson">Tucson</span>
      <span class="pi">&pi;</span>
    </div>
  </body>
</html>
```

In Figure 19.10, you can see the layered effect, as each display box is placed over another. However, there's a problem! The boxes are not in a sensible order. The pi symbol covers everything else. There are two ways to fix this: first, by changing the order of the HTML tags, and second, by using the z-index property.

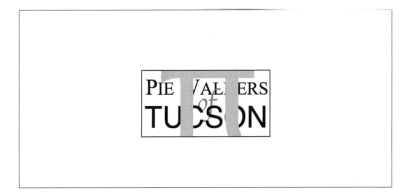

FIGURE 19.10
One box is laid over another, making the logo unreadable.

The z-index **Property**

Each layer is placed in the order it appears in the HTML source code, with subsequent layers placed on top of earlier ones. This order can be changed with the z-index property. Values for z-index are numbers that indicate the layering order. A lower number goes on the bottom, and a higher number goes on the top.

The property name z-index comes from basic geometry. Horizontal placement is said to be along the x-axis, vertical along the y-axis, and third-dimensional placement—out of the page or the screen—is along the z-axis.

Did you Know?

The style sheet in Listing 19.8 reassigns the layering order by using the z-index property. As you can see, you can skip numbers, so you don't have to assign them sequentially; all the layers are considered and then sorted so the highest are on top, even if there are gaps in the sequence.

LISTING 19.8   Style Sheet to Change the Order of Layering

```
/* layers-19.8.css */
.pwlogo .pi { z-index: 1; }
.pwlogo .pw { z-index: 10; }
.pwlogo .of { z-index: 3; }
.pwlogo .tucson { z-index: 5; }
```

Applying this style sheet to the HTML page in Listing 19.7 results in the layering order shown in Figure 19.11.

FIGURE 19.11
The layers are
now in the
desired order.

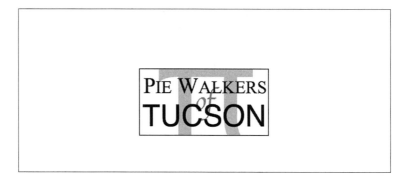

Fixed Positioning

In *fixed positioning*, a box placed on the screen doesn't move even if the rest of the page moves; it seems to float above the rest of the content without leaving its original position. This is useful if you want to create a menu bar or graphic that never leaves the page. A box placed according to fixed positioning is located in relation to the whole page, not to its containing block or its original position. Like absolute positioning (and unlike relative positioning), no space is set aside for the box in its normal flow location.

The style sheet in Listing 19.9 uses fixed positioning to set both a bar at the top that never goes away, and a "back to top" button that always stays fixed in the lower right corner. The full text of "The War Prayer" is omitted in Listing 19.9, but you can view the entirety on the book's website, to test scrolling with fixed positioning.

LISTING 19.9   Using Fixed Positioning

```
<!-- fixed-19.9.html -->
<html>
  <head>
    <title>Page with a lot of text</title>
    <style type="text/css">
      .section { margin: 0 8em; }
      .topbar {
        position: fixed; top: 0; left: 0;
        width: 100%;
        background-color: black; color: white; }
      .backtotop {
        background-color: white;
        border: 1px solid black;
        position: fixed; bottom: 1em; right: 1em; }
    </style>
  </head>
  <body>
    <div class="topbar">
      You are reading:
      <cite>The War Prayer</cite> by Mark Twain
    </div>
    <div class="section">
    <h1><a name="top">The War Prayer by Mark Twain</a></h1>
    <p> It was a time of great and exalting excitement.
        <!-- ... -->
    </div>
    <div class="backtotop">
      <a href="#top">Back to top</a>
    </div>
  </body>
</html>
```

The effects of fixed positioning are shown in Figure 19.12.

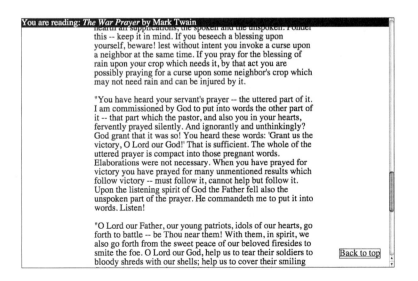

FIGURE 19.12
Objects fixed in position don't move when the rest of the page scrolls.

Summary

Display boxes can be moved from their original positions in the normal flow of layout by using the `position` property. The `position` property selects among four different types of positioning schemes. Absolute positioning places the HTML element in a new location within or relative to its containing block. Fixed positioning locates the display box on a set position on the screen, even if the page scrolls.

Placement of boxes in the context of their positioning schemes is determined by the values of the offset properties: `left`, `right`, `top`, and `bottom`. These can be measurements or percentages, with a positive value moving in the direction of the center of the containing block, and a negative value moving away from it. Care needs to be taken when placing boxes so that content isn't obscured or moved off the visible part of the page entirely. Absolutely positioned content that overflows its box can be clipped with the `clip` property.

In addition to existing in two dimensions, CSS boxes occupy a third dimension, as well, that determines which boxes are layered on top of other boxes if the content overlaps. The order of layering can be set with the `z-index` property.

Workshop

The workshop contains a Q&A section, quiz questions, and an exercise to help reinforce what you've learned in this hour. If you get stuck, the answers to the quiz can be found after the questions.

Q&A

Q. *My* `clip` *rule isn't working right, and I am following the CSS spec exactly! The clipped element doesn't appear at all. What's wrong?*

A. The problem here is an unclear specification. You might assume that the dimensions for `rect()` are like those of `relative` offsets—that each one specifies how to adjust the sides, with positive changes being toward the middle of the box. This is a natural assumption when you're working with positioning CSS, but it's not the case at all. Instead, a `rect()` defines a rectangle within the content box. As explained in this hour, it's easiest to think of the `rect()` values as a pair of coordinates for the upper-right and lower-left corners.

Quiz

1. Which of the following best describes absolute positioning?

    a. Subsequent text is flowed around the positioned box, relative to the box's new left or right location.

    b. The box is held in location relative to where it is located, even if the page is scrolled.

    c. Relative to the box's original location, the box is offset by a certain distance.

    d. The box is placed relative to its containing box.

2. The three <div> elements in the following snippet of HTML are placed with absolute positioning. What letter will be seen and why?

```
<div style="position: absolute; top: 0px; left: 0px;
   background-color: white; width: 2em; z-index: 10;">K</div>
<div style="position: absolute; top: 0px; left: 0px;
   background-color: white; width: 2em; z-index: 1;">L</div>
<div style="position: absolute; top: 0px; left: 0px;
   background-color: white; width: 2em; z-index: 6;">B</div>
```

3. You have an <img> tag that is 450 pixels wide and 300 pixels tall. The graphic is composed of nine images of television actors in a three by three grid, each cell 150 pixels wide by 100 pixels tall. You want to show only the face of the youngest one, in curls, in the lower left cell. How do you use clip to show only that portion of the image?

Answers

1. Absolute positioning is choice (c). Choice (c) is a description of relative positioning (from Hour 18), (a) describes floating content (from Hour 15), and (b) describes fixed positioning.

2. The letter *K*. Because they are all placed in the same location, the one that is displayed will be the <div> on the top of the stacking order. The highest z-index value is 10, and so the letter *K* will be visible. (Technically, the other letters are visible, too; we just can't see them.)

3. Here is the type of rule you would write:

```
img#bunch {
    overflow: hidden;
    clip: rect(150, 200, 0, 300); }
```

Did you remember that you needed to change the `overflow` value from the default of `visible` to be able to use `clip`? The values for `rect()` come from the coordinates for the upper-left corner and the lower-right corner of the portion that should be displayed—the points (150,200) and (0,300), respectively.

Exercise

Placing boxes on the screen can seem arcane until you get plenty of practice with it. In Hour 20, "Page Layout in CSS," you're going to see how to bring together what you've learned to lay out a page effectively. But you have the tools already to get started on positioning content blocks, and exercising your use of absolute and fixed positioning will help you prepare.

Begin by creating a simple HTML page with a number of different elements—some headers, a few images, <div> elements containing sections of text, some lists of links—and start placing them with absolute (or fixed) positioning. After you've got them where you want them...move them! The power of CSS-based positioning lets you move sections of your page around the screen by simply changing offset property values, thus enabling you to re-order the entire page without changing the HTML. Try it, and practice it until you've fully grasped the implications; then you'll be ready for the next hour!

HOUR 20

Page Layout in CSS

What You'll Learn in This Hour:

- ▶ The different strategies for laying out a page in CSS
- ▶ Why it's a bad idea to use `<table>` for page layout
- ▶ The steps to replacing a table-based layout with a CSS-based structure
- ▶ How to write HTML code for CSS-based layouts
- ▶ How to use positioned content to lay out a page
- ▶ How to use floating columns to lay out a page

One of the major draws of modern CSS—as supported by recent, more compliant browsers—is the freedom to replace clunky HTML layout tables with structured HTML markup, styled by CSS rules. In previous hours, you've learned how to place individual portions of your web page in specific locations using absolute positioning or floating content. You can use the same types of style rules to build the visual structure of the page.

Laying Out the Page

This hour will bring together many of the techniques you've learned in previous hours for using CSS properties to lay out an entire page or even an entire website. You won't need to misuse HTML `<table>` elements for page layout now that you have reliable CSS techniques for layout in your repertoire.

The examples this hour use a redesigned version of the website for the Dunbar Project (http://www.thedunbarproject.com). Dunbar School in Tucson, Arizona, was a segregated school for African-American students from 1918 until 1951, and was closed in 1978. Since then, a community group has been working to restore the school and make it into a community cultural center.

The Dunbar Project has graciously allowed the author to use their website in this book for a sample website redesign in CSS. The Dunbar Project site as it appeared in early 2006 is shown in Figure 20.1. It is mostly a dark teal color, and although it's not bad, it could be improved through the use of Cascading Style Sheets, as you'll see this hour.

FIGURE 20.1
The Dunbar Project's original website.

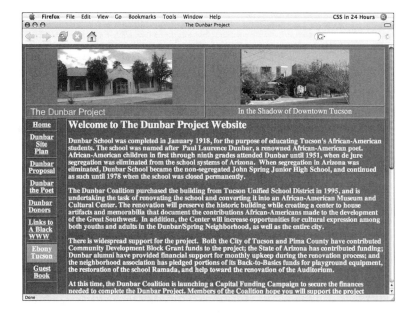

The Problems with Layout Tables

Figure 20.2 shows the source view for the original version of the Dunbar Project website, which was not designed with CSS. Instead, multiple nested `<table>` tags provide the page layout, and `<font>` is used extensively.

Tables for layout are problematic for a number of reasons. HTML purists argue against tables on principle: The `<table>` tag is meant to identify data in rows and columns of information, and is not intended for page layout. Accessibility mavens will tell you that screen readers employed by visually impaired users struggle with table layout.

Table-based layouts are often harder to maintain than CSS-based layouts, requiring extensive rewriting of HTML tags to make simple changes. Later this hour, you'll see how a few CSS rules can easily move entire sections around without touching the HTML document at all.

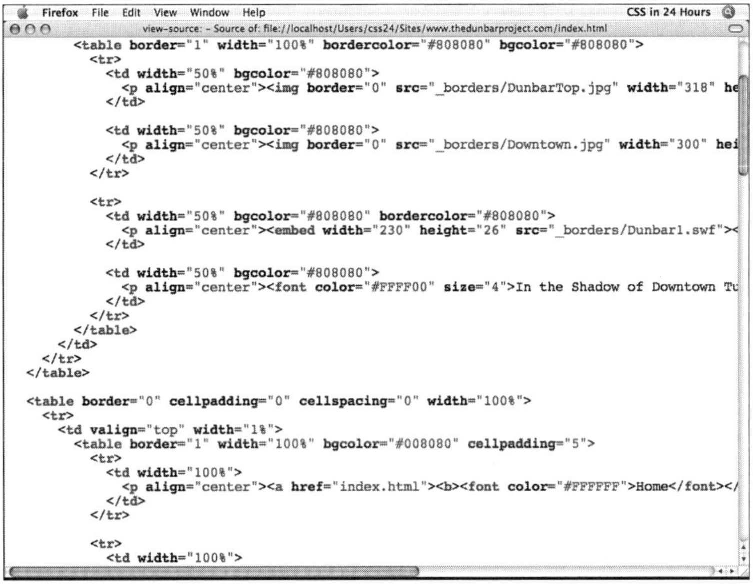

FIGURE 20.2
Table-based layout can be very convoluted.

CSS-based layouts make it easier to maintain your HTML pages without cluttering them up with <tr> and <td> tags, and make for simpler transitions to new layouts by just swapping in a new style sheet. Your web pages laid out with CSS will be smaller (and thus load more quickly) than table-based pages. You can write web pages with the main content first in the HTML source and the navigation and footer information after, making your page more friendly to screen readers and search engines.

Writing HTML with Structure

The first step to laying out a page is to start with well-written HTML that is divided into sections for styling. This is commonly done with <div> tags that have id attributes set on them, corresponding to the different sections of the page.

In Listing 20.1, you can see a redesign of the Dunbar Project home page, which uses simple markup to store the site navigation, the content, the side navigation links, and the page footer.

LISTING 20.1 Using <div> Tags to Create Sections for Positioning

```
<!-- dunbar-20.1.html -->
<html>
  <head>
    <title>The Dunbar Project</title>
  </head>
  <body>
    <div id="header">
```

LISTING 20.1   Continued

```
  <h1>The Dunbar Project</h1>
  <h2>In the Shadow of Downtown Tucson</h2>
  <div id="sitenav">
    <ol><li><a href="index.html">Home</a></li>
        <li><a href="about/">About the Dunbar Project</a></li>
        <li><a href="gallery/">Photo Galleries</a></li>
        <li><a href="donate/">Donate</a></li>
        <li><a href="contact/">Contact</a></li></ol>
  </div> <!-- sitenav -->
</div> <!-- header -->
<div id="main">
  <div id="content">
    <h3>Welcome to The Dunbar Project Website</h3>
    <img src="DunbarTop.jpg" alt="[Dunbar School]">
    <p>Dunbar School was completed in January 1918, for the
       purpose of educating Tucson's African-American students.
       The school was named after <a href="poet.html">Paul
       Laurence Dunbar</a>, a renowned African-American poet.
       African-American children in first through ninth grades
       attended Dunbar until 1951, when de jure segregation was
       eliminated from the school systems of Arizona.  When
       segregation in Arizona was eliminated, Dunbar School
       became the non-segregated John Spring Junior High School,
       and continued as such until 1978 when the school was
       closed permanently.</p>
    <!-- ... more content omitted ... -->
  </div> <!-- content -->
  <div id="sidebar">
    <h3>Dunbar Project</h3>
    <ol><li><a href="plan/">The Dunbar Site Plan</a></li>
        <li><a href="auditorium/">Dunbar Auditorium</a></li>
        <li><a href="history/">School History</a></li>
        <li><a href="proposal/">Project Proposal</a></li>
        <li><a href="donors/">Dunbar Donors</a></li>
        <li><a href="poet.html">About Paul Laurence Dunbar,
               Poet</a></li>
        <li><a href="links/">Related Links</a></li></ol>
    <h3>Coalition Partners</h3>
    <ol><li>The Tucson Urban League</li>
        <li>The Dunbar Alumni Association</li>
        <li>The Dunbar/Spring Neighborhood Association</li>
        <li>The Juneteenth Festival Committee</li></ol>
    <h3>Individual Members</h3>
    <ol> <!-- ... list of donors omitted ... --> </ol>
  </div> <!-- sidebar -->
  <div id="footer">
    <p id="note501c3">The Dunbar Project is a 501c(3) organization,
       and your contributions are tax deductible.</p>
    <p id="copyright">Copyright &copy; 2006 by the Dunbar
       Project. Questions?
       <a href="mailto:webmaster@thedunbarproject.com"
       >Mail the Webmaster.</a></p>
  </div> <!-- footer -->
</div> <!-- main -->
</body>
</html>
```

You can download a full copy of this HTML file from the book's website; the content has been cut for space in this listing.

The structure of this page is defined by the <div> tags with id attributes. The general skeleton (with content omitted) consists of the following:

```
<div id="header">
  <div id="sitenav"></div>
</div> <!  header  >
<div id="main">
  <div id="content"></div>
  <div id="sidebar"></div>
  <div id="footer"></div>
</div> <!  main  >
```

Comments are used with the closing </div> tags as reminders about which <div> is being closed; it makes the page easier to edit later.

The page is constructed of two sections: a header and a main body. Each of these has one or more subsections. This structure provides what's needed to redesign and lay out the page.

Why this particular structure? There are actually many ways you could structure such the page, inserting <div> tags appropriately. This skeleton is simply the method chosen for this example, to get the specific styles used later on. During the web development process, you might go back to your HTML and add or remove <div> tags while styling to give more flexibility when creating page layouts.

The number of <div> tags you use will vary from layout to layout. Some web designers believe strongly in using only a minimum number of <div> tags, whereas others add them freely whenever needed. The approach for this example is down the middle between those extremes: There are enough to make it easy to illustrate how CSS-based layout works, but not so many that we're adding extraneous <div> tags just because we can.

Figure 20.3 shows the new HTML page without any styles applied.

Writing a Layout Style Sheet

With an HTML page ready for styling, the next step is to write the style sheet. There are several questions to consider regarding how to lay out the page.

The first is a technical question: Will you use absolute positioning for layout, or will you use floated columns? You can get the same general layout effects from both techniques. Positioning is a little bit easier to grasp, at first, so this example uses absolute positioning. Later this hour, however, you'll learn how to lay out the same HTML page with the float property.

FIGURE 20.3
An unstyled
page, ready for
layout.

You need to figure out how many columns you want. There's a slight increase in complexity when you have more columns, but the specific techniques remain the same whether you're using two columns, three columns, or more. In this redesign, two columns are used to avoid making the example overly complex.

Finally, you need to determine whether you are using a fixed layout or a liquid layout. A fixed layout is one that defines a specific width for an entire page; for example, it may be always 700 pixels across, and excess space in the browser simply becomes wider margins. A liquid layout is one that grows larger (or smaller) based on the user's screen resolution and browser window size.

There are advantages and disadvantages to both fixed and liquid layouts. A fixed layout may be easier to create and easier to read on larger monitors; a liquid layout is more adaptable but could result in overly long lines, which are harder to read. In this example, the Dunbar Project site will use a liquid design with margin size based on em units.

Listing 20.2 is a style sheet that starts to set up the layout choices.

LISTING 20.2   A Style Sheet for Page Layout

```
/* dunbar-layout-20.2.css */

body        { margin: 0; padding: 0;
              background-color: silver; }
#header     { background-color: black; color: white; }
```

LISTING 20.2 Continued

```
#sitenav ol { padding: 0; margin: 0;
             display: inline; }
#sitenav li { display: inline; padding-left: 1em;
             margin-left: 1em; border-left: 1px
             solid black; }
#sitenav li:first-child
             { padding-left: 0; border-left: none;
             margin-left: 0; }
#sitenav li a { color: white; }
#main        { padding: 0 12em 2em 2em;
             position: relative;
             background-color: gray; }
#content     { background-color: white; }
#sidebar     { position: absolute; width: 10em;
             right: 1em; top: 1em; }
#sidebar h3 { color: white;
             background-color: black; }
#sidebar ol { margin: 0 0 1em 0;
             background-color: white;
             border: 2px solid black; }
#footer      { background-color: white; }
```

This style sheet is deliberately plain and simple, with colors of black, gray, silver, and white to make it easier for you to identify the various sections of the page.

So what's happening here?

▶ The first rule sets the margin and padding of the <body> to 0. This is an important first rule for layout because browsers typically add one or the other (or both) to any web page.

▶ The #sitenav rules in Listing 20.2 are used to turn the ordered list of links into a horizontal navigation bar.

▶ The #main section is set to position: relative to become the containing block around the #content, #sidebar, and #footer sections.

▶ The #main section is also given a large padding on the right, 12em. This is where the #sidebar will be located.

▶ Absolute positioning is used to move the #sidebar into the margin, out of its place in the normal flow of content. It is positioned 1 em to the left of the right edge of its containing block (#main) by right: 1em, and 1 em down from the top edge of the containing block by top: 1em.

Figure 20.4 shows the results of linking this style sheet to the HTML file from Listing 20.1.

FIGURE 20.4
Positioning prop-
erties define
the rough out-
line of the page.

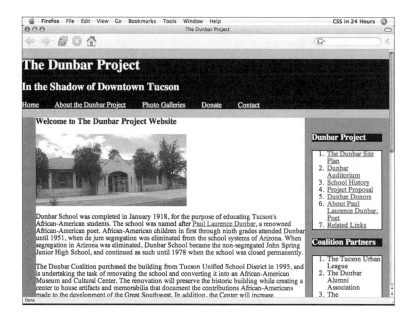

FIGURE 20.4
Positioning properties define the rough outline of the page.

It's still quite rough, but you can see the different sections moved into place. You should note the silver bars above and below the header. Where did they come from, and why?

The silver bars are the result of the background color set on the <body> showing through. They are formed because of the default margin properties set on the <h1> and <h3> headings used on the page. Remember that margins are outside of the border of an element's box, and the background-color property on a box colors only the interior content, not the margin. This applies even when you have a <div> wrapped around a heading, such as <h1>. The margin extends beyond the edge of the <div>'s background-color.

To fix this, we explicitly set the heading margins to zero on the heading tags. Listing 20.3 is a style sheet that not only does that, but also assigns colors, fonts, and other styles on the site. The teal, purple, white, and yellow colors were chosen to reflect not only the original design of the website, but also the actual colors used at the Dunbar school auditorium as well.

LISTING 20.3   A Style Sheet for Colors and Fonts

```
/* dunbar-colors-20.3.css */

body        { font-family: Optima, sans-serif; }
a:link      { color: #055; }
a:visited   { color: #404; }
```

LISTING 20.3 Continued

```
#header      { text-align: center;
               color: white; background-color: #055; }
#header h1, #header h2
             { margin: 0; }
#header h1   { color: #FFFF00; font-size: 250%; }
#header h2   { font-weight: normal; font-style: italic; }

#sitenav     { color: white; background-color: #404; }
#sitenav ol  { font-size: 90%; text-align: center; }
#sitenav li  { margin-left: 1em;
               border-left: 1px solid #DD0; }
#sitenav li a:link, #sitenav li a:visited
             { color: white; text-decoration: none; }
#sitenav li a:hover
             { color: #DDDD00; }

#main        { background-color: #055; }

#content     { background-color: white; padding: 1em 5em; }
#content h3  { margin-top: 0; }
#content p   { font-size: 90%; line-height: 1.4; }

#sidebar h3  { font-size: 100%; color: white; margin: 0;
               font-weight: normal; padding: 0.125em 0.25em;
               background-color: #404; }
#sidebar ol  { background-color: white; border: 2px solid #404;
               border-top: 0; margin: 0 0 1em 0;
               padding: 0.125em 0.25em; }
#sidebar li  { font-size: 85%;
               display: block; padding: 0.125em 0; }
#sidebar li a:link, #sidebar li a:visited
             { text-decoration: none; color: #055; }
#sidebar li a:hover { color: #404; }

#footer      { background-color: #404; color: white;
               padding: 0.5em 5em; }
#footer p    { margin: 0em; font-size: 85%; }
#footer p a:link, #footer p a:visited
             { color: #DDDD00; }
```

Figure 20.5 shows the HTML file from Listing 20.1 with both the layout style sheet from Listing 20.2 and the colors and fonts style sheet from Listing 20.3.

As you can see, the styled page in Figure 20.5 looks quite different from the unstyled version in Figure 20.3.

Re-Ordering Sections with Positioning Styles

The page in Figure 20.5 looks okay, but let's say that you got this far into the web design process and you suddenly decided that you want to have the site navigation bar located on top of the headline, rather than below it.

FIGURE 20.5
Fonts and col-
ors help define
the website's
look.

You could go in and change your HTML source around. This would work, but it would introduce a problem. The order of the HTML in Listing 20.1 is sensible—the name of the site is given first, and then the navigation menu. This is how users of non-CSS browsers such as Lynx will read your page, and also how search engines and screen readers will understand it as well. Moving the title of the page after the list of links doesn't make much sense.

Instead, you can use CSS positioning properties to reformat the page without touching the HTML file. Listing 20.4 is a style sheet to do exactly that.

LISTING 20.4   Moving One Section Before Another

```
/* dunbar-move-20.4.css */

#header    { padding: 1.25em 0 0.25em 0;
             position: relative;
             background-color: #404; }
#sitenav   { position: absolute;
             top: 0; right: 0;
             border-bottom: 1px solid #DDDD00;
             width: 100%;
             background-color: #055; }
```

What's happening here?

▶ The #header section encloses the #sitenav in the HTML source, so by setting it to position: relative, it now becomes the containing block for the site navigation links.

▶ Padding is added to the top of the #header section. This is where subsequent rules will place the site navigation menu; the padding reserves the space for it.

▶ Absolute positioning properties align the top-right corner of the #sitenav section with the top-right corner of its containing block, the #header.

▶ Giving a width of 100% to the #sitenav ensures it will reach across the full width of its containing block, which is, in this case, as wide as the browser display window.

▶ Finally, colors are swapped on the #header and the #sitenav to make them fit in better with the overall design in their new locations, and a yellow border is added to the bottom of the navigation links.

You can see the effects of these changes in Figure 20.6.

FIGURE 20.6
The navigation menu is now above the page headline.

Try it Yourself

Redesign the Layout of a Page

You just learned how to move the site navigation menu around. What if you want to make further changes to the page? Try these steps to get familiar with how easy it is to change the layout with CSS:

▼

1. Download a copy of the Dunbar Project page for editing. You can get all the files used in this hour from the book's website. The file dunbar.html contains the complete HTML page, and dunbar-full.css has all the style rules listed in this chapter combined into a single style sheet.

2. Move the sidebar to the left side of the page instead of the right. To do this, you need to make space for it in the left gutter by changing the padding rule on the #main section to

   ```
   #main { padding: 0 2em 2em 12em; }
   ```

3. Then change the positioning offset properties the #sidebar. You don't even have to change the rule for the top property; just replace the property name right with left.

4. Reload the page. You should now see the menu bar on the left side of the screen.

5. Next, move the #footer section. Even though the id of the <div> is "footer", there's nothing magical about that name that means it needs to be at the bottom of the page. Place it on the right side, where the sidebar used to be located. First clear some space:

   ```
   #main { padding: 0 12em 2em 12em; }
   ```

6. Then reposition the footer with these rules:

   ```
   #footer { position: absolute;
             top: 1em; right: 1em;
             width: 10em;
             padding: 0; }
   #footer p { padding: 0.5em; }
   ```

7. Reload the page. The #footer is now no longer a footer, but a third column on the right side of the page.

▲

The Floated Columns Layout Technique

You can also lay out a web page by using the float property rather than positioning properties. This method is a little bit more complex, but is favored by some designers who prefer the versatility. In addition, floated columns can be written with fewer <div> tags, and in some cases deal better with side columns that are shorter than the main text.

Listing 20.5 is a style sheet demonstrating how you can float entire columns on a page with CSS. This is a replacement for the dunbar-layout-20.2.css style sheet in Listing 20.2. The new style sheet places the menu bar on the left instead of the right, just for variety's sake—there's nothing inherently left-biased about floated columns (or right-biased about positioning).

LISTING 20.5 Float-Based Layouts in CSS

```
/* dunbar-float-20.5.css */

body        { margin: 0; padding: 0; }
#sitenav ol { padding: 0; margin: 0;
              display: inline; }
#sitenav li { display: inline; padding-left: 1em;
              margin-left: 1em; border-left: 1px
              solid black; }
#sitenav li:first-child
            { padding-left: 0; border-left: none;
              margin-left: 0; }

/* This is what positions the sidebar: */
#main       { padding: 0 2em 2em 12em; }
#content    { float: left; }
#sidebar    { float: left; width: 10em;
              position: relative;
              right: 11em; top: 1em;
              margin-left: -100%; }
#sidebar ol { margin: 0 0 1em 0; }
```

What does this style sheet do?

▶ The first section simply duplicates the site navigation bar code from Listing 20.2, so that the entire style sheet can be replaced by this one.

▶ Starting at the second comment, the code for positioning the columns appears. The first rule sets the #main section to have a wide gutter on the left, which is where we will be placing the sidebar.

▶ Both the #content and #sidebar sections are set to float. This means that they line up on the left side of the #main section, just inside the padding.

▶ A width is given to the #sidebar of 10em—the same width as in Listing 10.2. The size was chosen because that allows 1 em of space around it, after it is placed inside the 12 em gutter set by the padding rule on #main.

▶ A negative margin is set on the left side of the #sidebar, which actually makes it overlay the #content section. Relative positioning is then used, via the right and top rules, to push the sidebar into the correct place in the gutter.

Figure 20.7 shows this style sheet applied to the HTML file in Listing 20.1, along with the colors and fonts style sheet in Listing 20.3 and the style sheet from Listing 20.4, which relocated the site navigation menu.

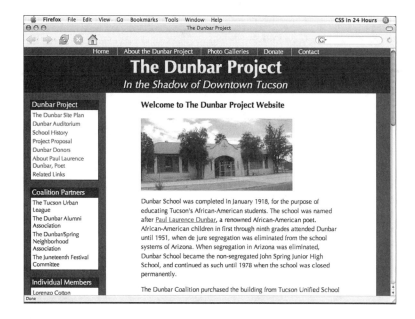

Summary

Tables have long been used in web design to lay out a web page. However, this misuse of <table> markup introduces a plethora of complications, from accessibility concerns to complexity problems. Using CSS for layout can clean up your HTML code and produce flexible designs that can be updated easily to new styles.

Laying out a page with CSS starts with adding sections to the HTML, using <div>s with ID selectors. These are then arranged in vertical columns, through the use of either positioning rules or the float property. With CSS layouts, it's not difficult to re-order and reshape the page simply by changing the style sheet.

Workshop

The workshop contains a Q&A section, quiz questions, and activities to help reinforce what you've learned in this hour. If you get stuck, the answers to the quiz can be found after the questions.

Q&A

Q. *Is it ever okay to use tables for layout?*

A. Never, ever, ever! Well, almost. CSS layouts generally are more efficient and versatile than `<table>`-based code, but if you are careful to test your layout tables in a browser such as Lynx to make sure that the site is usable without tables, you can probably get away with it. Tables aren't awful for laying out a page, and CSS can be tricky when you're dealing with grid-based designs. In general, though, you're better off using CSS whenever you can.

Q. *Which are better measurements for layouts, pixels or percentages?*

A. Some web designers, especially those from a print background or who have picky clients to please, swear by pixels. With some patience (and possibly work-arounds for browser quirks, as described in Hour 24, "Troubleshooting and Browser Hacks"), you can get close to pixel-perfect designs in CSS. Other designers like percentage measurements, which scale with the size of the text window. Personally, I prefer em measurements, which are based on the user's chosen font size. There's no clear-cut advantage to any approach, however; all have their pros and cons. You can experiment with a variety of measurement types, and don't be afraid to mix and match them sensibly on your site—for example, designating column widths in percentages but also setting pixel-based `min-width` and `max-width` values.

Q. *Are there problems with using ems for layout?*

A. Only if you're not careful. The biggest problems result from setting margins, padding, or positioning properties based on em values, and then changing the font size of those values. For example, you might overlook the effects of the `font-size` rule buried in these declarations:

```
#sidebar { right: 1em; top: 1em;
           text-align: right; color: white;
           font-family: Verdana, sans-serif;
           font-size: 50%; }
```

This won't actually be located 1 em in each direction from the corner of its containing block; it will be 0.5 em from the right, and 0.5 em from the top. If you are going to change the font size within a section that uses ems for dimensions or placement, set the `font-size` rules on the contents of the box, as done in this chapter's style sheets with `#sidebar h3 { ... }` and `#sidebar ol { ... }` rules. You could also add an extra `<div>` inside the sidebar, and set the `font-size` rule on that `<div>`.

Quiz

1. Which property tells the text to start flowing normally again, after a floated column?

2. How do you designate the containing block for an absolutely positioned element?

3. What kind of rules would you write to change an ordered list of navigation links into a horizontal navigation bar?

Answers

1. The `clear` property, which was introduced in Hour 15, "Alignment," can be used after floated columns—for example, if you want a footer to reach across the entire browser window below the floated columns.

2. As explained in Hour 19, "Absolute and Fixed Positioning," you set the containing block by changing the `position` property, usually to a value of `relative` (with no offset properties designated).

3. Listing 20.2 has an example of a style sheet with rules to do that, using the display property as described in Hour 16, "Borders and Boxes."

Exercises

Practice the following exercises:

▶ What kind of layouts can you create with CSS? Choose your favorite sites— either your own or some you enjoy using—and duplicate their layout styles with CSS. Existing sites make good models for doing your own practice, but keep in mind that unless you get permission, you shouldn't simply steal someone else's code. Start with the visual appearance as you see it on the screen, and draw out boxes on paper as guidelines showing you where various columns are located. Use that as your model to write the HTML and CSS for building a similar layout.

▶ Try both of the techniques described in this hour—using absolutely positioned content and using floating columns. Start with one version and convert it over to the other. Find a style of page that looks right to you, and the CSS code that you feel is easiest to understand, apply, and modify consistently.

PART V

Mastering CSS

HOUR 21

Web Design with CSS

What You'll Learn in This Hour:

▶ Why it's important to design for your audience and to test carefully

▶ How to incorporate style sheets into your web design practices

▶ Which questions you need to ask yourself before starting on a style sheet

▶ How to organize your style sheets to make them easier to use and edit

▶ How to create alternate style sheets that can be selected by your site visitors

The web developer's role is more than just that of a programmer or code author. In addition to understanding properties, values, selectors, and the cascade order, a CSS developer needs to be conversant in the art of design and the craft of usability.

Basic Principles of Web Design

In previous hours, you've learned the "what" of using Cascading Style Sheets. You can write your own rules, set your own fonts, choose your colors, and lay out a page.

In this hour, you'll look at the question of "when," which is what design principles are all about. It's not enough to know the method of doing something; you also need to know the right times to do it and when it's best to not do it.

Web development is a complex field, even if some of the component parts seem simple at first. Designing a website is all about balance; it's a complicated balancing act between the desires of the site operator and the needs of the audience. Even basic issues such as how much content to place on each page require finding the right balance between too much and too little. Web developers spend a lot of time making compromises, often choosing an alternative that isn't necessarily the absolute best but that works for the greatest amount of people.

Designs that reflect an understanding of the audience and put their needs first are referred to as *user-centric* designs. Some site designs are *designer-centric,* meaning that the web developer's need for artistic expression comes first; for some sites, such as a personal website, this may make sense. More common are *content-centric* designs, which are focused on the site information and functionality. Content-centric sites are usually more effective than designer-centric sites, but their designs sometimes fail to fully understand how their content is used in practice. An effective designer utilizes all these techniques to create web designs.

Color, Fonts, and Layout

Presentation isn't everything, but it's a whole lot of something. In an information-intensive medium such as the Web—accessed visually by most users—it's important to have an effective presentation that supports the purpose of the site. Rather than being mere window dressing, style sheets can be an integral part of a website, crucial to understanding and using the site.

Some people think that because the Web is a completely new medium, the old rules of offline design don't apply. Although the Web does introduce new challenges because of the nature of the medium, it's not so revolutionary that everything can be discarded. The disciplines of graphic design and user-interface design have a lot to teach, but few web developers learn it. For example, graphic design can tell you much about the effective use of color and whitespace, and user-interface design informs you how computer users make choices.

On the other hand, some designers make the opposite mistake of assuming they can just put the same design on the Web as on paper, and this often leads to disastrous results. "Brochure" websites gained a bad reputation early, and in most cases it was deserved, based on sites that were barely more than a scanned pamphlet posted on the Internet. The flexible nature of web design, where the user's choices can influence the final presentation as much as the author's, can prove frustrating and incomprehensible to graphic artists who are used to working in a fixed, printed medium.

As noted in previous hours, font and color rules should be used sparingly; don't go nuts simply because you can. A restrained presentation usually looks better than an overly complex one that is awash in every hue under the sun and set with dozens of fonts.

CSS rules can be used for a number of effects in combination, including simulating buttons and logos with styles. This is generally a good idea, although in some cases you'll be unable to get the exact effect you want. For example, if you need a rare font with a drop shadow, you're in trouble because the user may not have the same font on her browser, and text shadow effects are tricky in CSS. In those cases, you should use a GIF or JPEG with text to gain the desired effects.

Did you Know?

Navigation menus created with CSS instead of graphics are much easier to maintain and load faster than images. If you need to add a new link, just add the HTML—no need to open a graphics program.

Usability

Not all attractive web pages are created equal. Some great-looking sites are hard to use, whereas others are elegantly straightforward and a joy to use. The difference isn't found in the appearance alone—although the visible look can affect ease of use—but instead in a somewhat nebulous quality called the *usability*. The usability of a website is a measure of how easy it is for people to use that site. Usability is also the name of a field of study concerned with understanding and improving how people use computers, websites, and other technologies.

Did you Know?

Jakob Nielsen's website at http://www.useit.com/ has good information on usability. You may also notice that his site is very plain. This is more a reflection of Jakob's personal aesthetic than of a strict usability principle. A website can (and should) employ good visual design in addition to adherence to usability; there's not a conflict between the two, and a great visual design is actually a boon to usability.

Cascading Style Sheets can be used to enhance usability by producing web presentations that are simple and distinct. Your styles should reflect how the information is used, highlighting information that is most essential to the site's purpose and the user's needs while still allowing access to all the content.

For example, you can make your site's navigation system stand out by giving a distinct appearance to that part of the page—visible enough that it can be found, but not so intrusive that the design overwhelms the rest of the content.

Many popular conventions observed on the Web are so widespread that they are second nature to use, making your site easier for visitors. As an example, placing a row of links with distinct styles on the left or top of your page lets users instantly recognize those as navigation links. Don't be afraid to reuse existing web design elements in this manner; often a site that is too creative can inadvertently become amazingly difficult to use.

Knowing Your Audience

To create user-centric designs, you need to be aware of who your audience is. In some cases, you may be in luck, as you may know everything there is to know about your users. For example, if you are working on an intranet site for your employer, and the company has standardized on Firefox, your task suddenly becomes a lot easier. You can use advanced features found only in Firefox and you don't have to worry about quirks in Internet Explorer, Opera, or other browsers.

> However, there's a danger in taking intranet "freedom" too far. You may have to recode your entire site if there's a policy change mandating a new browser or a new version of the same browser. Some users may prefer to use familiar software, such as the Internet Explorer browser they used at their last job. Employees with disabilities might employ special assistive technologies to access the intranet. It usually saves you time and effort in the long run if you design your site to be generally accessible by everyone and not dependent upon a single browser.

If you don't know exactly who your audience is, you can still make some educated guesses. Web servers dutifully record all accesses, and the information they save includes the browser type (name, version, and platform) of each person who downloads a file. These are stored in a web server log, a long listing of all connections to the server; you can then run a log analysis program, such as Analog (http://www.analog.cx/), to collate and summarize this information. If your ISP or web host doesn't provide you with this information, ask for it; it's important data for anyone running a website.

The information you're looking for is not only the type of browser, but also which pages are being used. By looking at site usage patterns you can discern which pages are most popular and also measure the effectiveness of your navigation systems. You can also learn other useful information such as screen resolution from your browser statistics. This is useful for knowing how to design your page layouts and font sizes.

Another useful tactic for getting information on your users is to simply ask for it. Put up a survey on your site to gather responses from your current users so you can serve their needs better. In addition to gathering technical browser information, you should consider other demographics that can also affect the way you design the site. For example, generational differences among audiences can influence whether you build your site for younger or older users. Users with disabilities may have specific needs; in Hour 22, "Accessibility and Print Media," you'll find out more about how to satisfy those needs.

Organization and Planning

Before you write one line of HTML or CSS code, you need to spend some time planning out your site and organizing the information contained on it. A carefully planned site is much easier to maintain and update than one that grows organically, out of control. Websites have a natural tendency to evolve, and this is a good thing, but planned growth is always better than accidental growth.

You may want to draw your site out on paper; you might want to create a diagram with software that creates flow charts. The exact way in which you plan your site will depend on your own preferences. Building a chart of your web content and the links between pages will help you visualize the information and group it into natural sections. The better you organize the page, the easier it will be for users to find your content.

Testing Your Website

After you've got the site up and running, it's time for testing. The first testing will be your own browser tests, using your suite of browsers. In Hour 3, "Browser Support for CSS," I recommended building up a standard set of browsers, ideally on different platforms if you can manage it, which represent a broad spectrum of web users. After you start using a browser with decent CSS support, such as Opera, Netscape 6, or Internet Explorer, you may not want to use older or broken browsers regularly. However, it's still important to test on those because, for whatever reason, people are still out there using them!

After you've given your pages a once-over, you're not really finished. For the same reason that writers can't edit their own work, you can't be the only one to test your web pages. A writer will often miss mistakes she's generated, because she knows how something's supposed to be written, and her mind fills in the correct version instead of what's really on the page. For the same reason, you'll want to have others test your site.

One thing you can do is to ask some fellow web developers for a critique. Because they understand the code behind the designs, they can often point out not only mistakes, but also how to fix them. If you don't know any other web developers, consider joining a local group or a mailing list.

Another way to test your site is by doing user testing, one of the core techniques employed by usability experts. In a formal usability test, you get a number of people and have them attempt to use specific site features, filming them and taking notes from behind a one-way mirror. As explained by Jakob Nielsen, a formal usability test may be overkill; a small sample of around five representative users should be enough, and you can get by without the camera and the mirror.

Here's how you do it:

1. Look over your site and choose several primary functions that users would want to accomplish. Write up several of them (five is a good number again) as tasks or questions; select a variety of functions ranging from easy to difficult. For example, to do such a test on http://www.css24.com/, I might choose, "Who is the technical editor of this book?" and "Order this book from Amazon.com" as two of the questions. (On the latter task, I wouldn't require that the transaction actually be completed.)

2. Find your test subjects. Ask them politely, and if possible, offer them compensation or a latte. As much as possible, choose representative users, but don't get obsessed about making sure they're "really" representative. For example, I wouldn't choose my mom for a test of the book's site because she's not a web developer and won't be using CSS, but I might ask my dad, who has done web design himself. If you work for a large company, find some users outside your workgroup who can spare a few minutes.

3. Invite each user to access the website and have them attempt the list of tasks you've created. Stress to your users that you're testing the site, not them; if they get something wrong, that's great because it points out a weakness in your design. Watch the users and take notes as they move around your site. No matter how strong the temptation, don't jump in and help them; if they can't figure something out, write that down.

4. When the test is over, thank your test subject and buy that latte. Then sit down with the results and make sure your ego is safely locked away; every site can be made better. Look at all the comments and notes you made and look for patterns across your users. If a certain function is hidden or confusing for several of them, it's likely a good candidate for redesign.

As you can see, this kind of easy user testing isn't a formal science, but it can still produce very useful results. It's certainly better than doing no user testing at all, which is sadly the case for many websites.

The Role of CSS in Web Design

As a web developer, skilled in HTML, Cascading Style Sheets, and possibly other web languages and technologies, you have a web development process. Even if you haven't planned it out formally, you've got a method that works for you, whether it's as simple as sitting down and designing whatever strikes your fancy or as complex as working in a multi-developer corporate development system for a large employer.

Adding CSS to your repertoire has made you an even better web developer than before; your skill set has expanded and the types of designs you can create are nearly limitless. The next step is to integrate your CSS skills into your web development process. I'm not going to tell you exactly how you'll do that—people have their own methods—but I'll help you think about how you can go about using CSS in your web designs.

In a few cases you may be able to develop your style sheets completely separately from your HTML pages. More commonly you'll employ an iterative process, where you make changes to the style sheet, then changes to the HTML page, and then go back to the style sheet for a few more tweaks until you're satisfied with the results. The adaptive nature of style sheets makes it easy to create these kinds of changes, and you may find yourself continuing to perfect your styles even after you post your content on the Web.

By the Way

You may not be starting with a blank slate and an uncreated website when you begin using CSS. Redesigns are very common in web development, and you may want to take advantage of a new site design to convert to a CSS-based presentation. It can sometimes be harder, but it's certainly possible to keep the same look and feel of your site when converting it to use CSS. If you're using a content management system (CMS) that automatically generates your website from a database, converting to style sheets may be a snap. CSS is very compatible, on a conceptual level, with the idea of templates as used by content management systems.

As mentioned at the start of this hour, CSS design involves balancing a number of factors to arrive at the best compromise for your site and its users. Questions will arise as you work with CSS on any site, and you'll need to answer them before you go on. I've listed several of these key questions here to help you plan your site:

▶ Will you use Cascading Style Sheets, and if so, to what effect? You certainly aren't required to use CSS, even after reading this entire book. You can create websites that are usable, accessible, attractive, and effective without a single CSS property anywhere in evidence. However, using CSS will make your site more flexible and easier to maintain and will give you access to presentation effects you couldn't get through HTML alone.

▶ What "flavor" of HTML will you use? As you may recall from Hour 4, "Using CSS with HTML," there are three varieties of HTML: Strict, Transitional, and Frameset. The Strict variety relies upon CSS for all styling effects, whereas Transitional (and Frameset) HTML can mix CSS rules with presentational markup. If you're concerned about older browsers that don't understand CSS, you may want to choose Transitional.

► Which browsers will you support? By "support," I mean investing the effort to work around the quirks of certain browsers. (By "certain browsers," I mostly mean Internet Explorer 6 and earlier.) This book has a number of workarounds, plus ways to exclude certain browsers from viewing styles. If you are designing just for CSS-enabled browsers, such as recent Firefox, Safari, or Opera versions, those workarounds become less important.

► Are you using positioning CSS for layout? It's relatively easy to use CSS for formatting text, controlling fonts, and setting colors. Using it for layout is trickier, especially with inconsistent browser support among some of the older versions. Don't assume that you must use positioning CSS; even in 2006, many sites are still using tables extensively for page layout. Using CSS for positioning is still more tricky for some developers than misusing the `<table>` tag.

► Will you use embedded or linked style sheets? Here, I'll give you advice: Use linked style sheets whenever you can. Many of the examples in this book use embedded style sheets, but that's mainly because it's easier to give you one listing than two.

The preceding list isn't exhaustive; you'll encounter more choices to make when designing and using CSS, but you should have learned enough by now to answer them.

Style Sheet Organization

The way you organize your style sheet can affect how easy it is for you to use and maintain your CSS, even if the effects are not evident in the presentation. This becomes even more critical if you're in a situation where someone else may have to use your styles in the future. You may work with an organization where multiple people will be working on the same site, or perhaps when you move on to another job your successor will inherit your style sheets.

To make a great style sheet, be organized and clear in what you're doing, and above all, use comments. Web developers often overlook comments in CSS, but if you have to come back later and try to figure out why you did something, they're invaluable. Comments can also be used to group related styles together into sections.

Reasonable names for `class` and `id` attributes can make your style sheet easier to read; choose names for these important selectors that reflect the functions of the elements. If you can, avoid selectors based solely on appearance characteristics, such as the `boldtext` or `redbox` classes; instead try something descriptive of why you've chosen those styles, such as `definition` or `sidebar`. That way, if you change your page styles later, you won't have to rewrite your HTML; there are few things as confusing as a rule like the following:

```
.redbox { color: blue; background-color: white; }
```

In what way is that box red? Well, it probably was red in some prior incarnation of the style rules, but not now.

When you list your rules in your style sheet, do them in a sensible order. Generally speaking, it's best to start with the body rules first and then proceed down from there, but because the cascade order matters only in case of conflict, it's not strictly necessary to mirror the page hierarchy. What's more important is that you are able to locate the rules that apply to a given selector and to discern which styles should be applied.

An example of bad style sheet organization is shown in Listing 21.1. This is part of the style sheet from the author's personal website, but with the rules in a scrambled order. How hard is it for you to figure out what is going on here?

LISTING 21.1   A Randomly Organized Style Sheet

```
#sidebar0 .section, #sidebar1 .section { font-size: smaller;
border: 0px solid lime; text-transform: lowercase;
margin-bottom: 1em; }
gnav a:link, #nav a:visited, #footer a:link, #footer
a:visited { text-decoration: none; color: #CCCCCC; }
#nav .section, #nav .shead, #nav .sitem, #nav h1 { display:
inlinc; }
#sidebar1 { position: absolute; right: 2em; top: 3em;
width: 9em; } a:link { color: #DD8800; text-decoration: none; }
#main { } a:hover { color: lime; }
#nav .shead, #nav .sitem { padding-left: 1em; padding-right:
1em; }
#nav { position: fixed; top: 0px; left: 0px; padding-top:
3px; padding-bottom: 3px; background-color: #333333; color:
white; width: 100%; text-align: center; text-transform:
lowercase; }
#nav .section { font-size: 90%; } #layout { padding: 1em; }
body { background-color: white; color: #333333; font-family:
Verdana, sans-serif; margin: 0; padding: 0; }
#nav h1 { font-size: 1em; background-color: #333333; color:
white; } a:visited { color: #CC8866; text-decoration: none; }
#nav { border-bottom: 1px solid lime; } #main { margin-left:
11.5em; margin-right: 11.5em; border: 0px solid lime;
margin-bottom: 1.5em; margin-top: 1.5em; }
#nav a:hover, #footer a:hover { color: lime; }
#sidebar0 { position: absolute; left: 2em; top: 3em;
width: 9em; text-align: right; }
```

If that was hard to follow, don't feel bad; the difficulty was intentional. CSS rules are very easily obfuscated if you're not careful. Most style sheets grow organically as piecemeal additions are made; discipline is necessary to keep the style sheet readable.

The style sheet in Listing 21.2 is really the same style sheet as in Listing 21.1. Both are valid style sheets and both produce the same results when applied to the web page, but the second one is easier to understand. Comments make clearer what each section of the style sheet does, indentation and whitespace are used effectively, and the order is much easier to follow.

LISTING 21.2   A Better-Organized Style Sheet

```
/* default styles for the page */
body      { background-color: white;
            color: #333333;
            font-family: Verdana, sans-serif;
            margin: 0;
            padding: 0; }

a:link    { color: #DD8800; text-decoration: none; }
a:visited { color: #CC8866; text-decoration: none; }
a:hover   { color: lime; }

/* layout superstructure */
#layout   { padding: 1em; }

/* top navigation bar */
#nav      { position: fixed;
            top: 0px;          left: 0px;
            color: white;      width: 100%;
            padding-top: 3px;  padding-bottom: 3px;
            background-color: #333333;
            text-align: center;
            text-transform: lowercase; }
            border-bottom: 1px solid lime; }
#nav .section, #nav .shead, #nav .sitem, #nav h1
            { display: inline; }
#nav .section
            { font-size: 90%; }
#nav .shead, #nav .sitem
            { padding-left: 1em; padding-right: 1em; }
#nav h1   { font-size: 1em;
            background-color: #333333; color: white; }
#nav a:hover, #footer a:hover
            { color: lime; }
#nav a:link, #nav a:visited,
#footer a:link, #footer a:visited
            { text-decoration: none; color: #CCCCCC; }

/* main content section */
#main     { margin-left: 11.5em;  margin-right: 11.5em;
            margin-bottom: 1.5em;  margin-top: 1.5em;
            border: 0px solid lime; }

/* two sidebars, absolutely positioned */
#sidebar1 { position: absolute;
            right: 2em; top: 3em; width: 9em; }
#sidebar0 { position: absolute;
            left: 2em; top: 3em; width: 9em;
            text-align: right; }
```

LISTING 21.2   Continued

```
#sidebar0 .section, #sidebar1 .section
        { font-size: smaller;
          border: 0px solid lime;
          text-transform: lowercase;
          margin-bottom: 1em; }
```

Site-wide Style Sheets

The style sheet given in Listing 21.2 was created to be used on the entire site, not just on one page. Linking to an external style sheet is an easy way for you to apply style sheets over your entire set. You simply use the `<link>` tag on every page, with the `href` attribute set to the location of your site-wide style sheet.

A site-wide style sheet can be used to enforce a consistent appearance on the website, even if you have multiple web developers working on different parts of the same site. Additional styles can be added in embedded style sheets or in additional linked CSS files that are created for each department or business unit. For example, each department at a school may use the school's global style sheet for design elements common to the entire site, and individual departmental style sheets for that department's unique color, layout, and font choices.

Alternate Style Sheets

Not all style sheets are going to appeal to everyone. Some users might prefer a smaller font, letting more fit on the screen, whereas other visitors to your site might require large print with high contrast.

The CSS specification allows you to create alternate style sheets that can be switched out by the user upon request. This allows you to create sites which offer a variety of "skins" that are selectable in browsers that support alternate style sheets.

There are actually three types of linked style sheets—persistent style sheets, preferred style sheets, and alternate style sheets. A *persistent style sheet* is one that can't be switched for another style sheet through use of the browser's mechanism for alternate style sheets; it is always on. The style sheets you have created so far have all been persistent.

A *preferred style sheet* is loaded automatically by the browser, but if an alternate style sheet is selected, the preferred sheet switches off, and the *alternate style sheet* is used instead. You can have multiple alternate style sheets, but only one preferred style sheet.

To designate an alternate style sheet that can be swapped out for the main style sheet, you change the attributes of the `<link>` property. A name must be assigned to a preferred or alternate style sheet and must be set as the `title` attribute on the link, as shown in Table 21.1.

TABLE 21.1   Attributes for `<link>` That Determine Style Sheet Type

Style Sheet Type	`rel` **Attribute**	`title` **Attribute**
Persistent	`"stylesheet"`	Unset
Preferred	`"stylesheet"`	*"Name of the style sheet"*
Alternate	`"alternate stylesheet"`	*"Name of the style sheet"*

For example, imagine that you have basic rules that should always be used in `base.css`, the preferred styles in `default.css`, and an older version of your style sheet in `old-2005.css`. You would write the following HTML to allow users to switch between these style sheets:

```
<link type="text/css" rel="stylesheet"
      href="base.css">
<link type="text/css" rel="stylesheet"
      href="default.css" title="Current Site Style">
<link type="text/css" rel="alternate stylesheet"
      href="old-2005.css" title="Last Year's Style">
```

These attributes establish `base.css` as a persistent style sheet, `default.css` as the preferred style sheet, and `old-2005.css` as an alternate style sheet.

Browser Support for Alternate Style Sheets

You know how to designate alternate style sheets with the `<link>` tag, but what browsers will use them? Not all web browsers fully implement the CSS specification, and alternate style sheets are one example of this.

On a browser that supports alternate style sheets, the user can select which style sheets to use from a menu option. In Firefox, this is found on the View menu, under Page Style. As shown in Figure 21.1, the title properties from the `<link>` tag are used as menu choices; the user can also view the page without any style sheets.

As of early 2006, only Firefox and Opera support selection of alternate style sheets from the browser interface. Other browsers apply persistent and preferred style sheets, but don't allow switching out the preferred style sheet for an alternate style sheet.

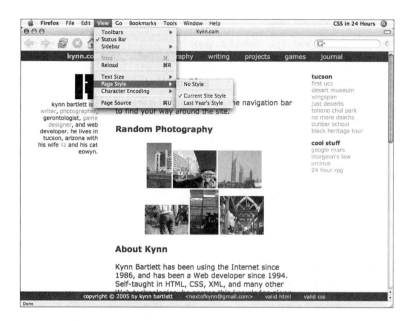

FIGURE 21.1
Firefox allows
selection of
alternate style
sheets.

Creating an Alternate Style Sheet

Why would you want to create an alternate style sheet? There are a number of valid
reasons, including showing off your ability to use CSS to reformat and restyle a website easily. A better reason might be to meet specific user needs. Web accessibility
proponent Joe Clark has promoted the use of "zoom" layouts to accommodate users
with visual disabilities; see http://joeclark.org/access/webaccess/zoom/ for a full
explanation.

> You'll learn more about CSS and web accessibility in Hour 22.

By the Way

A zoom layout is simply a style sheet that has been designed to show a page in a
single column, with high contrast, scalable large fonts, and simple navigation controls. Listing 21.3 is an example of a zoom style sheet, written for the Dunbar Project
website, which was introduced in Hour 20, "Page Layout in CSS." The colors yellow,
violet, and lime are used as brighter versions of the colors in the original design of
the site.

LISTING 21.3   A "Zoom" Style Sheet

```
/* dunbar-zoom-21.3.css */

body        { background-color: black; color: white;
              font-size: 125%; line-height: 1.25;
```

LISTING 21.3   Continued

```
                font-family: Verdana, sans-serif;
                letter-spacing: 1px; /* one pixel extra */
                word-spacing: 1px;
                margin: 0; padding: 0; }

a:link        { color: violet; }
a:visited     { color: lime; }
a:link:hover  { color: black; background-color: violet; }
a:visited:hover
                { color: black; background-color: lime; }

#header, #content, #sidebar, #footer
                { padding: 1em; margin: 1em;
                  border: 0.15em solid white; }
#header       { border-color: lime; }
#sidebar      { border-color: lime; }
#footer       { border-color: violet; }
#header h1    { color: yellow; }

#sitenav ol   { padding: 0; margin: 0;
                  display: inline; }
#sitenav li   { display: inline; padding-left: 1em; }
#sidebar li   { display: block; }
table         { border-collapse: collapse;
                  border: 0.15em solid yellow;
                  margin: 1em; }
table th, table td
                { vertical-align: top; text-align: left;
                  padding: 0.2em 1em 0.2em 0.2em;
                  font-size: 125%; line-height: 1.25;
                  border-bottom: 0.15em solid yellow; }
th            { color: lime; }
.mailingaddress
                { margin: 0 2em; color: lime; }
```

As you can see, this does not use any CSS for layout, and it makes for a larger, bolder presentation with bright colors against a dark background. Such a style sheet is useful for certain users with specific visual impairments. Figure 21.2 shows this style sheet displayed in a web browser; compare with the figures from Hour 20 to see the difference that an alternate style sheet can make.

Making Alternate Style Sheets Stick

There's one problem with alternate style sheets—they don't last. You can choose an alternate style sheet in your browser, but the minute you go to another page, or even reload the current page, you're back to the preferred style sheet.

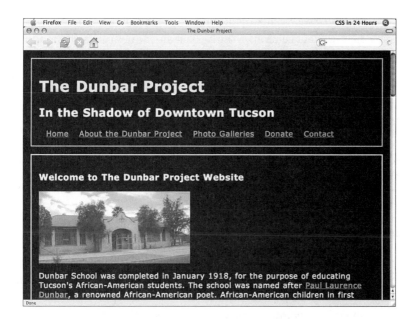

FIGURE 21.2
A zoomed version of a website.

One way to get around this limitation is to use HTML cookies, and server-side or client-side programming. A cookie is small bit of information stored by a web browser, associated with a specific website. Programming languages on both the server side and client side can access these cookies. JavaScript is an example of a client-side programming language that can manipulate cookies; for more about JavaScript, see Bonus Web Hour 1, "CSS and JavaScript."

Try it Yourself ▼

Create a Zoom Style Sheet

Creating an alternate style sheet for users who need high contrast is a good exercise in minimalism. Learn how to do it by following these steps:

1. Start with a website you've created, perhaps in the course of reading this book.

2. Keep your original style sheet handy for reference, but start over with an empty style sheet to begin creating your zoom style sheet.

3. Set a dark background and light text with a body rule. Add some extra line spacing, letter spacing, and word spacing, as these can help make the page more readable.

▼

▼

4. Add additional styles, but keeping within the general philosophy of simple, bold design without columns. Which elements such as colors and fonts can you preserve from the original design? Try to work those in so that the zoom version seems like a sibling of the original, rather than an unrelated design.

5. Link the style sheet with `<link type="alternate stylesheet">` and be sure to add a `title` attribute as well. When choosing a `title`, web designer jargon like "zoom" may confuse users. How about simply "High Contrast"?

▲

6. View your creation in Firefox or Opera, and use the browser's style sheet switcher to test your new creation!

Summary

When creating any web pages, whether using CSS or not, it's important to keep the needs of your users in mind. Providing them with an attractive website is not in conflict with giving them an easy-to-use site. In fact, the two approaches are both complementary and necessary for making a truly great site.

Testing plays a major role in any CSS design, and you can't rely on your own judgment when catching possible mistakes. Three important resources are other web developers who can give advice about your design efforts, users in informal tests who point out unexpected errors, and CSS validation services that check your syntax and warn of omissions.

Web development using CSS is a balancing act, and the factors you'll have to weigh include using CSS for layout, supporting older browsers, and accounting for browser quirks. Because each site is unique, there's no universal answer; you need to use your own judgment to figure out what works for you.

Organizing your style sheets in a sensible manner will make life easier for you and anyone else who has to read your style sheet. Use comments whenever you think of it, and group your styles together in natural groupings. You'll thank yourself later, when you need to maintain the style sheet.

Alternate style sheets can give your users a choice of appearance, enhancing the site's overall usability and meeting specific needs, such as zoom text. Cookies can be used with PHP, JavaScript, or other programming languages to make these choices persistent.

Workshop

The workshop contains a Q&A section, quiz questions, and activities to help reinforce what you've learned in this hour. If you get stuck, the answers to the quiz can be found after the questions.

Q&A

Q. *I've created a design that is 1024 pixels wide but my web stats tell me that 35% of my audience is still using 800×640 resolution. What should I do?*

A. You have several options here. The first is to simply give up the idea of fixed-width designs and redesign a more fluid site. Site designs that are fluid can expand or shrink to fit the user's screen, but they offer you less control over the end result.

You could redesign the same look to fit in an 800-pixel-wide window. Fixed-width resolution designs look best when they're around 700 pixels or so across. You could also make your page adaptable with minimum and maximum widths so that the content scales down better on smaller resolutions.

Finally, you could use server-side or client-side programming, such as PHP or JavaScript, respectively, to provide alternative style sheets based on the browser's resolution. One style sheet could take advantage of the full-width displays and offer your original 1024-pixel design, whereas the fallback would be designed simply, with fluid layout.

Q. *How can I learn more about web programming?*

A. Client-side and server-side programming practices are beyond the scope of this introductory book on CSS, but the Sams Teach Yourself catalog offers a wide range of books on web programming topics, such as *Sams Teach Yourself JavaScript in 24 Hours, 4th Edition* and *Sams Teach Yourself PHP in 24 Hours, 3rd Edition*.

Quiz

1. Which of these is not a benefit of a well-organized style sheet?

   a. It's easier to make changes later on, after the design goes live.

   b. The download time is quicker if your style sheet is nicely formatted.

   c. You can spot problems such as unexpected cascading or inheritance consequences more easily when you've grouped your style rules sensibly.

   d. If you hand the website off to someone else, it's easier for them to understand how the site's style rules function.

2. What do you need for effective user testing?

   a. Nothing. Just follow your own instincts because you're a user too. You'll find out after the site goes live whether it's working or not.

   b. Five people, five tasks, and five lattes; have your volunteers attempt to accomplish specific goals at the site, and thank them with a bribe of an appropriate beverage.

   c. A usability lab with one-way mirrors, video cameras, and a million-dollar budget; if you have less than that, don't bother.

3. Why would you want to use cookies and server-side or client-side programming with alternate style sheets?

Answers

1. All the listed benefits are the result of having a well organized style sheet, with the exception of (b). A style sheet that compresses together all your CSS rules on one line or otherwise lacks white space may actually load fractionally quicker because it is a few bytes shorter in size than one with more readable formatting—but this benefit is very small compared to the advantages of using indentation in readability and maintenance.

2. The answer is (b), but the lattes are optional. I prefer a nice cold cherry cola myself.

3. When a browser lets you pick an alternate style sheet, it doesn't save that choice, which means the next time you view the page, or another page on the site, you're back to the original. Using cookies lets the designer code client-side or server-side solutions that save a user's style sheet choice.

Exercises

Here's a list of projects you can undertake to reinforce what you've learned this hour:

▶ Look at a website you've worked on, or one that you've used before, and design a hypothetical usability test. Create at least five questions that could be answered by using the site, in the form of tasks that would be performed by an average user to the site. Some should be difficult, and some can be easy.

▶ In fact, if you've got the time and the inclination, do an informal user test as described earlier this hour. The results are always educational, even if they just tell you that you're on the right track.

▶ Look at some of the style sheets you've worked on, and see whether you can reorganize them to be easier to understand. Comments, comments, comments!

HOUR 22

Accessibility and Print Media

What You'll Learn in This Hour:

▶ What hurdles people with disabilities face and how your use of CSS design can increase their accessibility to the Web

▶ Which standards relating to accessibility the W3C and the U.S. government have published

▶ How Aural Cascading Style Sheets are used and which browsers for visually impaired users support them

▶ How to specify rules for specific media types

▶ Which media types are supported by CSS and when they are used

▶ What kinds of things to consider when making a print style sheet

The promise inherent in the name "World Wide Web" is an information network that can be used by everyone across the entire world. To a large degree this promise has been fulfilled, although there are still many groups of users whose needs aren't adequately met. To address these needs, the Cascading Style Sheets recommendations included specific support for accessibility by people with disabilities and for internationalization and non-English languages.

Related to universal accessibility is the concept of alternate media types. Most style sheets are written for onscreen display in a web browser. However, CSS isn't restricted only to screen display; style sheets can be applied to printed versions of a page as well as to other media types.

What Is Accessibility?

When we talk about web accessibility, we're talking about the interaction between content and presentation and about ensuring that people who may have disabilities can use the result of that interaction. The content is the information you want to convey to your audience; it's not even necessarily the HTML code, but rather the information embodied by the HTML code—or by a Flash animation, GIF image, or multimedia movie. The presentation is the specific way you choose to express that information to your audience.

A basic principle of accessibility is that these two types of information, the content and the presentation, should be separated from each other. This allows for alternate versions of the presentation to be constructed, conveying the information in a way that the user can perceive it. If the content cannot be extracted from the presentation easily, an alternate version can be provided.

The classic example of this is the `alt` attribute on the HTML `<img>` tag (and the `<area>` tag as well). The content of a visual image is obviously going to be inaccessible to user who is blind; she simply can't see it. However, if a text equivalent of the image is supplied (by the `alt` attribute), her computer has information about what the image means, and it can provide that to the user—for example, by reading it out loud to her.

Users with disabilities often use assistive technology (AT) to enable access. Assistive technology is a broad category that not only includes Braille terminals and screen readers for blind users, but also includes magnification devices, voice recognition software, specialized input devices for those who can't type or use a mouse, and other hardware and software solutions.

Although assistive technology can solve many problems for users with special needs, it can't solve them all because it can work only with the information that is available. For example, if there is no `alt` attribute for an image, the assistive technology has no clue what to tell the user about the image's function and purpose. AT alone can't enable access; it requires cooperation from the web developer as well.

How People with Disabilities Use the Web

Most of the time when you hear about web accessibility, the focus is on blind and visually impaired users. The Web is commonly thought of as a visual medium; however, it's more accurate to say that it's an information medium, and the visual representation of information is simply the most common. A mistaken insistence that the Web is meant to be only visual can lead many web developers to inadvertently create websites that are inaccessible to users who can't see well.

A user who is blind commonly uses a screen reader, a software program that uses a synthetic voice to read the output of other programs. Examples of common screen readers include JAWS for Windows (http://www.freedomscientific.com/) and WindowsEyes (http://www.gwmicro.com/). Screen readers depend on a web browser to retrieve and process web pages; for example, JAWS is integrated with Internet Explorer for web display.

Another option is a speaking web browser, which is essentially a browser with a specialized screen reader built into it; examples are IBM's Home Page Reader (http://www.ibm.com/able/) and EmacSpeak for Linux/Unix (http://emacspeak.sourceforge.net/). Also in use are Braille terminals, which display around 40 characters at a time using raised dots in a row.

All these access solutions for blind users dramatically change the experience of using the typical website. Rather than experience the content as a two-dimensional visual display, a user hears (or feels) the content in a sequential, linear order. On most page designs this means having to wade through the navigation options and banner ads before finally reaching the main content of the page.

Users who can see, but not necessarily see well, often employ other solutions to access web content. For some, screen magnification software, which allows sections of the screen to be increased to many times their original size, may be necessary for ease of reading. A user with less severe requirements may simply increase his default font size to allow for comfortable reading.

Color blindness may cause someone to be unable to distinguish content within color graphics or to have difficulty discerning text against the background colors. The use of color as the only means of conveying information can restrict access by users who are color-blind or who can't see at all.

Compared with users with visual disabilities, deaf or hearing-impaired users are relatively fortunate when using the Web because most sites don't make heavy use of sound. However, those users can miss sound cues, audio files, and the sound tracks of multimedia presentations.

Users who are unable to use a keyboard or a mouse often employ creative means to provide equivalent input to their computers. For example, a quadriplegic user who is unable to use his arms or hands may move the mouse pointer by moving a pointer wand worn on his head.

One of the broadest groups of users with disabilities is also the least understood when it comes to web accessibility—users with cognitive disabilities. This wide category includes everything from relatively simple dyslexia to extreme mental retardation. Many individuals with varying cognitive impairments regularly use the Web as a primary information source, and they should not be discounted as a potential audience for your site simply because of their disabilities.

CSS Enables Access

Because the W3C created the CSS specifications with the needs of disabled users in mind, Cascading Style Sheets, if applied correctly, have great potential to meet the needs of those users. The primary benefit of using CSS is the separation of presentation from content; using CSS with HTML (especially Strict HTML) makes it clear which code is meant for presentational effects and which is the structured information of the page.

The CSS language has many features specifically intended to benefit users with visual disabilities, mainly because style sheet properties primarily define visual appearance. Media-specific alternate style sheets and rules can be created for screen readers, Braille terminals, and Braille printers. Aural CSS properties, described later in this hour, give control over the pitch, frequency, and even apparent location of synthesized speech.

Using relative measurements, such as ems instead of absolute font sizes, allows your style sheets to adapt to user preferences, either in browser settings or in a user style sheet. This lets users with special needs for font or color choices continue to access your site even if the styles you've set are not sufficient for their needs.

Style sheets do little to benefit deaf, hard of hearing, physically restricted, or cognitively impaired users, although a CSS-styled website based on sound usability and design principles will provide benefits for users both with and without these disabilities. Many cognitively disabled users specifically benefit from nontextual information cues, such as color, layout, and graphics.

Accessibility Standards and CSS

To fully test your CSS designs on all possible web browsers and AT devices, you'd have to spend a fortune; you already know how hard it can be to fully test a CSS design on mainstream browsers, and adding assistive technology software and hardware to the mix makes the task nearly impossible. So what is a web developer to do?

The solution is for those with expertise in assistive technologies to gather information on accessibility and create a set of recommendations for web developers to follow. By learning these standards, a web developer won't have to spend time researching every possible access method, but can instead be reasonably sure that a page created according to those principles will be accessible to a broad audience of users.

W3C's Web Content Accessibility Guidelines

The World Wide Web Consortium, in addition to publishing CSS, HTML, XHTML, XML, and other language specifications, also established the Web Accessibility

Initiative (WAI). The purpose of the WAI is to create and distribute information on making the Web more accessible to people with disabilities. The WAI has issued guidelines for browser programmers, web editing tool programmers, and web developers that suggest how to improve web accessibility.

Most of us aren't programming browsers or authoring environments, so the WAI recommendation we're concerned with is the Web Content Accessibility Guidelines (WCAG), a list of checkpoints that can be used to measure the accessibility of your website.

Each WCAG checkpoint has a priority rating of one, two, or three, where priority one checkpoints are the most important and priority three the least. The WCAG checkpoints most applicable to CSS design are:

▶ **Provide text alternatives for non-text elements (priority one)**

Most images used in style sheets, such as backgrounds or list bullets, are purely decorative, and thus don't require additional alternatives.

▶ **Don't use color as the only way to convey information (priority one)**

Make sure that the content can be understood if CSS colors aren't displayed.

▶ **Design pages that function even if style sheets are turned off (priority one)**

Test your page in Lynx, or with styles turned off in your browser, to ensure the pages still function properly.

▶ **Style sheets should be used instead of presentational markup (priority two)**

After reading this book, this should be an easy one for you to meet! See also Appendix A, "Replacing Presentational HTML with CSS."

▶ **Use relative values for styles instead of absolute values (priority two)**

For example, use x-large, smaller, or 3em instead of pixels or points for fonts; this is more responsive to users' own preferences.

▶ **Use foreground and background colors that contrast well with each other (priority three)**

Colors that don't stand out well cause problems for users with poor vision or color blindness.

This list is far from complete, but these are the checkpoints that are most relevant for CSS developers. If a web page or site conforms to all the priority one checkpoints (not just those listed here), it is said to be Single-A accessible. Meeting the priority one and two checkpoints equates to Double-A accessibility, and Triple-A accessibility means that all checkpoints of any priority level are met.

Many governments, schools, and other public institutions around the world have adopted Double-A accessibility as a standard for their sites; Single-A accessibility is considered the minimum for a public website.

You can use several websites to measure the accessibility of your website. These automatic checkers don't discover every problem, but they can help you get started on solving accessibility hurdles you may have accidentally introduced.

Examples of accessibility evaluators include Access Valet at http://valet.webthing.com/access/, Cynthia Says at http://www.cynthiasays.com/, TAW Online at http://www.tawdis.net/, and WAVE at http://wave.webaim.org/. You can find a full list of accessibility evaluators and other useful online tools on the World Wide Web Consortium's site (http://www.w3.org/WAI/ER/tools).

U.S. Government's Section 508

As part of employment and civil rights regulations, the U.S. Federal government requires all agencies to make their public and internal sites accessible to people with disabilities. Known as Section 508 (from the applicable section of the Rehabilitation Act), these regulations affect how agencies can purchase and use information technology—accessibility is a requirement for hardware, software, and websites employed by the government.

By the Way

If you're not an American or don't work for the U.S. Federal government, you might think these rules don't apply to you—and you're right. Section 508 is not an attempt to regulate the private sector, just Federal agencies. However, as the U.S. Federal government is the largest employer of information technology in the world, these rules have far-reaching influence and may be considered as a model for future accessibility standards. Therefore, it's important to be familiar with these requirements and how they apply to web development that uses CSS.

The requirements for web page accessibility are based on the W3C's Web Content Accessibility Guidelines; specifically, most of the priority one checkpoints with a few additions. Those include the following:

▶ Make online forms compatible with assistive technology.

▶ Inform users whether a timed response is required, and if so, allow for extra time to be requested.

▶ Allow users to skip over lists of repetitive links, such as a navigation bar. A common way to do this is to create a link that jumps ahead in the page to the main content.

Many of these requirements—and the WCAG checkpoints—don't deal directly with Cascading Style Sheets and should be handled by the way you create your HTML (and are thus beyond the scope of this book). However, even in those cases, CSS can still be used to enhance the style and accessibility of your page.

Try it Yourself ▼

Disable Your Web Access

What's it like to be a computer user with disabilities? Most of us who are visually dependent—we are forced to use our eyes to access the Web—don't have a good idea of what it's like to have limitations on our Internet access. Here's a simple exercise you can try that doesn't exactly mimic any specific disabilities, but is useful in raising your awareness:

1. Sit down at your computer and open up your web browser.

2. Go into the preferences or configuration section of your browser and start turning things off. Anything you can turn off that relates to displaying content, do it.

3. Turn off images. Turn off JavaScript and Java. Figure 22.1 shows how you do this in Firefox; it's similar in most other browsers as well.

FIGURE 22.1
Disabling content preferences in Firefox on Mac OS X.

4. While you're at it, if you can disable style sheets, or force your own fonts and colors, do that too. (In Firefox, set the Advanced and Colors options under Fonts and Colors.)

5. Mute your computer's speakers.

6. Unplug your mouse and throw it out the window. No, don't really do that; just set it aside for now, and eschew the use of it for this exercise.

7. Now visit your favorite websites and see how well you can use them. Try sites you've designed as well. Are you able to accomplish the basic functions of each site easily? Is it designed to be easily usable by someone with limitations, or does it shut out users with special needs?

8. You may want to read up on your operating system's accessibility features such as keyboard access. Most of us don't realize how to turn them on and off until we actually need them. Remember, we're all getting older—it's quite likely that you will need accessibility features yourself as you age! Will the Web be usable by you then?

Aural Cascading Style Sheets

Aural properties for Cascading Style Sheets were first proposed as an extension to CSS level 1 and were incorporated into the CSS level 2 specification. In the CSS 2.1 update, they've been assigned to an optional appendix; they're not widely applicable to, nor supported by, existing browsers. These properties enable you to control the sound properties of spoken text, just as the visual properties control the visual properties of text and other elements.

Browsers That Understand Aural CSS

Unfortunately, this list is quite short. There are no mainstream browsers that support aural CSS properties. The EmacSpeak browser, developed for Linux and Unix by one of the primary authors of the aural properties of the CSS level 2 specification, is the only browser that supports aural CSS.

If you're running a Unix-based system, you can download EmacSpeak from T.V. Raman's website at http://emacspeak.sourceforge.net/.

Currently, screen readers and speaking browsers, such as JAWS for Windows and Home Page Reader, do not support aural CSS either; they use their own rules, which are not fully CSS compliant, to determine how to speak each page. Future versions may support aural CSS, though.

Because of this lack of support, there's little reason today to spend much time with aural style sheets; this is unfortunate because many of the properties are quite useful both for disability access and potentially for general use. Because these properties don't cause any problems in existing browsers—they're all completely ignored—it doesn't hurt anything to include them; there is a very low cost of failure when an aural CSS property is not supported.

Future versions of browsers, screen readers, and other access methods may support aural CSS; one particularly interesting proposal is for multi-modal access methods that would provide both visual and aural renditions simultaneously.

Aural CSS Properties

Rules using aural CSS properties are written just like rules for any other property, with a selector and a declaration of property names and values. You could use the @media selector described later in this hour to limit these rules only to media type aural, although by their very nature these properties apply only to text that is spoken by the computer.

You might think that simply setting rules with the `aural` media type would allow you to create separate style sheets for blind users with screen readers. For example, this seems a natural way to hide "skip navigation" links:

```
@media aural { .nav { display: none; } }
```

The problem here is that screen readers aren't fully `aural` browsers; what most of them do is literally read the screen out loud. Thus many times something that is hidden in the visual presentation is also hidden in the screen reader's audio output. This rule simply won't work as desired, even if it's encapsulated in a style sheet linked with `<link media="aural">`, on most modern assistive technology. This is disappointing and limits the effectiveness of CSS for overcoming accessibility barriers; for some work-arounds, see Hour 24, "Troubleshooting and Browser Hacks."

Watch Out!

Because aural CSS is so poorly supported, I won't give an extensive tutorial on each property; if you want specifics, you can consult the aural properties section of the CSS specification. In this hour I'll just tell you enough to know the general capabilities of aural CSS.

Volume and Voices

The characteristics of the voice speaking the content of the page are determined by several properties relating to volume, pitch, and other qualities. These properties are listed in Table 22.1 along with the range of values allowed.

TABLE 22.1   Volume and Voice Aural Properties

Property Name	Values
pitch	*frequency*, x-low, low, medium, high, x-high, inherit
pitch-range	*variation-number*, inherit
richness	*richness-number*, inherit
speech-rate	*words-per-minute*, x-slow, slow, medium, fast, x-fast, faster, slow, inherit
stress	*stress-number*, inherit
voice-family	*specific-family*, *generic-family*, inherit
volume	*volume-number*, *percentage*, silent, x-soft, soft, medium, loud, x-loud, inherit

The voice-family property is similar to font-family; you can define a specific voice, which may or may not be supported by the aural CSS browser, or you can use one of three generic voice families: male, female, or child. There's no standard list of voice types beyond this, and so the use of specific voices (such as robot, Spock, or "Britney Spears") depends on the browser.

Pausing and Cues

Aural CSS properties enable you either to insert pauses to break up the aural reading, either before or after an element, or to insert specific sound files, called *audio cues*. These properties are shown on Table 22.2.

TABLE 22.2   Pausing and Cues Aural Properties

Property Name	Values
cue	Shorthand property, setting cue-after and cue-before
cue-after	*sound-url*, none, inherit
cue-before	*sound-url*, none, inherit
pause	Shorthand property, setting pause-after and pause-before
pause-after	*time-measurement*, percentage, inherit
pause-before	*time-measurement*, percentage, inherit

Cues are normal sound files, usually .wav or .au files, and are indicated by url() notation. Pauses are measured in seconds (s) or milliseconds (ms), such as 2s or 30ms.

Three-Dimensional Sounds

Most humans without hearing impairments hear sound in three dimensions. Aural Cascading Style Sheets enable you to designate a specific location, within three dimensions, from which a sound could originate. Consider a transcript of an interview, marked up with voice properties similar to those of the appropriate speakers, where the interviewer's voice is heard on the left side, and the subject of the interview is heard on the right. A question from the audience could come from behind and below while an overhead announcement originates from directly above the listener.

The properties that place each sound in a specific location are shown on Table 22.3.

TABLE 22.3 Three-Dimensional Sound Aural Properties

Property Name	Values
azimuth	*angle*, left-side, far-left, left, center-left, center, center-right, right, far-right, right-side, behind, leftwards, rightwards, inherit
elevation	*angle*, below, level, above, higher, lower, inherit

Angles are measured in degrees (deg), grads (grad), or radians (rad), such as 90deg, 100grad, or 1.571rad, which are all (approximately) a right angle. A 0deg azimuth is directly in front of the listener, and 0deg elevation is level with the listener.

Choosing What to Speak

Just as the display and visibility properties let you hide what is shown visually, aural CSS also lets you control what is vocalized and how that's done. You can even add the equivalent of a background image by specifying a background sound to be played while an element is spoken. These properties are shown in Table 22.4.

TABLE 22.4 Speaking Method Aural Properties

Property Name	Value
play-during	*background-sound*, mix, repeat, auto, none, inherit
speak	normal, none, spell-out, inherit
speak-header	always, once, inherit (table cells only)
speak-numeral	continuous, digits, inherit
speak-punctuation	code, none, inherit

The `play-during` property enables you to specify whether a background file is mixed in with any other background sounds already playing (from a containing element) or whether it replaces the other sound.

Media-Specific Style Sheets

Using CSS, you can create style sheets that are media specific, meaning that they should be applied to only one particular type of output device. An *output device* is any physical hardware device that can present web content—visually or otherwise—as well as the software necessary to allow for that presentation, such as a printer driver or a screen reader.

In Hour 4, "Using CSS with HTML," you learned the basics of the `<link>` element and its attribute `media`, which enable you to tie style sheets to categories of output media. In this hour, you'll expand your knowledge of media types and learn how to write rules within one style sheet that apply to different media.

Categories of Media Types

The full list of media types defined in CSS is listed on Table 22.5. A given browser is required to support only those media types appropriate for that browser. For example, a set-top box doesn't need to support screen, aural, or print media types. The typical visual browser uses two media types: `screen` and `print`. Opera also supports the `projection` media type in full-screen kiosk mode.

TABLE 22.5   Media Types in CSS

Media Type	Description
aural	Pages read out loud by synthesized voice; for example, screen readers for the blind.
braille	Content represented by raised dot characters on Braille terminals for blind users.
emboss	Pages printed out as raised dots in Braille, on thick paper.
handheld	Content displayed on a limited-size handheld screen.
print	Pages printed out on paper.
projection	Content displayed as slides or transparencies projected on a large screen.
screen	Pages displayed on a color monitor.

TABLE 22.5 Continued

Media Type	Description
tty	Content printed on teletype devices or other media with limited display capabilities, which print only characters of a fixed size and type.
tv	Pages displayed on a television screen, possibly taking advantage of sound capabilities but with limited interaction.

Media type values are used in `<link>` tags and `@import` rules for the purpose of specifying which style sheets to use, and they are also used to classify certain rules within a style sheet as applicable.

Did you Know?

The media types described here are obviously not enough to fully capture the diversity of access methods available to web users of the 21st century. For example, the handheld media type assumes that a handheld device will be monochrome, but we've already seen a number of color handheld devices become available. Also, there is a large difference between a PDA, a pocket computer, and a cell phone, although these are all grouped under the term "handheld."

The W3C realizes these deficiencies and is developing a better classification system for the CSS level 3 recommendation; you can read the current drafts at http://www.w3.org/Style/CSS/current-work. Also, the W3C's Composite Capabilities/Preferences Profile (CC/PP) work is moving toward a standardized way of describing end-user device characteristics; see http://www.w3.org/Mobile/CCPP/ for more.

Linking and Importing Media-Specific Style Sheets

You've already seen in Hour 4 how to use a media type with the `<link>` tag in HTML:

```
<link type="text/css" rel="stylesheet"
     media="print, emboss" href="paged-output.css">
```

Such a link would load only the style sheet if the browser were currently printing to a standard or Braille printer.

An `@import` rule at the beginning of a style sheet can also be set to specify style sheets applicable to certain media types:

```
@import url("site.css");
@import url("screen.css") screen, tv;
@import url("dots.css") braille;
```

These rules always load the `site.css` file, and load `screen.css` for display on a computer or television screen and `dots.css` for a Braille display terminal.

> Internet Explorer on Windows does not support `@import` rules with media types. For compatibility with Internet Explorer, you should use some other method of linking media-specific style sheets, such as the `<link>` tag or the `@media` rule described next.

Using the `@media` **Rule**

Within the same style sheet, you can mix rules for different media types by using an `@media` rule. This is a special type of rule that surrounds your other CSS rules and applies them only to certain media types. The basic form of this rule is

```
@media media-type {
   selector { declaration; }
   selector { declaration; }
   ...
}
```

That last curly brace is important because it marks the end of the `@media` rule. Any rules within the `@media` rule's braces are applied only to the media type listed. Listing 22.1 has several examples of the `@media` rule limiting certain rules to only certain types of output devices.

LISTING 22.1   A Style Sheet with `@media` Rules

```
/* media-rules-22.1.css */

@media print {
  body    { font: 10pt "Times New Roman", serif;
            color: black; background-color: white; }
  .footer { border-top: 1px solid black;
            font-size: 8pt; }
  }

@media screen {
  body    { font-family: Verdana, sans-serif;
            color: white; background-color: #330000; }
  .footer { padding: 2em; font-size: smaller;
            border: 1em solid green; color: #330000;
            background-color: white; }
  }
```

CSS Properties for the `print` Medium

By far the most common medium you'll be concerned with—besides `screen`—is `print`. Nearly all computers have printers attached, and it's common for users to print a page as a way of making a permanent copy of the content.

CSS rules can be used to format the appearance of the printed page. You can control the layout, fonts, line spacing, display characteristics, and more, separately from the way a page is displayed on the screen. A specific style sheet for printing is a nice addition to any CSS-based website.

Browsers and Printing

Printing a web page is often a risky proposition. The combination of text, tables, style rules, frames, and low-resolution GIF images often results in a poor-looking printed document. Most of the time, browsers don't print nearly as well as they display onscreen. You can overcome some of these problems with a print style sheet.

To link in a style sheet for printing, simply use the HTML `<link>` tag as described previously. You can also use an @import rule or an @media rule in the main style sheet with the appropriate media type. Multiple `<link>` tags let you provide one style sheet for rules common to all media types—one for screen display and one for printing, like the following:

```
<link type="text/css" rel="stylesheet"
     media="all" href="all.css">
<link type="text/css" rel="stylesheet"
     href="screen.css">
<!-- default value for media attribute is screen -->
<link type="text/css" rel="stylesheet"
     media="print" href="print.css">
```

Measurements for Printing

When you're creating a style sheet for printing, you can use additional units of measurement that would be inappropriate or meaningless on a computer monitor. These units correspond to real-world units of measurement used in printing and are listed in Table 22.6.

TABLE 22.6   Units of Measurement Appropriate for Printing

Unit	Measurement
cm	Centimeters
in	Inches (1in = 2.54cm)
mm	Millimeters (1mm = 0.1cm)

TABLE 22.6   Continued

Unit	Measurement
pc	Picas (1pc = 12pt)
pt	Points (72pt = 1in)

These units can be used with any CSS property that requires a measurement value. For example, the following rule sets a padding value in centimeters:

```
@media print { h1 { padding: 1cm 2cm 1cm 1cm; } }
```

Designing CSS for Print

When creating style rules or style sheets for the print medium, it's important to remember how the medium differs from the computer screen. The point of using a different style sheet for print is to make the resulting hardcopy easier to read and use.

Many printers out there will be black-and-white, although color printers are used often. However, many users avoid printing in full color simply to save ink. Therefore, you want to make sure you're not relying on color entirely.

A printed page is clearly not interactive. When someone is printing a page, they're usually doing it for the content. Therefore, things such as navigation bars and hypertext links are pretty useless. You can't click on a piece of paper.

The display, visibility, and text-decoration properties can help with this. You may want to enclose your navigation bar in a <div class="nav"> and set rules like the following:

```
.nav { display: none; }
a:link, a:visited { text-decoration: none; }
```

Areas with dark backgrounds and light colors consume a lot of black ink. Changing these to black text on a white background, is a friendly thing to do when creating a style sheet for print. You'll save a lot of ink for your users who choose to print your pages out.

As described earlier in the hour, you can use exact units such as centimeters or inches when printing, as well as points for font sizes. Be careful not to assume that your users' papers will be the same size as yours, though. For example, a user may just decide to print out your web page in landscape mode (wider than it is long) instead of portrait.

Summary

Users with disabilities are as entitled to use the Web as anyone else, but often they are unable to access sites because of careless web design. Using Cascading Style Sheets is an excellent first step toward developing a site that can be used by everyone, as style sheets separate presentation from content.

Assistive technology devices and software can often enable access by disabled users, but only if sites are designed in accordance with web accessibility standards. The W3C has produced Web Content Accessibility Guidelines that are an invaluable resource for web developers and that form the basis of the U.S. Government's Section 508 regulations for Federal agency sites.

Aural CSS properties let you determine qualities of the voice used to read content out loud, such as the pitch, speed, and "family" of the voice. Unfortunately, almost no browsers support aural CSS currently, thus limiting its usefulness.

Alternate style sheets for different access devices are classified by the media types to which they apply. You can set the media type of a CSS rule in several ways: by linking to a style sheet containing the rule with the `<link>` element in HTML; by using `@import` to import a style sheet with that rule; or by wrapping the CSS rule in an `@media` rule. Visual browsers support the `screen` media type, and nearly all of them also support the `print` media type.

Designing for the print medium requires a different approach than doing so for the screen. Scrolling, links, interactivity, and paging are all changed, so you need to think carefully about how to devise your print styles.

Workshop

The workshop contains a Q&A section, quiz questions, and an exercise to help reinforce what you've learned in this hour. If you get stuck, the answers to the quiz can be found after the questions.

Q&A

Q. *Is Section 508 the same as the Americans with Disabilities Act (ADA)? What are the ADA requirements for web accessibility?*

A. Section 508 and the ADA are different sets of regulations. Section 508 applies only to Federal agencies, whereas the ADA is applicable to a number of private and public sector entities. There are no formal ADA regulations for web accessibility as there are for Section 508; however, the ADA requires organizations to avoid discrimination on basis of disability when providing services. For detailed commentary on legal requirements for accessibility, see Cynthia

Waddell's essays on the website of the International Center for Disability Resources on the Internet (http://www.icdri.org/).

Q. *Can tables be made accessible? Frames? JavaScript? Java? Flash? PDF?*

A. Yes. You can make tables and frames accessible by using HTML markup carefully and by providing additional attributes or elements, such as `<noframes>`. If a certain technology or file format can't be made accessible directly, the content within it can be presented in an alternate, accessible format, such as a transcript or HTML version.

Q. *I need more control over the print layout than what CSS gives me (and the browsers don't support). What other options are there?*

A. As an alternative to CSS's print-related properties, you may want to investigate Extensible Stylesheet Language Formatting Objects (XSL-FO). Formatting objects use XML elements with attribute values related to CSS and are usually created by applying an Extensible Stylesheet Language Transformations (XSLT) sheet. Obviously, this is advanced stuff, but if you need advanced layout capabilities for print, this may be what you are looking for. See the W3C's XSL page at http://www.w3.org/Style/XSL/ for more.

Quiz

1. Do the Web Content Accessibility Guidelines suggest that color should be avoided in web design?

2. Which of the following is *not* an aural CSS property?

    a. `voice-family`

    b. `stress`

    c. `accent`

    d. `speak-numeral`

3. Your navigation bar has a class of navbar, and you've decided you don't want it to appear when the page is printed. How do you write such a rule using `@media`?

4. Which of the following is *not* a unit of measurement in CSS?

    a. `in`

    b. `mm`

    c. `ft`

    d. `pc`

Answers

1. No. This is a common misunderstanding; the restriction is on using color as the only way to convey information. If you also provide that information in the HTML tags or the text content, your colors are not a problem at all.

2. **c.** There is no accent property in CSS.

3. Here is one way to write a rule to hide the `navbar` class:

```
@media print { .navbar { display: none; } }
```

4. **c.** Feet are not a valid unit of measurement in CSS; inches, millimeters, and picas are.

Exercise

Because most browsers don't have good support for printing CSS styles, it can be rather hit-and-miss designing a print style sheet. However, this is still probably one of the best exercises: It forces you to think through some of the assumptions you make when designing a page. For example, you've probably laid out your page in percentages or pixels, for online display. Do those measurements work well in print, or would it be better to use centimeters or inches? What do you want to do about links on the page? Present them as underlined text, even though they can't be clicked on? Remove the underlines? Or remove the navigation bar entirely? Choose a style sheet you've worked on in the past and redesign it for printed output.

Next, how would you redesign the same style sheet for the aural media type?

HOUR 23

User Interface and Generated Content

What You'll Learn in This Hour:

▶ How you can change the appearance of the mouse pointer

▶ Which properties allow you to create outlines, and how an outline is different than a border

▶ How to use the system colors and fonts in your design, and why you'd want to in the first place

▶ How you can add content to a page, before or after specific elements

▶ Which properties let you control the appearance of quotation marks

▶ How to use generated content to add shadows to text

▶ How counters can be used to number lists and other elements automatically

The properties defined in the Cascading Style Sheets specification allow you to do more than simply place and present content. Specific properties also enable you to shape the user's experience directly through interaction with the operating system and browser; other properties let you add to the content of the page to build an appropriate presentation for the user.

User Interface Properties

The *user interface* (UI) of a computer program is the part that interacts with the person using the program. This interaction includes not only the visual output, but also the method of providing information to the program via mouse, keyboard, or other input device.

When talking about web content, you're dealing with several layers of user interface. The operating system—be it various versions of Windows, Mac OS, or Linux running XWindows—provides a basic graphical user interface (GUI) layer, which creates the windows, menus, and boxes onscreen. The browser's user interface is built upon the operating system's UI and generally is designed to mesh with the operating system while adding appropriate controls for web surfing. A third layer of user interface is created by the content itself; a web page can be thought of as a UI for the information contained in the markup.

CSS Level 2.1 has several user interface properties examined in this part of the hour. These are not enough to fully control all interactions with the user, but they do enable you to alter some UI components and use information provided by the operating system to style the page.

Changing the Cursor Appearance

A key part of the web-user experience is showing what part of the GUI is currently being pointed to by a pointing device, such as a mouse. The mouse cursor could be controlled by a mouse or by another tool, such as a track-ball, a joystick, or a virtual mouse via the keyboard, for people who can't operate a normal mouse. For users with severe disabilities, mouse control can be approximated by pointer wands attached to the head, or even by eye-tracking sensors.

A mouse cursor is applicable only in certain contexts; in print or Braille, for example, there is no mouse cursor. The mouse cursor is disabled or ignored by screen readers for blind users, and it's also inapplicable for kiosk systems with touch panels or for small devices with touch screens, such as Palm or Pocket PC organizers.

It's important to keep in mind that a mouse cursor is just an indicator of potential action and not necessarily a choice that's been acted on; the cursor's location corresponds to the :hover pseudo-class in CSS, not to the :active or :focus pseudo-classes.

The CSS property cursor can be used to change the appearance of the mouse cursor; this change occurs whenever the mouse cursor is over the part of the page display corresponding to the display rule's selector. Because :hover is implied, it's not necessary to use that pseudo-class with the selector.

A cursor rule is written like this:

```
selector { cursor: cursor-type; }
```

The values that can be assigned to the cursor property are shown in Table 23.1. The default value is auto, and if this value is set on a containing box, it is inherited by that box's children elements.

TABLE 23.1 Values for the `cursor` **Property**

Value	Effect
auto	Lets the browser decide the shape of the cursor
crosshair	Displays a crosshair cursor
default	Displays the default cursor (usually an arrow)
e-resize	Indicates that the object can be resized eastward
help	Displays a help-available cursor (usually a question mark)
move	Indicates a movable object's cursor (usually crossed arrows)
n-resize	Indicates that the object can be resized northward
ne-resize	Indicates that the object can be diagonally resized to the northeast
nw-resize	Indicates that the object can be diagonally resized to the northwest
pointer	Displays a link pointer cursor (usually a pointing hand)
s-resize	Indicates that the object can be resized southward
se-resize	Indicates that the object can be diagonally resized to the southeast
sw-resize	Indicates that the object can be diagonally resized to the southwest
text	Displays a text editing cursor (usually an I-shaped bar)
wait	Displays a waiting cursor (usually an hourglass)
w-resize	Indicates the object can be resized westward
url(*address*)	Displays a cursor image from a given URL
inherit	Uses the cursor value for the containing box

Many of the values listed in Table 23.1 refer to compass directions. These cursors are intended to be used with client-side programming techniques such as JavaScript and AJAX to mark objects that are resizable when clicked and dragged. The compass directions are a bit misleading—"north" simply means up, toward the top of the screen; "west" means left; "south" means down; and "east" means to toward the right. Therefore, a cursor with the value of se-resize indicates the object is resizable in a lower-right direction.

The url() value is written in a special format; you can write as many url() values as you like, and the browser displays the first one it is able to load and understand. After the last url() value, you should provide a "generic" cursor value from the list in Table 23.1, in case the url() cursors can't be displayed; for example, if the file format isn't understood by the browser. The concept of a generic default is similar to that of the font-family property and so should be familiar to you.

Because there is not a universal format for cursor files, you should use multiple url() values to provide cursor images in several file formats. For example, give a version of the cursor in SVG, .tiff, .cur, and .gif formats, in addition to supplying a generic value. Cursor images should usually be small—no more than around 40 by 40 pixels, and usually around 16 by 16.

Watch Out!

Only Internet Explorer 6 for Windows supports the url() method for specifying a cursor image, so be sure to provide a backup cursor type as you would for fonts. Opera has limited support for cursor changes, especially the -resize values. The progress cursor was introduced in CSS 2.1, and is currently supported only by Firefox.

Listing 23.1 is an HTML file that demonstrates the various cursors available in CSS. You can test these out yourself and see how your operating system and browser display each cursor type.

LISTING 23.1 The Different Styles of Cursors

```
<!-- cursors-23.1.html -->
<html>
  <head>
    <title>Changing Cursors</title>
    <style type="text/css">
      table { border-spacing: 0.5em;
              width: 100%; margin: 0;
              empty-cells: hide; }
      #a td { width: 25%; } #b td { width: 33%; }
      td { padding: 1.5em 1em; text-align: center;
           font-family: Verdana, sans-serif;
           border: 3px solid silver;
           text-align: right; }
      td:first-child { text-align: left; }
    </style>
  </head>
  <body>
  <table id="a">
    <tr><td style="cursor: crosshair;">crosshair</td>
        <td style="cursor: default;">default</td>
        <td style="cursor: help;">help</td>
        <td style="cursor: pointer;">pointer</td></tr>
    <tr><td style="cursor: progress;">progress</td>
        <td style="cursor: text;">text</td>
        <td style="cursor: wait;">wait</td>
        <td style="cursor: url('k-small.cur'),
                           url('k-small.tiff'),
                           url('k-small.gif'),
                           auto;">url()</td></tr>
  </table>
  <table id="b">
    <tr><td style="cursor: nw-resize;">nw-resize</td>
        <td style="cursor: n-resize;">n-resize</td>
```

LISTING 23.1   Continued

```
        <td style="cursor: ne-resize;">ne-resize</td></tr>
    <tr><td style="cursor: w-resize;">w-resize</td>
        <td style="cursor: move;">move</p></td>
        <td style="cursor: e-resize;">e-resize</td></tr>
    <tr><td style="cursor: sw-resize;">sw-resize</td>
        <td style="cursor: s-resize;">s-resize</td>
        <td style="cursor: se-resize;">se-resize</td></tr>
  </table>
</body>
```

The screenshot in Figure 23.1 is actually a composite of several screenshots; obviously, only one cursor can usually be displayed at a time, so I've combined images together to show you how one browser displays these cursors.

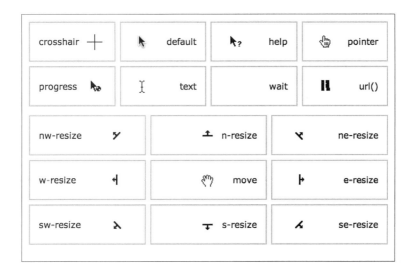

FIGURE 23.1
A variety of cursors on display.

Now you know how to change the cursor, but why would you want to? In most cases, the web browser automatically sets the style of the cursor to something sensible, which actually serves as a useful cue to the user. A `pointer` finger cursor, for example, lets users know that they are over a link. In general, you should change the cursor appearance only if you have a very good reason. For example, if you're using Asynchronous JavaScript and XML (AJAX) client-side programming to load information dynamically, you can change the cursor to `progress` or `wait` so the user is aware of the change. If you're using graphics for cursors, don't just set one for the whole page; create different graphics for links and input fields, and write appropriate rules to call them. Otherwise, your users will be confused when the cursor doesn't change over a text field or a hyperlink.

Did you Know?

Creating Outlines

An outline is a visual line surrounding an element. This sounds similar to a border, doesn't it? Unlike a border, an outline doesn't actually take up any space in the box model. Instead, it's laid over other elements. The outline is placed just outside of the border, and thus it will be displayed over the margin or even over other content if the margin is small and the outline is wide.

The appearance of the outline is set with the `outline-width`, `outline-style`, and `outline-color` properties, or the `outline` shorthand property that sets them all at once. The `outline-width` property can take the same types of values as the `border-width` property; the `outline-style` can accept `border-style` properties. Unlike the border properties (which are covered in Hour 16, "Borders and Boxes"), there are not outline properties for each side of a box; the outline must be consistently the same color, width, and style on all sides.

The `outline-color` value can be any normal color value, or `invert`, which means the outline is displayed in the opposite colors of the margins (or other content) over which it lies. Unlike borders, there is only one outline; you can't set separate outlines for different sides of the outlined element.

An outline is most useful for indicating focus or hover, although you can use it without the `:focus` or `:hover` pseudo-classes to simply draw an outline around anything. For example:

```
a:focus, a:hover { outline-width: medium;
                   outline-style: dotted;
                   outline-color: invert; }
h2 { outline: green 1px solid; }
```

Outlines can be very useful if you are debugging your style sheets. Because an outline doesn't affect the width of the box model, this means that your outlines don't change the way the page is laid out. You can use outlines to highlight specific boxes and watch how they react with each other.

Internet Explorer (as of version 6.0) doesn't support the `outline-width`, `outline-style`, `outline-color`, or `outline` properties. Don't rely on your outlines being visible on someone else's browser—but if you're using Firefox, Safari, or Opera, you can still use outlines for troubleshooting.

Using the System Colors and Fonts

The CSS language enables you to access certain qualities of the system or browser user interface and use these for color or font values. You can do this by using special keywords that correspond to the current system settings.

The system color keywords can be used with any CSS property that can be set to a specific color value—color, background-color, border-color, and so on. These are listed in Table 23.2. These keywords are traditionally written in mixed case, with capital letters at the beginning of words for greater legibility. However, CSS is not case sensitive for color values, so if you write activeborder or ACTIVEBORDER, it means the same thing as ActiveBorder.

TABLE 23.2 System Color Keywords

Value	Effect
ActiveBorder	The border color around the active window
ActiveCaption	The background color of the caption on the active window
AppWorkspace	The background color within the application's main window
Background	The background color of the desktop
ButtonFace	The background color of a three-dimensional button
ButtonHighlight	The border color for the dark edge of a three-dimensional button
ButtonShadow	The shadow color of a three-dimensional button
ButtonText	The text color for a three-dimensional button
CaptionText	The text color in a caption
GrayText	The text color for disabled options (grayed out)
Highlight	The background color for selected items
HighlightText	The text color for selected items
InactiveBorder	The border color around an inactive window
InactiveCaption	The background color of the caption on an inactive window
InactiveCaptionText	The text color of the caption on an inactive window
InfoBackground	The background color for tooltips
InfoText	The text color for tooltips
Menu	The background color for menu items
MenuText	The text color for menu items
Scrollbar	The color of the scrollbar
ThreeDDarkShadow	The dark shadow for a three-dimensional element
ThreeDFace	The background color for a three-dimensional element
ThreeDHighlight	The highlight color for a three-dimensional element
ThreeDLightShadow	The border color for the light edge of a three-dimensional element
ThreeDShadow	The shadow color for a three-dimensional element

TABLE 23.2   Continued

Value	Effect
Window	The background color of a window
WindowFrame	The border color of the frame around a window
WindowText	The text color within a window

For each of the values in Table 23.2, a descriptive adjective such as *highlight*, *border*, *background*, or *text* is given before the word *color*. These describe how the colors are used within the system user interface, but you don't have to use them for only those purposes in your style sheet. For example, you could set the text color to Window, and the background-color to WindowText; the AppWorkspace value could be used to set a box's border. Here are examples of how to use these values:

```
.showthis { color: window;
            background-color: windowText;
            border: 2px solid AppWorkspace; }
```

You can also use the system font settings for various types of text within your style sheet. You do so by setting the font shorthand property to one of the system values shown in Table 23.3. For example, to make a <div> use the font qualities for a system message box, use the following:

```
div { font: message-box; }
```

TABLE 23.3   System Values for the font Property

Value	Effect
caption	Uses the same font values as system captions
icon	Uses the same font values as system icons
menu	Uses the same font values as system menus
message-box	Uses the same font values as system message boxes
small-caption	Uses the same font values as small system captions
status-bar	Uses the same font values as the status bar

Each use of font in this manner sets the font-size, font-style, font-weight, font-variant, and font-family to the same values as the specified kind of system text. Subsequent rules can change those values, as shown here:

```
div { font: message-box;
      font-weight: bold;
      font-size: larger;
      color: window;
      background-color: windowText;
      border: 2px solid AppWorkspace; }
```

Why would you want to use system colors and fonts? Usually you wouldn't, actually. Websites have good reason to express their own individuality and style, and utilizing the user's system appearance doesn't mesh well with that. However, there are some cases, such as alert boxes, where you may very well want to mimic the effects of an operating system prompt.

There is a potential accessibility benefit: In general, you can be sure that system colors will be usable by someone with visual impairments because otherwise she couldn't operate her computer at all. Most users with special needs set their computers to high contrast, large fonts, and any other required properties.

However, the accessibility benefit of system styles is small compared with the negative effects of "sameness" and bland design; even users with poor vision can benefit from an attractive website design. User style sheets and alternate style sheets provide better accessibility options for all users in the long run.

Creating Content

In CSS terminology, *generated content* consists of text or images that aren't present in the HTML markup but are added through CSS rules. The ability to generate content allows for even more flexibility in designing style sheets and alternate style sheets that effectively convey the information on the page to the user.

In overview, generating content depends on using the :before and :after pseudo-classes as selectors for rules with content property declarations. Text, attribute values, images, quotation marks, and numbered counters can all be added to HTML using CSS content generation.

Because of browser deficiencies, users who have turned off style sheets, or devices that can't display CSS, generated content is not always going to be available, so you shouldn't rely on generated content unless you know the browser on the other end can display it. Generated content is therefore only safe when you can be sure that it will actually be displayed to the end user—for example, if you are serving content to a specific browser. In some cases, you can use generated content to enhance the presentation without being dependent upon it as the only way to convey important information. In this hour, you will see an example of using generated content to create a specific text effect that enhances the web page for display in browsers that support CSS, but doesn't leave out users whose browsers don't produce generated content.

The :before and :after **Pseudo-Classes**

To generate content, you must use the :before and :after pseudo-classes. These pseudo-classes define the point where you place additional material. Content can be added at the beginning or the end of an element.

To add content at the beginning of an element, you would write a rule like this:

```
element:before { declarations; }
```

To insert the content after the element, the rule looks like this:

```
element:after { declarations; }
```

You can combine this with any other CSS selectors, such as class, id, attribute, relationship, or pseudo-class selectors. You can't write a single rule that has both :before and :after selectors, but you can write one rule putting content before the element and another adding content after it.

The content **Property**

The material generated at the insertion point (either before or after the selector) is defined by the content property. This CSS property can be used only within a rule with a :before or :after pseudo-class selector. The values for content are shown on Table 23.4.

TABLE 23.4   Values for the content Property

Value	Effect
"*quoted-text*"	Inserts the specified text
attr(*attribute*)	Inserts the value of the specified attribute
close-quote	Inserts an appropriate closing quote mark
counter(*name*)	Inserts a counter's value
counter(*name*, *marker-style*)	Inserts a counter's value
counters(*name*, *string*)	Inserts a counter's value and a string
counters(*name*, *string*, *marker-style*)	Inserts a counter's value and a string
no-close-quote	Suppresses the printing of a closing quote mark
no-open-quote	Suppresses the printing of an opening quote mark

TABLE 23.4 Continued

Value	Effect
open-quote	Inserts an appropriate opening quote mark
url(*address*)	Inserts the contents of the specified URL

The content property allows for multiple values, separated by spaces. Here is an example of a complex content rule:

```
.note:before { content: url('note.gif') "Note "
           counter(notes) ": (" attr(title) ")"; }
```

The content inserted consists of an image, quoted text, a counter reference, another bit of quoted text, an attribute value, and a final snippet of quoted text.

The specified content is added at the designated insertion point and becomes a virtual child element. Although the generated content inherits all appropriate properties from the element into which it was inserted, it can also be styled separately, as well.

> Internet Explorer versions 6.0 and earlier don't display generated content. As suggested before, you should use generated content only if you can be certain which browser will be used or if you are using the generated content only to enhance, rather than to provide the full presentation.

Watch
Out!

Listing 23.2 and is a brief (and deliberately incomplete) list of books by J.R.R. Tolkien, which will be used to demonstrate how content generation can be used.

LISTING 23.2 A Simple HTML File Listing Some Works of Tolkien

```html
<!-- generated-23.2.html -->
<html>
  <head>
    <title>Author Data: J.R.R. Tolkien</title>
    <style type="text/css">
      /* Insert style rules here */
    </style>
  </head>
  <body>
    <h3>J.R.R. Tolkien</h3>
    <ul id="works">
      <li class="book">The Hobbit</div>
      <li class="series" >
        <ul title="Lord of the Rings">
          <li class="book">The Fellowship of the Ring</li>
```

LISTING 23.2   Continued

```
              <li class="book">The Two Towers</li>
              <li class="book">Return of the King</li>
            </ul>
          </li>
          <li class="book">The Silmarillion</li>
        </ul>
      </body>
</html>
```

The HTML file in Listing 23.2 defines a simple structure wherein book titles are identified by <li> list items with the book class, and related books are grouped within
titled <ul> tags. There is no styling information provided, so the list appears plain
and straightforward, as shown in Figure 23.2. Note that the series title *Lord of the
Rings* isn't shown because it is an attribute value and not text content.

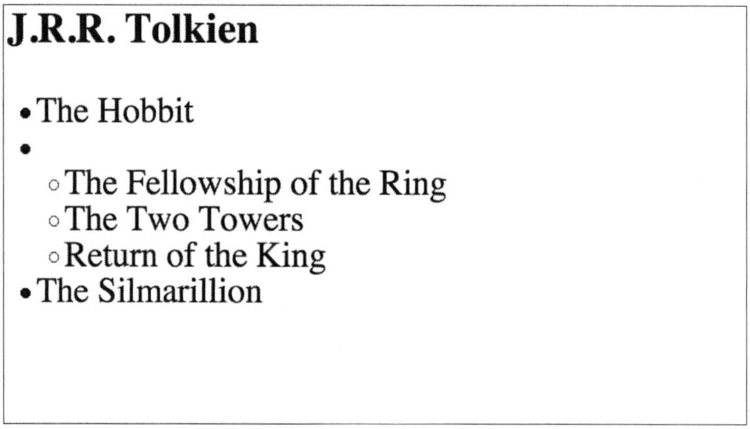

FIGURE 23.2
No styles
applied to the
Tolkien book
list.

J.R.R. Tolkien

- The Hobbit
-
  - The Fellowship of the Ring
  - The Two Towers
  - Return of the King
- The Silmarillion

Adding Text and Images

You can insert text into a page by giving a quoted text value to the content property. The quotes around the value can be either double quotes (") or single quotes (');
they have to match. You can use double quotes to surround single quotes (or apos-
trophes), or single quotes to surround double quotes. For example:

```
h1:before { content: "Kynn's Headline: "; }
h2:before, h2:after { content: '"'; }
```

You can also insert text by using an attribute's value via the attr() function, which
inserts the value of a specific attribute on the element. Here is an example combining quoted text with an attribute value to make the alternative text of an image visible, which is useful for testing your web pages:

```
img:after { content: " [ALT: " attr(alt) "]"; }
```

If you want to insert an image before or after an element, you give a url() value. This is similar to providing a bullet image with the list-style-image property, although it can be done with any element.

> Opera doesn't display images inserted with the url() function, although it displays generated text and attribute values just fine.

Listing 23.3 is a style sheet that adds explanatory text, as well as a small graphic, to the HTML file's presentation. The most important rules here are the content rules, listed first after each selector.

LISTING 23.3   Style Sheet Generating Text for Book List

```
/* generated-23.3.css */

body { font-family: Verdana, sans-serif; }

h3:before
  { content: "BookBase: ";
    font-size: small;
    font-family: cursive, sans-serif;
    color: white; background-color: black; }
h3:after
  { content: " (author index)";
    font-weight: normal; font-size: small; }

.series ul:before
  { content: "Series: " attr(title)
            "  " url('series_l.gif');
    font-weight: bold; }

.book:after
  { content: "  " url('book_l.gif'); }

.series .book:after
  { content: "  "url('bookinseries_l.gif'); }

li { list-style-type: square; }
li.series { list-style-type: none; }
.series ul li:first-child { margin-top: 0.5em; }
.series ul { margin-bottom: 0.5em; }
.series li { margin-left: 1em; }
```

Not all browsers support generated content, but Firefox, Opera, and Safari do. The results of applying the style sheet to the Tolkien listing are shown in Figure 23.3. You'll notice that separate books are followed by one icon, the name of a series with another icon, and books within a series by a third icon. The word *series* has also been added to further identify books within a particular series.

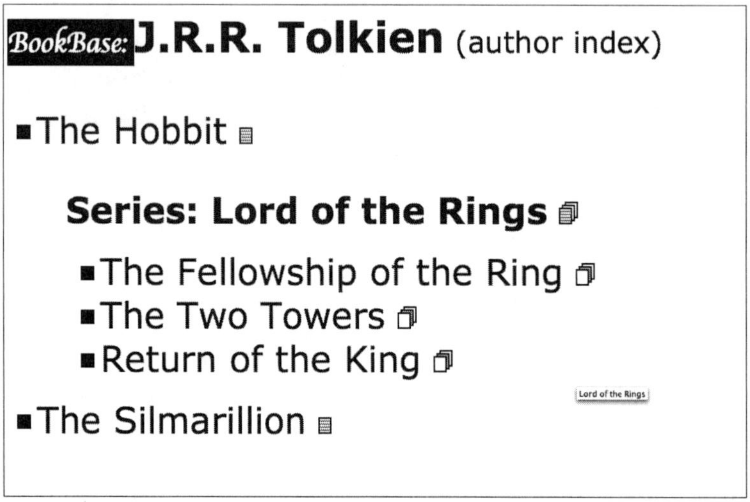

FIGURE 23.3
Firefox generating content for Tolkien list.

Generating Quotation Marks

You can use CSS to add quotation marks to your web page. This is most useful when you're dealing with multiple languages on the same site, where different languages have different quotation symbols. It's also applicable if you use the HTML element <q> to mark up your quotations.

To add quotations, first you must define which quotation marks should be used by using the quotes property. The values for quotes are pairs of symbols enclosed in double quotes themselves (or single quotes if they contain double-quote characters). The first pair is considered the outer pair of quotation symbols; inner quotes use the next pair in, and so on. Listing 23.4 gives an example, using doubled left-ticks and right-ticks for some quotes and square brackets for others. Your values for quotes don't have to be actual quotation marks; you can use any symbols or text.

LISTING 23.4   Style Sheet That Adds Quotes to the Book List

```
/* generated-23.4.css */

/* Set values for quotes */
ul { quotes: "[" "]"; }
ul li { quotes: "`" "'"; }

.series ul:before
  { content: "Series: " open-quote attr(title)
            close-quote "  " url('series_l.gif');
      font-weight: bold; }

.book:before
  { content: open-quote; }
```

LISTING 23.4 Continued

```
.book:after
  { content: close-quote "  " url('book_1.gif'); }

.series .book:after
  { content: close-quote "  " url('bookinseries_1.gif'); }
```

As shown in Listing 23.4, the open-quote or close-quote values for content designate the types of the quote marks to be generated. You can see the effect of these rules in Figure 23.4, which applies the updated style sheet to the HTML file from Listing 23.2.

BookBase: **J.R.R. Tolkien** (author index)

■ ` The Hobbit ' ▤

Series: [Lord of the Rings] ▤

  ■ ` The Fellowship of the Ring' ▤
  ■ ` The Two Towers' ▤
  ■ ` Return of the King' ▤

■ ` The Silmarillion' ▤

FIGURE 23.4
Quote marks inserted as generated content.

Counters and Numbering

Generated content can also consist of counter values. A CSS counter is like a very simple variable from a programming language. Each counter is identified by a name and holds a numeric integer value, such as 1, 2, 335, or -5. The counter can be set to a specific value, increased or decreased by a certain amount, or displayed as part of a content rule.

You set a counter to a specific value by using the counter-reset property; whenever a CSS rule containing counter-reset is applied to a selector, the counter is reset to the specified value, or to zero if no value is given. The name of the counter must be specified in the counter-reset declaration. The counter increases whenever a counter-increment property is applied that designates a counter of the same name. The general syntax for counter-reset and counter-increment looks like this:

```
selector { counter-reset: name amount name amount ... ; }
selector { counter-increment: name amount name amount ...; }
```

The *amount* can be omitted; for counter-reset this resets the counter to zero, and for counter-increment this increases the counter by one. You can reset or increment multiple counters by giving *name-amount* pairs (or just multiple counter names if you want to use the default *amount* values).

To display the counter value, use the function counter() or counters() within a content declaration. Each counter has a scope over which the counter applies, which consists of the element in which it was declared and its children; you can have multiple counters with the same name. The value of the current counter with a given *name* is specified by counter(*name*); the values of all counters with that *name* within the scope are given by counters(*name*, *delimiter*). The *delimiter* option specifies a string to be displayed between values. This lets you create nested lists with proper numbering.

An additional option can be supplied to the counter() and counters() functions, which selects a list style to be applied to the display of the counter. This can be any list-style-type value as covered in Hour 12, "Styling Links."

An example of counters in a style sheet can be seen in Listing 23.5. This example counts books within a series and the total numbers of books from the HTML Tolkien book list.

LISTING 23.5   Style Sheet for Adding Counters to the Book List

```
/* generated-23.5.css */

#works         { counter-reset: Total; }
.series        { counter-reset: BooksInSeries; }
.book          { counter-increment: BooksInSeries Total; }
.series:after  { content: "Books in Series: "
                         counter(BooksInSeries, decimal);
                 margin-left: 2em;
                 text-decoration: overline;
                 display: block; }
#works:after   { content: "Total books in index: "
                         counter(Total);
                 margin-top: 1em; display: block;
                 font-weight: bold; }
```

Some browsers do not support counters; Opera and Firefox display counters, whereas Safari and Internet Explorer (as of version 6.0) do not. Figure 23.5 shows how Firefox displays the HTML file from Listing 23.2 with the styles from Listing 23.5 sheet applied.

■ `The Hobbit ' 🗎

Series: [Lord of the Rings] 🗇

■ `The Fellowship of the Ring' 🗇
■ `The Two Towers' 🗇
■ `Return of the King' 🗇

Books in Series: 3
■ `The Silmarillion' 🗎

Total books in index: 5

FIGURE 23.5
Firefox displays counts for Tolkien's books.

Generating Text Shadows

The original CSS Level 2 specification included a property, `text-shadow`, that allowed drop shadows to be generated around text, giving a three-dimensional look. Only one browser, Safari, supports `text-shadow`, and so the property was removed in CSS 2.1.

However, you can use generated content to create your own text shadows around certain text elements. Listing 23.6 has the code that creates text shadows; the explanation follows after.

LISTING 23.6 Adding Shadows to Text

```
<!-- text-shadow-23.6.html -->
<html>
  <head>
    <title>Text Shadows</title>
    <style type="text/css">
    body {font-family: Verdana, sans-serif; }

    .shadow:before { color: gray; }

    .shadow[title] {
       line-height: 2em;
       margin: 0; }

    .shadow[title]:before {
       display: block;
       margin: 0 0 -2.10em 0.20em;
       content: attr(title); }

    h1.shadow { color: white; }
```

LISTING 23.6   Continued

```
   h1.shadow:before { color: black; }
  </style>
</head>
<body style="text-align: center;" >
  <h1 class="shadow" title="Announcing...">
    Announcing...</h1>
  <h2 class="shadow"
     title="Teach Yourself CSS in 24 Hours!">
    Teach Yourself CSS in 24 Hours!</h2>
  <p>Want to learn Cascading Style Sheets the easy way?
    Read this book! It's fun! Give it a try!</p>
  <p class="shadow" title="Tell all your friends!">
    Tell all your friends!</p>
</body>
</html>
```

So what's going on here? Look carefully at the HTML—each element that is to receive a text shadow has a class of shadow, as well as a title attribute that repeats the text of that element. This is then used in the content rule for the .shadow[title]:before selector in an attr() rule. That produces a copy of the text to be shadowed. Thanks to the .shadow:before rule, the color of this text will be gray.

Because the .shadow[title]:before rule sets the display to block, we end up with a repeat of the text on two lines—one line in black (default) text, one in gray text. The margin rule of the .shadow[title]:before selector moves the gray text behind the black text, and the line-height rule on the .shadow[title] text is there to ensure there's enough room to do that.

Figure 23.6 shows exactly how these rules come together and display a text shadow in a browser.

FIGURE 23.6
Shadows behind text, thanks to generated content.

Announcing...

Teach Yourself CSS in 24 Hours!

Want to learn Cascading Style Sheets the easy way? Read this book! It's fun! Give it a try!

Tell all your friends!

You can tweak the parameters here by changing the values for the margin rule; the difference from 2.0em is the vertical offset for the text shadow, and the difference from 0.0em is the horizontal offset. In this example, the final two rules set up a different color scheme—white on black—for <h1> text shadows, as shown in Figure 23.6.

This method for text shadows works well as long as your text is all on one line. If it wraps around, everything is thrown off. You can insert a white-space: nowrap rule to prevent text wrapping.

If this method of creating text shadows seems arcane, don't feel too bad—it is quite complicated, and is an example of the type of hoops that web designers are often willing to jump through to gain a specific effect. You'll learn more about the types of accommodations necessary for browser quirks and bugs in Hour 24, "Troubleshooting and Browser Hacks."

Summary

Cascading Style Sheets enable your web designs to incorporate elements of the user interface into the presentation. Through CSS, you can change the cursor with the cursor property or draw highlights around certain items with the outline properties.

Colors and fonts can be tuned to fit the operating system or the user's browser preferences if you employ special keywords for the color, background-color, border, and font properties.

Additional information can be added to the HTML by style sheets using content generation. Quoted text, attribute values, images, quotation marks, and counters can be included via the content property. The quotes property specifies the styles of quotes to be used, and the counter-reset and counter-increment properties manage the values of the counters.

As with many advanced CSS features, content generation may be supported sporadically by the browsers. If the primary content of the site is supported or explained only by generated content, users without access to the style sheet are left out, so care should be taken whenever using these techniques.

Workshop

The workshop contains a Q&A section, quiz questions, and exercises to help reinforce what you've learned in this hour. If you get stuck, the answers to the quiz can be found after the questions.

Q&A

Q. *Can I use content generation to insert HTML tags before and after an element? That would be really cool.*

A. It would indeed be cool, but the answer is no, you can't. Quoted text is inserted directly as text, not as markup, which means that if you wrap HTML tags around something, they won't be interpreted by the browser. Instead you'll just see those tags, in angle brackets, when viewing the page.

Q. *Generating content doesn't sound reliable. It would be easier to just add the content to the HTML, and that works in Internet Explorer and every other browser! Why would I ever use generated content?*

A. Content generation is useful and powerful, but as you say, it can be unreliable. In general, you're right; if you need to include some text in your output, you should put it in the HTML. There are a few cases where generated content is particularly useful, though, including sites where you may not have access to the content but can style it; alternate style sheets for specific presentations, such as a screen reader style sheet for visually impaired users; and XML files that don't inherently contain explanatory text. For more on XML and generated markup, see Bonus Web Hour 2, "CSS and XML" (available on this book's website).

Quiz

1. Which of these options is not a valid declaration for the `cursor` property?

    a. `cursor: hourglass;`

    b. `cursor: ne-resize;`

    c. `cursor: url('target.cur'), crosshair;`

    d. `cursor: text;`

2. Your HTML contains `<a>` links of the class `button3d` that you want to style to look like three-dimensional buttons. How do you make members of this class appear as such, using the system `color` and `font` properties?

3. What does each of the following content rules accomplish?

    a. `a[href]:after { content: "[LINK: " attr(href) "]"; }`

    b. `h1:before { "#" counter(item); counter-increment: item; }`

    c. `blockquote p:before { content: open-quote; }`

Answers

1. (a). hourglass is not a proper value for cursor; to display an hourglass or timer cursor, use the value wait.

2. Here is one way to write the appropriate style rules:

```
a.button3d:link {
    display: block;
    font: menu;                    color: ButtonText;
    background-color: ButtonFace;
    border-width: medium;      border-type: outset;
    border-color: ButtonHighlight; }
```

3. The rules generate the following types of content:

a. All links are followed by an indication of their link target. This is a very handy rule if you are printing out documents.

b. This numbers all <h1> elements.

c. This starts all paragraphs within a <blockquote> with the opening quote character.

Exercises

Here are some projects that will help you get practice using the properties from this hour:

1. Experiment with changing the cursors on your website. Does it make it easier to use or harder to use if the cursors aren't set by the browser?

2. Using the :active pseudo-class, extend the style rules from Quiz question 2 to create three-dimensional buttons that appear to depress when clicked.

3. Use content generation to add notes to a web page explaining the function of each element. Style these notes in a different color or with a border around them.

HOUR 24

Troubleshooting and Browser Hacks

What You'll Learn in This Hour:

▶ How to detect errors in your style sheets or HTML code by using validators

▶ What browser hacks are and how they work

▶ How to write CSS rules that filter out specific browsers

▶ What conditional comments are, and how to use them with Internet Explorer

▶ How to reliably hide content from visual browsers while still making it available to screen readers for blind users

▶ Four ways to change the transparency of any element with proprietary CSS rules

▶ How to produce a variety of visual transformations that will appear only in Internet Explorer

▶ How to create rounded corners in Gecko-based browsers with proprietary CSS rules

Writing style sheets can feel like an arcane art when the style rules don't have quite the effect you want. Sometimes it will be a problem with the way you've written the rules, and other times you've just run into a browser bug or quirk. This hour teaches you how to identify your own mistakes, work around browser quirks, and use certain browser deviations from the standard to benefit rather than break your CSS-based designs.

Troubleshooting Style Sheets

When you're writing a style sheet, sometimes the results you get in your browser don't match what you were hoping for. Don't worry—this happens to everyone. To correct these problems, you can follow a strategy of eliminating syntax errors though validation, simplifying the possible sources of errors, and working around browser bugs and quirks.

HTML and CSS Validation

Everyone makes mistakes, even you and I. Mistakes in writing CSS can be benign, producing a minor effect such as putting a block of text in the wrong font, or they can be much more serious and prevent people from using your page at all.

The first step to making sure that your style sheet contains no mistakes is ensuring that your HTML isn't broken. As you learned in Hour 4, "Using CSS with HTML," you can validate your HTML by using the World Wide Web Consortium's HTML validator at http://validator.w3.org. Figure 24.1 shows the validator inspecting the author's website.

FIGURE 24.1
The W3C's HTML validator locates problems in web pages.

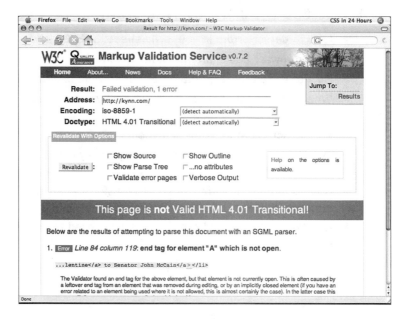

As you can see, the validator discovered a problem—there is an extra closing tag, </a>, that is not matched by an opening tag. This was the result of a simple HTML editing problem—I changed the spot at which I wanted my link to end, but forgot to remove the original closing tag. Thanks, validator, for spotting that!

The W3C provides a free CSS validation service, as well, for checking your CSS syntax. This is located at http://jigsaw.w3.org/css-validator/.

By the Way

Another CSS validator, this one from the Web Design Group, can be found at http://www.htmlhelp.com/tools/csscheck/.

To use the W3C CSS validator, you can specify a web page that contains CSS code, give the direct URL of a style sheet, or paste your style rules directly into a text box. The validator analyzes your CSS rules and notifies you of errors. It also gives useful warnings.

An example of CSS validation is shown in Figure 24.2, which shows the results of validating the style sheet for the author's website. As you can see, it caught an error and gave a warning about some possible errors.

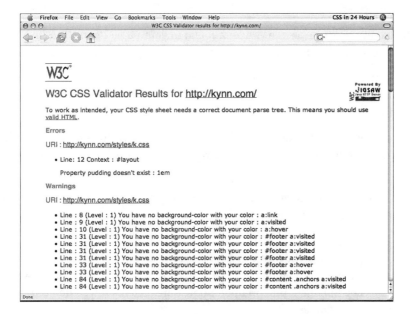

FIGURE 24.2
Using the W3C's CSS validator on a style sheet.

Validation is a useful strategy for a number of reasons. The biggest benefit is that it enables you to spot errors in your style sheet syntax. For example, in Figure 24.2, the CSS validator noticed a problem with the style sheet. The style sheet contained a reference to a pudding CSS property; this was a typo for the padding property.

The warnings issued by the CSS validator are quite useful for spotting accidental omissions, such as setting a foreground color without a contrasting background color. However, you have to interpret those results carefully. The CSS validator can't fully account for inheritance and transparency in your web page, and so you need to determine for yourself whether a warning is an actual problem.

A validator is like a spell-checker or grammar-checker in a word processor. It can spot potential problems and you wouldn't think of submitting a document without checking it first, but blind reliance on an automated checker without using human judgment is just as bad.

▼   **Try it Yourself**

Check for Valid HTML and CSS

Get some hands-on experience with the W3C's validators by following these simple steps:

1. Choose a web page you've worked on that uses CSS.

2. First, validate the HTML at http://validator.w3.org/ and take note of any problems you find.

3. Fix any HTML errors the validator found in your page; clean HTML is a solid foundation for CSS work.

4. Next, run the page's style sheet through the CSS validator at http://jigsaw.w3.org/css-validator/. You'll get two types of responses—errors and warnings.

5. Fix any errors that appear, such as mistyped property names or poorly formed CSS rules. It's not uncommon to leave out closing curly braces or have extraneous ones, for example.

6. Then go through each warning and analyze what it's trying to tell you. You may not need to change your style sheet at all, if you can check against your HTML and determine whether the warning calls for action or not.

7. Fix any warnings that are helpful, and ignore any you don't need to fix. For example, if it tells you that you need to set a background color, but it will always be inherited from an appropriate parent element, you don't need to
▲   make that change.

Narrowing Your Focus

Validation won't find all your mistakes, just as a spell-checker in a word processing problem won't catch factual errors in a term paper. So just because your page is designated as syntactically valid, that doesn't mean it won't have additional problems that can affect how it appears on the screen.

After you have validated your CSS, it's time to start stripping it out. Save the original version of your HTML and CSS, and work on a copy off it. Remove sections of the CSS step by step, reloading the page in the browser each time. You can remove these rules from the page by editing them out of the source, or you can comment them out.

Your goal in this process is to identify exactly which rules are causing problems for you. Cut away any extraneous style rules that you suspect have nothing to do with your problems—but be sure to reload after each removal, because it's possible that something that appears completely unrelated might be causing your problems! Style rules sometimes have unintended consequences.

Problems involving the cascade are particularly hard to spot at first glance because the individual rules look right, and the effects of the combination can be tricky to figure out. If you need to, review Hour 7, "Cascading and Inheritance," for details on how selectors are given higher specificity based on the types of selectors used. The more selectors of each type used, the more specific the rule; id selectors beat class (and pseudo-class) selectors, and class selectors beat element type selectors.

You should also watch for shorthand properties, such as font, background, border, margin, and so on. These properties not only set the values given, but also reset to the default (by the CSS specification, not by other rules on your page) any of the properties they represent. Consider this rule:

```
.sidebar { font-weight: bold; font: 12pt Verdana, sans-serif; }
```

This certainly looks as if it would give you Verdana text, 12 points high and in bold. But it won't. Because the font rule listed here is a shorthand property, it is actually identical to the following:

```
font-style: normal;
font-variant: normal;
font-weight: normal;
font-size: 12pt;
line-height: normal;
font-family: Verdana, sans-serif;
```

Because the font rule follows the font-weight: bold; rule, the weight of the font is effectively set back to normal from bold. The sidebar text would be 12 point Verdana, but it would not be bold.

Narrowing down your rules to a smaller set and checking the cascading, inheritance, and shorthand properties can identify many of these kinds of mistakes in your style sheets.

Ruling Out Browser Bugs

Now, it may be that you've made no mistakes at all in your CSS rules. As discussed throughout this book, especially in Hour 3, "Browser Support for CSS," no browser has perfect support for the CSS standards and all have quirks and bugs ranging from minor to serious. So it's possible that a problem just isn't your fault.

To identify whether a CSS problem is the result of a browser quirk or bug, you'll first need to do some browser testing in alternate browsers. This should be part of your normal routine anyway, but you use a slightly different approach when hunting down a problem. Your goal is not to make it appear the same, but to see whether or not you can reproduce the problem on other browsers with different layout engines, including mostly compliant browsers (such as Firefox, Opera, or Safari).

Use the simplified version of the style rules you developed when narrowing down the rules to a smaller subset, and see whether you can confirm what the correct behavior should be. If two or three other browsers agree on the way your CSS code should be presented, they're probably right; however, if there's one browser that's just doing it all wrong, you most likely have stumbled onto a browser bug or quirk.

When you are trying to hunt down problems in Internet Explorer, make sure you are aware whether or not you are in "quirks mode." By default, Internet Explorer 6 is in a quirky, backwards-compatible mode that matches IE 5 and 5.5, but you can put it into a more standards-compliant mode by using a `<!DOCTYPE>` definition, as you learned in Hour 4.

If you think you've found a bug, you may be right—and you may not be the only person to find it. Check on some of the very valuable websites that document browser bugs, such as Position Is Everything (http://www.positioniseverything.net/), or simply do a web search with keywords such as the name of your browser, the name of the CSS property, and "bug." You'll likely find other people who have encountered the same problems, and advice on how you can use other browser quirks to get yourself out of your difficulties.

Browser Hacks

In a perfect world, you could sit down with this book, a copy of the CSS specification, and your computer, and write style sheets that display properly on every browser in the world. Unfortunately, as discussed in Hour 3, we don't live in that perfect world yet. Each browser has its own quirks and bugs, some very minor and some quite serious.

To work around these quirks and bugs, web designers have developed certain techniques for dealing with browsers that don't always behave as they should. Somewhat ironically, these techniques themselves rely on quirks and bugs themselves to get around other quirks and bugs.

A *browser hack*, therefore, is any technique that uses CSS rules (or sometimes HTML tags) in a quirky way to address a known problem in a browser. If a CSS rule wouldn't be included in that perfect world, but is included because, for example, Internet Explorer 5.5 has a bug, then that rule is the result of a browser hack.

A hack isn't all bad, mind you. The term "hack" has both negative and positive connotations in the English language, depending on the context in which it is used. A hack writer is a bad writer, but in computer programming, a hacker is a deft manipulator of the computer system—as opposed to a cracker, which is someone who maliciously breaks in and steals your data.

In the sense we're using it here, a browser hack is an unfortunate compromise forced upon web designers because of browser limitations. Nobody likes to use a browser hack; we'd rather live in a CSS utopia where rules work correctly. A browser hack is therefore a compromise we live with because we have to.

Browser hacks have several identifying features. First, they are targeted at specific web browsers. One browser hack might be aimed at Internet Explorer 5.5, whereas another works to correct a quirk in Opera 7. Secondly, browser hacks are almost always valid CSS, especially if they're well-written hacks. Thirdly, they exploit bugs or limitations in the targeted browser that deal with how it handles proper CSS.

Some browser hacks use selectors that are not implemented in the target browser, and thus will be ignored. For example, if you want to write a rule that won't be understood by Internet Explorer 6, an easy way to do this is to use one of the selectors from Hour 8, "Advanced Selectors," such as an attribute selector. Other browser hacks depend on bugs in the way the layout engine reads through the style sheet and parses out the CSS rules. For example, certain browsers have problems with comments stuck in the middle of property names, and these bugs can be exploited to write rules targeting those browsers.

The vast majority of browser hacks depend on at least two bugs: one in the way the rule is read by the layout engine, and one in the way the layout engine places the content on the page. The combination of these two bugs results in a hack to use the former as a fix for the latter. These double-bug browser hacks are useful only as long as each bug is unique to only that browser.

The examples in this hour use Internet Explorer—currently the most commonly used quirky browser, as described in Hour 3—to illustrate how filtering works. You can find specific hacks for specific browsers at Position is Everything (http://www.positioniseverything.net/) and Centricle (http://centricle.com/ref/css/filters/), among other sites.

Filtering Out Specific Browsers

As you learned in Hour 18, "Box Sizing and Offset," there is a bug in the way certain versions of Internet Explorer calculate the width (and height) of a box. This is called the *IE box model bug*. Versions of Internet Explorer prior to 6 (and IE 6 in quirks mode) miscalculate the box dimensions by including the border and padding in the width and height.

If you use CSS to set a box's width to 600 pixels, plus another 300 pixels of border and padding, most browsers correctly display this as 900 pixels wide. Internet Explorer makes the box 600 pixels across. If you set the width to 900 pixels, it displays as desired in Internet Explorer, but is suddenly 1200 pixels wide in compliant browsers. Figure 24.3 shows exactly this scenario—the width has been set to 600 pixels, and Internet Explorer displays it incorrectly.

FIGURE 24.3
This box should be 900 pixels wide, but IE miscalculates.

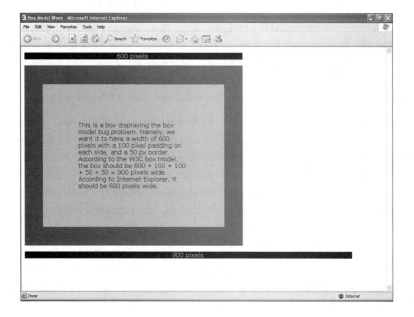

It would be nice if there were a way to feed separate values for width to Internet Explorer and to browsers that respect the standards. This desire has led to the development of browser filters. A filter is a kind of browser hack that targets certain browsers by writing rules that either are ignored by only those browsers, or understood by only those browsers.

You can use browser filters to address the box model bug in Internet Explorer. One way to do this is by using a rule other browsers understand, but that Internet Explorer cannot understand, and will therefore ignore.

Did you Know?

As explained in Hour 18, there are several other ways to deal with the IE box model bug. One method is to simply never set the padding and border on any object that has the width set. Use nested <div>s instead of a single <div>, assign the (larger) width to the outer <div>, and the padding and border to the inner <div>. This makes your HTML more complex, which offends some markup purists because the extra <div> is extraneous.

Another method is to force Internet Explorer out of the default "quirks mode" and into "standards mode" by using a <!DOCTYPE> statement; this works only in Internet Explorer 6, which means you will still have to do something about IE 5.0 and 5.5. The filters in this hour can help you in that regard.

The Direct Child Selector Filter

In Hour 8, you learned that Internet Explorer (even version 6) does not understand the direct child selector, represented by a > symbol between the parent and child elements. This means that any rule written with a direct child selector will not be understood by current versions of IE. Therefore, you can write two rules: first, a rule setting the width to the Internet Explorer dimension, and then a second rule that updates that width to the "real" value, for browsers that understand direct child selectors. Listing 24.1 is an example of this type of filter.

LISTING 24.1 Using Child Selectors to Filter Out Internet Explorer

```
<!-- box-model-24-1.html -->
<html>
  <head>
    <title>Box Model Woes</title>
    <style type="text/css">
      body { font-family: Verdana, sans-serif; }
      .bar { color: white; background: black;
             text-align: center; margin: 1em 0; }
      #six { width: 600px; } #nine { width: 900px; }

      #box { width: 900px;    /* The width for IE */
             background-color: silver;
             padding: 100px; border: 50px solid #555; }

      html>body #box { width: 600px; }
                 /* The "real" width value */
    </style>
  </head>
  <body>
    <div id="six" class="bar">600 pixels</div>
    <div id="box">
      <p>This is a box displaying the box model
         bug problem. Namely, we want it to have
         a width of 600 pixels with a 100 pixel
         padding on each side, and a 50 px border.
         According to the W3C box model, the
         box should be 600 + 100 + 100 + 50 + 50
         = 900 pixels wide. According to Internet
```

LISTING 24.1   Continued

```
        Explorer, it should be 600 pixels wide.</p>
    </div>
    <div id="nine" class="bar">900 pixels</div>
  </body>
</html>
```

The results of displaying this page in Internet Explorer 6 (not in "quirks mode," because there is no <!DOCTYPE> in Listing 24.1) are shown in Figure 24.4. As you can see, the box is now the right size. A browser such as Firefox would also display the box at the same size because it would understand and use the real value of 600px given in the child selector rule.

FIGURE 24.4
Internet Explorer
uses the 900px
value to pro-
duce a box of
the proper
dimensions.

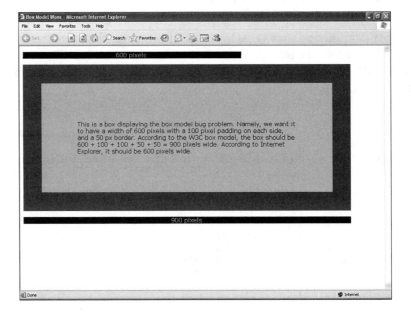

The embedded style sheet in Listing 24.1 first sets the width to the wrong value of 900px, and then corrects it with the subsequent rule, which IE ignores. Another way to use a browser filter is to write a rule that is ignored by all other browsers, but understood by only the targeted browser. This is the opposite approach to the method in Listing 24.1.

The Star HTML Filter

Internet Explorer, up to and including version 6, has a minor bug. IE believes that there is an invisible, unknown element that contains the <html> element. No other browser has this quirk, but if you write a rule such as the following, Internet Explorer will apply it:

```
* html p { color: blue; }
```

Such a rule will make your paragraph tags blue, but only in IE. Any other browser would look first at the universal selector (*) and then at the html element selector, and conclude that there's no parent element that contains html—so the rule won't apply to anything. Web designers call this the *star HTMLfilter* or *star HTML hack*.

Listing 24.2 is a style sheet that uses this particular quirk to write a style rule just for Internet Explorer; this style sheet is a replacement for the embedded style sheet in Listing 24.1.

LISTING 24.2   A Style Sheet That Uses the Star HTML Filter

```
body { font-family: Verdana, sans-serif; }
.bar { color: white; background: black;
      text-align: center; margin: 1em 0; }
#six { width: 600px; } #nine { width: 900px; }

#box { width: 600px;    /* The correct width */
      background-color: silver;
      padding: 100px;
      border: 50px solid #555; }
* html #box { width: 900px; }
      /* The width for only Internet Explorer */
```

Internet Explorer displays the box correctly when this rule is used. IE actually reads both rules in this case, both the width of 600px and the width of 900px. It chooses to use the latter rule because of the specificity calculations that you learned about Hour 7. A rule with more selectors of a given type is more specific.

> There isn't a screen capture of Listing 24.2 displayed in a browser because it would look identical to Figure 24.4, which illustrated the direct child filter. Later in this hour you will learn yet another way to fix the box model problem, and again it will look just like Figure 24.4.

By the Way

So which method should you use? There are advantages and disadvantages to both. The technique in Listing 24.1 makes the assumption that any browser that understands direct child selectors will not have the Internet Explorer box model bug, and vice versa. So far this is true, but it is somewhat shaky ground. The star HTML hack in Listing 24.2 presumes that every browser that recognizes the nonsensical * html selector will also have a broken box model algorithm. Each hack therefore depends upon two unrelated bugs or quirks to function.

What if the next version of Internet Explorer fixes one of the bugs used in a hack but not both? For example, what if Internet Explorer 7 stopped believing in a fictional parent for <html>, but still had the box model bug in quirks mode? What if Internet Explorer suddenly understood child selectors?

In fact, it appears that exactly this situation has come true—as this book is being written, Internet Explorer 7 is available in only a preview release, but Microsoft's developers have warned that the star HTML selector won't be recognized by IE7, and direct child selectors will be understood. However, not all CSS bugs in IE6 will be fixed in IE7. Some web designers are upset by this—their browser hacks will break in IE7.

Conditional Comments

Microsoft has recommended that web developers stop using filters that target Internet Explorer for inclusion or exclusion, such as the direct child hack or the star HTML hack. Instead, they promote the use of conditional comments.

Conditional comments are HTML markup following the general syntax of normal comments—they begin with <!-- and end with -->. This means that most browsers ignore anything between those markers, even if it looks like normal HTML tags.

However, Internet Explorer will look inside certain comments if they contain a conditional statement. These conditional statements enable you to embed within the comments some HTML tags that will be read only by Internet Explorer. You can even refine these conditional statements further by requiring that only IE browsers of a certain version read the HTML that is contained.

Here are several examples that illustrate the syntax for conditional comments:

```
<!--[if IE]>
  <p>Internet Explorer detected!</p>
<![endif]-->
<!--[if IE 6]>
  <p>Congratulations (or condolences), you're using IE 6.</p>
<![endif]-->
<!--[if lte IE 5.5]>
  <p>I'm sorry, you're using an earlier version of IE.</p>
<![endif]-->
```

If you viewed this HTML code in a non-Microsoft browser, such as Firefox, you wouldn't see any of these messages, as anything between the <!-- and the --> is ignored as a comment. But if you view this in Internet Explorer, you will see a message dependent upon your browser version.

Conditional statements can be as simple as [if IE] (to match all versions of Internet Explorer from 5.0 onward, when conditional comments were introduced), or more complex statements with the modifiers lt (less than), gt (greater than), lte (less than or equal to), or gte (greater than or equal to) matching against specific browser version numbers.

For more details on using conditional comments, read about them at the Microsoft Developer Network at http://msdn.microsoft.com/workshop/author/dhtml/ overview/ccomment_ovw.asp.

By the *Way*

HTML-style comments aren't allowed inside style sheets, including embedded style sheets, so you can't use conditional comments mixed directly into your CSS rules. To use conditional comments with CSS, create one or more extra `<style>` or `<link>` elements containing style rules for Internet Explorer, and then wrap them in an appropriate conditional comment. Listing 24.3 contains an example that illustrates how to use conditional comments instead of the star HTML hack to fix box model problems.

LISTING 24.3   An HTML File Containing a Conditional Comment

```
<!-- box-model-24.3.html -->
<html>
  <head>
    <title>Box Model Woes</title>
    <style type="text/css">
      body { font-family: Verdana, sans-serif; }
      .bar { color: white; background: black;
             text-align: center; margin: 1em 0; }
      #six { width: 600px; } #nine { width: 900px; }

      #box { width: 600px;    /* the real width */
             background-color: silver;
             padding: 100px; border: 50px solid #555; }
    </style>

    <!--[if lte IE 6]>
      <style type="text/css">
        /* the width for Internet Explorer */
        #box { width: 900px; }
      </style>
    <![endif]-->

  </head>
  <body>
    <div id="six" class="bar">600 pixels</div>
    <div id="box">
      <p>This is a box displaying the box model
         bug problem. Namely, we want it to have
         a width of 600 pixels with a 100 pixel
         padding on each side, and a 50 px border.
         According to the W3C box model, the
         box should be 600 + 100 + 100 + 50 + 50
         = 900 pixels wide. According to Internet
         Explorer, it should be 600 pixels wide.</p>
```

LISTING 24.3   Continued

```
    </div>
    <div id="nine" class="bar">900 pixels</div>
  </body>

</html>
```

The net result of this style sheet is identical to that in Listing 24.2, which used the star HTML filter. Most browsers receive only the first width rule, and Internet Explorer receives both. In this case, both rules have the same selector (#box) and thus the same specificity; therefore, the one defined later in the HTML source code is used. The result of displaying this web page is identical to that shown in Figure 24.4.

Hiding Content Meant for Screen Readers

When you are designing a web page, it's important for you to consider the needs of users with disabilities, as you learned in Hour 22, "Accessibility and Print Media." Using CSS means you're already off to a good start toward meeting those needs as a natural consequence of good web design techniques.

Sometimes there is a perceived conflict between designing a page that is accessible and designing one that is visually attractive. For example, web accessibility check-lists such as the U.S. government's Section 508 requirements (http://www.access-board.gov/sec508/guide/1194.22.htm) require web designers to provide links that skip over navigation lists and go directly to the main content of the page. Such a link might look like this:

```
<p class="skiplink"><a href="#content">Skip Navigation</a></p>
<ul>
  <!-- navigation links would be listed here -->
</ul>
<h1><a name="content">Main Content</a></h1>
```

This provides easy access for users with screen readers, giving them a shortcut to avoid listening to long and possibly repetitive lists of links before getting to the main content of the site. However, this method also presents a problem: The text Skip Navigation is visible onscreen to all users and is a clickable link, but it doesn't actually seem to do anything, and the meaning of the text Skip Navigation is undoubtedly opaque to the average visually dependent web user. A web designer concerned with the visual appearance of the page is likely to want to hide these links.

Another example would be the ubiquitous search box. As you learned in Hour 14, "Forms," the <label> tag can be used to provide a text label for an HTML form element. But what about a short form like this?

```
<form method="post" action="search.php">
  <input type="text" id="searchtext">
  <input type="submit" value="Search!">
</form>
```

This type of form can be found around the Web, and for most users it is quite obvious what it does: You type something in the box and press the button and it searches. You know this because you can see the button labeled Search! to the right of the box. Visually impaired users, however, don't hear the search button first because web pages are read in order by screen readers. They hear an announcement of the input box, and don't know what to type because they don't hear the word "Search!"

The obvious solution is to add a `<label>` element telling the user it it's a search box, like this:

```
<form method="post" action="search.php">
  <label for="searchtext">Search:</label>
  <input type="text" id="searchtext">
  <input type="submit" value="Search!">
</form>
```

This works great for screen reader users. However, to a web designer focused on the visual appearance, the label takes up extra space and unnecessarily repeats the word "Search."

The most obvious solution is to write a CSS rule to hide the display of the label text. That would be something simple such as

```
label { display: none; }
```

This seems straightforward and simple, and many web designers using CSS seem to think this would work. A very famous "image replacement technique" using this method was promoted by the big names in CSS-based web design—until it was discovered that it does not work. Why not?

Screen readers are a very specific type of technology; they read what is on the screen. If something is not displayed on the screen—which is what `display: none` does—then the screen reader doesn't read it. This is also why it doesn't work to simply add an `@media` rule; screen readers don't actually use the media type "aural" but instead read out the text as displayed visually by the browser.

A number of alternative methods for hiding material from visual browsers but still making it accessible to screen readers have been proposed over the years, many of them without being tested first in actual screen readers. Bob Easton has compiled a chart testing each of these methods in leading screen readers and makes the results available at http://www.access-matters.com/screen-reader-test-results/.

From those results, it has become clear that the most reliable method to hide content while keeping it accessible to screen readers is called the *off-left* technique. In short, you use absolute positioning to place the hidden content way off to the left side of the screen, where it can't be seen but is still read out loud by screen readers. Listing 24.4 shows how you can use off-left placement to hide the .skiplink and <label> in the example HTML fragments.

LISTING 24.4 **A Style Sheet That Visually Hides Content but Leaves It Available for Screen Readers**

```
.skiplink, label {
    position: absolute;
    left: -999px;
    width: 90px; }
```

You might wonder whether it's really necessary to go to these lengths to hide accessibility-related content. In many cases, you can meet the needs of users with disabilities by simply designing your page differently. For example, perhaps your search form will start with a <label> of Search:, but the Submit button will read Go! instead. Even so, you may find situations in which you want to hide certain parts of your page but still make them readable by screen readers, and this is currently the best way to do that.

Proprietary CSS

Many web browsers can understand and apply more CSS properties than simply the ones listed in the CSS 2.1 specification. These additional CSS properties can expand your capabilities to style a page, but are usually restricted to only one or two browsers. Such properties are called *proprietary* CSS styles. Rather than being part of the standards agreed to by all browsers and developed by the World Wide Web Consortium (W3C), these CSS properties were created by the browser companies themselves. As such, they can be rather unreliable; browsers that don't understand these additional properties just ignore them.

Most responsible browser companies give these properties names that make it clear they are not ordinary CSS properties, but something proprietary. The most common way to do this is with a prefix on the property name identifying the browser or browser company. For example, proprietary properties recognized by Mozilla's Gecko layout engine all begin with -moz- (for Mozilla).

In the remainder of this hour, you'll learn about some of the proprietary extensions to the CSS language that can be used in current browsers. This isn't an extensive list; instead it's meant to make you familiar with the concept of proprietary CSS and the limitations involved as well. For more details on which specific proprietary values are supported by the browsers, see each browser's documentation website.

Opacity

One ability web designers greatly desire is to control the opacity of an object—how opaque or transparent it is. An object that is partially opaque is partially transparent—meaning that anything placed behind it can be seen through that object. Control over the opacity of a content block is not available in CSS 2.1. You can't do it under the current standards.

However, in the proposed drafts for CSS Level 3, there is an opacity property. This property can be assigned values from 0.0 (completely transparent) to 1.0 (completely opaque), with a default value of 1.0.

Some browser companies have implemented opacity in their browsers. However, as the CSS3 specification is still being written, it's not exactly prudent to use the draft as a reference. If the W3C's working group decided to change the definition of the opacity property—for example, to change it to a percentage scale—then web pages built with the early implementations would break.

To prevent these types of problems, the programmers working on the Gecko layout engine (used in Firefox and related browsers) chose to call this property -moz-opacity, and the creators of the KHTML layout engine (used in Konqueror) named it -khtml-opacity.

This is both responsible behavior and rather frustrating to web designers, because it means that to create an opaque content block, you need to set three properties: -moz-opacity, -khtml-opacity, and opacity itself, for those browsers such as Safari that jumped the gun and implemented the CSS3 version.

The situation is even more complex, thanks to Internet Explorer. Internet Explorer doesn't attempt to implement an opacity property a la the CSS3 standard. Instead, Internet Explorer provides what it calls the filter property, which lets you define IE-only transformations on any content block. One of those filters is the opacity filter, and that's what you use to get the same effect as the CSS3 opacity property.

> This is an all too common situation where you have the same term with several meanings. As defined earlier in this hour, a browser filter is a hack designed to keep certain browsers from applying specific rules. But as used here, filter refers to a proprietary CSS property implemented by Microsoft. This leads to confusing ambiguity—does "an Internet Explorer filter" refer to a browser hack to hide (or show) rules to IE, or to Internet Explorer's visual transformation `filter` property? In the rest of this hour, I will make it clear by context which sense of the word *filter* is being used.

The syntax for the `filter` property is very different from the `opacity` (and `-moz-opacity` and `-khtml-opacity`) property: It uses percentages instead of a decimal number between 0 and 1. The four methods for setting opacity to 65% are shown in Listing 24.5. Figure 24.5 demonstrates how this is displayed in a web browser.

LISTING 24.5   Four Different Rules to Modify Opacity

```
<!-- opacity-24.5.html -->
<html>
  <head>
    <title>Tucson Transfer Building</title>
    <style type="text/css">
      body { margin: 0; padding: 0;
             background-color: #6666CC;
             background-position: top center;
             background-repeat: none;
             background-image: url("tucson-transfer.jpg");}
      h1 { margin-top: 50px; margin-left: 5%;
           width: 40%; text-align: center;
           font-family: Optima, sans-serif;
           background: black; color: white; }
      #caption
           { width: 40%; position: absolute;
             font-family: Optima, sans-serif;
             top: 50px; right: 5%; padding: 0 0.5em;
             background: white; color: black; }
      #footer
         { font-size: small; margin: 1em;
           padding: 0 0.75em;
           border: 0.5em solid black; }
      /* opacity rules: */
      #caption, h1
         { opacity: 0.65;
           -moz-opacity: 0.65;
           -khtml-opacity: 0.65;
           filter: alpha(opacity=65); }
    </style>
  </head>
  <body>
```

LISTING 24.5   Continued

```
  <h1>Tucson Transfer Building</h1>
  <div id="caption">
    <p>The Tucson Warehouse and Transfer Company building is
       located at the corner of 6th Street and 7th Avenue
       in Tucson.</p>
    <p>The building is currently occupied by a number of
       businesses, including an architectural firm and a
       plumbing supply company.</p>
    <p>One of the early African-American pioneers of
       Tucson, Henry Ransom, worked at the Tucson Transfer
       Company from 1892 until his retirement in 1931.</p>
    <div id="footer">
      <p>This page is part of the
         <a href="http://kynn.com/projects/heritage-tour/"
           >Tucson Black Heritage Tour</a></p>
    </div>
  </div>
</body>
</html>
```

FIGURE 24.5
Firefox renders
the content
as partially
transparent.

Microsoft's `filter` Property

Microsoft's Internet Explorer understands a proprietary CSS property known as `filter`; the preceding section of this hour showed you how to use `filter` to change the opacity of a content box. Additional filters are supported by Internet Explorer versions 4 or later; these include those shown in Table 24.1.

TABLE 24.1   Types of Filters Available in Internet Explorer 4 or Later

Filter Value	Visual Effect
alpha(opacity=*percent*)	Changes the opacity
blur(direction=*degrees*, strength=*px*)	Applies a motion blur effect
chroma(color=*rgb*)	Sets one color as transparent
dropshadow(color=*rgb*, offX=*px*, offY=*px*)	Creates a shadow effect
fliph	Flips along the horizontal axis
flipv	Flips along the vertical axis
glow(color=*rgb*, strength=*px*)	Surrounds with a glow effect
gray	Converts to 256-color grayscale
invert	Displays in "negative" colors
light	Shines a light source on an object
mask(color=*rgb*)	Reveals transparent pixels and hides others
shadow(color=*rgb*, direction=*degrees*, strength=*px*)	Adds a shadow effect
wave(freq=*num*, phase=*percent*, strength=*px*)	Applies a sine wave distortion
xray	Displays in stark black-and-white

You use these filter values with the `filter` proprietary property, as you did earlier to change opacity. For example, to create a shadow in Internet Explorer, you can write the following CSS rule:

```
img.shadowed { filter: shadow(color=#808080, direction=135, strength=5); }
```

This creates a shadow around any `<img>` that has the `shadowed` class; the shadow will be gray in color, will be offset 135° (with 0° pointing toward the top of the screen), and will extend for 5 pixels.

Internet Explorer version 5.5 and later versions support additional filters and use a more complex syntax, although they also understand the IE4 versions. As an example, to write a rule using the `fliph` and `glow` filters in Internet Explorer 4 syntax, you can write

```
h3 { filter: fliph glow(color=lime, strength=5); }
```

The Internet Explorer 5.5 version of this rule is:

```
h3 { filter: progid:DXImageTransform.Microsoft.BasicImage(rotation=2, mirror=1)
             progid:DXImageTransform.Microsoft.Glow(color=lime, strength=5); }
```

For full details on Internet Explorer filters, see the Microsoft Developer Network Site page at http://msdn.microsoft.com/library/default.asp?url=/workshop/author/filter/reference/reference.asp, which has documentation and sample code.

Mozilla Corners

In Hour 19, "Absolute and Fixed Positioning," you learned how to create rounded corners on boxes by using images, absolute placement, and trimming. Browsers based on the Gecko layout engine, such as Firefox, Camino, or SeaMonkey, recognize proprietary CSS properties that enable you to create these effects entirely with styles instead of images.

Table 24.2 is a listing of these properties. Each property begins with the -moz- prefix to indicate that these are proprietary properties. Other browsers don't recognize these properties; they are ignored silently, and the corners of selected boxes remain square.

TABLE 24.2 Properties Creating Curved Corners in Gecko-Based Browsers

Property Name	Effect
-moz-border-radius	Sets the radius for all four corners.
-moz-border-radius-bottomleft	Sets the radius for the bottom-left corner.
-moz-border-radius-bottomright	Sets the radius for the bottom-right corner.
-moz-border-radius-topleft	Sets the radius for the top-left corner.
-moz-border-radius-topright	Sets the radius for the top-right corner.

The -moz-border-radius property is similar to the border, margin, and padding properties in that you can give it one, two, or four values. If one value is given, then the border radius for each corner is set to that value. If two are given, the first value is applied to the top-left and bottom-right corners, and the second value to the top-right and bottom-left. If four values are given, they are assigned to the top-left, top-right, bottom-right, and bottom-left corners respectively.

The values for the properties in Table 24.2 can be measurements such as 2em or 12px, or percentages based on the height of the box. These measurements indicate how far in from the corner, in both directions, the radius of a circle should be drawn. The edge of the box is then wrapped along that circle, and the border (if any) is drawn on that edge. If there is a background, the background ends at the newly drawn quarter-circle edge rather than continuing to fill out to the corner of the box.

Listing 24.6 gives an example of the corner properties in use. Each box is styled with a different radius for illustrative purposes.

LISTING 24.6 Boxes with Curved Corners

```html
<!-- rounded-corners-24.6.html -->
<html>
  <head>
    <title>Daily Reminder List</title>
    <style type="text/css">
      body { margin: 0; padding: 2em;
             font-family: Verdana, sans-serif;
             color: black; background: white; }
      h1 { padding: 0.5em; margin: 0;
           border: 2px solid black;
           background-color: silver;
           -moz-border-radius: 0.75em; }
      #todo { border: 3px solid gray; padding: 25px;
              width: 40%; position: absolute;
              left: 2em; top: 8em;
              -moz-border-radius: 0 10%; }
      #schedule { border: 3px solid gray;
                  width: 40%; position: absolute;
                  right: 2em; top: 8em; padding: 25px;
                  -moz-border-radius: 20px 300px 65px 0; }
      #schedule dl { margin-left: 20%; }
      #schedule dt { float: left; width: 20%;
                     margin-left: -20%; text-align: right;
                     font-weight: bold; font-size: small; }
      #schedule dd.empty { background-color: silver; }
      #schedule dd { margin: 3px 0; width: 60%;
                     height: 1.5em; padding: 2px 10px;
                     background-color: gray; color: white;
                     -moz-border-radius: 50%; }
    </style>
  </head>
  <body>
    <h1>Daily Reminder List</h1>
    <div id="todo">
      <h2>Things to Do</h2>
      <ul>
        <li>Feed the cat</li>
        <li>Pay bills</li>
        <li>Laundry</li>
        <li>Change the oil</li>
        <li>Call mom and dad</li>
        <li>Go shopping</li>
      </ul>
    </div>
    <div id="schedule">
      <h2>Today's schedule</h2>
```

LISTING 24.6   Continued

```
    <dl>
      <dt>9:00</dt><dd class="empty"></dd>
      <dt>10:00</dt><dd>Conference call</dd>
      <dt>11:00</dt><dd class="empty"></dd>
      <dt>12:00</dt><dd>Lunch</dd>
      <dt>1:00</dt><dd>Client Meeting</dd>
      <dt>2:00</dt><dd class="empty"></dt>
      <dt>3:00</dt><dd>Staff Party</dd>
      <dt>4:00</dt><dd class="empty"></dd>
      <dt>5:00</dt><dd class="empty"></dd>
    </dl>
  </div>
 </body>
</html>
```

Figure 24.6 shows how these boxes appear in a Gecko-based browser.

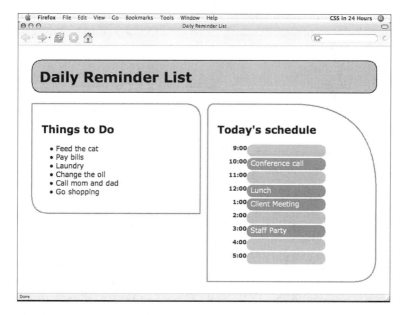

FIGURE 24.6
Firefox displays the box with rounded corners.

Summary

To properly troubleshoot your style sheet, you need to start with valid HTML and CSS. The W3C's online validators can check for problems in your code and offer warnings about possible problems. After you have eliminated syntax errors, you should simplify your code until you spot the source of your problems.

If it turns out that you're dealing with a browser bug or quirk, you may need to use a browser hack to fix the problem. Most browser hacks rely on using one bug to fix another, including browser filters that exclude or include targeted browsers. Examples include the direct child selector hack and the star HTML hack, which can be used in rules targeting Internet Explorer quirks and bugs. You can also use Microsoft's conditional comments to provide rules that are recognized by only Internet Explorer.

Some browsers have extended the CSS they recognize beyond the specifications written by the W3C; the results are proprietary CSS properties. Examples of proprietary properties include the various versions of opacity, Internet Explorer's visual transformation filters, and Gecko's rounded corners.

Workshop

The workshop contains a Q&A section, quiz questions, and an exercise to help reinforce what you've learned in this hour. If you get stuck, the answers to the quiz can be found after the questions.

Q&A

Q. *The HTML and CSS validators provide little buttons saying my code is valid. Should I use those?*

A. It's really up to you. As a matter of aesthetics, most websites aren't designed to look good with those graphics slapped onto them; the colors, fonts, and designs of the buttons aren't guaranteed to be compatible with any random site you might create. Furthermore, the information conveyed—"valid HTML!"—will mean nothing to your target audience for your site, unless you are designing a website for web developers.

On my personal sites, I usually use a simple text link to the validators. Keep in mind that by putting up one of these buttons or links, you are obligating yourself to validate your HTML and CSS each and every time you make a change. It's really embarrassing to proudly proclaim your compliance with the standards, then have someone email you that the site isn't really valid CSS because you wrote pudding for padding!

Q. *What should I use to filter for Internet Explorer?*

A. Before Internet Explorer 7 came on the scene, both of the CSS-based filtering techniques given in this hour would have worked well—direct child selectors and star HTML selectors. With IE7 promising to fix both of these bugs, hacks that rely on them will no longer function for version 7 (but will still work in earlier versions). For this reason, conditional comments seem to be the safest bet.

Quiz

1. Which of the following is not a benefit of validating your HTML and CSS?

    a. You will find typographical errors in the names of CSS properties.

    b. The validator will warn you about problems with unset background colors.

    c. You will be able to use proprietary CSS properties easily.

    d. Unclosed or prematurely closed HTML tags will be brought to your attention.

2. You want to make an image appear to be 50% transparent. Which set of rules accomplishes this on the widest variety of browsers?

    a. `img.fade { opacity: 50%; -khtml-opacity: 50%;`
       `-moz-opacity: 50%; -ie-opacity: 50%; }`

    b. `img.fade { opacity: 0.5; -khtml-opacity: 0.5;`
       `-moz-opacity: 0.5; -ie-opacity: 0.5; }`

    c. `img.fade { opacity: 0.5; -khtml-opacity: 0.5;`
       `-moz-opacity: 0.5; filter: alpha(opacity=50); }`

    d. `img.fade { opacity: 50%; -khtml-opacity: 50%;`
       `-moz-opacity: 50%; filter: alpha(opacity=50); }`

3. You want to send a style rule to Internet Explorer only (versions 6 or lower). Can you name at least three ways to do this?

Answers

1. (c) is not a benefit of validation; if you try to validate a style sheet with proprietary CSS properties, you will get an error message.

2. The correct answer is (c). There is no property named -ie-opacity, and the other opacity values must be written as decimal numbers between 0 and 1, not as percentages.

3. The three methods you learned in this hour were the direct child selector browser filter, the star HTML selector browser filter, and conditional comments.

Exercise

Your ability to test browser filters depends on which browsers and operating systems you have access to. To better understand browser filtering, use the Centricle listing of filters (http://centricle.com/ref/css/filters/) to discover hacks that target your specific browsers, and write rules that apply to those browsers only. Validate your code to see whether the browser filters are producing legitimate CSS. If your browsers support proprietary CSS properties, add those to your style sheet and then validate. What does the validator seem to think of your non-standard CSS?

PART VI

Appendixes

APPENDIX A

Replacing Presentational HTML with CSS

One of the goals of the Cascading Style Sheets language is to move presentational effects out of the HTML markup, achieving a separation of content from presentation. Such a separation has many benefits, especially for users with special needs, as discussed in Hour 22, "Accessibility and Print Media."

The HTML 4.01 specification defines three varieties of HTML—Strict, Transitional, and Frameset—as detailed in Hour 4, "Using CSS with HTML." Within this framework, specific HTML tags and attributes have been designated as deprecated. Deprecated tags are considered obsolete and are intended to be removed from future versions of the HTML language. Strict HTML disallows the use of these tags and attributes, instead relying on CSS rules for the same effects.

Table A.1 provides a list of deprecated tags and attributes, along with CSS equivalents for that HTML; also shown are cross-references to the hours of this book that discuss those CSS properties. You should use the CSS versions when designing web pages, especially if you are using Strict HTML.

TABLE A.1 Obsolete (Deprecated) HTML Tags and Attributes

Deprecated HTML	CSS Equivalent	Hour
`<basefont>`	`body { font-family }`	Hour 9
`<body alink>`	`a:active { color }`	Hour 12
`<body link>`	`a:link { color }`	Hour 12
`<body text>`	`body { color }`	Hour 2
`<body vlink>`	`a:visited { color }`	Hour 12
`<center>`	`text-align: center`	Hour 15
`<font>`	`font`	Hour 9
`<li type>`	`list-style-type`	Hour 13
`<s>`	`text-decoration: line-through`	Hour 10
`<strike>`	`text-decoration: line-through`	Hour 10
`<u>`	`text-decoration: underline`	Hour 10

TABLE A.1 Continued

Deprecated HTML	CSS Equivalent	Hour
align attribute	`text-align` or `margin: auto`	Hour 15
background attribute	`background-image`	Hour 11
bgcolor attribute	`background-color`	Hour 11
border attribute	`border`	Hour 6
clear attribute	`clear`	Hour 15
color attribute	`color`	Hour 2
height attribute	`height`	Hour 18
hspace attribute	`padding`	Hour 6
nowrap attribute	`white-space: nowrap`	Hour 15
valign attribute	`vertical-align`	Hour 15
vspace attribute	`padding`	Hour 6
width attribute	`width`	Hour 18

In addition to deprecated elements, HTML 4.01 also includes a number of presentational elements and attributes that are not considered obsolete but that are redundant with CSS properties. These HTML tags and attributes are allowed with Transitional HTML, but should be avoided with Strict HTML. Equivalent CSS rules are shown in Table A.2.

TABLE A.2 Using CSS Instead of Presentational HTML

Presentational HTML	CSS Equivalent	Hour
`<b>`	`font-weight: bold`	Hour 9
`<big>`	`font-size: larger`	Hour 9
`<hr>`	`border-top` or `border-bottom`	Hour 16
`<i>`	`font-style: italic`	Hour 9
`<pre>`	`white-space: pre; font-family: monospace`	Hour 15
`<small>`	`font-size: smaller`	Hour 9
`<table cellpadding>`	`padding`	Hour 6
`<table cellspacing>`	`border-spacing`	Hour 17
`<table frame>`	`border`	Hour 17
`<table rules>`	`border`	Hour 17
`<tt>`	`font-family: monospace`	Hour 9
char attribute	`text-align`	Hour 17

TABLE A.2   Continued

Presentational HTML	CSS Equivalent	Hour
charoff attribute	text-align	Hour 17
frameborder attribute	border	Hour 6
marginheight attribute	margin	Hour 6
marginwidth attribute	margin	Hour 6

Often, web developers use a valid HTML tag in a way that it wasn't intended to get a certain presentational effect. For example, someone might use <blockquote> because it provides right or left margins, even if the content wasn't actually a quote. With CSS allowing much more control over the presentation, there's no longer a need to resort to such tricks. HTML tags should be used only to represent the actual meaning of each tag, and CSS styles can be applied to change the formatting.

Examples of tags that are often misused are listed in Table A.3, and the CSS properties that can replace these tags are shown as well. Remember that these apply only to tags that aren't used for their intended meaning. The <blockquote> tag should still be used whenever a block of quoted text is provided; don't just blindly replace it with a margin rule in all cases. Ask yourself whether or not the original meaning of the HTML tag is appropriate.

TABLE A.3   Frequently Abused HTML Tags

Misused HTML	CSS Equivalent	Hour
<blockquote> for margins	margin	Hour 6
<dl> for margins	margin	Hour 6
<h1> for large text	font-size	Hour 9
<img> for list bullets	list-style-image	Hour 13
<ol> for margins	margin	Hour 6
<table> for layouts	Positioning properties	Hour 20
<textarea> for scroll box	overflow: scroll	Hour 18
<ul> for margins	margin	Hour 6

The first key to using CSS effectively is to use your markup properly. A solid foundation of valid, properly used HTML will enable you to make the most of your style sheet designs. For more on HTML tags, see the HTML specification at http://www.w3.org/TR/html4.

APPENDIX B

Glossary

accessibility—The process of making web content available to all users, regardless of disabilities. By using CSS, you can make your websites accessible to a broad spectrum of users.

Asynchronous JavaScript and XML (AJAX)—A technique of web page programming incorporating JavaScript, XML, and CSS to create interactive pages. AJAX-driven web applications exchange information with the web server using the JavaScript XMLHttpRequest object, but don't require reloading the entire page to update information.

attribute—A quality set on an HTML element in the opening tag, consisting of an attribute name and an attribute value. For example, in the HTML tag <h2 align="left">, the attribute name is align and the value is left.

Aural CSS (ACSS)—The group of CSS properties that dictate how a page should sound when read aloud by a screen reader or a talking browser.

block element—An element that is styled as a separate block; it is self-contained and starts and ends with new lines, such as the HTML <p> tag. *See also* Inline Element.

box model—The way in which CSS browsers display elements: element content, surrounded by padding, a border, and a margin. Not all elements have these properties, but all displayed elements are presented as boxes, either inline or block.

browser—A program that displays content of the type usually found on the Web—HTML documents, graphics, multimedia, and style sheets. Browsers are the most common type of user agent. Examples include Firefox, Internet Explorer, Safari, and Opera.

browser hacks—Specific techniques for getting around deficiencies in browser support for CSS or HTML standards. The term "hack" can be used in both a positive and negative sense; in this book, it carries no particular negative connotations.

calculated value—A property value that is calculated when it is applied; the actual value, rather than a relative keyword, is inherited by child elements.

cascade—The method by which CSS determines which of several conflicting property values should take precedence. The more specific a rule, the higher the priority granted to it.

Cascading Style Sheets (CSS)—A language created by the World Wide Web Consortium to describe presentation effects for HTML and XML documents.

child element—An element contained within another element. For example, within the HTML markup `<div> <img src="kynn.gif" alt="Kynn"> </div>`, the `<img>` element is a child of the `<div>` element.

class selector—A selector based on the HTML `class` attribute. A class selector can be used to assign styles to a specific set of elements that are defined in the markup.

comment—Text within a CSS or HTML file that is not displayed to the user but instead serves as notes or reminders to the web developer. In CSS, comments are indicated by `/* slashes and asterisks */`.

containing box—The box that contains an element and from which certain properties may be inherited. For example, in the HTML markup `<div> <img src="kynn.gif" alt="Kynn"> </div>`, the `<div>` element is the containing box around the `<img>` element.

content—Generically, any information that is prepared for display on the Web. In the case of HTML or XML, this is the text and any child elements between the opening and closing tags of an element. Content is usually meant to be presented to the user in some way.

declaration—The part of the CSS rule that specifies one or more styles to be applied. A declaration consists of pairs of property names and property values and is enclosed within { curly braces }.

deprecated markup—HTML tags that have been removed from the official language specification. Older versions may have included these obsolete items, but their functions have been replaced by newer elements or by CSS properties.

display box—A box, either visible or not, corresponding to an element in the markup. Boxes can be either inline or block and can contain text content or other boxes. Everything in CSS is conceptualized and displayed as a box according to the CSS box model.

Document Object Model (DOM)—A standard way of using programming languages to access parts of a web page. JavaScript can be used to manipulate the DOM and create dynamic HTML applications.

Dynamic HTML (DHTML)—The combination of HTML, CSS, and JavaScript to create presentations that change appearance as the user interacts with the content.

ECMAScript—The standardized version of JavaScript, a scripting language available in most browsers.

element—The basic component of a markup language such as HTML or XML. An element contains content, which can be text or child elements, between opening and closing tags, and elements can have attributes with values set in the opening tag. Elements are represented as display boxes in CSS browsers.

embedded style sheet—A style sheet that is contained within a web page. An embedded style sheet is enclosed within a `<style>` element in the `<head>` section of the HTML.

Extensible Hypertext Markup Language (XHTML)—The HTML language rewritten to conform to the rules of XML. Like HTML, XHTML 1.0 is available in three versions: Strict, Transitional, and Frameset.

Extensible Markup Language (XML)—A meta-language for creating other markup languages. XML is a set of rules for how languages or documents are constructed, and those rules promote interoperability between programs by defining a common format for information.

filtering—A type of browser hack that enables you to give specific CSS rules only to specific browsers. *See also* Browser Hacks.

font—A group of typefaces that share the same general appearance. CSS enables you to select a specific font family and then choose typefaces by specifying desired qualities, such as size, weight, and type.

Frameset HTML—The version of HTML 4.01 that allows sets of frames to be declared. CSS can be used with Frameset HTML to set the appearance of frames.

generated content—Text or other content inserted by style rules. Generated content does not appear in the HTML markup but is added when the style sheet is applied.

generic font families—The set of five font families that are browser defined and can be used as default values. The CSS generic font families are serif, sans-serif, cursive, fantasy, and monospace.

hexadecimal—A base-16 counting system using the digits 0 through 9 and A to F. Hexadecimal notation is used to write RGB color values in HTML and CSS.

Hypertext Markup Language (HTML)—A markup language for creating web pages. The current version of HTML is 4.01 and comes in three "flavors," Strict HTML, Transitional HTML, and Frameset HTML. CSS can be used with all flavors of HTML to set the appearance of the page.

id selector—A selector based on the HTML id attribute. An id selector uniquely identifies one specific element because all id values must be unique within a web page.

importing—The process of loading style rules from an outside file. The @import rule in CSS enables style sheets to be imported.

inheritance—The method by which elements take on the property values of their containing boxes. Properties in CSS are of two types: those that are inherited and those that are not. The inherit property value can be used with most CSS properties to force a value to be inherited from the containing box.

inline element—A markup element that appears within the flow of text across the page, rather than within a separate block box as block elements do. One example of an inline element is the HTML `<img>` tag.

inline style rule—A CSS rule set by using the HTML `style` attribute on any element. The inline style rule has only a declaration section; the selector is the element with the `style` attribute.

interoperability—The capability of different technologies to work together seamlessly. Interoperability is the primary goal of the World Wide Web Consortium and is possible only when all parties involved agree to implement the same standards.

JavaScript—A scripting language found in most web browsers. JavaScript allows manipulation of the DOM and styling properties to create dynamic HTML. The standardized version of JavaScript is known as ECMAscript.

layout—The way that information is spatially presented on a two-dimensional canvas, either onscreen or in printed material. CSS positioning properties enable users to lay out pages without resorting to HTML `<table>` elements.

linked style sheet—A file that contains style rules to be applied to a web page. The style sheet is external to the HTML file and is linked via the `<link>` tag in the `<head>` section of the page. A linked style sheet can be used by many web pages, and any given page can link to multiple style sheets.

list—A markup element designed to be displayed as a series of list elements, possibly with markers or counters. CSS enables you to change the appearance of HTML lists with the list item properties.

markup—Content consisting of normal text with tags added to define the meaning or presentation of the text. HTML and XML are the foremost examples of markup languages.

measurement—A property value that designates a linear distance or size. Measurements in CSS can be expressed in pixels, points, picas, ems, exes, inches, centimeters, or millimeters.

media types—The broad categories of devices that may display a document styled with CSS. Different media categories have different characteristics, based on the output and input capabilities of the device. The most common media categories are screen, print, and aural.

MIME type—A two-part code identifying the format of a specific file. The MIME type for a CSS file is `text/css`; for an HTML file, `text/html`; and for a JPEG file, `image/jpeg`.

positioning (CSS-P)—A subset of CSS properties that enables display boxes to be placed in a specific position within the layout of a page.

presentation—The appearance of content, independent of the actual information contained within that content. For example, the content of this glossary is the set of term and definition pairs; the presentation is the formatted, printed representation you hold in your hands, which we call a "book." CSS allows for the separation of presentation from content, increasing the accessibility of web designs.

property—One of the qualities that can be set, using CSS, on an HTML element to style it. Properties have property names and property values; the values are set in the declaration portion of a CSS rule.

pseudo-class selector—A type of selector that is based on the state of the web page but that functions as a class selector.

pseudo-element selector—A type of selector that identifies a virtual subelement, one that is not actually present in the markup but can be used to set style rules.

Recommendation—The official term for a W3C specification. The Cascading Style Sheets Level 1 recommendation created the CSS language; CSS Level 2 is the current recommendation, and as of this book's publication, CSS 2.1 is a working draft of an updated specification. A W3C recommendation is a specification that has been approved by the Consortium members and is considered a standard of the Web.

RGB—Red-Green-Blue; a designation for colors as used on the Web. Three numbers constitute an RGB triple. The first refers to the amount of red, the second to the amount of green, and the third to the amount of blue. Zero is the lowest value, and 255 (FF in hexadecimal) is the highest. In RGB notation, #FFFFFF is white, and #000000 is black.

rule—A complete styling instruction in CSS, consisting of one or more selectors to identify the elements to which the rule applies, and of one or more declarations to set property values.

selector—The portion of the CSS rule that identifies markup elements that receive the styling described by the rule's declarations. The selector comes before the curly braces that surround the declaration.

Strict HTML—The version of HTML 4.01 that relies upon Cascading Style Sheets for presentational information. Strict HTML disallows elements and attributes that are intended only for presentation.

structure—The internal order and logic of a file's content, as expressed through the markup. For example, if a document is divided into three sections with <div>, and each has an <h2> tag at the start of each section, that defines a very clear structure within the file. The CSS styles should be written to enhance and to supplement the structure to best convey the meaning of the content.

style—The qualities of display that collectively make up presentation. CSS is a style language, which means it is used to define how software should display web content.

style sheet—A collection of CSS rules. A style sheet can be external and can be linked via the HTML <link> tag or embedded within an HTML file inside a <style> element.

style sheet editor—A program specifically created for the creation of style sheets. Style sheet editors provide a visual interface for editing style rules and for tracking selectors.

tables—HTML markup elements that display information as cells arranged in rows and columns. Tables are used for two purposes: displaying columns of data or laying out a web page. CSS rules can be used to enhance the appearance of tables or to replace layout tables entirely.

tag—In a markup language such as HTML or XML, the text that identifies the beginning and end of an element, as well as the attributes set on that element. A tag is distinguished from other text by <angle braces>, and closing tags have a slash before the element name.

text editor—A program that provides simple text editing capabilities. Because HTML and CSS files are plain text, a text editor can be used for no-frills creation and maintenance of web pages and style sheets.

Transitional HTML—The variety of HTML 4.01 that allows presentation information to be included in HTML attributes and elements. Cascading Style Sheets can be applied to Transitional HTML pages, and if the CSS properties are not understood, the HTML presentation is available as a backup.

type selector—A selector that chooses all elements of a given type; for example, all <h1> elements or all <p> elements. Type selectors are very common in CSS and are often combined with other kinds of selectors.

user agent—Any software that retrieves a web document and does something with the information therein. The most common example of a user agent is the humble web browser, but indexing spiders, robots, intelligent agents, and proxies also fall into this category.

user-defined style sheet—A style sheet that resides on the user's hard drive and defines the user's preferences for viewing web content. A user-defined style sheet can override the author's styles, presenting the content in the method that is most accessible to the end user.

user interface CSS—The set of properties that interact with the user's environment. CSS allows access to system colors and fonts and also provides the capability to change the cursor type.

Web Content Accessibility Guidelines (WCAG)—A set of recommendations from the W3C for making web pages more accessible. Strategies for using Cascading Style Sheets to improve accessibility are detailed in the WCAG Techniques for CSS.

whitespace—Characters that are considered equal to a space character by a web browser; these include actual spaces, carriage returns, linefeeds, and tabs.

World Wide Web Consortium (W3C)—The international industry consortium that creates web specifications that promote interoperability. CSS, HTML, XML, and many more languages have been developed by the W3C and issued as W3C Recommendations. The W3C's website is http://www.w3.org/.

Index

alternate style sheet, 374

aural properties, 388-389

child selectors, 136

columns, 300

counters, 416

first-child pseudo-class, 97

focus pseudo-class, 210

generated content, 409, 413

text-based, 57

web pages, testing, 61

bugs. *See also* **troubleshooting**

browsers, 427-428

Internet Explorer

box model bug, 430-431

conditional comments, 434-436

direct child selectors, 431-432

star HTML hack, 432-434

bulleted lists

HTML, 220

markers

formatting, 222-223

images, 226-227

international, 224

virtual marker box placement, 227-229

<button> tag, 234

ButtonFace keyword, 407

ButtonHighlight keyword, 407

buttons

colors, 407

forms, 239-240

links as, 214

mouseover effects, 212-214

ButtonShadow keyword, 407

ButtonText keyword, 407

C

calculated values

defined, 456

inheritance, 126-127

Camino, 54

Canadian English language code, 98

capitalize value (text-transform property), 172

capitalizing text, 172

caption value (font property), 408

<caption> tag, 289, 298

caption-side property, 298-299

captions

tables, 289, 298-299

text color, 407

CaptionText keyword, 407

cascades, 10-11, 456

active links, 207

CSS Level One/Level Two, compared, 128

explicitly more important rules, 122

HTML presentational attributes, 121

imported style sheets, 124

ordering, 119-121

overview, 117

Cascading Style Sheets. *See* **CSS**

case

text, 172-173

sensitivity

class names, 74

id attributes, 76

CC/PP (Composite Capabilities/Preferences Profile), 393

cells

borders

collapsing, 294-296

separating, 296-297

viewing/hiding, 293-294

element type, 114

empty, 293

horizontal alignment, 301-302

spacing, 296-297

vertical alignment, 302-303

cellspacing attribute, 296

center center value (background-position), 198

center value (background-position), 198

centimeters (cm), 396

Centricle website, 429

check boxes (forms), 240-241

child elements, 456

child selectors, 136-137

choosing. *See* **selecting**

class attribute, 74

class selectors, 74-76

defined, 456

<div> tag combination, 84-85

absolute positioning, 350-351

colors/fonts, 352-353

floated columns, 356-357

HTML sections, 347-349

re-ordering sections, 353-355

style sheet, 349-353

tables, 346-347

dynamic actions, 17

Dynamic HTML (DHTML), 456

E

e-resize value (cursor property), 403

ECMAScript, 457

edge properties, 272

editing

environments, 26-27

style sheet editors, 459

text, 460

elements

attributes

adjacent siblings, 137-139

children, 136-137

existence, 131-132

values, 132-135

block, 455

child, 456

defined, 457

focus, 209-210

inheritance, 457

inline, 458

visual formatting method, 106-107

elevation aural property, 391

<em> tag, 106

EmacSpeak for Linux/Unix, 383

embedded style sheets

based on HTML, 70-72

converting to external, 71

defined, 457

emboss media type, 392

empty cells, 293-294

empty-cells property, 293-294

ems, 112, 115, 277

en (English language code), 98

en-ca (Canadian English language code), 98

en-uk (British English language code), 98

en-us (American English language code), 98

English language code, 98

Epiphany, 54

Evolt, 61

exclamation points (!), 122

Extensible Markup Language. See XML

Extensible Style Sheets (XSL), 13

Extensible Stylesheet Language Formatting Objects, 398

external style sheets

based on HTML, 68-70

embedded conversions to, 71

F

families (fonts), 145, 152-153

common, 161

generic, 153-157, 161, 457

cursive, 160

fantasy, 160

Firefox, 154

HTML file listing, 153

Internet Explorer, 154

monospace, 159-160

Opera 8.5, 155

Safari, 157

sans-serif, 158

serif, 157-158

selecting, 34

family-based selectors

adjacent sibling, 137-139

child, 136-137

fantasy fonts, 160

<fieldset> tag, 234

filter proprietary property, 441-443

filtering, 457

finding mistakes, 426-427

Firefox

forms, support, 245

generic font families, 154

overview, 52-53

first-child pseudo-class, 93-97

first-letter pseudo-element, 99-101

first-line pseudo-element, 99-100

fixed background images, 199-200

472

HTML

multiple properties, 200-202

positioning, 196-198

shapes with tiling, 202

tiling, 190, 194-196

URLs, 191-192

borders, 216

bulleted lists, 226-227

text as, 163

thumbnail galleries, 265-266

@import rule, **394**

@import statement, **125**

!important rules, **122**

importing

rules, 457

style sheets, 124-125

in (inches), **396**

inactive windows, **407**

InactiveBorder keyword, **407**

InactiveCaption keyword, **407**

InactiveCaptionText keyword, **407**

inches (in), **396**

indenting text, **253-257**

InfoBackground keyword, **407**

InfoText keyword, **407**

inherit value

background-color property, 188

background-image property, 194

border-style properties, 278

border-width property, 276

clear property, 263

clip property, 334

cursor property, 403

display property, 280

float property, 261

font-style property, 149

font-variant property, 148

font-weight property, 148

letter-spacing property, 175

line-height property, 180

margin property, 274

offset properties, 319

overflow property, 315

position property, 317

text-decoration property, 170

text-indent property, 256

text-transform property, 172

visibility property, 283

white-space property, 178

word-spacing property, 176

inheritance

calculated values, 126-127

elements, 457

link styles, 206

properties, 126

specifying, 127

tables, 291-292

values, 126

inline block, **280**

inline elements, **107**

inline styles

based on HTML, 72-73

rules, 458

selectors, 78

inline value (display property), **280**

inline-elements, **458**

<input type=""> tag, **234**

inset value (border-style properties), **278**

international list markers, **224**

Internet Explorer

bugs

conditional comments, 434-436

direct child selectors, 431-432

IE box model, 430-431

star HTML hack, 432-434

width, 311-312, 322

filter proprietary property, 441-443

filters website, 443

forms, support, 247

generic font families, 154

Macintosh version, 58-59

older versions, 52

overview, 51

shells, 52

interoperability, **458**

italic fonts, **146-150**

italic value (font-style property), **149**

J

JavaScript

AJAX, 455

defined, 458

476

listings

offset properties, 319, 329

text-indent property, 256

vertical-align property, 258

word-spacing property, 176

media attribute, 70

@media rule, 394-395

media types, 392-393, 458

media-specific style sheets, 392

   linking, 393-394

   media types, 392-393

   multiple rules, 394-395

medium value (border-width property), 276

menu colors, 407

Menu keyword, 407

menu value (font property), 408

MenuText keyword, 407

message-box value (font property), 408

Microsoft FrontPage, 27

middle value (vertical-align property), 258

millimeters (mm), 396

MIME files, 458

mistakes, finding, 426-427

mm (millimeters), 396

monospace fonts, 159-160

mouseover events, 208

   example listing, 213

   links

      buttons, 212-214

      colors, 208-209

      underlines, 212

move value (cursor property), 403

Mozilla, 53, 443-445

Mozilla Firefox

   forms, support, 245

   generic font families, 154

   overview, 52-53

multiplier value (line-height property), 180

multipliers, 181

MySoft Maxthon, 52

N

n-resize value (cursor property), 403

names

   classes, 74

   colors, 166

   style sheets, 28

navigation bars

   mouseover effects, 213

   styling, 281-282

ne-resize value (cursor property), 403

negative measurement value

   letter-spacing property, 175

   text-indent property, 256

   vertical-align property, 258

   word-spacing property, 176

negative-measurement value

   margin property, 274

   offset properties, 319, 329

negative-percentage value

   offset properties, 319, 329

   vertical-align property, 258

nesting lists, 223

Netscape

   older browsers, 54

   version 8.1, 53

no-close-quote value (content property), 410

no-open-quote value (content property), 410

no-repeat value (background-image property), 194

none value

   border-style properties, 278

   clear property, 263

   display property, 280

   float property, 261

   text-decoration property, 170

   text-transform property, 172

normal flow, 325

normal value

   font-style property, 149

   font-variant property, 148

   font-weight property, 148

   letter-spacing property, 175

   line-height property, 180

   white-space property, 178

   word-spacing property, 176

nowrap value (white-space property), 178

numbered lists, 219

nw-resize value (cursor property), 403

repeat-x value (background-image property), **194**

repeat-y value (background-image property), **194**

replacing

    <body> tag attributes, 210-211

    misused HTML tags, 453

    presentational HTML, 452-453

resources (browser support), 61

RGB (Red Green Blue), 40, **166-167**, **459**

rgb() function, **167**

richness aural property, 390

ridge value (border-style properties), **278**

right center value (background-position), **198**

right property values, 318, 328

right value

    background-position, 198

    clear property, 263

    float property, 261

rounded corners proprietary properties, **443-445**

ru (Russian language code), **98**

rules

    background/foreground color, 119

    basic structure, 29-30

    combining, 30-31

    comments, 31-33

    conflicting, 79

    creating in HTML, 74-76

    declarations, 456

    defined, 13, 459

    explicitly more important, 122

    HTML attributes, 121

    @import, 125, 394

    importing, 457

    inline, 458

    links

        <body> tag replacements, 210-211

        mouseover effects, 212-214

        underlines, deleting, 211-212

    @media, 394-395

    ordering, 119-121

    priorities, 122

    sorting, 120

    text formatting, 33-34

run-in value (display property), 280

Russian language code, 98

S

s-resize value (cursor property), **403**

Safari, 55-57

    forms, support, 246

    generic font families, 157

sans-serif fonts, 158

saving style sheets, 28

screen magnification software, 383

screen media type, 393

screen readers, 382

    browser support, 59

    content, hiding, 436-438

scroll value (overflow property), 315

scrollable panels, 316

Scrollbar keyword, 407

scrollbars, 407

se-resize value (cursor property), 403

SeaMonkey, 53

Section 508, 386-387, 436

sectional styling

    class selectors, 84-85

    id selectors, 85-86

<select> tag, 234

selecting

    attributes

        adjacent siblings, 137-139

        children, 136-137

        existence, 131-132

        values, 132-135

    font families, 34

selection lists (forms), 242-243

selectors

    adjacent sibling, 137-139

    attribute

        adjacent siblings, selecting, 137-139

        children, selecting, 136-137

        existence, 131-132

X-Z